READERS AND WRITERS
WITH A DIFFERENCE

READERS AND WRITERS WITH A DIFFERENCE

A Holistic Approach to Teaching
Struggling Readers and Writers

LYNN K. RHODES

AND

CURT DUDLEY-MARLING

HEINEMANN
PORTSMOUTH, NH

Heinemann
A division of Reed Elsevier Inc.
361 Hanover Street
Portsmouth NH 03801-3912
Offices and agents throughout the world

The authors and publisher thank those who generously gave permission to reprint borrowed material.

Fig. 8–2, from "Critical reading/thinking across the curriculum: Using I-charts to support learning" by James V. Hoffman, in *Language Arts.* Copyright 1992 by the National Council of Teachers of English. Reprinted by permission.

Fig. 9–1, from *Neat and Scruffy* by J. Gale. Copyright © 1975. Published by Ashton Scholastic Ltd. Reprinted by permission of the Publisher.

Fig. 9–2, from *A Risky Trip* by J.E. Richardson. Copyright © 1976. Published by Benziger. Reprinted by permission of Glencoe Publishing Company.

Excerpt from "A response-based approach to reading literature" by J.A. Langer in *Language Arts*. Copyright 1994 by the National Council of Teachers of English. Reprinted with permission.

Fig. 10–1, from "Teaching Question Answer Relationships, Revisited" by Taffy E. Raphael. From *The Reading Teacher* (February 1986). Reprinted with permission of Taffy E. Raphael and the International Reading Association.

Library of Congress Cataloging-in-Publication Data

Rhodes, Lynn Knebel.
    Readers and writers with a difference: a holistic approach to
teaching struggling readers and writers / Lynn K. Rhodes and Curt
Dudley-Marling.—2nd ed.
        p. cm.
    Includes bibliographical references and indexes.
    ISBN 0-435-07215-3 (alk. paper)
    1. Learning disabled children—Education—United States.
2. Language arts (Elementary)—United States. 3. Reading
(Elementary)—United States. 4. Inderdisciplinary approach in
education—United States.   I. Dudley-Marling, Curt.   II. Title.
LC4705.R5 1996
371.9'0973.—dc20   96-5894
                                                                     CIP

Editor: *Scott Mahler*
Production: *Melissa L. Inglis*
Cover design: *Jenny Jensen Greenleaf*
Cover image: *Emily Berg/The Fringe*
Manufacturing: *Louise Richardson*

Printed in the United States of America on acid-free paper
02 01   EB   5 6 7 8 9

CONTENTS

Introduction to the First Edition   ix

Introduction to the Second Edition   xi

SECTION I   WHAT IS WHOLE LANGUAGE?   1

1   An Introduction to Whole Language Theory   5
    Language as a System
      Graphophonic Cues
      Syntactic Cues
      Semantic Cues
      Pragmatic Cues
    Language as a Process
      Language as a Psychological Process
      Language as a Social Process

2   Whole Language: It's a Matter of Principles   17
    Some Pedagogical Principles
      Children Are Always Learning
      Children Learn Best What's Meaningful and Relevant to Them
      Students Learn Most Easily When They Have Some Measure of Control
        over the Decisions Affecting Their Learning
      Children Learn to Read and Write by Reading and Writing
      Errors Are Critical to Learning
      Children's Learning Should Be Celebrated, Not Rewarded
      Learning Is Social
      Teachers Must Practice What They Teach
      Teachers Are Learners, Too
    Whole Language and "Readers and Writers with a Difference"
      The Model of Unique Instruction
      Eclecticism: The Best of All Worlds?
      Whole Language and Struggling Learners

SECTION II   ONGOING ASSESSMENT: THE BASIS OF LITERACY INSTRUCTION   31

3   Literacy Assessment: An Overview   33
    Relating Literacy Assessment and Instruction

Principles of Literacy Assessment
Aspects of Literacy to Assess and Teach
Collecting and Recording Assessment Information
   Ways to Collect and Record Information
   Managing Assessment

4   **Assessing Aspects of Literacy**   52
   Assessing Reading Performance: Comprehension and Processing Words
   Assessing Writing Performance: Composition and Conventions
   Assessing Early Reading and Writing Development
   Assessing Other Aspects of Literacy
      Attitudes and Interests
      Perceptions
      Social Aspects
      Procedural Aspects
      Literary Aspects
      Flexibility
      Metacognitive Aspects
      Environment and Instruction

5   **From Assessment to Planning and Adjusting Instruction (and Back Again)**   81
   Written Goals or Objectives
   A Holistic Approach to Planning Instruction
      Developing Summary Statements
      Developing Learner Objectives
      Developing Teaching Goals
      Revision of Summaries, Learner Objectives, and Teaching Goals
      The Individual Education Plan: A Note to Special Educators
   Gradual Release of Responsibility
      Clarifying the Goal for Independent Use
      Discovery and Demonstration
      Guided Use
      Independent Use

SECTION III   READING INSTRUCTION: A FOCUS ON STRUGGLING READERS   99

6   **Environments That Facilitate Reading and Reading Development**   101
   The Physical Environment
      Selecting Reading Material
      Trade Books and Paperbacks
      Predictable Books
      "Big Books"
      Song and Wordless Picture Books
      Textbooks
      Student-Published Books and Nonbook Materials
   The Organizational Environment
      Routines That Facilitate Reading Instruction
      Reading Across the Curriculum
   The Interpersonal Environment

7   **Before the Book Opens: Prereading Instruction**   128
   Learning to Choose Reading Material
   Establishing Purposes for Reading
   Activating Student Knowledge About Text
      Previewing the Topic
      Book Introductions

Previewing Vocabulary
Previewing Text
Increasing Student Knowledge About Text
"Hands-On" Exploration
Using Alternative Presentation Modes
Related Reading

8   **Reading Fluently and Making Sense of Text: In-Process Reading Instruction**   150
Oral Reading or Silent Reading?
Developing Fluency in Reading
Confronting Students' Perceptions About Reading
Instructional Strategies for Developing Reading Fluency
Making Sense of Text
Reading Conferences That Assist Students in Learning to Make Sense of Text
Strategy Lessons That Assist Students in Learning to Make Sense of Text
Increasing Knowledge of Text Structure

9   **Making Sense of Words and Text Features: In-Process Reading Instruction**   185
Learning to Make Sense of Words in Text: Strategy Lessons
Sources of Information
Reading Strategies
Instructional Cloze
Teacher Feedback to Miscues
Retrospective Miscue Analysis and Reader-Selected Miscues
Learning Words and Other Text Features
Pointing
Graphophonic Prediction Check
Sequencing Text Parts
Matching
Games
Regenerating a Text
Innovating on an Author's Structure
Writing
Reading Alternate Versions of a Text

10   **Sharing and Extending Text: Postreading Instruction**   209
Sharing and Extending a Text
Oral Sharing and Extending
Written Sharing and Extending
Sharing and Extending Through Graphic Representation and Visual Art
Sharing and Extending Through Games
Sharing and Extending Text Sets
Learning to Answer (and Ask) Questions
Interpreting the Question
Locating Information to Answer Questions
Formulating an Answer
Questioning the Author
Study Reading

SECTION IV   WRITING INSTRUCTION: A FOCUS ON STRUGGLING WRITERS   235

11   **Writing Instruction: The Writing Workshop**   237
What Students Do: A Writing Process
Rehearse
Draft
Revise

Edit

Share

What Teachers Do: Elements of the Writing Workshop

   Creating an Environment for Writing

   Immersing Students in Literature

   Conducting Minilessons

   Conferences

   Encouraging Students to Share Their Writing

12   Transcription: Choices and Instruction   271

Spelling

   Instruction for Prephonemic Spellers

   Instruction for Phonemic Spellers

   Instruction for Letter Name Spellers

   Instruction for Transitional Spellers

   What Do You Do When You Don't Know How to Spell a Word?

   Unusual Spelling Difficulties

Punctuation

Usage

Handwriting

SECTION V   WORKING TOGETHER   301

13   Developing Collaborative Relationships   303

Collaboration Among Teaching Colleagues

Collaborating with Parents

   Engaging Families

   Some Guiding Principles for Working with Parents

Collaborating with Administrators

Collaborating with Students

Collaborating with Others

Strategies for Dealing with Imposed Curricula

14   Sharing Expectations About Reading and Writing Development   322

The Expectations of Parents

   The Printed Word

   Phone Calls

   Parent Conferences and Open Houses

   The IEP Conference

   Classroom Visits

   Home Visits

The Expectations of Teachers and Administrators

The Expectations of Students

References   335

Author Index   369

Subject Index   377

INTRODUCTION
TO THE FIRST EDITION

Before you begin reading this book, we'd like you to think about what it means to be a holistic teacher, and how the instructional strategies presented throughout this book should be viewed.

Holistic teachers are concerned with more than reading and writing. Holistic teaching extends to all areas of learning and the curriculum. Holistic education is a philosophy of teaching, not an approach to reading and writing instruction. It is as applicable to science, math, geography, and history as it is to teaching written and oral language. Holistic teachers endeavor to place students' learning within the context of their own experiences. When learning is meaningful, students learn. In fact, in a meaningful environment, it is difficult to stop children from learning.

When learning is not meaningful, artificial rewards must be used to encourage students' efforts. No artificial rewards were needed, however, to help children learn to talk, walk, or want to play with their friends because learning to talk or walk fulfilled important social and emotional needs. Holistic teachers seek to ensure that reading and writing also meet the emotional and social needs of their students.

Holistic teachers do not fragment learning, nor do they divide and subdivide learning into artificial time periods. Just as holistic teachers encourage reading, writing, and oral language across the curriculum, they attempt to integrate all areas of the curriculum. They will be just as likely to take advantage of an opportunity to teach a geography lesson during reading as the other way around.

Holistic teachers are themselves learners, learning with and from their students. At the same time, teachers are students of learning, regularly observing their students as they learn and respond to instruction. As a result, holistic teachers learn about literacy development and modify their instruction according to their students' needs. Teachers also reflect on their own teaching, and on themselves as readers and writers, so that they can share their own literacy experiences with their students.

Holistic teachers respect the learning capabilities of students. They recognize that students will learn what is personally meaningful to them. For this reason, they carefully consider the literacy environment they create with students, striving to mirror the purposes, audiences, and materials of the literate world. They also recognize that students must have plentiful opportunities for reading and writing if they are to become readers and writers.

In this text we present strategies that we believe will encourage the reading and writing development of learning disabled and remedial readers. We focus upon those strategies with which we are personally familiar or which teachers we know have shared with us. You will certainly encounter many other strategies elsewhere. And we have no doubt that you already have or will invent successful strategies worth sharing with us.

The strategies in the forthcoming chapters should be considered only as models for written language assessment and instruction. It may be that some of them will work for you without adaptation while others may not work at all; in general, most will have to be modified in accordance with teachers' individual styles and the unique needs of each of their students. We hope that teachers will use the strategies presented in this book productively and not prescriptively. Those who use the information presented here as another experience in their continued learning and growth will obtain the greatest benefit from this text. We have not provided and cannot provide teachers with *the* answers for meeting the needs of their students. What we can do is help promote their growth as teachers by stimulating their thinking and sharing some of our ideas. We hope that our readers will use our ideas this way, continue to seek the ideas of others, and, more important, integrate these ideas into their own experiences with students. We wish our readers the best in their continued growth.

We'd like to conclude this introduction by thanking our colleagues who have contributed to our ongoing learning, especially the many teachers who have talked with us and challenged our thinking about literacy development and instruction and who continue to do so.

INTRODUCTION TO THE SECOND EDITION

When we wrote the first edition of *Readers and Writers with a Difference* we worried if we'd sell enough books to pay back the advance Heinemann had given to us. Thankfully, *Readers and Writers with a Difference* has been popular with teachers and has been used as a text in many undergraduate and graduate courses in the United States and Canada (and beyond). We are grateful for the opportunity this has given us to share our ideas and experiences with so many teachers. But with the continued success of *Readers and Writers with a Difference* comes a problem. Theoretical developments in literacy and literacy education mean that some of the material in the first edition is now dated. Developments in the writing process, for example, have left the two chapters on writing in the first edition out of date. Research in the area of literacy as social practice, which has enriched the theoretical underpinnings of whole language, highlights shortcomings in the theoretical foundation we presented in the first edition. It is no longer possible to talk about approaches to teaching students to read (and write) *once and for all.* Instead we have to think about supporting students as they learn a range of literate practices including learning reading and writing practices unique to schooling.

Our own development as teachers and researchers also means that we are no longer comfortable with parts of the first edition, including, for example, the tone of our discussions about working with parents, which, it seems to us now, puts parents in the role of passive recipients of teachers' knowledge. We have also learned much more about literacy and literacy instruction over the past eight years as we have read the work of others, observed countless teachers, engaged in many discussions of reading and writing, and listened to teachers' questions and comments about what we had written in the first edition of *Readers and Writers with a Difference.* These personal developments and developments in the field of literacy instruction argued for a revised edition of *Readers and Writers with a Difference,* which is what we have undertaken here.

The most obvious difference between the first and second editions is that the second edition has been updated to take account of the various developments in language arts since we first wrote this book. This necessitated, for example, that the chapters on literacy theory and written language composition be almost totally rewritten. The chapter on assessment has also been significantly revised to take advantage of the work Rhodes has been doing on assessment over the last several years. In some chapters revised sections stand alongside other sections which have been left much as they appeared in the original edition. In other places we've merely reorganized and/or updated. Some sections have been deleted as a reflection of changes in our beliefs or an effort to be more concise. The list of predictable books lists which appeared at the end of the first edition has been deleted because the widespread availability of predictable books made this section unnecessary (and, we should add, difficult to update). In all cases, we've tried to make our discussion clearer and, where possible, more concise without losing the detail that readers found valuable in the previous edition.

There are two other significant differences between the first and second editions we need to comment on. First of all, we broadened the audience we imagined for this book to include regular classroom teachers as well as resource room teachers and teachers of self-contained classes for students with learning disabilities. This change was motivated by a shift in the way schools are currently addressing the needs of remedial readers and students with learning disabilities. Increasingly, students with learning and literacy problems are being served within regular classroom settings, often with the support of remedial or special education teachers. Therefore, regular classroom teachers are assuming significant responsibility for the reading and writing instruction of many students who were previously the responsibility of special education or resource room teachers.

As you can tell from the new subtitle for the second edition, we have also broadened our discussion of whole language reading and writing instruction to include all students for whom reading and writing are a struggle, including students in Title I programs and students labeled learning disabled. This is a logical extension of the arguments we made in the first edition—and repeat here—that there is nothing unique about the instructional needs of students with formal labels. Students who struggle in school usually require *frequent*, *intense*, *explicit*, and *individual* support and direction from their teachers. We believe that whole language theory and practice provides a particularly useful perspective from which to provide that support.

We'd also like to reiterate our hope that the strategies we present in this book provide teachers with a productive resource and not a prescriptive one. As we said in the introduction to the first edition, effective whole language teachers adapt instruction to fit their needs and the unique instructional needs of their students. Since we've never met most of you or your students, it is unlikely that many of the strategies we present here will work without at least some modifications or adaptations.

Finally, we'd like to thank again all the teachers who have influenced us over the years. In most ways, this book is merely an effort to pass on what we have learned from them. We also wish to acknowledge the patience, love, and support of our spouses, Chris and Enno, and our children, Anne, Ian, Alec, and Kara. And thanks to all those who honored us by reading the first edition of this book. We are privileged to have been able to share our ideas with you.

WHAT IS WHOLE LANGUAGE?

As whole language educators we believe that the primary goal of literacy instruction is *to provide students with the literacy experiences, the support, and the direction they need to learn to use reading and writing to fulfill a range of personal intentions in a variety of social settings.* We expect that the instructional support whole language teachers provide will lead their students to discover the power of literacy to affect their lives in and out of school. We hope they will use that power to seek personal and vocational fulfillment and satisfaction.

In the highly literate and technological workplace of the late twentieth century literacy is one of the keys to economic success. We believe it would be a serious mistake, however, to accept the all-too-common view that reading and writing are merely commodities to be exchanged for vocational opportunities. Vocational success does help to fulfill basic needs for food, shelter, clothing, and self-respect, but it does not guarantee personal satisfaction, self-fulfillment, or happiness. Reading and writing provide a means for people to establish and maintain relationships and to examine and challenge the conditions of their lives and the lives of others. This makes literacy a powerful tool for addressing people's social and emotional needs as well as opening up vocational opportunities. Language arts instruction that emphasizes vocational literacy to the exclusion of personal and social uses of reading and writing will almost certainly exacerbate the sense of helplessness and alienation felt by so many men and women in Western societies at the end of the twentieth century.

We wish to emphasize that our goals for literacy instruction apply to *all* children, regardless of ability or economic, social, linguistic, or cultural background. Special literacy programs for poor and minority students (students often described as "at risk") that emphasize basic skills instruction and limit the purposes and audiences of students' reading can have the effect of reinforcing a status quo in which many people are disadvantaged because of their race, gender, class, ethnicity, or language. The practice of emphasizing vocational literacy in work-study programs for special educational and remedial students—whose numbers typically include disproportionate representation of poor and minority students—may deny some students a means for challenging the disadvantage and discrimination that restricts their vocational and social opportunities. Because of who or what schools imagine some students to be they may limit who they can become.

So our goal to expand the range of purposes for which and social settings within which students use literacy is political as well as theoretical and pedagogical. Working with struggling students inevitably means working with disproportionate numbers of poor, Black, Hispanic, Aboriginal, and bilingual students—students whose struggles in school have less to do with *their* capabilities than the ability of schools to recognize the range of individual, social, and cultural differences students bring with them to school. The standardized, one-size-fits-all curricula found in so many schools today imagine students to be pretty much the same, but they're not. Whole language classrooms can, we believe, create spaces that are congenial to the range of differences students bring with them to school and enable students to acquire a range of reading and writing practices that will help them overcome the disadvantage and discrimination that limit their vocational and social choices. But we also recognize that, to really make a difference in the lives of many struggling readers and writers, whole language teachers must also become social activists (see Shannon, 1993; Edelsky, 1994) who challenge the institutional racism, classism, and sexism that make it difficult for many students to succeed no matter how literate they become (Gee, 1990; Graff, 1979).

We believe that effective whole language instruction for struggling readers and writers begins with an examination and, perhaps, a reconsideration of our beliefs about literacy and literacy learning. Underpinning all literacy instruction are sets of beliefs, or assumptions, about the nature of written language and how children learn to read and write. Underlying the approach to teaching struggling readers that emphasizes the isolated decoding of words, for example, is the tacit belief that meaning resides in the print and the reader's task is to "unlock" the meaning. This contrasts with the assumption underlying whole language practice that readers' background knowledge, experiences, histories, and cultures all play a role in how readers go about making sense of written texts. Making our beliefs about literacy and literacy learning explicit also makes it easier for us to reflect on our teaching practice in order to provide useful support for struggling readers and writers, to grow professionally, and to avoid theoretical conflicts that confuse students, parents, and the public.

An understanding of written language and written language learning will also help teachers *adapt* and *invent* instructional and assessment strategies that are appropriate to their needs, the needs of their students, and the constraints imposed by the physical, social, and cultural context within which they work. This is an important point. We hope that teachers will take the assessment and instructional strategies presented in the chapters of this book as examples, not as prescriptions for whole language teaching. Many teachers have told us that the first of edition of *Readers and Writers with a Difference* is their "bible." This is flattering to be sure, but if teachers take the strategies in this book prescriptively, it's not likely they'll get very far. Good whole language teachers borrow and adapt strategies they've seen or read about, but they also draw on their theoretical understanding of language and language learning to invent their own strategies appropriate to the students with whom they work. From this perspective whole language isn't a method, but "a set of beliefs, a perspective. It must become practice, but it is not the practice itself" (Altwerger, Edelsky & Flores, 1987, p. 145). The use of "Big Books" or interactive journals, for example, is often associated with whole language practice. But these activities do not, by themselves, reflect whole language—they only have the *potential* to fit a whole language framework (Edelsky, Altwerger & Flores, 1991). Whether something is or is not whole language can only be determined by considering the basic understandings about literacy and literacy learning that underlie whole language theory and practice.

In this section we examine the theoretical and pedagogical underpinnings of whole language that inform the assessment and instructional strategies that make up the bulk of this book.

1

An Introduction to Whole Language Theory

I n this chapter we lay out our theoretical beliefs about reading and writing as language processes—that is, what we believe reading and writing are and what we believe readers and writers do in the process of reading and writing—by discussing *language as a system* and *language as a process*.

Language as a System

From a holistic perspective, language is understood as a system. Readers and writers use their knowledge of language systems to make sense from and with texts by simultaneously drawing on their knowledge of sound-symbol relationships, word-ordering rules, the structure of written language genres (e.g., story grammar), the meanings of words and concepts, and their knowledge of how language is used in different contexts. Readers make sense of a particular word or phrase within a text, for example, by referring both to the text and context of the reading, including the social setting, the reader's purpose(s), experience, and social, cultural, and linguistic background. Since no readers have precisely the same experience or background, readers' responses to a given written text will vary greatly (e.g., Bloome, Harris, & Ludlum, 1991; Fish, 1980), regardless of the writer's intention. The meaning readers assign to the phrase "walked upon the water," for example, is a function of the text in which the phrase is found (e.g., New Testament versus a newspaper) and the reader's cultural and religious background. It is doubtful that many of us even have the same meaning for a text as seemingly straightforward as "STOP" on a stop sign, which, from our personal experience, can mean:

- Always stop

- Slow down

- Stop unless you're turning right

- Stop when there are other cars in the intersection

- Stop when there is a police car in sight

- Stop except in an emergency

- Stop unless you're on a bicycle

It's worth repeating that reading and writing are not simply matters of knowing about graphophonics (sound-symbol relationships) *and* syntax (word-ordering rules) *and* semantics (roughly: the meaning of words and concepts) *and* pragmatics (rules governing the use of language in context). Readers and writers apply their knowledge of all of these cueing systems simultaneously as they actively construct meaning from and with texts within a sociocultural context (Bloome, Harris, & Ludlum, 1991; Bloome & Egan-Robertson, 1993; Gee, 1990).

In the following section we consider the various cueing systems of written language—graphophonics, syntax, semantics, and pragmatics—and how readers and writers use these cues to construct meaning. We discuss these cueing systems separately only for the convenience of our readers. It's our view that these cues aren't learned, nor should they be taught, separately. If they are taught separately, what is learned may have little relevance beyond the context of instruction (Edelsky, 1991; Edelsky & Smith, 1984; Myers, 1992).

Graphophonic Cues

Graphophonics refers to the knowledge readers and writers have about the marks on the page—the sound/letter relationships represented there, the white spaces denoting word boundaries, and so on (see Goodman, 1993). Graphophonic rules are enormously complex. Therefore, readers' and writers' knowledge of these rules is largely intuitive; that is, readers and writers have no difficulty using their knowledge of graphophonics rules in the process of reading and writing, but usually only linguists are able to explain how this all works explicitly.

Readers and writers know, for example, which letter combinations in English are permissible (e.g., *la-*, *qu-*, *ee*, and so on) and which are "illegal" (e.g., *qi*, *Ix*, *yl*, and so forth) even though they may never have been explicitly taught rules governing English orthography, nor could many people actually state these rules. Readers and writers also know which letter combinations are permissible, or even likely, in certain positions within a word. Readers would be very surprised, for example, to encounter a word that began *rv* even though this is a permissible letter combination within a word (e.g., *curve*). Again, it is doubtful many of us could explain why it isn't permissible to begin English words with *rv*, even though we know this is so.

Since graphophonic rules are so complex—and most of the phonics rules we were taught in school grossly underestimate this complexity—there is little reason to believe that many of these rules can be taught explicitly or that readers or writers would benefit from such instruction. In general, there is an uneven relationship between knowing about language and knowing how to use it. Still, teachers can offer support and direction to help students learn to make better use of graphophonic cues. (See Weaver, 1994; Wilde, 1992; and Chapter 9 in this text.)

Clearly, readers and writers use their knowledge of graphophonic rules to construct meaning, but effective readers and writers do not overrely on this aspect of written language. Instead, they combine their knowledge of graphophonics with their knowledge of other language cues to make sense of texts.

Syntactic Cues

Syntax refers to the morphological and word-ordering rules that affect our use and understanding of oral and written language. It is a syntactic rule that tells us that in the sentence, "Alec kicked Kara," it is Alec who did the kicking and Kara who felt the pain. It's also a syntactic rule that tells us that a similar ordering of words, "Alec was kicked by Kara," has an entirely different meaning. Children come to school with a considerable store of syntactic knowledge and, as they learn to read and write, they draw on this knowledge to help them make sense with and from texts.

The following exercise illustrates how readers use syntactic cues to construct meaning from printed texts. Try reading the following story (from Goodman, 1968) and then answer the questions that follow it using complete sentences and the same "language" in which the story is written. As you read and answer the questions, pay attention to the specific cues you use.

The Marlup

A marlup was poving his kump. Parmily a narg horped some whev in his kump. "Why did vump horp whev in my frinkle kump?" the marlup jufed the narg. "Er'm muvvily trungy," the narg grupped. "Er heshed vump horpled whev in your kump. Do vump pove your kump frinkle?"

1. What did the narg horp in the marlup's kump?

2. What did the marlup juf the narg?

3. Was the narg trungy?

4. How does the marlup pove his kump?

As you read and answered these questions, you certainly used syntactic cues as well as graphophonic cues. You probably used your knowledge about the meaning of word position, modifiers, and so on. In addition, you used your knowledge of how morphological markers like -s, ed, and ly affect meaning. Undoubtedly, punctuation and capitalization also played a role in your ability to answer the questions because they helped you determine where sentences began and ended. The presence of quotation marks indicates that there are characters talking with each other. Question marks and periods also gave you some sense of the purposes for which the characters were talking to each other (to seek information, for example). Additionally, function words like *a*, *in*, and *the* also provided some clues about what's going on in this piece by helping you take advantage of other syntactic cues in the text.

Even though few readers would claim to understand *the meaning* of "The Marlup," most people are able to make sufficient sense of the syntactic cues to answer the questions at the end of the story. (In many school settings such knowledge often *counts* as reading.) The degree to which you were able to make sense of "The Marlup" and answer the questions is related to your knowledge of English syntax. We know the Marlup "poved his kump" because we understand how word endings and word-ordering rules operate in English even if we can't state these rules explicitly.

The ability of readers to make use of syntactic information can lead teachers to misjudge students' reading abilities. Teachers sometimes assume that, if students can answer comprehension questions following a basal story, for example, they understood what they've read. It may be, however, that students are simply drawing on their knowledge of English syntax to answer questions, just as you did, without really "understanding" anything. But even this level of understanding demonstrates students' extraordinarily sophisticated knowledge of the workings of English syntax.

Semantic Cues

Semantics refers to the world knowledge shared by readers and writers and how that knowledge is represented by language. Semantics refers not only to vocabulary, but also to the concepts represented by that vocabulary and how those concepts are organized into schema—our structured knowledge about the world.

The following exercise offers a feel for the role of semantics in making sense of text. Try reading the following passage from Stephen Hawking's best-seller, *A Brief History of Time*, and then retell the passage to yourself or to someone else.

> The laws of science do not distinguish between the past and the future. More precisely, as explained earlier, the laws of science are unchanged under the combination of operations (or symmetries) known as C, P, and T. (C means changing particles for antiparticles. P means taking the mirror image so left and right are interchanged. And T means reversing the direction of motion of all particles: in effect, running the motion backward.) The laws of science that govern the behavior of matter under all normal situations are unchanged under the combination of the two operations C and P on their own. In other words, life would be just the same for the inhabitants of another planet who were both mirror images of us and who were made of antimatter, rather than matter (1988, p. 144).

If you're like us, you were able to pronounce all the words in this brief excerpt from *A Brief History of Time,* but the passage as a whole didn't make much sense. And it probably didn't help much that you "knew" the meaning of the individual words (except, perhaps, for *antimatter*). Being able to pronounce the words, knowing the syntax and the meanings of individual words is insufficient to make sense of this text or any other text. Unless you possess the relevant conceptual background, this passage will never make much sense.

This doesn't mean that people can't learn something new by reading about it. Every text has the potential to teach us something. However, whether we learn something new through reading is a function of our ability to make connections between the new information in the text and what we already know. If connections cannot be made—if we lack the relevant background knowledge to make the connection—then learning will be difficult, as in the case of the passage from Stephen Hawking. Because of differences in our background knowledge and experience not all texts have the same potential to teach us, and again, because of differences in what we already know, we will all learn different lessons from any particular text. Some of you may, for example, have learned something from Stephen Hawking. Regrettably, we did not.

Pragmatic Cues

Pragmatics refers to the rules that govern the use of language in context. Writers (and speakers) refer to the context of language use (e.g., the physical setting, the writer's purpose, the physical and social distance between readers and writers, readers' background knowledge, and so forth) to determine appropriate topics, syntax, word choice, and so on. Consider, for example, the following sentences which have roughly the same meaning.

- Teachers of students with learning disabilities have shown increasing interest in whole language theory and practice as a framework for teaching reading and writing.

- Lately LD teachers have shown much more interest in whole language.

- I know a lot of LD teachers who are into whole language.

Even though these three sentences have similar meanings, we wouldn't expect them to be used interchangeably. The first sentence is most likely to be written in a formal paper. (In fact, this is the opening sentence of an article by Dudley-Marling.) It could be spoken, but probably only in a very formal setting like a conference presentation. The second version could be written or spoken, but it's still somewhat formal, signaling some distance between the writer (or speaker) and the audience. The third sentence is likely to be spoken, probably in a less formal setting, maybe a school staffroom. There are probably an infinite number of ways to convey this meaning, but the forms we choose depend on our linguistic and cultural background, our assessment of the language context, and our purpose(s). If, for example, our purpose includes enhancing our own status as *someone who knows* about trends in learning disabilities—and this is one of the purposes of academic writing—we may prefer the first sentence. If we wish to signal a friendly informality, the third sentence, "I know a lot of LD teachers who are into whole language," is more appropriate.

Readers and listeners also use their knowledge of pragmatic rules to make sense of what they read or hear. Imagine you read in *Newsweek* that Bill Clinton's press secretary responded to persistent press inquiries by saying: "The president is aware of the issue and will consult his advisors to study the problem further." Most of us understand this as meaning the president will do no such thing. His press secretary is just trying to avoid answering a question. In a different context, however, we might conclude that the president really was going to "consult his advisors to study the problem further." (See Grice, 1978, for a detailed explanation of the operation of pragmatics.)

How the context of language use affects the meaning of oral or written language is often very subtle and frequently accounts for the fact that children from different cultural or language backgrounds often get very different meanings from texts they read or from what their teachers say. Shirley Brice Heath (1983) reports, for example, that students from working-class Black communities were confused by teachers' indirect requests for action (e.g., "It's time to put away our toys.") In their experience the assertion ("It's time . . .") did not count as a request for action the way it did for middle-class students. Similarly, different expectations about how language works in various sociocultural contexts may lead some students to miss the humor in a story or see humor where none was intended. Whenever misunderstandings occur in our classrooms, especially among students and teachers from different cultural or language backgrounds, we would do well to consider the possibility that there is a conflict in expectations about how language operates in different social settings.

There is much more to reading and writing, however, than our knowledge of graphophonics, syntax, semantics, and pragmatics. Written language is an active process by which readers and writers combine their knowledge of the world with their knowledge of language within a social, historical, and cultural context to transact meaning. This is the topic of the next section.

Language as a Process

Reading and writing are transactive, sociopsycholinguistic processes in which people use active strategies for constructing meaning as they interact with print as readers or writers (Rosenblatt, 1978; Shanklin, 1981; Weaver, 1994). Written language is transactive in the sense that both readers and writers contribute something (through texts) to the act of making meaning. Rosenblatt puts it this way: "Transaction designates . . . an ongoing process in which the elements or factors are . . . aspects of a total situation, each conditioned by and conditioning the other" (1978, p. 17). As transactions, reading processes cannot be described as either top down or bottom up since they are clearly both. We mention this because whole language is sometimes misrepresented as a top-down process that ignores graphophonic cues. This will be important to remember when we discuss the role of phonics in whole language instruction later in this chapter.

Reading and writing are sociolinguistic processes in that they are always used and understood in sociocultural contexts that shape the meaning of texts. As Halliday puts it:

> Language comes to life only when functioning in some environment. We do not experience language in isolation—if we did we would not recognize it as language—but always in relation to a scenario, some background of per-

sons and actions and events from which the things are said to derive their meaning. (1978, p. 28)

The meaning of language, written or oral, derives not so much from the content of words as from the social and cultural context within which it is used, including the "interplay of what went before and what will come later" (Bloome & Egan-Robertson, 1993, p. 309). From this perspective, words have meanings independent of the intentions of writers or speakers. (See Gee, 1990.) A remark about skin color or physical appearance, for example, derives its meaning from the historical and cultural context independent of the speaker's intention. Language can be racist or sexist even if the speaker or writer isn't. In this way, writers and speakers get some meanings "for free" (Gee, 1990), something not understood by critics of politically correct language.

In this section we'll discuss *language as a psychological process* and *language as a social process* separately. Again, this is merely a matter of convenience for our readers since language—reading, writing, speaking, and listening—always involve people in psychological and social processes.

Language as a Psychological Process

Each instance of written language behavior is a complex sociopsycholinguistic event requiring the orchestration of graphophonic, syntactic, and semantic cues within a language context in order to construct meaning (Harste & Burke, 1978). That is, reading and writing demand that readers and writers make use of graphophonic, syntactic, semantic, and pragmatic cues simultaneously. The various cues interact with each other to facilitate the production or reception of other language cues. Edelsky observes that language systems "not only operate in context; they also are interdependent, each one having consequences for the other. In any instance of genuine . . . language use, a choice in one system has ramifications for what choices or interpretations are possible in another" (1984, p. 9). Because available cues and processing requirements vary according to the context of use, each composition-comprehension transaction between writer and reader is unique. Therefore, we would never expect a reader to assign precisely the same meaning to subsequent readings of a given text given changes in setting, the reader's background knowledge (which is changed by each reading of the text) and purpose, and so on.

In reading and writing we use a variety of strategies to process language cues to make sense of texts. Readers/writers use these strategies—*predicting*, *confirming*, and *integrating*—as they find them useful, and often simultaneously. These strategies help readers orchestrate graphophonic, syntactic, semantic, and pragmatic cues at both focal and global levels. Writers must also be aware of these strategies if they are to anticipate the needs of readers.

Predicting is a strategy we use in all aspects of our lives. Before we open our eyes in the morning, we may make global predictions about what we expect to happen that day. We may also make focal predictions about what we expect to see when we open our eyes. We predict our way through the events of our lives, only becoming conscious of our predictions when we are surprised that they are not confirmed. The same thing happens during reading. In reading, we predict what the author will say next and how she will say it depending on our experience (including experience with authors, genres, and so forth) and our linguistic, social, and cultural backgrounds. We might globally predict the next event in the story at the same time that we make a more focal prediction about the next sentence. We may also predict how the author will use language in the rest of the sentence and what letters are likely to be in the rest of a word.

Our enormous store of knowledge about the world, the structure of language, and print allows us to make predictions with enough confidence that we need only sample the print on the page (Smith, 1973). We sample only those cues we need to make sense of a text. On the basis of our experience with print, we usually know which cues are significant and need to be considered. When we are on the same wavelength with the author and have shared backgrounds and language, predicting is an easy task. When we do not share the author's background and/or language, predicting is not easy and we find ourselves sampling more cues from the text in an attempt to construct meaning. In other words, when our background knowledge and the text do not match, we are forced to depend more heavily on graphophonic cues, which will always make reading more difficult.

In writing, we also use prediction strategies that are based on the context of the writing situation and on the text we have produced once we begin writing. Prior to and during writing, we make global predictions about what we need to say and what we don't need to say in order to fulfill our communicative intentions toward our readers. As we write, we continue to make global predictions, but we also make focal predictions about content and language—what we'll say next and precisely how we'll say it. "As in reading, prior text constrains what one may write in upcoming text" (Shanklin, 1981, p. 81). As we read what we've written, we predict again, this time partly as an outside reader of our own writing and partly as an inside reader, considering other options available to us in composition.

Confirming is another strategy we use regularly in our lives. As we experience life, we monitor whether our experiences make sense. When an experience doesn't make sense, we may dissociate ourselves from the experience; we may rethink the experience; we may seek the experience again, hoping to make sense of it this time; or we may seek outside help in attempting to make sense of the experience. Again, the same is true of reading and writing.

Proficient readers constantly monitor whether they are making sense of the author's cues and their purposes for reading. In essence, they ask themselves, "Does this make sense?" and when it does they keep reading. When a text doesn't make sense, readers have several options. They may decide not to read the text. They may read the text again in hopes that it will provide more cues or that they'll think of something that hadn't occurred to them before. They may continue reading in hopes that the author will provide more cues; they may rethink what they have read. Or they may look outside the text for help in understanding what they are reading.

In writing, we also use confirmation strategies to monitor whether we are making sense to ourselves and to our potential readers. When we read our own text and think we are making sense, we keep writing. When we don't think we're making sense, we may decide to stop writing, we may revise our text so that it does make sense, or we may keep writing in hopes that we'll eventually figure out how to make sense. At the same time writers consider whether they're making sense to potential readers, they also consider whether they're making sense to the first reader of any piece, the writer himself. If it doesn't make sense to me, the thinking goes, it can't possibly make sense to anyone else.

In reading and writing, the strategies of predicting and confirming (or disconfirming) not only help readers/writers process language cues and solve meaning construction problems, they also provide continual feedback. Readers or writers keep a constant check on their own comprehension or composition monitoring until the text has been read or written.

A third strategy we use in our lives and apply to reading and writing is *integrating*. That is, as we read, we integrate what we already know, believe, and feel with our interpretations of what the author knows, believes, and feels. We choose which information will be remembered or integrated on the basis of whether the information is important for the reading purposes we have established and on the basis of the relationship between our schema and the author's schema. Because all of us approach a text with different backgrounds, beliefs, and feelings, the strategy of integrating renders the reading transaction unique each time a text is read.

As we write, we must keep in mind our potential readers' needs. If we wish to persuade our readers to a particular point of view with a piece of writing, for example, we have to think about how what we say and how we say it will be perceived by readers. Essentially, we have to integrate what it is that we know, believe, and feel with what it is that we perceive our readers know, believe, and feel in order to make decisions about what to write and how to write it. If we can't do that, our attempt to present a particular point of view to our readers is likely to fall flat. We choose which information will be included in the piece of writing on the basis of whether the information is important for the writing purposes we have established and on the basis of the relationship between our own schema and what we perceive to be the readers' schema.

As we have described the strategies used in the reading and writing processes, we have attempted to explicate the parallels between reading and writing. Our description of reading and writing as processes can be graphically represented, as shown in Figure 1-1 (adapted from Y. Goodman & Burke, 1980).

The notion that reading and writing are analogous processes provides an important basis for the evaluation and instructional chapters of this book. It is not only the end products of reading and writing that we are concerned with observing, but also the processes themselves. What students do during reading and writing provides data from which instructional decisions about reading and writing can be made, including how to positively affect reading and writing products. Likewise, we have found that instructional attention to the process of reading/writing—in particular to the strategies of predicting, confirming, and

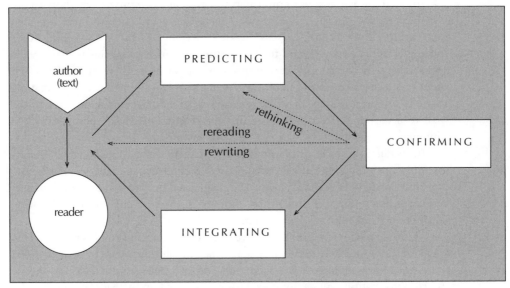

FIG. 1-1 *Reading and writing as processes (adapted from Goodman & Burke, 1980)*

integrating—has a positive impact both on reading and writing and on reading and writing products. If students learn to process language cues and solve meaning construction problems more effectively in the process of reading/writing, their comprehension and composition improve as well.

In summary, readers and writers simultaneously orchestrate various cueing systems and problem-solving strategies as they attempt to make sense of texts. But since the sociocultural context of any reading or writing event imposes different demands, readers and writers don't always do the same things as they manage these cueing systems and problem-solving strategies. Some reading activities require readers to rely more or less on graphophonics and syntax, for example. Students who are drilled on isolated word lists or "nonsense" words rely on graphophonic cues virtually to the exclusion of syntactic or semantic cues. A reading passage and comprehension questions may enable students to rely more on syntax and graphophonics as in our Marlup example.

Language as a Social Process

As social and cultural practices reading and writing also "involve specific ways of interacting with people, specific ways of using language (including written language), specific sets of values for various kinds of behaviors, and specific sets of interpretations for understanding and guiding behavior" (Bloome et al., 1991, p. 22). A Gospel read to a congregation and reading bits from the newspaper at the breakfast table, for example, involve people in different ways of talking, interacting, thinking, valuing, and believing (Gee, 1990). Similarly, school reading lessons often require that students display behaviors appropriate to doing school—how to act, think, and talk like a student (Bloome et al., 1991). Wortham, for example, observed how students in high school English classes learn to display reading comprehension to their teachers by relating assigned reading to their personal experience during class discussions (1993). In this context reading *means* summoning personal experiences to signal comprehension independent of whether students understood the story in the conventional sense. Viewing reading and writing as social practices has a number of important implications for teachers of struggling readers and writers. First of all, literacy as social practice indicates that *people do not learn to read once and for all.* Gee argues that the verb *read* can never be used intransitively. (The same can be said of *write.*) Instead, people learn to read particular texts in particular ways appropriate to the social and cultural context (Gee, 1990). As Gee puts it, people do not learn to read, but learn to read texts of type X in way Y. Importantly:

> One does not learn to read texts of type X in way Y unless one has had experience in settings where texts of type X are read in way Y . . . One has to be socialized in a *practice* to learn to read texts of type X in way Y, a practice other people have already mastered (Gee, 1990, p. 43).

If we expect students to be able to use reading and writing for a range of purposes in a variety of settings (recall our primary goal for literacy instruction) then we need to provide students with a wide range of literacy experiences. Otherwise, the range of texts and the way students are able to "read" them will not support their needs for literacy in out-of-school contexts.

Viewing reading and writing as social practices also enables us to recognize that schools often privilege certain literacy practices and, therefore, the children who come from homes in which those literacy practices are prevalent. The schools' valuing, for example, of storybook reading, the telling of fanciful stories, talking *about* language (e.g., explicitly stating phonics rules), and "essay-text" literacy (which assumes that speakers/writers should ignore what listeners/readers know and explicitly say it anyway) mirror literacy practices in many middle-class homes (Gee, 1990; Heath, 1983).

Many middle-class children appear to learn to read and write so easily because school literacy practices so closely match their literacy experiences at home. Conversely, children from nondominant linguistic and cultural backgrounds often come to school with a range of literacy experiences (see Gee, 1990; Heath, 1983; Schieffelin & Gilmore, 1986; Scollon & Scollon, 1981), but more often their "ways with words" are not valued by the schools (Heath, 1983). So, for many struggling readers and writers, the problem isn't simply learning to read or write, but learning to read and write in ways valued by the schools. We imagine that at this point some of you are thinking something like, "This is all very interesting, but if I don't teach my students to read and write in the ways society and schools expect they will have little chance of succeeding in school, and, like it or not, for now school success means vocational success." We agree. Viewing literacy as social practice doesn't change the reality that many students—especially students from nondominant social and cultural groups—are having serious difficulty learning to read and write in school. But it does suggest a somewhat different response from teachers. Based on our belief that reading and writing are social practices and that schools (unfairly) favor the literacy practices of some students over others, we suggest the following strategies.

In the long term, teachers of struggling readers and writers must work to expand the range of reading and writing practices valued in their classrooms and their schools. Expanding the range of literacy practices in our classrooms—encouraging students to expand the range of texts they read (and write), the purposes for which they read and write, and their stance (e.g., critical, interpretive, and so on) benefits all of our students since the "skills" acquired learning (some) school literacy practices may not generalize to other settings.

> Defining literacy skill as a collection of socially constructed practices . . . suggests that the traditional skill-based school instruction cannot transfer to literacy use in other contexts. The skills of exercises are not the same as the skills of literacy in other social contexts (Myers, 1992, p. 302).

In the short term, teachers of struggling readers and writers may need to apprentice students from nondominant cultural and linguistic background into the middle-class literacy practices favored by schools. This may, as Lisa Delpit suggests, require some explicit instruction in traditional school literacy practices such as learning to talk about literacy and storybook reading (1988). But it is important to remember that such instruction supports students learning *school reading* and *school writing*, though it may do little to help students discover and use the power of literacy in their social and vocational lives outside of school.

2 Whole Language
It's a Matter of Principles[1]

E merging from our theoretical understanding of written language, our own experiences as teachers, our reading of research on whole language instruction (see Rhodes & Shanklin [1989], Stephens [1991], and Weaver [1994] for summaries of research on whole language practice), and our work with whole language teachers across North America is a set of pedagogical principles which inform our work with struggling readers and writers. In this chapter we attempt to detail these foundational principles and their relationship to current understandings of language development. We conclude this chapter by discussing the appropriateness of whole language instruction for struggling readers and writers including remedial students and students with learning disabilities.

Some Pedagogical Principles

The first pedagogical principle informing whole language practice is:

Children Are Always Learning

When we look at struggling readers and writers we don't see deficits or deviance. We see students who may not always learn what their teachers want them to or who may not always learn as quickly as their parents and teachers expect, but who are capable learners nonetheless. One of us has a niece named Pam. When Pam was in first grade she was diagnosed as having an Attention Deficit Disorder and put on Ritalin by her family doctor. Apparently, Pam had difficulty following her teacher's directions and completing her school work. When she visited Anne Dudley-Marling at her grandmother's farm (free from the influence of Ritalin), Pam and Anne spent an afternoon catching and studying butterflies, sometimes consulting a butterfly guidebook to learn more about the butterflies they caught. It

---

1 These principles were first presented in an article, "Whole language: It's a matter of principle(s)" by Curt Dudley-Marling (1995), which appeared in *Reading and Writing Quarterly*.

was not the case that Pam *couldn't* attend. It's just that she *didn't* attend to what her teacher expected when she expected it.

All children, except for the most severely retarded, are marvelous learners. Frank Smith points out that by age four most children have vocabularies of over 10,000 words and are adding 20 words to their personal lexicons each day (1986). Those same four-year-olds have also mastered a bewildering number of word-ordering rules of nearly indescribable complexity, as well as the remarkably subtle rules for using what they know about language in a range of social settings. Four-year-olds have also developed complex understandings of the worlds in which they live. They still have much to learn to be sure, but what they have learned leaves no doubt about their native abilities as language learners.

Because we believe that all students are capable, productive learners, we prefer to view the students with whom we work in terms of what they know and not what they don't know (i.e., deficits). Consider, for example, the spellings in the following piece of writing produced by Charles, a third grader who spent part of his school day in a learning disability resource room.

> I whent to the curcrse with my famale and my cuson and we hab fyn togeter andb we saw peole jamping on the hrempin.
> (I went to the circus with my family and my cousin and we had fun together and we saw people jumping on the trampoline.)

Adopting a deficit view (What's wrong with this child?) focuses our attention on the numerous spelling errors in this writing sample. An alternative view assumes that, whatever his difficulties in school, Charles is a bright young boy. Viewing Charles's writing from this perspective we note that over half of the words are spelled correctly. Many words would be spelled correctly if just one letter were changed (e.g., "jamping," "fyn"), added (e.g., "togeter," "peole") or omitted (e.g., "whent," "andb"). His other misspellings represent good phonetic approximations (e.g., "curcrse," "famale," "cuson"). Despite his numerous spelling errors, Charles demonstrates a sophisticated understanding of the English spelling system. (See Read, 1975; Temple, Nathan, & Burris, 1982; Wilde, 1992.) We focus on what students like Charles know because we assume that this is the foundation on which we can build. Focusing on his deficits, on the other hand, would frustrate and discourage both Charles and his teachers.

Children Learn Best What's Meaningful and Relevant to Them

Our work with struggling readers and writers is informed by a constructivist view that defines learning as the integration of new knowledge with old knowledge (Piaget, 1971; Poplin, 1988; Smith, 1975). As Mary Poplin puts it, "Two or more learning experiences transform one another and transform the structure of present knowledge. *Thus, learning is not merely additive, it is transformative*" (1988, p. 414, emphasis added). From a constructivist point of view, students learn most easily when they're able to draw on their background knowledge and experience to make sense of school lessons. Meaningfulness is one of the principal reasons language learning is so effortless for children, at least before they come to school. Meaningfulness also facilitates learning in school. The teacher who begins a unit on plants, for example, with a discussion of what students already know about plants helps her students activate their existing knowledge to make sense of new information presented in the unit. Similarly, a geography lesson that starts with a study of the neighborhood around the school gives students a schema for understanding other geographical regions.

When students are not able to draw on their background knowledge to make sense of school lessons—when, for example, learning has been fragmented for purposes of instruction—learning becomes more difficult. Here we have in mind the fragmenting of reading and writing for the purpose of making learning to read and write easier which, from our point of view makes learning harder by making it less meaningful to learners. Of course, it is possible to learn things that aren't personally meaningful or relevant, but such learning will certainly be more difficult and is much more likely to be forgotten (Holt, 1982; Poplin, 1988).

Students Learn Most Easily When They Have Some Measure of Control over the Decisions Affecting Their Learning

Ken Goodman observed that "Language development is empowering: the learner owns the process, makes the decisions about when to use it, what for and with what results" (Goodman, 1986, p. 26). Even the casual observation of young children reveals how they use language to control the environment and assert their identities and independence. No doubt the power of language plays a major role in children's desire to learn language and the speed with which they gain control over its uses.

Literacy is also empowering *"if the learner is in control of what's done with it"* (Goodman, 1986, p.26, emphasis added). Teachers who allow their students to select their writing topics, the audiences for their writing, their reading materials, and so on, permit students to exercise some measure of control over the content and purpose of their reading and writing experiences. Students who read and write to fulfill *their* intentions are far more likely to discover the power of literacy to affect their lives in and out of school. When students take control over their reading and writing they learn skills and conventions—like punctuation, spelling, decoding, and predicting—as a means of supporting their goals.

On the other hand, students whose reading and writing experiences are carefully managed by teachers through the use of worksheets and basal readers, for example, learn only how to use reading and writing to "do school" (Bloome et al., 1991). Under these conditions, in which students have little stake in school learning beyond earning grades and pleasing their parents and teachers, teaching (and learning) can be difficult. Holt concludes: "Why *don't* they learn what we try to teach them? The answer I have come to boils down to this: *Because* we teach them—that is, try to control the contents of their minds" (1982, p. 231).

Permitting students more control over their literacy learning does not mean that teachers need to abdicate their responsibility to support students' reading and writing development. In our opinion, teachers who withdraw their instructional support for fear of interfering with student "ownership" create a laissez-faireism which is the worst perversion of whole language instruction. If anything, our experience indicates that teachers who share responsibility for literacy learning with their students are even more involved in students' reading and writing development as they offer their expertise and experience to support students' intentions (e.g., Calkins, 1994; Weaver, 1990) as in the following example:

> In October Jennifer, Wayne, Troy, Nicholas, and Hugh—students in Mr. Marling's third-grade class—started bringing fan magazines to school so they could read and talk about their favorite TV and movie stars. When they started writing letters to the cast of *Beverly Hills 90210,* Mr. Marling brought these five students together to share with them the format for writing personal letters. He also displayed an example of a personal letter in the appropriate format for their reference.
>
> Mr. Marling didn't teach his students the format for personal letters because a curriculum guide indicated third grade was the appropriate time for learning this skill. Nor did he postpone teaching this skill because the curriculum guide indicated that third grade was not the appropriate time. Rather, Mr. Marling taught students a skill because *they* needed it. He offered his expertise as a way of supporting his students' intention to write a friendly letter. The work of Calkins (1983, 1994), Atwell (1987), and Graves (1983), among others, demonstrates how well children learn effective writing skills when teachers work to support students' intentions and not the other way around.

Children Learn to Read and Write by Reading and Writing

We believe that children learn to talk because they are immersed in a "veritable language bath" before coming to school (Lindfors, 1987). During their early years children have frequent opportunities to use talk and hear talk used in a range of settings, for a variety of purposes. This principle of language learning also applies to literacy learning; that is, children learn to read and write by reading and writing (Edelsky, 1991; Gee, 1994). Therefore, children must spend a great deal of time reading and writing in order to become effective readers and writers (Allington, 1993; McGill-Franzen & Allington, 1991; Smith, 1981; Weaver, 1994). Explicit reading and writing instruction is often necessary—especially for struggling readers and writers—but it is insufficient for students to develop into effective readers and writers. Reading and writing instruction must be embedded in an environment in which students have frequent opportunities to use reading and writing and to see reading and writing used for a variety of purposes, in a range of settings. Frequent reading and writing provide students with opportunities to build on, consolidate, and extend knowledge gained from reading and writing lessons.

This is a good place to comment on one of the most common misconceptions about whole language instruction: that whole language teachers do not teach skills, especially phonics. (We do acknowledge that there are "whole language teachers" who do eschew any explicit teaching, but, from our perspective, this is not good teaching.) Ken Goodman comments:

> Whole language is the term given to instructional curriculum that builds on the view that readers and writers integrate all available information in authentic literacy events as they make sense of print. Whole language teachers don't reject phonics; they put it in its proper place (1993, p. 108).

Whole language teachers recognize the value of a rich literacy learning environment, but they also acknowledge that struggling readers and writers often need frequent, intensive, and explicit support and direction from their teachers. Therefore, despite claims to the contrary (e.g., Spiegel, 1992), *good whole language teachers do teach phonics* (e.g., Dudley-Marling, 1995; Newman & Church, 1990; Weaver, 1990) and many of the strategies presented later in this book support students' developing uses of orthographic cues. Whole language teachers do, however, tend to avoid the isolated drilling of phonics rules which demands that students rely on orthographic information to the near exclusion of semantic, syntactic, and pragmatic cues. This kind of instruction prepares students only for the narrowly defined literacy they will encounter nowhere else but school and, in the case of struggling readers and writers, may only exacerbate their learning problems. In any case, holistic literacy instruction may be at least as effective at teaching the skills of school literacy as programs focusing on isolated skill instruction (e.g., Dahl & Freppon, 1995; Freppon & Dahl, 1991; Goodman, 1993; Weaver, 1994).

Errors Are Critical to Learning

Those of us trained in the behavioral tradition were taught that errors were to be avoided. Our instructors told us that mistakes, if practiced, would be learned. This notion has a commonsense appeal which is probably behind parents' concerns about teachers who don't correct their children's spelling errors. Children's early language learning demonstrates, however, that even years of producing unconventional forms like "runned" and "brang" doesn't interfere with children's ability to acquire standard forms. Arguably, repeatedly correcting children's language "errors," by responding to the form and not the content of what they have to say, may discourage children from talking at all. If children learn to talk by talking, anything that discourages children from talking would certainly interfere with children's language development.

Additionally, from a Piagetian perspective, children's "errors" are hypotheses which are crucial to their learning (Gruber & Voneche, 1977). From this perspective, students who are unwilling to risk errors may be disadvantaged as learners. Charles, the third-grade student with learning disabilities who wrote the piece about the circus, had been reluctant to write words he couldn't spell and, therefore, wrote very little. Early in the school year Charles was also reluctant to tackle books he couldn't read independently. There are lots of Charleses in our classes, students whose reluctance to take risks further delays their written language development. These students' learning needs would be better served by a willingness to risk mistakes and to learn from them.

Whole language teachers endeavor to encourage students to take risks as readers and writers by creating an atmosphere of trust—free from the tyranny of constant evaluation. These teachers see errors as data that provide insights into students' knowledge and abilities, not as evidence of problems. But whole language educators don't ignore students' errors. Errors are used to plan lessons. Whole language teachers may not automatically correct students' oral reading errors, but may follow the reading with a minilesson that calls attention to consonant blends or long vowels, for example. We'll talk more about this in later chapters.

Children's Learning Should Be Celebrated, Not Rewarded

Children learn language because it works, and parents encourage their children's language development by providing appropriate responses to children's language (i.e., they make sure it *works*). If little Ian asks for a drink ("Joos, pees.") Dad gets him a drink. He does not say, "Good talking, Ian." Certainly, parents get excited over their child's first words, which may be celebrated with a call to aunts, friends, and grandparents. But these "rewards" are incidental to language learning. It's the appropriate response of listeners that keeps children on the road of language learning.

Whole language teachers celebrate students' reading and writing by encouraging students to share their reading and writing with classmates and parents. Students may share their writing by publishing it and adding it to the classroom or school library, by displaying it prominently in the classroom, or by orally sharing their writing with classmates. Similarly, teachers may celebrate a student's fluent reading of a book by inviting the student to read it to the class or by sending the book home so the student can read it to her parents. Celebrations such as these recognize students' achievements and offer students authentic responses from audiences.

Whole language teachers do not, however, believe that learning requires coercion or irrelevant rewards (F. Smith, 1978, 1986). From a holistic perspective, the need for extrinsic rewards most likely indicates that what's being learned has little value for the learner and is not, therefore, worth teaching. Conversely, if what we teach has the potential to satisfy students' natural curiosities and to fulfill their needs in and out of school, learning will be its own reward.

Learning Is Social

Oral and written language are complex social acts which can only be learned in social settings. Therefore, whole language teachers seek to situate reading and writing within a community of learners in which students learn *with* and *from* each other. As part of a community of learners, struggling readers and writers have frequent opportunities to talk about their reading and writing. These interactions demonstrate the purposes for which people read and write, suggest topics for writing and new authors to be read, reveal the struggles of readers and writers as they try to make sense with and from print, and illustrate problem-solving processes readers and writers use. Social interaction also provides opportunities for students to use talk to extend their reading comprehension (Short & Pierce, 1990; Peterson & Eeds, 1990) and to obtain authentic responses to their writing (Dyson, 1989). In social settings students will also be able to provide direct support for one another's learning (Hansen, 1987).

Literacy learning is also facilitated when students are able to use language to share, discuss, debate, collaborate, and question. In general, if students do not have opportunities to engage in social interaction with others who offer a range of alternative points of view, there will be no new viewpoints to incorporate into students' thinking and, therefore, no intellectual development (Bayer, 1990). Throughout this text we will make every effort to situate instructional strategies within the context of classroom communities.

Teachers Must Practice What They Teach

Teachers who write regularly discover that writers rarely follow a linear process of pre-writing, writing, revising, and editing. Sometimes writers do not pre-write and often they revise *as* they write (see Murray, 1990). And some writing (e.g., letters to friends, grocery lists) may not be revised at all. As writers, teachers will also discover the kind of feedback from readers that they find useful. Teachers who write will also learn that both the content and form of writing are functions of the writer's purpose, topic, genre, and audience.

Similarly, teachers who regularly read and reflect on what they do in the act of reading discover the processes readers use to make sense of texts. They learn that even effective readers produce miscues (i.e., errors), but that the miscues of effective readers rarely change the meaning of texts. And, if miscues do change the meaning of texts, effective readers correct them (Goodman, Watson & Burke, 1987). Reflecting on their reading also enables teachers to discover various sense-making strategies readers use as they read including, for example, predicting, confirming, and integrating. As readers, teachers will also discover that the processes readers employ vary according to their purposes, the content and structure of texts, and the social context. Teachers who reflect on their reading may notice that they don't always finish books they choose, which may affect their expectations of their students.

We firmly believe that teachers will find it difficult to teach reading and writing effectively if they don't read and write themselves and take the time to reflect on what they do in the process of reading and writing. We know how difficult this can be. Teachers are overworked and it seems to be getting worse, but without regular experience as readers and writers, teachers won't know what they are aiming for in their students' reading and writing.

Teachers Are Learners, Too

Whole language teachers share a set of beliefs about language and language learning. Whole language teachers do not, however, share a common set of instructional practices. In fact, whole language theorists reject the notion that there can ever be a uniform set of whole language practices (Edelsky et al., 1991). Instead, whole language teachers create and adapt instructional strategies based on the needs of their students, the settings within which they teach, their needs and interests as teachers, models provided by other whole language teachers, professional literature, and their shared beliefs. In this sense teachers learn to teach by observing their students as they read and write and as they respond to reading and writing instruction. And, of course, what teachers learn in the practice of teaching continually informs whole language theory, which is itself in a constant state of development.

Teachers learn to teach by teaching and, as learners, they must be given the same consideration as other learners. Teachers must be free to take risks and learn from their experience. Teachers who themselves have little control over their work may find it difficult to offer much freedom to their students (Five, 1995). Teachers must also be free to draw on their background knowledge and experience to support the learning of their students. Ways must also be found to celebrate teachers' achievements. And teachers must be given the time they need to reflect on their teaching practice and to share their experiences with colleagues. From this perspective, teachers' working conditions become a factor in the development of effective whole language teachers.

Whole language theory and practice has had a tremendous influence on reading and writing instruction all over the world. Instruction for struggling readers and writers, however, especially students placed in remedial and special education programs, tends to be informed by behavioral principles and the assumption that written language instruction needs to be slowed down and made more concrete (i.e., broken into instructional "bits") for these students (McGill-Franzen & Allington, 1991). Continued resistance to whole language instruction by special education and remedial reading teachers is, we think, based on the honest belief that whole language is not appropriate for many struggling readers and writers and on misunderstandings about the possibility of explicit instruction within a whole language framework (e.g., Shapiro, 1992, 1993; Siegel, 1992). This book is, of course, based on our assumption that whole language theory and practice is particularly appropriate for struggling readers and writers. Therefore, in the final section of this chapter, we consider the relevance of whole language theory and practice to the instruction of struggling readers and writers.

Whole Language and "Readers and Writers with a Difference"

In the first edition of this book "readers and writers with a difference" referred specifically to students identified as learning disabled or remedial readers (e.g., students in Title I programs). In this edition we've broadened our notion of "readers and writers with a difference" to include all students for whom reading and writing are a struggle whether or not they've been formally identified (i.e., labeled) and whether they are served in a self-contained classroom, a resource room, or the regular classroom. This decision is based on our belief that reading and writing instruction should be informed by our assessment of individual students' needs and their knowledge and use of literacy. Responding to students on the basis of their assignment to general categories (e.g., learning disabled, remedial, and so forth) ignores students' individual needs by assuming broad commonalities among children with similar labels. We also believe that good reading instruction ought to be informed by sound theory—our notions of reading and reading theory do not change because a child happens to have been assigned to an administrative category for purposes of funding or grouping. The theoretical perspective and pedagogical principles we outlined in the previous chapter apply to the instruction of all children, although we acknowledge the struggling readers' and writers' needs for more frequent, explicit, intensive, and individual support and direction.

In this chapter we review three versions of instruction for struggling readers and writers, each informed by different sets of assumptions, which emerge from our reading of the special education and language arts literature. We discuss these three versions of literacy instruction as a means of taking up the broader issue of the appropriateness of whole language instruction with struggling readers and writers.

The Model of Unique Instruction

One version of instruction for struggling readers and writers is that some students, especially those who have been labeled learning disabled, require *qualitatively* different sorts of instruction (see, for example, Hallahan & Kauffman, 1976; Lerner, 1993). Proponents of this point of view sometimes appeal to evidence of neurological dysfunction to support arguments for unique instruction. The work of Gerald Coles, among others, has called into question much of the research linking learning disabilities to neurological dysfunction (1987).

We believe, however, that identifying the cause of reading and writing failure is educationally relevant only if the cause can be related to a set of instructionally relevant characteristics. If, for example, students with learning disabilities shared a set of characteristics and, therefore, needs different from non–learning disabled students, it might be arguable that these students require reading and writing instruction qualitatively different from other students. In reality, however, there is no set of characteristics that apply to *all and only* students with learning disabilities, which is why current assessment practices often fail to discriminate between students with learning disabilities and other underachievers (Epps, McGue & Ysseldyke, 1982; Epps, Ysseldyke & McGue, 1984; Ysseldyke, Algozzine, Shinn & McGue, 1982; Deshler, Schumaker, Warner, Alley & Clark, 1980), normally achieving students (Dudley-Marling, Kaufman & Tarver, 1981; Haber, 1979, 1982; Hare, 1977; Weener, 1983). What all students identified as learning disabled share is the experience of struggling in school and not a common set of behavioral, psychological, or neurological characteristics. The characteristics attributed to students with learning disabilities apply only to a statistically constructed "average" LD child and, therefore, have little instructional relevance. These sorts of findings led Ysseldyke and Algozzine to conclude that the argument over what is and is not a learning disability is fruitless and misses the more important point about how to teach struggling students. "To ponder, argue, quibble, and mix about what to call them and who they are has merely served to sidetrack interest from the bigger, more important question—what do we do with them?" (1983, p. 29). We agree. There are significant numbers of children who are failing in school, children in need of our help, some of whom are labeled "learning disabled," some of whom are called "remedial," others of whom are referred to as "at risk." Certainly, our goal must be to identify effective instructional strategies for students who struggle in school and, if possible, eliminate structural barriers that contribute to so much school failure in the first place. (See Skrtic, 1991, for a discussion of the role administrative structures play in creating school failure.) It is doubtful, however, that engaging in endless polemics over what to call students for whom school is a struggle will ever get us very far.

Perhaps following the reasoning of Ysseldyke and Algozzine the case for unique instruction is more often put this way: Since these students did not profit from the "normal" curriculum, something fundamentally different is needed. Special education was founded on, and is sustained by, this assumption. Typically, that "something different" has taken the form of behavioral approaches to reading and writing instruction, although research by Allington and McGill-Franzen (1989) raises doubts about whether instruction in special and remedial classes really differs—either quantitatively or qualitatively—from what goes on in the regular classroom (Allington, 1993; McGill-Franzen & Allington, 1991). To the degree that instruction in special and remedial programs has been different, it hasn't always been very effective although there is no doubt such programs have benefited individual children (e.g., Carlberg & Kavale, 1980; Glass, 1983). Some critics have concluded that special education programs may actually harm both students and their families (e.g., Granger & Granger, 1986; Taylor, 1991).

There is, however, a more fundamental problem with the notion of unique instruction for struggling readers and writers based on our earlier discussion of reading and writing as social practices. You'll recall our position that each reading and writing event places readers and writers within a sociocultural context in which they must orchestrate various cueing systems and strategies to make sense with and from print. You will also recall the argument that the skills of literacy in one social context are not the same as the literacy skills of other social contexts (Myers, 1992). There is no reason, therefore, to expect that the literacy skills students acquire in a unique instructional context equip students to participate in reading and writing anywhere but in that unique and, therefore, atypical setting. A behavioral approach to reading instruction that focusses narrowly on the decoding of letters, syllables, and words, for example, may prepare students to read in similar contexts (e.g., reading tests), but not in settings where they encounter extended texts that demand readers who draw on a range of linguistic and cognitive resources to construct meaning. This explains why there is often little relationship between students' reading test scores and qualitative evaluations of students' extended reading of texts (Altwerger & Resta, 1986).

There is a more sinister side to unique instruction, however. For struggling readers and writers unique instruction has usually meant, as we noted earlier, instruction that is slowed down and more concrete (McGill-Franzen & Allington, 1991). Summarizing research on the reading instruction offered to poor readers, Weaver (1994) concludes:.

- Readers in lower reading groups spend approximately 70–75% of their instructional time reading orally trying to say words correctly while their teachers listen and correct. Conversely, good readers spend 70–75% of their time reading silently for meaning and enjoyment. When readers in higher groups make a reading error—what is often called a miscue—teachers typically ignore the miscue or "suggest how the context may help to clarify the meaning. But when readers in lower reading groups make a miscue, teachers typically stop them and often call attention to the letter/sound cues exclusively, or correct the miscues immediately, giving the students in lower groups much less time to discover a lack of continuity in meaning and to correct themselves." (Weaver, 1994, pp. 300–301)

- Reading lessons for lower groups "are more teacher-centered, more tightly monitored, and more likely to focus on literal interpretation of text rather than upon drawing inferences, analyzing, evaluating, and extending or relating to what has been read" (Weaver, 1994, p. 301).

- Readers in lower reading groups "receive much more drill on isolated words than do readers in higher groups. The lower-group readers are kept busy practicing skills with workbooks and dittos, and they may be drilled on word lists and flash cards. The higher-group readers read whole books and participate in creative ways of enhancing and expressing comprehension" (Weaver, 1994, p. 301).

We aren't aware of research on differential writing instruction for good and poor writers, but our experience indicates that writing instruction for struggling writers is far more likely to focus on mechanical skills like spelling, punctuation, and handwriting while instruction for more able writers includes more opportunities to write extended texts.

The differential instruction afforded poor readers and writers, whose numbers include students assigned to special educational and remedial programs, has the effect of limiting the range of reading and writing practices to which struggling learners are exposed. As a result, able readers and writers learn to use reading and writing in a variety of settings for a range of purposes. Struggling readers and writers do not. Successful readers and writers learn to use literacy to establish and maintain social relationships and to examine and improve the conditions of their lives. Poor readers and writers learn the drills and exercises of school literacy. In this way, "unique," or differential, instruction may exacerbate the differences between successful and less successful learners. Put another way, the rich get richer and the poor get poorer.

This brings us back to the sinister side of unique instruction. Poor, Black, and Hispanic students—students who are especially likely to be disadvantaged by the effects of poverty and discrimination—are disproportionately represented among struggling readers and writers. To the degree that differential reading and writing instruction limits the literacy experiences of some students, such instruction also helps to maintain a status quo in which people's vocational and social opportunities are closely tied to their race, culture, and language. Unique instruction for struggling readers and writers—based in part on the assumption that whole language is appropriate only for more able learners—is not only theoretically and pedagogically unsound and ineffective, but it is also unjust.

This reasoning has led to initiatives like California's OLE (Optimal Learning Environment) Project, which is attempting to replace the slowed-down and concrete literacy instruction in resource room programs in school districts with large Hispanic populations with a holistic model of teaching and learning (Figueroa, Ruiz & Garcia, 1994). The assumption underlying the OLE project is that students disadvantaged by the effects of poverty and discrimination will make much better progress if they are offered the same literacy opportunities as successful learners. Like us, the developers of the OLE project assume that there are language learning principles that apply to all learners. The early results of this project, by showing significant gains in student reading, support these assumptions (Figueroa et al., 1994).

Eclecticism: The Best of All Worlds?

A common alternative to the model of unique instruction is eclecticism, which holds that "*multiple* perspectives and approaches will be necessary to accommodate the needs of children who possess differences in abilities and learning histories" (Kameenui, 1993). Here teachers select the "best" teaching and learning activities from various approaches to literacy—regardless of the theoretical underpinnings of these approaches— as a means of meeting the diverse needs of learners. Obviously, this approach appeals to our common sense, but eclecticism assumes that the task of teachers is to teach students to read and write once and for all, by whatever means. As we argued earlier, however, people do not learn to read once and for all. Reading and writing are social practices and different approaches to reading and writing instruction entail different social practices. The eclectic teacher who selects teaching strategies from skills-first and meaning-centered approaches to literacy instruction, for example, involves herself and her students in contradictory and, from the students' perspective, confusing assumptions about *how people learn* to read and *what it means* to read.

Whole language practice, for example, emphasizes the reader's role in meaning making. If a student is confronted with a word she doesn't know when reading, a whole language teacher will suggest a variety of strategies to the child—all of which stress the child's role in making sense. Other approaches to reading, however, emphasize the reader's responsibility to "break the code" as a means of "unlocking" the author's meaning. Here the reader's role in making meaning is relatively passive compared to the more active sense-making emphasized in whole language classrooms. Eclectic teachers who freely borrow "best" instructional practices from whole language and reading instruction emphasizing isolated decoding instruction risk involving students in significant contradictions on the role of readers in making meaning.

Whole language teachers also endeavor to help students develop a repertoire of reading and writing strategies as a means of supporting students' intentions to use reading and writing within a range of sociocultural contexts. This contrasts with the assumption underlying other approaches to literacy instruction that reading is a matter of learning a finite set of skills that apply to reading in all situations. The assumption is that readers learn to read once and for all by mastering a set of autonomous skills (Gee, 1990). Ultimately, eclecticism assumes that reading and writing instruction is a matter of acquiring requisite skills and, therefore, has more in common with skills-first models of literacy instruction than whole language theory and practice. Eclectic teachers who *borrow* whole language practices in the name of common sense distort the meaning of those practices by integrating them with other reading practices based on radically different assumptions about the meaning of literacy.

Whole Language and Struggling Learners

A third version of instruction for struggling students assumes that there are models of literacy learning which best describe the reading and writing development of all children. From the perspective of whole language theory and practice there are universal language learning principles from which instructional practices derive (e.g., Dudley-Marling, 1995; Edelsky, Altwerger & Flores, 1991; Weaver, 1990). This perspective is informed by considerable research on oral and written language learning and language instruction including research with struggling readers and writers (e.g., Rhodes & Shanklin, 1989; Stephens, 1991; and Weaver, 1994).

The assumption of universal language learning principles does not mean that all learners should be treated the same, however. Whole language practice recognizes individual differences in students' learning and life histories as the foundation upon which teachers can build, but not as the basis for qualitatively different sorts of instruction. But even though whole language advocates do not believe that struggling readers need qualitatively different instruction, they recognize that struggling students usually require *frequent*, *intensive*, *explicit*, and *individual* support and direction from their teachers. Whole language teachers do not ignore the teaching of skills, as has been suggested by critics. Whole language teachers do teach the skills of literacy in support of students' intentions. They differ, however, from many teachers in terms of *how*, *when*, and *why* they teach skills as well as the meaning they attach to "skills." (Whole language teachers do not, for example, find much use for the endless drilling of word analysis skills outside the context of reading real texts.) It may be true that some teachers hide behind whole language as a means of explaining their failure to provide students with explicit support and direction. This is poor teaching, however. Whole language teachers do teach. Whole language teachers carefully assess their students. Whole language teachers provide explicit support and direction based on students' needs. Good whole language teaching is, in our opinion, just what struggling readers and writers need. This book offers a sampling of strategies teachers may use within regular classrooms or resource rooms to support the needs of struggling readers and writers, including students currently served in remedial programs or classes for students identified as learning disabled.

ONGOING ASSESSMENT
The Basis of Literacy Instruction

If teachers are to make a difference with students for whom reading and writing are a struggle, information from ongoing assessment must be the primary basis of instructional planning and delivery. Teachers who continually gather information about the students they teach—how they feel, their lives outside of school, their experiences in school, and their academic development—can most effectively teach the whole child. Although we focus in this section specifically on the assessment of literacy, it should not be forgotten that teachers who can best help students with literacy learning are those teachers who get to know and appreciate the child in his larger world. Of course, literacy teachers have an excellent opportunity to come to know the child well, since sharing thoughts and stories in writing and talking about powerful books open the student and teacher to a great deal of information about each other's lives and values.

In this section on assessment, we have assumed the teacher's perspective on assessment (Farr, 1992). That is, we are concerned with helping teachers understand how they can most effectively collect and use information that assists them in guiding the literacy development of students, and in making instructional decisions that assist in that goal. We believe that it is these kinds of assessment efforts that make a difference in students' learning. Although accountability is important, using assessment information for purposes of informing instruction is more important to teachers and ultimately to students, and it is thus what we have elected to focus on in these pages.

This section on literacy assessment contains three chapters. Chapter 3 gives an overview of literacy assessment including the relationship between assessment and instruction, principles important to keep in mind as literacy assessment occurs, aspects of literacy that can be assessed and taught, and various means of gathering assessment data during instruction. Chapter 4 includes specific information and assessment examples of each of the aspects of literacy outlined in Chapter 3. In Chapter 5, we consider how teachers might use assessment information to plan instruction. In particular, we discuss how classroom teachers and resource teachers, including both remedial and special education teachers, can plan for struggling readers and writers on the basis of assessment information.

3 Literacy Assessment
An Overview

Teachers often equate assessment with report cards and standardized tests. Teachers who think about assessment in this way usually consider it to be a formal testing process, conducted infrequently, and conducted for the sake of parents and administrators. Teachers who have worked with students in special education or remedial reading programs (including Title I programs in the United States) are likely to think about assessment as a means of identifying students for special programs. Today, many teachers are taking a new look at assessment, especially the assessment of literacy, and discovering that:

- Assessment is key to child-centered instruction. Information gathered about students' literacy during daily instructional events can be used to plan instruction that addresses students' needs, expands their interests, and challenges them. With carefully collected assessment information, teachers can individualize instruction for struggling readers and writers, even in busy classrooms.

- Assessment is an integral part of instruction. Every lesson that involves students in literacy offers teachers assessment data. Some of this assessment information may be recorded for later planning but much of it is available for immediate adjustments in instruction. Most of what an effective teacher knows about a student's literacy comes from observing the student during instruction, not from giving tests.

- The same assessment information gathered to plan instruction can also be used for traditional purposes such as communicating students' progress to parents, for writing educational plans and so on. Parents and others who work with struggling students appreciate the detail with which teachers who record assessment information can describe a student's literacy interests, development, and processes.

- It is valuable to involve students, including young ones, in self-assessment. Students are wonderfully perceptive and honest about themselves as readers and writers. If we want students to become responsible for their learning, we can use self-assessment to involve them in setting reading and writing goals and in assessing their progress toward these goals. Students' views about themselves as readers and writers enlarge our understanding of children's attitudes and performances.

In this chapter, we'll explore these and other ideas about literacy assessment. We'll consider why assessment is important, what principles guide literacy assessment, what aspects of literacy can be assessed, and methods and tools teachers can use to collect and record information.

Relating Literacy Assessment and Instruction

The fact that we are addressing literacy assessment prior to discussing reading and writing instruction may be taken to reinforce the conventional assumption that assessment always precedes instruction. This is often the case in remedial and special education programs (but even here assessment data is collected throughout the year). On the other hand, regular classroom teachers tend to begin the school year by providing instruction and then collect assessment information during instruction.

Of course, there are reasons why resource and classroom teachers begin the school year differently. Resource teachers are often bound to identify students for their programs on the basis of assessment before they can begin instruction. For example, Title I teachers in the United States typically review standardized test results from the previous year or give fall standardized tests, using the results to select which students they will work with. They may then assess students individually or in small groups to determine their final case load. Instruction itself often doesn't begin until several weeks into the school year. Thus, the fact that students must be identified for the program drives the assessment-first sequence.

In contrast, classroom teachers begin teaching immediately, often meeting their students for the first time as they arrive the first day. Seemingly, they begin without assessing students. But do they? In a sense, they have general information about students. First, the grade level curriculum is based on an assessment of what experienced educators have determined that the majority of students at that grade level can be expected to learn. In addition, an experienced teacher has knowledge of what students at that grade level know and can learn, especially if they have taught in the same community previously. In addition, teachers who want to take advantage of them (not all do, often for sound reasons) have access to the cumulative files of students, files that often provide assessment information. All of this information is based on someone's assessment of students.

In either case, it is not long before assessment and instruction become intertwined in both resource and classroom teachers' actions, especially when they take a student-centered approach to teaching. Assessment informs the instruction the teachers provide and what happens during instruction is the source of most of their assessment information. Although this occurs to a greater degree in student-centered classrooms, we don't know any teachers who do not adjust their instruction to some degree on the basis of what they observe about students' interest and learning during instruction.

It may be obvious that we have adopted a broad notion of literacy assessment. In fact, we use the word *assessment* to include the mental activity that good teachers continually engage in as they observe students in activity. Often, assessment information is collected mentally and then immediately used to adjust the content, pace, and density of instruction in the midst of a lesson. Other assessment information may be recorded to help teachers remember events that they believe will help plan future instruction or that they think they may want to share with others interested in students' progress. Whether or not assessment information is recorded, assessment also includes the analysis of the information in a way that assists in instructional planning. Thus, for us, literacy assessment implies the process of collecting (and sometimes recording) and analyzing students' literacy products and processes in a way that establishes a connection between the assessment data and the teacher's immediate instruction and future instructional plans. We want to argue that this connection between assessment and instruction is especially important for struggling students. Neither we nor our students can afford to follow pre-planned curricula and assume that students will learn from the experiences. We must continually observe students' interest and learning during instruction so that instruction can be adjusted to accelerate the students' learning as much as possible.

Underlying our notions about the relationship between assessment and instruction is the idea that the most informative kind of assessment is that which occurs on a daily basis during everyday reading and writing instruction. It is not necessary to separate instruction and assessment. This has two benefits. One is practical—teachers cannot afford to steal time from instruction for assessment. Additionally, assessment is most likely to inform instruction if it takes place within the contexts of instruction, which are always affected by students' reading and writing performances, attitudes, and so on.

Principles of Literacy Assessment

The following assessment principles will help teachers go beyond specific examples of assessment practices we share in this book and guide their decision making about the kinds of assessment to conduct, when to assess, and who should be involved. The principles (adapted from Rhodes & Shanklin, 1993) are:

Assess Reading and Writing in a Variety of Contexts

Because students are expected to be able to participate in a multitude of literacy practices within and outside of school, we're interested in gathering information about a range of reading and writing behaviors, including: how well students read and write informational and narrative material, how well they persuade someone to their point of view through their writing, if they know authors who portray their own and others' cultures, how well they find and correct their own misspellings in a piece of writing, and so on. Since reading and writing abilities and attitudes vary with the context in which they occur, we need to observe students in a wide variety of contexts in which they actually use reading and writing for purposes like these. Only then can we ensure that we are able to describe their reading and writing well.

Assess the Literacy Environment, Instruction, and Students

It is not sufficient to assess various aspects of students' literacy such as performance, attitude, and perceptions; we need to also collect information about the students' past and present literacy environments and instruction, particularly when students are struggling in school. If the literacy environment and instruction are not attended to, there is a danger of looking for and finding literacy problems only *within* students, overlooking the influence of the learning context. That may mean adjusting how we teach the student, what we focus on in our instruction, what material we encourage the student to read, what kinds of texts we encourage the student to write, and so on.

Assess Processes as Well as Products

It is typical to focus assessment on the products of students' reading and writing, namely reading comprehension and written compositions. However, we also need information about what students do in the process of reading and writing. In reading, that means that we ask students to think aloud and to read aloud in order to understand their thinking strategies, their miscues, and how they relate to what they have read. In writing, that means observing students while they write and talking to them about what they do in the process of composing texts. This gives us insights that just aren't available when we focus on the products of reading and writing.

Analyze Error Patterns in Reading and Writing

Errors provide insights into students' understandings about the world of print. Errors are not random—they are usually based on rules that students have generated about print that are different from the conventional rules of mature readers and writers. Reading miscues provide us with information about the cueing systems students use as they read, what reading strategies they are using, and why they may be having difficulty understanding text. Writing miscues provide us with information about students' understandings of spelling, grammar, capitalization, and punctuation. We can also interview students to find out if they are aware of their miscues, if they know how to correct them, and the thinking underlying their miscues. Observing error patterns and figuring out the underlying thinking or rules allows teachers to guide students to more sophisticated understandings about how print works.

Consider Background Knowledge in the Assessment of Reading and Writing

Too often, educators conclude that students don't read or write well when in fact, the students read and write quite adequately as long as they are reading or writing topics and genres about which they have sufficient knowledge. In fact, everyone's reading is limited to a finite range of topics and genres. Few of us can comprehend legal contracts or insurance, for example. When students lack sufficient background knowledge, the teacher needs to help students develop this background knowledge as a means of supporting the students' reading and writing. In the case of struggling readers and writers, background knowledge may need to be a focus of assessment.

Base Assessment on Normal Developmental Patterns and Behavior in Reading and Writing

Interpreting the reading and writing behaviors of struggling students depends on an understanding of the literacy development of normally achieving students. This knowledge can be gained in two ways—by learning what researchers have discovered about developmental patterns and behaviors as well as by carefully observing normally achieving students. Teachers who have the best sense of students' literacy development are often those who have taught grade levels above and below the one they are currently teaching. Special education teachers who have not worked with normally achieving students are clearly at a disadvantage in this regard and might do well to take advantage of opportunities to observe students reading and writing in the regular classroom.

Clarify and Use Standards in the Assessment of Reading and Writing

Increasingly, professional organizations and federal, state, provincial, and local education agencies are defining the standards by which students' reading and writing are to be evaluated. Teachers who have the opportunity to serve as members of a group that writes standards can clarify their personal standards for reading and writing in the process. Using clearly defined and consistent standards in analyzing students' reading and writing will go a long way toward helping others, including students, to view your assessment as trustworthy. Educators who have come to agree on standards by talking through a shared vision of what students need to know and be able to do will be better able to communicate to students and others what their expectations are and why.

Base Educational Decisions on Multiple Sources of Data

Assessment information is more trustworthy (i.e., valid) if it emerges from multiple data sources. Gathering information from various instruments, perhaps even formal tests, will provide far richer, fuller, and more trustworthy information from which to make decisions about assistance for students. Information gathered using different methods—observation, interview, and performance assessment—also increases the richness and credibility of our assessments. The same is true if the previous principle about multiple contexts is kept in mind. Teachers know a great deal more about a student who doesn't perform well on a test because they know this student can readily retell what has been read to a classmate who was absent and can offer creative insights in literature discussions. It is easier to counter the conclusions of assessment based narrowly on formal tests if our own assessment information comes from a variety of contexts.

Involve Students, Parents, and Other School Personnel in the Assessment Process

The perspectives of others, especially students themselves, are invaluable to understanding literacy development and attitudes. Other teachers and parents often see the student in different contexts—contexts which may be more or less conducive to supporting literacy. For example, parents might be asked to respond to a brief questionnaire about specific homework assignments, what progress they expect or want to see in reading and writing, or what they observed about their child during a classroom observation (Fredericks & Rasinski, 1990; Hill & Ruptic, 1994). Involving the students themselves in literacy assessment has multiple payoffs. Not only does self-assessment information provide a fresh perspective, self-assessment encourages greater awareness of one's own literacy and eventually, greater responsibility for literacy. Especially for struggling students who have established behaviors of "learned helplessness," becoming involved in self-assessment helps them understand the importance of setting and achieving realistic goals for their learning.

Make Assessment an Ongoing Part of Everyday Reading and Writing Opportunities and Instruction

Generally speaking, assessment cannot be separated from instruction. Whenever teachers instruct they almost always reflect on students' reading and writing development. In this chapter, we will argue that "mental" assessments need to be recorded if they are to be more useful for planning instruction. But recording assessment information in the midst of instruction requires two conditions: routines that allow students to become increasingly independent readers and writers, and teachers who can effectively manage the collection, recording, and analysis of assessment information. Both conditions are addressed later in this chapter.

Aspects of Literacy to Assess and Teach

In this section, we'll address aspects of reading and writing that can be assessed. Teachers who have relied on traditional assessment practices may be surprised at the range of assessment data available to them.

The assessment of reading and writing can and should go beyond the assessment of achievement or performance (i.e., what students *do* on tests). We know, for example, that students' literate performances are affected by their attitudes toward reading and writing. Students who enjoy reading and writing will, for example, read and write more and, therefore, become more effective readers and writers. In some cases, we can affect students' reading by helping them find books they're interesting in reading or revalue themselves as readers. Thus, it is important to assess students' attitude toward reading and writing. In addition to attitude, there are a number of aspects of literacy that we think are worthy of assessment, and of course, worthy of attention during literacy instruction.

- *Comprehension.* Comprehension is the heart of reading. When we concern ourselves with the assessment of reading performance, this aspect of reading is the most important. For example, what kind of sense do students make of the texts they read? How do they use background knowledge in constructing meaning from text? What comprehension strategies (e.g., predicting, skimming, rereading) do they use in order to construct meaning?

- *Processing words and other text features.* Another aspect of reading performance has to do with how students process words and other text features (e.g., italics, punctuation) as they read. Processing text features affects comprehension but comprehension also affects processing. For example, what kinds of miscues do students make as they read text and how do these miscues seem to affect comprehension? What do the miscues reveal about the strategies and cues they use to process text? Do students use other text features such as capitalization, apostrophes, and so on to comprehend text?

- *Composition.* The content of a piece of writing and its organization is the heart of writing. When we concern ourselves with writing performance, this aspect of writing is most important. Students need to learn how to communicate meaning effectively through writing and they need to use composition strategies (e.g., considering audience, revising) that help to communicate meaning. For example, does the writer say enough and not too much for the intended audience? Is the piece organized in such a way that it is both clear and interesting? How sophisticated is the writer's use of revision?

- *Writing conventions.* Another aspect of writing performance is how students utilize the conventions of written language—spelling, capitalization, punctuation, grammatical usage—for the effective realization of their intentions and the convenience of readers. For example, what strategies do students use to spell words, especially when they encounter difficulty? At what level of spelling development are the students operating?

- *Attitudes and interests.* Because attitudes toward reading and writing affect the time students choose to spend reading and writing, and therefore their reading and writing performance, it is important to attend to how students feel about reading and writing in general and what their specific interests are or might be. It is no accident that good readers and writers are those who spend a great deal of their own time engaged in reading and writing materials of interest to them. We might ask, therefore, how have the students' reading and writing interests broadened over the course of the school year? Do the students choose to read and write outside of school?

- *Perceptions.* Students' perceptions of reading and writing processes and what good readers and writers do affect how they interact with text and what they set as personal reading and writing goals. For example, the perception that good readers are "good" because they "know all the words" will influence students to set goals for their development as readers that may actually interfere with their reading development. So we are interested in students' beliefs about how they read and write.

- *Social aspects.* Reading and writing are inherently social acts. We frequently share what we've read and written with others, and our comprehension or composition of texts is always influenced by social and historical voices. Writing, for example, is influenced by what we perceive others need and want to read. Our reading attitudes, interests, and perceptions are influenced by those with whom we spend time reading and talking about what we read. Here we want to know, for example, how effectively do students talk with each other about what they've read and written, and how does such talk influence what they do and think?

- *Procedural aspects.* Students' understandings of procedures used to engage in reading and writing can affect the reading and writing they do, including the amount of reading and writing they do. For example, a student who doesn't know how to obtain a library card will not be able to use the public library. A student who understands the instructional procedures in Writing Workshop has more potential for taking advantage of the time and support offered. Among the questions we might be interested in is: Do the students understand the procedures for using the school's Publishing Center?

- *Literary aspects.* Text comprehension and composition are facilitated by knowledge of literary aspects such as who authors are and how they work, genres, text structures, formats, and literary elements such as character development, problem/solution, and foreshadowing. What knowledge do students have of Mother Goose rhymes and how do they use that knowledge to understand political cartoons, for example?

- *Flexibility.* Good readers and writers adjust their effort, rate, and other aspects of reading and writing according to their purposes and the nature of the text. Poor readers and writers tend to approach all reading and writing events in the same way. So we want to know things like: Can students skim to locate factual information in text? Can students quickly record information in note form while watching a videotape?

- *Metacognitive aspects.* Students who talk and think about various aspects of reading and writing are better able to draw on their own resources to solve problems they encounter as readers and writers. For example, can writers talk about composition strategies they use, and about how to access information that will add to their writing? Can they identify word recognition strategies?

- *Environment and instruction.* The previously listed aspects of literacy all focus on what the student knows and does. As we suggested earlier, however, we cannot limit our assessment to what is "in" the student. We must also consider how the environment in the school, home, and elsewhere contributes to the student's literacy development and what role past and current instruction plays in the student's growth in reading and writing. Some of these outside factors can be adjusted more readily than we can "adjust" the student.

Collecting and Recording Assessment Information

Teachers continually gather information about students as they work with them. However, much of this information is never recorded. If teachers are to use assessment information for purposes of planning instruction and communicating progress to others, much more information needs to be recorded than most teachers now record. We suggest a variety of ways to gather and record information about literacy. Teachers need to select those means that best suit their requirements and their communicative and management needs. Teachers who decide that it is important to record more information can only do so if they learn how to manage the task in an already crowded day.

Ways to Collect and Record Information

Teachers use a variety of means to collect and record information about students' literacy: tests, performance samples, observations, interviews, and portfolios. Tests, the assessment practice most familiar to teachers, are usually separated from instruction and usually involve students in narrow, school-based definitions of literacy. Here we'll focus on less familiar assessment practices that rely on students reading or writing whole texts and are a natural part of instruction.

PERFORMANCE SAMPLES   Performance samples include writing samples, taped oral reading, written retellings, taped oral reports, and so on. Performance samples can be collected primarily for purposes of assessment or collected as students engage in reading and writing tasks during everyday instruction. When the focus is on assessment, performance samples are often conducted in a one-to-one teacher-student setting with standardized procedures for administration and scoring. Collecting a performance sample in this way may be useful on occasion when a student's reading or writing is a puzzle that requires more information to solve or when it might be helpful in situations like special education staffings.

However, most teachers find that they can gather performance samples in the midst of everyday instruction. Students could be asked, for example, to select what they consider to be their best piece of writing over the last grading period. That will allow the teacher and students to assess their best performance. Or students could be asked to organize all the notes, scribbles, drafts, and so forth that led to the final draft of a report they have just completed, allowing teachers to assess the process students used in writing an assigned report. Performance samples can be collected from targeted students, typically the students who struggle the most with literacy. You might, for example, collect an oral reading performance sample every other week from several students as they read aloud in reading conferences. This will allow you to identify the strategies they are using as readers and their progress toward using more effective strategies.

OBSERVATION   Most teachers rely heavily on assessment information they collect mentally as they observe students reading and writing. However, if teachers are to use observations to more fruitfully plan instruction, these observations must be written down. We also recommend that students record what they observe about themselves for the teacher's use as well. There are several ways to record observational data about students' literacy: checklists, anecdotal records, status of the class/self, and self-assessments.

Teachers who already have a good knowledge base about the development of reading and writing may prefer anecdotal records over checklists because they are able to record whatever occurs during a literacy event that is significant. On the other hand, teachers who feel they need to learn more about the development of reading and writing may decide to rely on checklists conceived by someone else in order to learn what to look for as they observe students reading and writing. Teachers who have a strong background in literacy development may construct their own checklists, taking advantage of the structure that a checklist provides. However, checklists also constrain teachers' observations—teachers who use checklists are less likely to attend to literacy aspects outside of the realm of the checklist items. Thus, surprising or unexpected aspects of literacy may be overlooked.

There are two types of *checklists* we find useful. First, there are general development checklists that often span a number of years of observation and provide a longitudinal picture of a student's development. The *English Profiles Handbook* (1991), for example, provides descriptors of reading and of writing from early stages through sophisticated stages. For teachers who need guidance in what to observe about students' reading and writing development, or for teachers who want to communicate with each other through an agreed-upon checklist, this is an excellent resource. This sort of checklist is useful to keep in a portfolio of a student's work as an overview of reading and writing progress.

The second type of checklist is directly linked to current instruction. The checklist in Figure 3-1 was developed by a teacher who had taught students various ways to respond to literature and wanted to gather information about their responses in literature logs. The checklist allowed her to provide individual specific feedback to students about other responses she'd like them to try out, and she was able to identify which responses most of the class needed to see demonstrated again. Checklists like this one serve the function of providing some teachers with ideas about what to teach students in order for them to respond to literature logs effectively. Of course, it is possible that you have different ideas about how students should respond in literature logs, and if so, your checklist should reflect what it is that you are teaching your students.

Checklists are commercially available (see, for example, Rhodes, 1993) but should be adapted to reflect what is actually being taught. Checklists can be found or constructed for a wide variety of aspects of reading and writing: reading comprehension, word recognition strategies, spelling strategies, discussion skills, amount and level of revision, and so on. Almost anything we teach can be converted to a checklist for purposes of assessment (although we need to be careful that constructing the checklist doesn't change the nature of what's taught). Generating or adapting others' checklists often serves to clarify what we want students to learn.

```
┌─────────────────────────────────────────────────────────────────┐
│                                                                   │
│   Name                                      Date                  │
│                                                                   │
│   Title of Book                                                   │
│                                                                   │
│   _____ Wonders                                                 │
│   _____ Reflects on important points                            │
│   _____ Ties book to self                                       │
│   _____ Ties book to other books                                │
│   _____ Thoughtful reasons for likes/dislikes                   │
│   _____ Appropriate response length                             │
│                                                                   │
│   Comments:                                                       │
│                                                                   │
│                                                                   │
└─────────────────────────────────────────────────────────────────┘
```

FIG. 3-1   *Literature log checklist*

Gathering the assessment information will help you understand what you still need to teach and to whom.

Routine *anecdotal records* are another means to document progress and plan instruction. They also tell the story of a student's literacy development over time. As such, anecdotal records on the same student written over time contain convincing detail that can be shared with parents and other teachers to help them understand what the student has learned and how, as shown in Figure 3-2.

Anecdotal records describe specific events or products. In this record, the teacher reported both. In recording the child's product, the teacher retained the child's capital letters and lack of spacing in the writing, and showed how the writing was read. She also described the event in detail—how she helped the student discover the relationship between print and sound, and how Eleanor responded to the teaching. If Eleanor's teacher's comments had been evaluative (e.g., "Eleanor sounded out words in writing for the first time today and will continue to need lots of help in doing so.") instead of descriptive, she might have forgotten the detail of this interaction, which is crucial to understanding what sort of help Eleanor is going to need in the future and what kind of progress she can be expected to make. We like to think we'll remember such detail but we won't.

It can also be helpful to use anecdotal records to relate observations to other information about students. In this instance, the teacher might have indicated that it was already February of first grade and that Eleanor had been writing random strings of letters on the pages of her journal for several months. On the other hand, the teacher didn't have any need to record this information for herself because she kept all of her anecdotal records organized chronologically in a notebook student by student; it was simple enough to look back at previous anec-

---

ELEANOR
(1st grade)

STRDAIPADENBSNO (Yesterday I played in the snow.)
Yesterday = STRDA
I = I
played = PAD
in = EN
the = B (said "du" and thought she was writing "D")
snow = SNO

Showed her how to stretch her words out like a rubber band—doing it almost on own by SNO. E. does have a fairly good grasp of sound–letter relationships. However, has a hard time isolating words and tracking words in sentences in her mind. That may hold up progress for a while. Asked her—at end—what she did in writing today that she hadn't done on other pages. She said, "I listened to sounds." I told her to do it in her writing again tomorrow.

FIG. 3-2   *Observation of Eleanor, Grade 1*

dotal records about Eleanor and understand that this was indeed a landmark day in Eleanor's learning.

In a classroom where students work together, it's often more economical to make anecdotal notes on groups of students. In working with a small group of students on writing research reports, for example, a teacher noticed that all the students had difficulty recording the information they had learned from books in their own words. Instead of recording this observation for each child, she made a single entry which she photocopied for each child's section of her anecdotal record notebook. When the group is a stable one, anecdotal notebooks can be organized by group. When teachers plan for the group, they can review not only the group's anecdotal records but also the anecdotal records of the individuals in the group. This will help teachers to figure out who in the group can be a resource to the other students and who may require additional support.

If anecdotal records are new to you, you may want to review techniques for writing them and keeping them organized as well as analysis techniques and uses of anecdotal records (Rhodes & Nathenson-Mejia, 1992). In addition, Afflerbach has developed a systematic approach to anecdotal records, an approach intended to help teachers carefully analyze struggling readers (1993). The system could be easily adapted for the assessment of writing as well.

Teachers with many students to keep track of, whose students may be reading and writing a wide variety of materials at any given time, may find *status of the class/self* entries helpful for keeping track of individual students. Status entries can be kept by the teacher or by students. Teachers who keep them typically make a three- to five-minute round of the classroom as students are working, often at the beginning or end of Reading or Writing Workshop. The teacher who made the status of the class entries in Figure 3-3 did so at the beginning of Writing Workshop almost daily, especially focusing on those students who seemed stuck on a piece of writing for a long time. She also used her status sheet to reflect on the needs of individuals. Check marks in some boxes indicate students she wanted to gather together in order to teach them how to punctuate the dialogue they were using in their stories. We've found that recording status of the class in the last few minutes of Reading Workshop (recording book titles and where students are in their books) also serves as an unobtrusive signal to the students that they need to find a place to stop in their reading. Of course, students can do this kind of recording by keeping status of the self sheets in their Reading and Writing Folders on which they record books they've read, titles of pieces they've written, and other information useful in tracking their progress.

Finally, students can use *self-assessments* to record their observations of their progress. They can be invited into whatever assessment process you decide to use. We know teachers, for example, who ask students to fill out and/or react to teacher-completed assessment checklists. Other teachers make anecdotal records available for students to read (their own entries only), react to, and add to. In addition, teachers can construct formative self-assessments that reinforce what they are teaching. For example, students might be asked to complete the self-assessment in Figure 3-4 at the end of DEAR time (Drop Everything and Read).

The whole class might be asked to fill out the form once as a means of evaluating the nature of the reading environment for the students. Students who are having trouble staying engaged during DEAR time could be asked to use this form repeatedly to reinforce expectations and help them to think about their responsibilities during DEAR time.

Students can also be asked to participate in summative self-assessments. One third-grade teacher we know, for example, asks students to complete self-assessments like the one in Figure 3-5 at the end of each grading period, requiring the students to reflect on what they've learned and what they hope to learn. (This assessment was completed by a struggling student.) Students' perceptions about what has been important to them and what they want to learn enriched the teacher's planning and broadened her notion of what students were learning in her classroom.

INTERVIEWS   Interviews can be conducted with individuals or groups, directly related to or in the midst of instructional events, or separate from those events but related to teaching concerns. In general, interviews are designed to uncover students' thinking and perceptions about reading and writing and to help teachers understand more about what students do and why when they are engaged in reading and writing.

Interviews can be based on prepared questions by using, for example, Burke's *Reading Interview* (in Y. Goodman, Watson & Burke, 1987). This is a series of ten questions, including, "When you are reading and you come to something you don't know, what do you do?" These questions help teachers uncover students' perceptions of the reading process and how they help themselves during reading. Other

Week of _____   Subject_____

Karisha	Heather	Mischa	Kim E.	Brandy
"I just U.S."	a b.	finished editing "published"	Dog story	"my favorite thing to do..." book
Angela "My Day at the Zoo"	"The World" Travels Jody	Castle & the Queen	new story "The World"	absent
Kim K. Guinea pig	Co author collaborate w/	Stephanie a want auto-	Michelle	Mollie Co Authoring w/ Dave
Kristin Rubishing Auto	David "New pubishd"	Nicole "Magic Horseshoe"	Kathy Auto- still	Patrick Guinea pig book, published
Aaron Choopi "chrummm"	Sean Co/Authoring w/ "Dolphins"	Janni	Caleb Auto still	Rebecca Scary) Dolphins
	Jennifer	Trisha Allison	Missy	Cody

FIG. 3-3

Name _____   Date _____

1. How much time did you spend reading during DEAR time today?

   all the time   most of the time   some of the time   not at all

2. If you didn't spend all the time reading, why didn't you?

3. What will help you so that you'll spend all your time reading the next time we have DEAR time?

FIG. 3-4   *Drop Everything and Read (DEAR)*

interviews, like the *Content Reading Interview* (by Vacca & Vacca in Wixson et al., 1984) are designed to gather more specific information—in this case, how students read content area materials. Although both interviews were designed to be given orally and individually, students can be asked to respond in writing; then they can share and discuss their responses to make it an instructional activity as well.

We find interviews that occur during instruction—or directly related to instruction—to be the most enlightening. We find it useful, for example, to ask students to describe what they are doing as they are reading or writing. If a student is summarizing a book the teacher might ask, "Tell me how you are going about this." In this way, teachers may uncover misperceptions about reading and writing processes, or they might uncover profitable strategies worth sharing with the rest of the class.

We also find it useful to encourage students to talk about the process they've used once they've finished something. For example, one of us interviewed a ninth-grade student receiving learning disabilities services about the process he had used to write a report for his English class (see Rhodes & Shanklin, 1993, pp. 102–107). As he talked, it was clear he didn't understand the function of brainstorming about a topic, he had little understanding about how to read resource material or write information in his own words, he didn't consider revision a part of the writing process, and he didn't understand his own role in and responsibility for editing his work. It was also clear that he was interested in and knowledgeable about his topic, he had put a lot of time into writing the report, he was aware of and had fulfilled the teacher's requirements in writing the report, his mother was willing to assist him with the writing, and he was aware of his punctuation difficulties. All of this information would be useful to the student's learning disabilities teacher and his English teacher the next time he was asked to write a report. They would have

NAME _BJ_ DATE _11/6/90_

These are some things I do well in reading.

I am good at reading
Beverly cleary books.

This is a problem I have.

my problem is thet I orbluams
in choling books

This is what I plan to work on next quarter.

To read choling books.

WRITING

These are some things I do well in writing.

macking up ides

This is a problem I have.

riting sentins with Kapitils and perids

This is what I plan to work on next quarter.

rit moor and thinking whar perids and
kapitals go

FIG. 3-5 *BJ's reading and writing reflection*

a clear idea about where in the writing process to offer assistance, what to teach, and what strengths they could rely on.

FOLDERS AND PORTFOLIOS   Portfolios are places, like folders, where students and teachers collect products. We think of *folders* as places to collect all or most of each student's ongoing work and of *portfolios* as places to collect work that is selected to represent something—the student's best work, work that reveals the student's learning, and/or work that exemplifies the process the student used to produce a product (for example, all the notes and drafts that culminated in a report). It is best to think of each piece selected for a portfolio as a product that should be assessed in some way by students themselves, by teachers, and/or by parents. Portfolios can also contain observation records, sometimes summarized, as well as interviews with the student, preferably with analysis.

If teachers don't collect the sort of assessment information we've talked about in these pages and then use the information to help students reflect on progress and to plan instruction, portfolios are more like cold warehouses rather than an opportunity for teachers and students to reflect on, celebrate, and improve reading and writing. Think about them as something that teachers, students, and parents *use* to help each other think about what students are capable of and what they need to learn next. In this way, portfolios themselves become an integral part of instruction just as do those pieces—such as analyzed performance samples, observations, and interviews—that make up the portfolios.

There are multitudes of issues that need to be addressed if portfolios are to be used in the classroom. Some of the issues are:

> What is the general purpose of the portfolio? Is the portfolio to be used to reflect on growth, to share information or growth with others, for accountability purposes, to document program effectiveness, or is there some other purpose?

> What is the specific purpose of the portfolio? Is it to store students' best works, representative works, or works that reveal specific accomplishments?

> Who decides which items are placed in the portfolio? Students? Teachers? Parents? All of these parties?

> How is the portfolio to be used for assessment purposes? Who will assess the contents and what aspects of literacy will be assessed? What is the end result of this assessment—to plan instruction, to document growth, to arrive at an evaluation?

> What items are to be placed in the portfolio? A portfolio could include many kinds of student work and analyses of student work in different forms (e.g., paper, video, audio, computer disk).

Managing Assessment

In order to find time to collect, record, and analyze assessment information, teachers need to think carefully about where the assessment process fits into their busy lives. There is no doubt that recording and reviewing assessment information will take more time initially since anything new always takes more time. But, once learned, the assessment process should fit neatly into your day without extending it. Of course, that may mean that it will displace some other things you do, but we are confident that you'll find that some things are not as important in light of the benefits of assessment. We think it's likely that your perspective about how to spend your time will change.

Generally, there are three points in a teacher's day when assessment can take place: during *planning,* during *instruction,* and during *review* (and/or grading) of *student products. Planning time* can be used in one of two ways. First, it can be used to review and analyze assessment information to determine what future instruction should address. Planning based on assessment (not teachers' guides or textbooks) is the heart of student-centered teaching. Second, it sometimes makes sense to spend some planning time collecting focussed assessment information from students who puzzle you—ten minutes spent interviewing a child is often more economical than instructional time trying to get the child to write or time spent talking with parents.

As we've said before, most assessment information can be gathered during *instruction.* We're not suggesting that teachers abandon instruction in order to keep records (as one teacher worried aloud to us), but that assessment and record keeping become a natural part of teaching. Often, this takes no extra time. If you are listening to a child orally read, it takes no more time to record what the child does as you listen. If you are listening to a literature discussion group, you can record some of what the students say in the discussion while you listen. We find that we listen much better as a result of recording information. On the other hand, there are times when you'll need to record what happened during a conference (like the previous one with Eleanor) before moving to another child. Most teachers learn to do this quickly and efficiently.

We also think that gathering and recording assessment data is a useful way to *review student products.* Again, this requires that you approach the tasks of responding to and/or grading students' work from an assessment perspective. Teachers who respond to students' journals, for example, might consider what they're learning about a child's life, interests, or writing and make a record of it. Similarly, teachers who grade papers might ask, "What am I learning about this child from her work?" and, if there's something significant, record it. This brings us back in the assessment-instruction cycle to planning instruction. By the time you have finished responding to or grading papers and recording what you learned about the students, you're probably well on the way to planning follow-up lessons for a student or a group of students.

It's helpful to remember that it is not necessary to collect the same assessment information—or the same amount of information—on all students. Students who struggle are often a puzzle to teachers. To solve the puzzle, teachers frequently need more and a wider variety of information before they feel confident that they can help the students progress more rapidly than they have in the past. On the other end of the continuum, it is often helpful to collect assessment information on the students who excel not only because it allows us to tap their strengths for their benefit and the benefit of other students, but also because it encourages us to consider what we can do to challenge them with what we offer to the class.

Teachers who aren't in the habit of recording assessment information can begin by focusing on a few students, perhaps those who struggle with literacy. If learning more about the developmental nature of reading and writing is an assessment goal, it makes sense to focus on students representing a range of reading and writing attitudes and abilities. Once teachers learn to manage the assessment of a few students, it will be easy enough to broaden the scope of their assessment and include other students.

4   *Assessing Aspects of Literacy*

In this chapter, we'll offer specific examples of assessments designed to gather information about each of the aspects of reading and writing discussed in the previous chapter, referring to assessment principles underlying these practices. We'll also discuss various ways of collecting and recording assessment information and foreshadow our discussion in the next chapter on using assessment data to plan instruction.

Assessing Reading Performance: Comprehension and Processing Words

Assessing reading achievement or performance should include attention to comprehension and to how the student processes words during reading. Since comprehension is usually *the* priority for teachers, we'll begin our discussion there.

Comprehension

Since comprehension can be observed only indirectly, it must be inferred from whatever students say or do that reveals their understanding. We find that more open-ended methods of assessing comprehension offer a much broader understanding of students' comprehension than more traditional (though easier to score) multiple-choice comprehension questions or even the open-ended, short-answer questions found in many informal reading inventories. No matter what method of comprehension assessment we use, it's important to remember that the data may be only a partial representation of what students know from reading the text. Students' response to reading comprehension tasks may partially represent their best guesses about what they think we want to hear, rather than what they actually know.

Comprehension performance samples can be obtained through interviews, think-alouds, and retellings. All these methods of assessing comprehension can be incorporated into everyday literacy events. For example, students often retell text as a way to review what has been read the previous day or as part of literature discussions. Here we'll focus on *retelling* since it's the most common method used to assess comprehension. (See Rhodes & Shanklin, 1993, for more information about interviews and think-alouds.)

The following questions (mostly from Griffin & Jongsma, 1980) can guide teachers' assessments of retellings, whether they are performance samples elicited by teachers or arise naturally in the course of everyday reading instruction.

1. How much of the material presented in the text did the reader retell?

2. Did the reader's retelling include information not stated explicitly in the text, that is, information that was inferred? Were inferences appropriate and logical?

3. Did the reader's retelling reflect the structure and logic of the text? Texts, both narrative and expository, are typically organized in ways characteristic of their genre (see Chapter 8). Children as young as five may demonstrate an awareness of basic story structure (Marshall, 1983).

4. What background experience or knowledge did the reader bring to his understanding of the material? For example, a student's retelling of a story about camping may include information or attitudes from the student's own camping experiences.

5. Did the reader merely state details or were they related to each other in the retelling? For example, if a student read a story about forest animals did she relate information about each animal in the forest separately or did she relate the animals to each other and to the forest?

6. Did the reader's retelling represent an adequate understanding of the text? This may seem to be a subjective criterion for judging retellings, but judging meaning is always subjective (even if meaning is compared to some standards as in the case of the comprehension questions on standardized reading tests). If the retelling seemed inadequate, what seemed to be the problem?

These questions are merely guidelines. Other important aspects of students' retellings may be worth recording. After students have finished sharing what they've read, it may be helpful to ask some questions to elicit additional information about the reading. Ideally, these questions will naturally arise from the teacher or other students because they are interested in what they are hearing when they haven't read the same texts. As you listen to retellings, consider the impact of the context on students' retellings. Students may find it odd to retell stories to teachers who already know the story. Sensing that this may really be about evaluation, some students may offer little information. To encourage retellings, teachers can model their own retellings by sharing what they're reading with students from time to time, including how what they've read relates to personal experience.

Although performance samples are useful if a detailed analysis of comprehension is needed for particular students, teachers can usually assess students' comprehension within the context of everyday literacy events in the classroom. A student can be asked to tell yesterday's absentees about a chapter that they missed in the class read-aloud book, affording the teacher an opportunity to take notes as she listens to this functional retelling. Book talks offer teachers another opportunity to assess students' retellings. Teachers can also eavesdrop on literature-discussion groups as a means of learning about students' reading comprehension. Literature logs (discussed in Chapter 10) are another source of data on students' reading comprehension as are students' artistic responses to text (dioramas, sketches, maps). In these cases, teachers can take anecdotal records about students' comprehension or they can utilize checklists that enable them to focus on particular aspects of comprehension. (Rhodes & Shanklin, 1993, and Rhodes, 1993, contain many items that may be used in developing comprehension checklists.) The checklist for literature logs included in the previous chapter (Figure 3-1) illustrates the use of a checklist to assess comprehension as students respond in written form.

We often assume that if a student is having comprehension difficulties, the "fault" lies in the student. In fact, all readers occasionally face comprehension difficulties that are frequently related to background knowledge or the text itself. Thus, assessment should focus not only on the reader but also on textual and situational factors surrounding the reading. When proficient readers have trouble understanding a text, we typically blame their comprehension "difficulties" on the author (density of ideas, obtuse style, lack of clarity, and so forth), situational factors (distractions, testing pressure, and so on), or personal factors like background knowledge or lack of interest (which we might also blame on the text, i.e., the *text* isn't interesting). To the degree that these factors play a role in the reading comprehension of struggling readers, the problem isn't the student's ability to comprehend text. We cannot "automatically assume . . . instruction in understanding text is primarily what is needed" (Schell, 1988, p. 14).

Processing Words

Another important aspect of students' reading performance to assess is how they process words *as* they read, traditionally referred to as word recognition. Since the vast majority of the reading we do involves whole text or messages (versus isolated word recognition), we are most concerned with how students make sense of words in the process of reading whole texts. This can be done through *miscue analysis*. The extent to which students use various cueing systems and strategies to construct meaning from texts can be ascertained by examining their oral reading performance, focusing particularly on their miscues (i.e., deviations from the expected response). While reading text, successful readers use graphophonic, syntactic, semantic, and pragmatic cues to construct meaning. Research indicates that struggling readers tend to overrely on graphophonic information (e.g., Cambourne & Rousch, 1982; Hammond, 1982), thereby producing miscues that are more likely to change the meaning of texts (Pflaum & Bryan, 1982). In situations where they are reading familiar or predictable texts, other poor readers may depend too heavily on their previous knowledge of a story, ignoring graphophonic information.

Consider the following example. Two students orally read the sentence, "The second little pig made a house of straw." The first student read, "The second little pig made a horse of streets." The second student read, "The second little pig made a home of sticks." Some might be tempted to conclude that these two students had similar reading performances since both made two oral reading errors. Moreover, they had difficulty with the same two words, *house* and *straw*. However, the reading performances of the two students differ in an important way: The miscues of the first student significantly changed the meaning of the text, resulting in nonsense. The second student's miscues did not significantly affect the meaning. It is likely that the first student is experiencing comprehension difficulties related to his miscues while the other student is not.

Kenneth Goodman coined the more neutral term *miscue* to describe oral reading errors. A miscue is any oral reading response that does not match the text (K. Goodman, 1973). All readers produce miscues when they read, but miscues aren't random. They follow a pattern (K. Goodman, 1973; Hammond, 1982) that reveals readers' thought and language processes during reading (K. Goodman, 1973). For example, if the miscues in the previously cited sentences are typical of the two readers, we can conclude that the first student was using graphophonic and syntactic cues while the second student was using graphophonic, syntactic, and semantic information.

Y. Goodman, Watson, and Burke have published the *Reading Miscue Inventory* (RMI), which involves the intensive examination of a single reading performance (1987). Students are asked to read orally a text that is challenging but not so difficult that it frustrates them. Miscues are coded and classified according to a detailed taxonomy, e.g., "Is the miscue syntactically appropriate?", "Was it corrected?", "Does it change the meaning of the text?" The RMI manual contains three different miscue analysis procedures, with variations in the detail of analysis required. We find Procedure II most useful when an in-depth analysis of a reader is required but Procedure III is more useful for day-to-day use. Even less time-consuming than RMI Procedure III is the Classroom Reading Miscue Assessment (see Figure 4-2; from Rhodes, 1993), developed to provide busy teachers with a way to record miscue and retelling information (discussed below) during everyday oral reading and discussion events in the classroom. Computer software has been developed to aid the recording and analysis of miscues (Altwerger & Resta, 1994; Woodley, 1990).

For purposes of illustration we include here a coded sample of oral reading along with a brief descriptive analysis. The codes are explained in the legend for the sample.

It is obvious that this reader produced a large number of miscues. What's more interesting, however, is that over half of the miscues sounded or looked like the word in the text (the graphophonic system). Although most of his miscues sounded like language (the syntactic system), many do not (e.g., he read "From my on, stay own your side" for "From now on, stay on your side."). Many of his miscues resulted in meaning changes (the semantic system) but few of these were corrected, while miscues that differed from the text in terms of sound and appearance

- A word with another word written atop it indicates a substitution—for example, V*isitor* / Victor.

- A circle around the word indicates an omission—for example, (said).

- An encircled C indicates a correction—for example, ©said.

- An encircled R indicates a repetition—for example, ®said Victor to Billy.

The student read as follows:

Visitor *Bill*
Victor and Billy were brothers.

"Look what you ©*do*did," (said) ®Victor to Billy one day. "You broke my plane."

mind *Bill*
"I didn't mean to," Billy said.

Visitor *pick* *the* *He*
Victor picked up his broken plane. "I told you not to get into my things," he said.

want *that* *Bill*
"I just wanted to see it," Billy said.

"This is my new plane!" Victor said.

©*Is* *tore* *Bill* *his*
He took Billy by the arm. "Say you're sorry."

©*his* *Bill*
"You can't make me say anything," said Billy.

Victor took something out of his pocket.

"See this roll of tape?" he said. "I'm going to put a line of tape right down the middle of the room!"

Bill ©*want* *how*
"What for?" Billy wanted (to) know.

What ©*s—*
"Wait and see," Victor said.

Then Victor made a line with tape right down the middle of the room.

"Now," Victor said. "This is better."

"How come?" said Billy.

watch *ore*
"Now you'll know which is your side and which is mine. I don't want you * my* *own* ever to step over that line. From now on, stay on your side."

FIG. 4-1   *A coded sample of a student's oral reading*

(the graphophonic system) were likely to be corrected. Miscues that didn't look like language and that changed the meaning of the text were often uncorrected. For example, he read "Bill want how" for "Billy wanted to know," indicating that, for this reader, the physical similarity between *know* and *how* was more compelling than meaning. In general, this student gives more of his attention to graphophonic cues without concurrently attending to syntactic and semantic information. More seriously, he is all too willing to accept miscues that seriously disrupt meaning. When the student was asked to retell the story following oral reading, his comprehension was poor and, arguably, this was related to his miscue performance. The teacher recorded the information from the student's oral reading of the text (the

Reader's name _____   Date _____

Grade level _____   Teacher _____

Selection read _____

Classroom Reading Miscue Assessment

I.   What percent of the sentences read make sense?

	Sentence by sentence tally	Total
Number of semantically acceptable sentences	~~HHT HHT~~ IIII	14
Number of semantically unacceptable sentences	~~HHT~~ IIII	9

% Comprehending score:

$$\frac{\text{Number of semantically acceptable sentences}}{\text{Total number of sentences read}} \quad \text{x } 100 \quad = \quad \underline{61} \; \%$$

II. In what ways is the reader constructing meaning?

	Seldom	Sometimes	Often	Usually	Always
A. Recognizes when miscues have disrupted meaning	1	(2)	3	4	5
B. Logically substitutes	1	(2)	3	4	5
C. Self-corrects errors that disrupt meaning	1	(2)	3	4	5
D. Uses picture and/or other visual clues	1	2	(3)	4	5

In what ways is the reader disrupting meaning?

	Seldom	Sometimes	Often	Usually	Always
A. Substitutes words that don't make sense	1	2	3	(4)	5
B. Makes omissions that disrupt meaning	1	(2)	3	4	5
C. Relies too heavily on graphophonic cues	1	2	(3)	4	5

III. If narrative text is used:

	No		Partial		Yes
A. Character recall	1	2	(3)	4	5
B. Character development	1	(2)	3	4	5
C. Setting	1	2	3	(4)	5
D. Relationship of events	1	(2)	3	4	5
E. Plot	1	(2)	3	4	5
F. Theme	(1)	2	3	4	5
G. Overall retelling	1	(2)	3	4	5

If expository text is used:

	No		Partial		Yes
A. Major concepts	1	2	3	4	5
B. Generalizations	1	2	3	4	5
C. Specific information	1	2	3	4	5
D. Logical structuring	1	2	3	4	5
E. Overall retelling	1	2	3	4	5

FIG. 4-2   *Classroom Reading Miscue Assessment (from Rhodes & Shanklin, 1993)*

portion of it excerpted here) and the student's retelling on a Classroom Miscue Reading Assessment form (Figure 4-2).

This example, of course, is based on a single reading episode. More examples of reading behavior are necessary before we can make confident judgments about any student's reading abilities. We need to observe oral and silent reading over time, with different reading materials, done for different purposes. Multiple samples of reading performance will help us understand what we need to teach the student, and how we can adjust textual and situational factors to provide the student with opportunities to use more effective comprehension strategies.

One of the limitations of miscue analysis is that it relies on students' oral readings, rather than on silent readings. Oral reading focuses students' attention on graphophonic information and may, therefore, interfere with meaning construction (Newman, 1978). *Reader selected miscues* (Watson, 1978—which we discuss as an instructional strategy in Chapter 9) is a useful assessment strategy that enables teachers to explore students' miscues during silent reading. Students are given bookmarks and instructed to place their bookmarks at any place in the text where they're having difficulty and then continue reading. When they've finished reading, students are instructed to select miscues that were particularly troublesome for them, miscues that caused a loss of meaning or distracted them from their reading. Students then write each sentence containing a miscue on a bookmark and underline the trouble spot.

Some students may mark no miscues at all because they haven't had any difficulties with the text. But if you suspect that this isn't the case, you may wish to talk with the student about whether they have understood the instructions. Some students may pay so little attention to meaning, they don't know when the meaning they construct doesn't make sense. In these cases, the only way to assess miscues is to ask students to read the text orally. In any case, knowing the types of words and contexts that cause students difficulty can be very useful for teachers in planning instruction.

The use of *cloze exercises* (discussed further in Chapter 9) can also provide insights into students' reading behaviors. Students' choices in cloze exercises indicate the degree to which they use contextual information to construct meaning and the sources of contextual information they use. For example, a student who completed a cloze sentence as "The girl *is* to the store" produced a meaningful response in terms of what came before, but not after, the blank. Cloze exercises can also indicate whether students use information from adjoining sentences or paragraphs to make predictions about meaning. In general, many of the questions used to analyze students' oral reading miscues apply to their performance on cloze exercises.

We recommend the use of cloze exercises for assessment only when cloze is also used as an instructional strategy to encourage students to make predictions. There is no need to contrive tasks for purposes of assessment. It's sufficient to observe students as they read, and, in the case of cloze exercises, as they respond to instruction.

Assessing Writing Performance: Composition and Conventions

For our purposes, the assessment of students' writings is guided by two general questions: 1) How well does the writing fulfill its purpose—to report, persuade, elicit feeling, and so forth? and 2) What do students know about writing, including writing conventions, that helps them fulfill their intentions?

Graves suggests that assessment of students' writing be based on routine examination of their written work, including observing members of the whole class as they write (1983). As part of this, Graves recommends about five minutes of "close in" observation of individual students, which involves sitting right next to or in front of students as they write, and suggests that students be told its purpose. Teachers may wish to say something like, "I'm going to watch what you do while you write for a few minutes. It'll help me figure out how to help you better. Just go on with what you're doing as if I'm not here." Just as for reading, it's desirable to observe students writing for a variety of purposes and audiences on a variety of topics, including topics they have chosen.

We suggest some more specific questions below that will help teachers better understand students' writing and assist them in planning instruction. Many of these questions can only be answered by carefully observing students as they write. Although the questions can be used to guide observation, they are not exhaustive. Of course, it's unnecessary to address all these questions each time a student writes. Understanding writing performance will accumulate as you observe students in numerous settings in which they are writing.

1. Who initiated the writing? It could be the student, the teacher, or someone else. Students are likely to produce better writing if they initiate the writing to fulfill their own purposes.

2. Who chose the topic for writing? If the student chose the topic, did she have difficulty choosing a topic? Did she choose to write on a topic she knew much about? Students' background knowledge and interests can dramatically affect their writing about a topic.

3. How much did the student write and how much of the writing time was spent writing? Did the student write without prompting? What role did drawing play in the writing? Students shouldn't be expected to write continuously for long periods of time since good writers often pause to compose their thoughts, review what they have already written, or they just get stuck. But it is worth noting exactly what students do as they write and occasionally asking them why they do what they do.

4. What, if anything, did the student say aloud while he was writing? Did he speak first, then write, or speak during writing? Did the student's utterances give you any insight into his writing strategies? For example, we overheard one young writer saying, "No, they'll never understand what this means" as she erased a line of text from her paper.

5. Was there anything about the student's body language as she wrote that provides insights into her feelings about writing? Continual squirming may be an indication of a student's feelings about writing, or at least about a particular writing assignment.

6. Did the student reread and/or revise and edit what had been written? What sorts of revisions and/or edits? Why? If you don't know why, ask the student. Knowing why students revise and edit their work (or don't revise and edit it) can provide important insights into how students go about writing and why.

7. For what audience was the piece of writing intended? Different audiences have different informational needs. Audiences also differ in their relationship to the author. The writer needs to adjust the amount of information, style, and even the use of conventions to her audience.

8. For what purpose was the piece written? How well a piece of writing fulfills its purpose can only be evaluated in terms of why and for whom the author wrote it. As is the case for audience, writers adjust the amount of information, style, and use of conventions to fulfill particular purposes.

9. How well does a piece of writing "hang together"? Is it a cohesive whole or does it read like a series of sentences related only by topic? Effective writers, like effective speakers, use a number of conventions to make their language flow. Conjunctions, transitions, and pronouns as well as organizational features serve this purpose.

10. How effectively does the student use language structures such as syntactic rules, word endings, and varying sentence patterns? Does the student's writing reflect the language structures of his speech or does the student use "book language"?

11. How effectively does the student use words in writing? Does she use a wide and sophisticated range of words? Does the student's writing vocabulary reflect her speaking vocabulary?

12. Does the student's "voice" come through in the writing? Voice is related to a writer's urge to express himself, his ownership of the writing, and efforts to put himself into the writing (Graves, 1983). Voice is often the difference between the dullness of writing to please someone else and the writing students do for themselves or audiences they consider important.

13. Is the student's writing performance fairly consistent? Each piece of writing will not be equally effective. Graves has found that children's writing performance is often variable, and he argues that variability is, in fact, a desirable quality (1983). It indicates that writers are taking risks in their writing.

14. What does the student know about punctuation, capitalization, and spelling? Understanding developmental patterns in these areas helps teachers describe students' uses of capitalization, punctuation, and spelling and determine appropriate instruction.

If others' recording forms will help you record assessment information about students' writings, you may find Shanklin's (in Rhodes, 1993) Authoring Cycle Profile useful. It can be used to collect information in one-to-one settings or in small groups and is designed to capture what the students do during writing as well as to assess the students' writing products. The Profile calls for assessing rehearsal, drafting, conferring in Author's Chair (see Chapter 11), revising, editing, and the final product.

In addition to observing students' writing processes and products, you can also learn about the processes they use by interviewing writers before and after they write. Before writing, you might ask questions like these:

- What are you going to be writing about?

- How are you going to put that down on paper?

- How did you go about choosing that topic?

- What problems do you think you might run into?

After writing, you might ask questions like these:

- How did you go about writing this?

- Did you make any changes?

- What are you going to do next with this piece of writing?

- What do you think of this piece of writing? Why? (Graves, 1983)

We recommend that teachers ask students to read what they've written aloud. This will provide a natural opportunity to ask students "after writing" questions like those above and will clarify any confusion that might arise because of poor handwriting or unrecognizable spellings. Students' comments, self-corrections, and oral revisions should also be observed. Self-corrections and oral revisions will help teachers understand the student's potential in revision and editing.

As with reading performance, teachers need to consider factors outside the student in assessing writing performance. Any of us who are assigned to write about an unfamiliar topic, for example, will face serious difficulties as writers. Situational factors such as the purpose for writing (i.e., writing for teachers instead of for themselves) may also affect students' writing performances. A student's instructional history can be an especially important—but easily overlooked—factor in students' writings. Students who have been embarrassed by poor spelling in the past may avoid words they don't know how to spell (or avoid writing altogether), giving the appearance of limited vocabularies.

In considering the assessment of writing conventions, it's useful to recall the role of conventions such as capitalization, punctuation, spelling, and usage in writing. These standardized forms are an important part of the written language code writers use to fulfill communicative intentions and are important for writers to be easily understood by their readers. This is an important consideration when assessing samples of students' writings since the appropriateness of forms depends on the writers' purposes, potential audiences, and so on. Appropriate spelling, for example, depends on the context of the writing. *Thru* may not be an appropriate spelling in a formal paper, but it is acceptable in a memo or a note. Similarly, rules governing capitalization and punctuation may be suspended or modified in a diary, a journal, or even a letter to a friend. The point here is this: It isn't sufficient just to find out whether or not students "know" the rules of punctuation, spelling, and capitalization. Writers must also know how to apply these rules flexibly depending upon the context of their writing.

Spelling Development and Assessment

Many educators express their frustration with what they perceive to be an irregular English spelling system. Why, for example, should there be a *g* in *sign* or an *e* in *gate*? And why is *phone* spelled *p-h-o-n-e* and not *f-o-n-e*? (Interestingly, the phone book in one large midwestern city uses both spellings.) This "irregularity" is often blamed for spelling difficulties and has generated considerable commentary on spelling reform. However, English spelling is quite regular and ideally suited for its purpose (Temple, Nathan, Temple, & Burris, 1993). It would not be desirable, for example, for the spellings of words like *sign* and *signal* to be significantly different (e.g., *sine, signal*) since this would mask the meaning relationship between them. Nor would we want spellings to be related to variations in pronunciation. If they were, Americans would spell *again a-g-e-n* and Canadians would spell it *a-g-a-i-n* (or *a-g-a-n-e*). Nor would we want the spellings of words to change as their pronunciation changed over the course of time. So, although English spellings may not be highly regular in terms of phonetic rules, they are rule governed and systematic. (See Goodman, 1993, for more information.)

Children demonstrate an early awareness of the regularities of English spelling and even the spelling of students with learning disabilities tends to be rule governed (e.g., Gerber, 1984; Invernizzi & Worthy, 1989). However, developing spellers, including many struggling writers, tend to rely on phonetic rules (Gerber, 1984; Read, 1975) rather than attending to the visual features of words. Developmentally, most children progress from a developing awareness of the phonological rules governing English spelling and a reliance on these rules to an ability to employ the visual features of standard English spelling. In the process of developing a knowledge of the rules governing English spelling, most children learn to apply developmentally more sophisticated strategies to their spellings over time. Since an understanding of spelling development is important in assessing students' spelling performances, we'll review the information here.

Prephonemic spellers use letters or letter-like symbols to represent language. However, random strings of letters, numbers, and other "markings" may also be used to represent words. Since prephonemic spellers are not usually readers, they have not developed the concept that there is a regular correspondence between print and oral language.

A wide range of writing is considered prephonemic. The example of prephonemic spelling presented in Figure 4-3 was written by a normally developing three-year-old. This child read a riddle she had written as: "It is green. You put food in it. You take it to picnics." (The answer: a cooler). The writing sample in Figure 4-4, written by a second-grade boy, is also prephonemic. When he was asked to read what he had written, he "read" Jack and Jill, a nursery rhyme that his Title I teacher had taught him. Although some of the words do begin with *J* as *Jack* and *Jill* should, this may be because his own name begins with *J*.

The second writing sample, unlike the three-year-old's riddle, contains only conventional letters to represent words. Other prephonemic spellers, especially those who are being taught to read, may incorporate some correctly spelled words they have learned in reading lessons. However, most words are represented by random strings of letters.

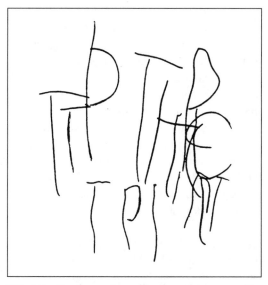

FIG. 4-3   *Prephonemic spelling by a three-year-old*

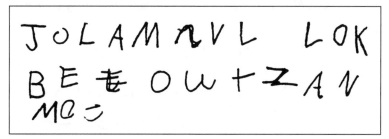

FIG. 4-4   *"Jack and Jill" by a second-grade boy*

Phonemic spellers have discovered phonetic principles of spelling and attempt to capture the sounds of words in their own writing. However, phonemic spellers represent only some of the sounds in words, often the first and/or last sounds, although they may recognize that they haven't represented all of the sounds. For example, a normally achieving kindergarten student wrote herself a note so that she'd remember to draw a picture of a rainbow the next day. She laboriously sounded out the word rainbow like this:

"R . . . r . . . r . . ." and then she wrote *R*.
"Ray . . . ray . . ." and then she wrote *A*.
"Bow . . . bow . . . b . . . b . . ." and then she wrote *B*.

She then looked at what she had written and announced, "It's not long enough!" and promptly added three more letters without sounding them out, ending up with the piece of writing in Figure 4-5.

Phonemic spellers represent more and more letter sounds until they represent all or most of the sounds in a word. When this happens they are called **letter name** spellers. Letter name spellers represent all of the sounds of words but do so on the basis of letter names—spelling, for example, *baby* as "*babe*" or *letter* as "*letr*." Once you catch on to the letter naming strategy, most spellings are fairly transparent. However, you need experience with young children's spelling before other letter name representations become apparent. For example, guess what word "yet" is supposed to represent? This is a letter name spelling for *went*. Why did the child use *Y* to represent the letter sound /w/? *Y* is the letter name that comes closest to representing the sound /w/—make the sound /w/ and the letter name *Y* with your mouth and feel the similarity. Similarly, letter name spellers frequently use the letter *H* to represent the sounds /sh/ and /ch/.

Readers may wish to try to decipher the note of a letter name speller to the tooth fairy explaining how she lost her tooth:

TOH FARE MY TOH WET DON EAE JAAN
BAT SO CAN I HAVE SAM MANE
[Tooth fairy, my tooth went down the drain but so can I have some money?]

This child's spelling of *drain* as "jaan" is an example of her reliance on a letter name strategy. Although *drain* is conventionally spelled with an initial *dr–* most

FIG. 4-5   *"Rainbow" by a kindergarten student*

speakers pronounce it "j-rain." Most of us cannot even hear this oddity in pronunciation, but young children do and often represent the /dr/ sound with the letters *J* or *G*.

Some older students, especially remedial students and students with learning disabilities, continue to use letter name strategies. A fourteen-year-old student with learning disabilities wrote the following entry in his journal:

I said after schooh to hip Mer Shagr part up sham hares.
[I stayed after school to help Mr. - put up some chairs.]

This student does not, however, rely exclusively on a letter naming strategy. For example, he does represent the /k/ sound in *school* with the appropriate *ch*, showing that he knows some visual features of words. But when he is uncertain about a spelling, he reverts to the letter naming strategy.

As students learn to read they may notice differences between their spellings and conventional spelling in books and begin to incorporate some of the visual features of standard English orthography into their own spelling. These students are *transitional* spellers. Although transitional spellers have begun to employ many of the visual features of standard English spelling, they may overgeneralize these features. They may, for example, spell *eat* "eet," *altar* "alter," *business* "busyness," and so on.

Correct spellers are students who regularly employ the visual features of standard English spelling. This doesn't mean that students are correct spellers only if they can spell all words correctly, only that they regularly spell words correctly.

A final word about these various points or stages in spelling development. Spelling stages are not discrete, and you may not observe students' progress through all of the stages (Hughes & Searle, in press). They merely serve to describe children's progress along a continuum of spelling development. Students may revert to earlier strategies when they attempt to spell less familiar words. The fourteen-year-old boy in one of the previous examples demonstrated an awareness of the features of standard English orthography (e.g., "said," "schooh") but relied on a letter naming strategy when he was uncertain.

Since instructional strategies for spelling differ according to students' spelling development, it's useful to determine the approximate point of students' spelling development in order to decide how to respond to students' spelling (Temple, Nathan, Temple, & Burris, 1993; Wilde, 1992). This can be accomplished by rating each spelling "error," or miscue, according to its developmental level:

1 = Prephonemic

2 = Phonemic

3 = Letter name

4 = Transitional

5 = Correct

Students' spelling can be categorized according to this taxonomy and then averaged to obtain a rough estimate of a student's developmental spelling level. The following is an example of an eight-year-old learning disabled student's written spellings of a word list (from J. W. Beers, 1980). This student's average rating is approximately a 3 indicating that, in general, she is using a predominantly letter name strategy.

Although this example uses student responses to a list of spelling words, spelling can just as easily be assessed within the context of students' writings. Spelling lists are only necessary for purposes of assessment if students play it so safe in their writing—for example by attempting only words they know how to spell—that there is no spelling data to observe. Also, it's best to assess students' spelling only after they've had the opportunity to edit their work since they may know more about spelling than is apparent in a draft where they have focussed on meaning. It's also useful to observe students as they spell or correct the spellings of words, especially during editing. Asking how they decided on a particular spelling and what strategies they used to correct spelling errors will provide additional insights into students' orthographic knowledge.

Word	Student's Spelling	Rating
hat	hat	5
back	bik	2
stack	sak	2
sap	sip	2
bed	bed	5
step	sep	2
wreck	rik	2
speck	pek	2
lip	lep	3
stick	sik	2
pit	pit	5
lid	led	3
gate	gate	5
lake	lak	3
spade	pad	3
drape	gap	3
week	wek	3
seat	sete	4
creek	kek	2
streak	set	2
ride	ride	5
light	lite	4
tribe	cib	3
dike	dik	3

FIG. 4-6   *Ratings of an eight-year-old LD student's written spellings of a word list (from Beers, 1980)*

Assessing Capitalization and Punctuation

The assessment of capitalization and punctuation is best conducted in the context of students' writings. We find it most useful to observe students when they edit a piece of work for capitalization and punctuation. This will reveal what students actually know and can do when their focus is no longer on composing meaning. We may find out that students don't need help in learning these conventions; they simply need to learn how to attend to their use when they edit. In addition, it isn't enough simply to compare children's use of punctuation and capitalization to some absolute standard. Instead, we need to describe how children apply these rules, to figure out what rules they are operating under so that we can help them replace those rules with conventional forms or extend their use.

Like spelling, capitalization and punctuation are developmental, with children gradually using more sophisticated hypotheses about how these aspects of written language work. Wilde explains that punctuation and capitalization mark grammatical units like sentences or clauses and signal specific meanings (1992). For example, capital letters signal the beginning of sentences while periods, question marks, and exclamation marks signal the end of sentences. On the other hand, capital letters can be used to alert readers that something is important or is being emphasized by the author—an example of how capitalization can be used to communicate meaning.

Writers have a lot to learn about punctuation: apostrophes, colons, semicolons, commas, quotation marks, parentheses, and the like. Although learning to punctuate seems simple on the surface, it actually is complex conceptual learning. Learning where to place a period, for example, is "a conceptual task that will reflect the writer's evolving sense (explicit and/or implicit) of what a sentence is" (Wilde, 1992, p. 18). "Sentence sense" seems to be fairly well understood by about fourth grade since even low-proficiency nine-year-olds only create an average of .6 sentence fragments per hundred words. Interestingly, high-proficiency seventeen-year-olds create an average of .5 sentence fragments per hundred words, a decrease of only .1 over a period of eight years (Mellon, 1975). From these data, it might be concluded that almost no learning takes place with regard to punctuating sentences during those years. In fact, Weaver indicates that the "data mask some significant changes that are occurring. Though the proportion of sentence fragments may remain fairly stable beyond a given age or grade, the types of fragments apparently change over the years as students attempt to express new kinds of semantic relationships and to employ new kinds of syntactic constructions" (Weaver, 1982, p. 443). Thus, as students learn to punctuate a syntactic construction that they've been using in their writing for a while, they also begin trying out new constructions that they do not know how to punctuate, and those errors replace the old ones. As Weaver puts it: "Growth and error go hand in hand."

The rules that students generate for capitalization and punctuation are systematic just as they are in spelling. Our job is to discover what the system is, what "rule" students have created for themselves, and help the students move closer to adult systems. When Kara Rhodes was in first grade, for example, each line of her writing began with a capital letter and ended with a period whether it was the end of a sentence or not. Her rules were quite systematic, and it became clear that she had generated the rules from being regularly exposed to basal reading primers at this stage of her school career. These books are typically written one sentence to a line, each line beginning with a capital letter and ending with a period. Kara made a reasonable guess about how to use capital letters and periods based on her experience with these books. Once her attention was called to how periods were used in other literature that was read to her, she began to experiment anew with capitalization and punctuation.

Examples of Writing Performance Assessment

For purposes of illustration we present two writing samples along with a brief descriptive analysis of each. The first writing sample, by a thirteen-year-old girl referred to a reading clinic, was written in response to a request from her clinic teacher to write on any topic.

> Love is like a game of football
> if you play the game right you both can win!
>   Summer was nice and fun. It's nice to be with your friend's, and in joy your salf. It's time to play and a time to go places. I alwas have fun in the summer. My friends and I do new thing and go new place. Sometimes I go out of town, its nice to go on vacasn and to get out of the house.

Although this piece of writing was on a topic chosen by the student, the writing was initiated by the teacher and probably viewed by the student as school writing since the audience for the writing was a teacher she had recently met and there seemed to be no other purpose than that of assessment. The student said she would write a love poem and produced the first two lines. Then, with encouragement, she produced more writing. Since the first two lines are topically unrelated to the rest of what she wrote, it may be that the teacher's encouragement sent her off in an entirely new direction. Overall, she wrote fairly quickly and without much hesitation. She edited while writing, making several erasures which she said were to correct her spelling or to improve her handwriting—a noticeable focus on conventions. None of her changes focused on revision that affected the meaning or structure of the story.

The topics of love and summer are of interest to this student, and she said she had written about them before. However, she does not rely on her personal experience in her writing. In fact, it seems that she doesn't understand love or football. Her paragraphs are reasonably well organized and her sentences follow in logical order, but she repeats herself and does not fully develop any of her ideas. She makes use of conjunctions and pronouns to achieve some degree of cohesion, at least at the sentence level, but she does not make use of transitions between ideas.

Her use of end-sentence punctuation and capitalization indicates that she has a fairly good grasp of the rules governing these conventions, but her use of an apostrophe with a plural noun shows some confusion about the rules for marking plurals. She uses appropriate yet simple syntax, although she omits *to* between *go* and *new* in line 6 and omits plural endings in line 5. Her spelling miscues indicate that she is a transitional speller; her misspellings employ visual features of standard English spelling.

Perhaps the most obvious characteristic of the content of this writing sample is its lifelessness. It conveys no conviction or urge to express, nor does it reflect the student's knowledge of language or her own personal experiences. Her erasures indicate more concern with producing accurate conventions than in communicating anything of real interest to her. This may be the result of the purpose and audience for the writing. Also, she might have produced a more effective piece of writing, and we could have learned more about her as a writer, if she had been asked to revise and/or edit her writing.

The second piece of writing is excerpted from a longer report written by Mary, a sixteen-year-old learning disabled student. It's noteworthy that Mary has been a reluctant writer and has never before produced writing of such length or conviction.

> My dream is to work with handicapped people I want to help them and know there troubles and care for them Because if no one will love them how will. I think they are very smart but they just need more help then others. You have to have the time to learn and understand them.

The report from which this excerpt is taken was written after Mary had written a summary of a book on dyslexia and had interviewed a handicapped teenager. She initiated the writing and chose the topic. Mary typed the composition herself, so some of her misspellings may be typographical errors, and it was written at home so we don't know how long it took her to write it or how much revision or editing, if any, she did.

The attention of most teachers and parents is probably drawn immediately to the problems Mary has with writing conventions. In this excerpt, she omitted periods at the end of two sentences and misspelled a homophone (*there their*) and substituted *how* for *who*. In another part of the report, she did not consistently mark the past tense of verbs ("I have interview him") and many of her sentences were awkward or even ungrammatical (e.g., "But what I've listen to what he says and does . . ."). Run-on sentences were also observed.

But these observations overlook strengths in Mary's writing and indicate only that she may need help in revising and editing her work, although this is uncertain until we've had more opportunity to observe her as she writes and to understand the role that typing may have played. In comparison to other writing Mary had done, she has made a marvelous breakthrough in her writing, a breakthrough not always achieved in the writing of "good" students. She has discovered that writing can be used to express and share her feelings with others. In relating what she learned from her interview of a handicapped adolescent, she attempted to persuade and move her audience, and her writing was full of life. Mary cares about what she has written. She has a reason to revise and edit her writing because she has something she wants to share. She also did an adequate job of organizing her writing; her ideas were well developed, and she used pronouns and conjunctions effectively to give her writing some degree of cohesion.

Readers will note that we haven't attempted to answer all the questions about writing we posed earlier as we assessed these two pieces of writing. It isn't necessary, or even possible, to address all the questions when assessing a single instance of a student's writing. They can be addressed by observing students' writings over a period of time. Analyzing these pieces of writing not only helped us understand both students' writing better, it also raised questions in our mind that we would want to answer in the future, especially in future observations of the students in the process of writing. Good assessment should not only answer questions but also raise new questions.

Assessing Early Reading and Writing Development

When Anne Dudley-Marling was two years old she was once observed carefully making scribbles on a piece of paper with a crayon. When she noticed the presence of an adult, she announced that she was writing. Asked what she was writing, she said that she was making a grocery list. Although no one would have recognized the marks Anne was making on her paper as writing, her comment revealed that she had made an important discovery about writing—"marks" on paper can be used to represent meaning. What she had not learned was how to use various written language conventions to convey her meaning and, therefore, her "writing" could not be read by others.

Teachers sometimes assume that students who can't read or write text in an independent and standard way know little, if anything, about reading and writing. Therefore, emergent reading and writing assessment tends to focus on "readiness" skills, perceptual and motor skills *presumed* to be necessary before written language instruction can begin. Since what we teach often reflects what we assess, the instruction for many emergent readers and writers has focused on these readiness skills, with little exposure to the print of texts. In light of what is known about the literacy development of young children, the traditional notion of readiness and the use of readiness tests are dubious at best (NAEYC, 1988; Rhodes & Shanklin, 1993; Stallman & Pearson, 1990). There's little doubt that reading and writing do require sophisticated perceptual and processing skills. However, any child who can discriminate cartoon characters probably possesses sufficient visual perceptual skills for reading and writing (F. Smith, 1973). In fact, most children come to school already knowing a great deal about print, and, as the example of Anne's grocery list demonstrates, children as young as two or three years of age usually know something about print (Y. Goodman, 1984; Harste, Woodward & Burke, 1984; Hiebert, 1981; Reid, Hresko & Hammill, 1981). The goal of early reading and writing assessment is to find out what they know.

As is the case with more experienced readers and writers, assessment information about emergent readers and writers can be gathered during everyday literacy events such as read–aloud time, shared reading or writing, independent reading or writing, drawing, language experience dictations, playing with environmental print, and so on. The following questions, some of them similar to those we'd ask about experienced readers and writers, may guide your observations. Of course, there are many more questions that could be asked.

1. Does the student enjoy being read to?

2. When the student is being read to what does she do? Does she ever finish a sentence or anticipate what's coming next? Does she demonstrate a concept of voice-print match?

3. How familiar is the student with literature? Does the student have favorite books?

4. Does the student ever talk about or use language or information from books that have been read to him? Does he refer to these books in different situations? For example, does the student talk about a dog he has read about when seeing a similar dog outside?

5. Does the student look at books on her own? write on her own?

6. As the student looks at books, how does she handle them? For example, does she point to words and turn the pages front to back?

7. What does the student say, if anything, while looking at books? while writing? Does what the student says relate to the book he is looking at? the writing he is doing?

8. Does the student recognize signs (e.g., stop signs), labels (e.g., Campbell's), or logos (e.g., McDonald's or Burger King)? attempt to use such print in play?

9. Does the student recognize her name? write it? know the names of the letters in it?

10. Does the student ask questions about print? What does he know about print?

If you would find it useful to use some published norm-referenced tests or performance samples to better understand a student or to learn what to observe in assessing emergent readers and writers, there are several available. The norm-referenced *Test of Early Reading Ability* or TERA (Reid, Hresko & Hammill, 1981) assesses children's knowledge of print in a variety of situations. A number of items are designed to observe children's abilities to read signs, logos, and other environmental print. For example, one item presents the familiar golden arches of Mc-Donald's. Other items assess children's knowledge of letters and words and their ability to read text orally and understand written language read aloud.

The Emergent Reading and Writing Evaluation (in Rhodes, 1993) is designed to help teachers carefully observe children as they engage in typical classroom lessons that involve drawing and writing, dictation of language experience stories, assisted reading over time, reading a predictable book, and retelling a book they have heard. In addition, the instrument guides teachers in understanding children's book-handling knowledge and their level of familiarity with literature.

Clay's Concepts About Print tests (two versions: *Sand* and *Stones*) are designed to help teachers uncover what it is that students know about print including such concepts as directionality, words, and letters (1970, 1972). Goodman and Altwerger (1985), McCormick (1981), and Hresko (1988) also have published procedures that help teachers in the assessment of emergent readers' and writers' concepts about print. Two other frameworks may also be useful in assessing aspects of literacy in students whose literacy is not yet conventional. Sulzby's categories of storybook reading assist teachers in determining a child's development with regard to their interactions with books (see Sulzby, 1991, or Rhodes & Shanklin, 1993). Morrow's scheme allows teachers to classify children's story reading responses with regard to the focus of the responses: focus on meaning, illustration, print, or structure (1990; also in Rhodes & Shanklin, 1993).

Parents of young children are an especially valuable source of information about reading and writing development as it has occurred in the years prior to school and as it occurs currently at home. Older students who are emergent readers and writers are also valuable resources about their own experiences. They are often able to provide insights about why they haven't learned to read and write and about the instructional experiences they've had and their reactions to them. Again, virtually all school-age students, including those from homes where literacy is not prized, will know something about print. Our task is to find out what that is. Once we have found out what emergent readers and writers know about literacy, we will be in a better position to plan instruction that assists their learning.

Assessing Other Aspects of Literacy

As we said earlier, the assessment of reading and writing can and should go beyond the assessment of performance or achievement. Other aspects of reading and writing are likely to have a significant influence on performance or may be important in their own right. In this section, we'll provide some ideas about how to assess other aspects of reading and writing: attitude and interests, perceptions, social aspects, procedural aspects, literary aspects, metacognitive aspects, flexibility, and environment and instruction.

Attitudes and Interests

A teacher who spends time talking with students about what they are reading and writing usually has a lot of information about the students' attitudes toward reading and writing and their reading and writing interests. However, further interviews with students who do not have positive attitudes about reading and writing may uncover details that will assist teachers in planning instruction. For example, a fourth-grade girl said this about why she continually had trouble getting started with her writing:

Diana: I don't like to write. I don't think I'm a good writer. I don't have a very good imagination.

Teacher: But you told me you like to tell your brothers and sisters stories.

Diana: Yes, that's fun. But I can't write them in here because we can't write bloody stories.

Teacher: What are you good at in writing?

Diana: The only stories I can write good are true stories. Things that have really happened to me. You know what happens to me? Once we start the story, I can't think of anything. And after the story's done, then I think of something, and I go, "Oh, no, I could have written that!"

Since Diana is known by her classmates as a "reading maniac," we wonder if she isn't assessing her writing of "imaginative" stories against the quality of commercial fiction. She reads little in the horror or biography genres and may not, as a result, have the same high standards for her writing (or telling) of "bloody stories" and "true stories" about herself. If we were Diana's teacher, we would probably give her free rein to write "true stories" about herself until she is more confident and ready to branch out into other kinds of writing. We might work to help her understand that fiction draws from real life. We would also help her understand that she can always go back to a previously written piece rather than starting a new one or that she can record things she thinks of on a topic list in order to remember them for possible future use. When the teacher sees Diana settle as happily into a piece of writing as she does into a book, she'll know that her attitude toward writing has changed.

It's possible to infer students' attitudes toward literacy from observations of students as they read and write. For example, Hunt notes that a number of behaviors may be observed during periods of sustained silent reading: 1) increased concentration during sustained silent reading, 2) a reluctance to stop reading when the period has ended, 3) greater spontaneous reaction during silent reading, 4) selection of reading material of increasing difficulty, and 5) greater impatience with disturbances (1970). An increase in any of these behaviors may indicate greater interest in reading, students' discovery of reading materials that interest them, and greater attention to meaning.

Students' interests in particular books can be directly accessed and then utilized to provide them with information about books they might want to read (Saccardi, 1993). In addition, general interest in reading and writing can be tapped via questionnaires such as The Denver Reading (Writing) Attitude Survey (in Rhodes, 1993).

Perceptions

Students' perceptions about reading and writing can have an impact not only on their performance but also on their attitudes toward reading and writing. Students' perceptions about reading and writing can often be accessed through interviews. Our favorite prepared interviews for this purpose are The Reading Interview

(Burke in Goodman, Watson & Burke, 1987, or in Rhodes, 1993) and a spin-off, The Writing Interview (Felknor in Rhodes, 1993). When there is only sufficient time to ask students the key question from each interview, the most important questions are:

> When you are reading and you come to something you don't know, what do you do? Do you ever do anything else?
>
> When you are writing and you have a problem (or get stuck), what do you do? Do you ever do anything else?

THE RESPONSES OF FOUR BOYS   The responses of four boys (collected by Carolyn Burke) illustrate the kind of information the question, "When you are reading and you come to something you don't know, what do you do?" can provide.

Rick: I ask someone. (Do you ever do anything else?) If someone's not around, I look up the word in the dictionary.

Shane: Try to sound it out. (Do you ever do anything else?) See if the vowels have an *e* marker on it—if there's a vowel marker. If the vowel is long, the *e* would be at the end of it. (Anything else?) Try to sound out all the other letters you can.

Seth: If it's an easy book, I skip it and then I'll probably catch what it is. If it's a hard book, I'll go ask someone. I really don't come to any words I don't understand because I have a pretty good vocabulary. Most of the things I've read, I've read before. (Do you ever do anything else?) Sometimes, if I find a couple words I don't know, I'll put the book away and go to another book—it'll probably be too hard for me.

Dave: Read back over it—the sentence I don't understand. (Do you ever do anything else?) Then, if I don't really understand that, I usually go back farther.

The boys' responses suggest quite different perceptions of reading. Rick, Shane, and Seth all appear to see reading as word-based, while Dave has a broader view that reading is the understanding of text. Rick's and Shane's responses both reveal that for them, reading is a matter of recognizing words; Seth views the understanding of the words' meanings as most important. Although Rick and Shane both seem to think that word recognition is what reading is about, they have very different approaches to it. Rick seeks outside help while Shane helps himself by sounding out the words. Both have a very narrow strategy base from which to operate when encountering difficulty.

In conjunction with observation of their reading, this interview provides information that can be very useful for planning instruction, especially when students like Rich and Shane have views of reading that are not meaning-based and so few strategies that they are aware of. Assuming that an observation of their reading confirms their descriptions of what they do and their views of reading, the boys' teacher can help them expand the range of strategies they use with a focus on strategies that help them begin to view reading as the construction of meaning.

Social Aspects

It is helpful to assess the social aspects of reading and writing, especially in classrooms that stress cooperative learning and/or high levels of student interaction in situations such as Author's Circle. After all, if students are to learn as much as possible from each other in these settings, it's important that the teacher assess how well students interact and what they offer each other.

Although teachers can take anecdotal notes about students' interactions in such settings, it is often profitable to involve students in assessing their participation in group activities. For example, a teacher might use a self-assessment like the one in Figure 4-7 on occasion following literature discussions.

Once the teacher has read students' responses, she can debrief them as a group with regard to how they seem to be expanding each other's understanding of the book under discussion. She can also help them look at how they are going about it, perhaps working with them to solve some problems that have arisen. She might

Name _____   Date _____

Title of Book Discussed _____

1. How much did you participate in the discussion today?

   about the right amount   too much   not at all   too little

2. What was an important contribution you made to the discussion?

   _____

   _____

3. What was an important idea expressed by someone else in the group during the discussion? (Identify the person and tell what he or she said.)

   _____

   _____

4. Is there an idea you have for improving the book discussions?

   _____

   _____

FIG. 4-7   *Book discussion form*

also work with or coach individual students who do not seem well-regarded by the group or who are having difficulty finding a place in the group.

Social aspects of literacy are likely to be a major focus in classrooms where students interact frequently with each other about their reading and writing. For example, Bath describes "trade-book minigroups"—groups of five or six students organized on the basis of books they have chosen to read (1992). Each group is facilitated by a student leader whose job it is to plan and execute a lesson or two to achieve the social goals (e.g., encouraging everyone to share) and discussion goals (e.g., summarizing) that the group has predetermined. At the end of each day's lesson and at the conclusion of each book, groups assess their learning using one of several assessment forms the teacher has prepared for their use.

Procedural Aspects

Procedural aspects of reading and writing can be assessed through observation, interviewing students, and self-assessments. In the self-assessment in Figure 3-4 (from Rhodes, 1993), students are asked to reflect on their engagement in reading during DEAR time and what they know about what they can do to help themselves be engaged. It might be useful to use this sort of self-assessment for a period of time with the students you know are having difficulty with engagement. It will provide students with a reminder of their responsibilities about how to proceed during DEAR time, and it will provide teachers with information that will help make the reading time we provide for our students more fruitful.

Literary Aspects

Students' knowledge of literary aspects of reading and writing can generally be observed as you talk with them about the reading and writing they are doing and as you observe the effect of your teaching about literary aspects on their knowledge of books and on their writing. Do students talk about favorite authors and/or genres with each other? Do they understand and can they locate such literary elements as story problems and solutions, flashbacks, foreshadowing, and themes? Do they consider various ways to begin a report in order to make it more interesting for the reader? Do they have ideas about how to make a written presentation such as a poster visually attractive? Observing students as they talk and work on various literacy tasks and asking them questions about literary aspects of the tasks will yield information about their knowledge and use of literary aspects in narrative and expository reading materials and their own writing.

In a research study one of us is involved in (Clarke, Davis, Rhodes, & Baker, 1995), we have observed the growth of an outspoken, frequently obstinate, and academically struggling fourth grader with regard to a particular literary aspect—the "rich language" of quality literature. Early in the school year, Takita publicly announced to her teacher that neither she nor her mother had any use for the "rich language" (literary language) that the teacher frequently pointed out when reading literature to the students. A few months later, she was observed commenting on the rich language of a story the teacher had read during read-aloud time and on the rich language of her classmates' writing during Author's Chair. In due time, Takita was attending to the use of rich language in her own writing and proudly accepting her classmates' praise of her attempts.

Flexibility

Good readers and writers adjust their effort, rate of reading and writing, and many of the other previously discussed aspects of reading and writing according to situational factors such as their purposes for reading and writing, their audiences, and the nature of the text they are reading or writing. We think of this as flexibility (Rankin, 1974). Poor readers, especially students with learning disabilities, may have difficulty adjusting their reading behavior according to their purposes for reading (Alley & Deshler, 1979; Rankin, 1974). The same is true for writing; we have met many writers who think that correct spelling is a necessity in all situations. In such a case, flexibility is probably affected by students' perceptions of the nature of writing.

Observation of students in many different reading and writing situations will help us understand if and how students adjust their reading and writing to the situation. Interview students about what you observe ("I noticed that . . . Why . . . ?"). Ask them how they operate differently from one setting to another (e.g., how they read differently when studying for an exam versus reading a novel). Their responses may add to your understanding of what might be needed to address with regard to flexibility in your instruction. Does the student read and write at the same speed for all types of material? For all purposes? Does the student ever use strategies like skimming and scanning as well as reading for detail? Does the student understand the importance of editing in formal writing situations? Does the student adjust the style of her writing in ways that are appropriate to the purpose and audience?

Metacognitive Aspects

Simply defined, metacognition is "knowing about knowing" (Brown, 1978) which, from the perspective of school literacy practices, means students being able to talk about, explain, or describe what they do in the process of reading and writing (Gee, 1990). Some of the previous examples of assessment revealed what students knew about various aspects of reading and writing. In the discussion on students' perspectives about reading, for example, Shane told us that he dealt with unknown words by sounding them out. Diana talked about her general attitude toward writing and how her attitude varied from one kind of text to another. Takita, another student, was able to recognize and discuss rich language before she came to appreciate it or use it in her writing. The assessment procedures we've discussed often rely on metacognition. For example, when students are asked, as they are in the self-assessment about DEAR time, to consider what will help them so they can spend all their time reading, they are required to reflect on what they know about their own reading and writing processes.

Some students have an easy time "knowing about knowing," as revealed in their explanations to others about what they do and think as readers and writers and why. Others have a more difficult time. We don't think students need to become consciously aware of everything they do and think but we do agree with Casanave's (1988, pp. 289–290) point that "by attempting to articulate . . . events, processes, and decisions, readers (and writers) become more aware of their existence and consequently of the need to pay attention to them while reading (or writing)."

Environment and Instruction

Assessment should lead to consideration of how we might adjust students' literacy environments and instruction, not just the students themselves. We would argue that the more a student struggles with literacy, the more teachers ought to try to figure out how to provide the kind of environment and instruction that helps the student compose and comprehend text as effectively as the student is capable of doing. We have it in our power as teachers—by adjusting the students' environments and instruction—to help students look and feel competent. The more we can do that and convince students that they are capable, the more they are willing to take risks and put forth effort, both of which lead to greater capability. Too often there is much about schooling that tells many of our students they are not competent readers and writers.

It is no accident that students who choose to read and write in their free time and who wholeheartedly engage in reading and writing in school are those who have had the advantage of literate environments. They are likely to have books at home, to be taken to the public library by their parents, to visit bookstores, to receive books, stationery, blank books or diaries as gifts, and to see the significant adults in their lives frequently engage in reading and writing. Given the importance of rich literacy learning environments in students' development as readers and writers, it is essential that we assess the quality of the literacy learning environment at school. The Survey of Displayed Literacy Stimuli (Loughlin & Martin, 1987; also in Rhodes & Shanklin, 1993), for example, enables teachers to examine the level of stimuli and support for spontaneous literacy behaviors in classrooms. Teachers can use the survey to assess their efforts to include books representing the students' cultures, writing materials, space, literacy invitations, environmental print, and so on. Of course, teachers can also assess environments outside of their immediate control. Do the students utilize the school library and the local public library? Do they have books in their homes? Do they trade books with each other? Do they write notes to each other?

Teachers can respond to information they have collected about the students' literacy environments, even those outside their immediate purview, in inventive ways. For example, one teacher who discovered that few of her students had books in their homes developed a two-pronged plan. She worked with her intermediate-grade students to help them figure out how to earn money in order to buy the inexpensive books offered by the school's book clubs, and she worked with the children to find and decorate heavy-duty cardboard boxes to serve as bookshelves for their newly purchased books. Toward the end of the year, she also helped them work out a plan to exchange books over the summer months.

One particularly important aspect of the literacy environment is the literacy instruction students currently receive and/or have received. Several instruments are available to help teachers examine their own literacy instruction or that can be used by others to assist teachers in examining their literacy instruction. Although not focused specifically on literacy, The Instructional Environment Scale (Ysseldyke & Christenson, 1987) is interesting in that it uses data from three sources to assess instruction: teacher interviews, classroom observations, and student interviews. Several other instruments rely on observation or self-analysis of literacy instruction, including the IAP Observation Checklist (in Rhodes, 1993), The Reading/Writing/Learning Self-Evaluation Form (Johnston & Wilder, 1992), and the Observation Guide Used to Develop an Integrated Reading/Language Arts Program (Vogt, 1991). An excellent discussion of factors that might be considered in assessing the instructional context may be found in Lipson & Wixson (1991). Students can also provide information about their educational environments. For example, Hill & Ruptic ask students to complete A Resource Room Evaluation each year (1994).

When instruction that's been offered to students is either poor or lacking, or doesn't match who they are as learners, it's important to understand the impact on the students involved. When students come from homes whose literacy practices closely resemble those of the schools, ineffective instruction may not have a lasting or significant impact. However, when the students must rely almost entirely on the school environment to learn about school-based reading and writing practices, the quantity and quality of classroom literacy instruction is important to assess.

The affective tone of the instruction received by struggling readers and writers is also worth assessing. One of the authors has been conducting a study (Davis, Clarke & Rhodes, 1993–94) of three teachers who are highly successful in helping minority, low-income students become literate, both with regard to their views of themselves and their skill as readers and writers. A key feature in each of these classrooms is that the teachers have convinced the children that they are capable students. They have high expectations, provide instructional situations in which those expectations can be met, and help students see the progress they are making in managing themselves and in becoming readers and writers. Although the teachers use different methodologies to achieve the results they do, they have all managed to convince their students that they're increasingly competent and that their efforts will make a difference.

Students themselves are valuable sources of information for understanding current and past instruction. If you are a resource teacher whose goal it is to help students gain as much as possible from regular classroom instruction, it's useful to understand the nature of that instruction. Since you spend most of your day with students and because their perceptions of instruction are important, talk with them about what happens during reading and writing in the classroom, what they do during that time, and how they do. One resource teacher we know discovered from talking with a small group of fourth-grade students that their teacher asked the students to produce a monthly composition, that she always assigned topics, that her assistance to the students was confined to spelling words for them and offering general comments of encouragement (e.g., "Good job!"), and that their monthly compositions were kept in a writing folder but not formally shared with anyone other than the teacher. On the other hand, she also discovered that their teacher expected students to do substantive writing across the curriculum on an almost daily basis and that she permitted students to talk informally with each other during almost all the writing they did. Because the resource teacher talked with the students who were experiencing the most academic difficulties, she also discovered how the teacher sometimes adjusted her writing requirements for these students.

In schools where collaboration is the norm, or in situations where the resource teacher and the classroom teacher have a good working relationship, the information gained from talking with struggling students in this fourth-grade classroom could be used by the two teachers as they experiment with writing instruction together. The resource teacher might offer, for example, to take the classroom teacher along to an in-service on conducting Writing Workshops, opening the door to conversation about writing instruction. Or the resource teacher might offer to co-teach Writing Workshop with the classroom teacher so that the two together could learn from each other and adjust the struggling writers' instruction in a way that would benefit them. The resource teacher could also learn more about the writing that the classroom teacher assigns across the curriculum and work with her students so that they can handle such writing more successfully.

In summary, there is much that we teachers can do to support and encourage students' views of themselves and their performances as readers and writers. It seems both practical—and ethical—to make every attempt to adapt the literacy environment and instruction to the needs of struggling students.

5 From Assessment to Planning and Adjusting Instruction (and Back Again)

Comprehensive assessment provides a firm foundation for instructional decisions which may range from instant adjustments during instruction to next-day plans and long-range plans, including Individual Education Plans for special education students. When assessment takes place in the midst of instruction, as we have recommended in the previous chapters, the assessment and instruction become indistinguishable. Assessment shapes instruction and instruction provides the contexts that make much assessment possible.

In this chapter we'll discuss using assessment information to plan and adapt instruction to the ever-changing needs of developing readers and writers. We'll begin by showing how we construct and continually review long-term plans for students in light of ongoing assessment, with special attention to using a holistic framework rather than the behavioral approaches ordinarily used in constructing such plans. The chapter will conclude with a discussion of a model of instruction that relies on assessment information to generate a sequence of lessons that encourages students to assume responsibility for what has been taught.

Written Goals or Objectives

Written goals or objectives are more than a good idea. Writing them helps teachers clarify what they want to teach and why, and encourages reflection on the needs of individual students. They also provide teachers with a focus for instruction that is responsive to students' development as readers and writers. Further, written goals and objectives reassure parents and administrators that students are receiving instruction tailored to their needs. Literacy goals or objectives are developed on the basis of assessment: what teachers have learned about various aspects of their students' reading and writing.

However, if written goals or objectives are going to be useful, they must be referred to often and revised on the basis of ongoing assessment. They must not be written and forgotten, something that happens all too often with Individual Education Plans (Dudley-Marling, 1985). Ongoing evaluation aids teachers in adapting instructional strategies in accordance with changing student needs. If a student who has been working on increasing writing fluency begins to produce writing fluently, the teacher's observations of these changes should lead to new goals such as writing for different purposes and audiences or learning the skills of editing and revision. The key is that the teacher is always aware of a student's current reading and writing performance, alert to evidence of continued development, and knowledgeable about the student's course of development. This awareness forms the basis for revising goals and objectives.

Further, if written goals or objectives are going to be useful, they must reflect the teacher's instructional philosophy. The problem for those whose teaching is based on a holistic philosophy is the behavioral nature of the goals or objectives written for students found in learning disability or remedial programs. In Canada and the United States, LD and remedial teachers are usually required to develop specific educational plans for each of their students. Many of these educational plans include specific, measurable, short- and long-term goals or objectives. But writing "measurable" (i.e., quantifiable) instructional objectives can lead to fragmented instruction.

"Johnny will pronounce the first one hundred words from the Dolch Word List with 80 percent accuracy by Jan. 1," for example, is a typical short-term, behavioral objective focused on literacy. The expected student performance is stated precisely and is measurable. It's clear what you and Johnny will have to do to show that this objective has been met: You will show Johnny the first one hundred words of the Dolch List and, if he pronounces 80 percent of the words correctly, the goal has been achieved.

Through task analysis teachers identify component parts of the learning process and teach those isolated tasks using appropriate reinforcement (Astman, 1984). Mastery of the task is defined in terms of learning those individual subskills thought to make up the task. It follows that writing behavioral objectives for reading and writing is a matter of identifying the component parts of the task of written language. Reading, for example, may be defined in terms of learning sight vocabulary, mastering a finite set of letter-sound correspondences, and learning a series of comprehension skills such as sequencing and locating the main idea. It's assumed that students can learn to read by learning these component skills.

But, of course, reading is not merely a matter of pronouncing words and applying comprehension skills nor is writing simply a matter of spelling, punctuation, and sentence structure. Reading and writing are sociopsycholinguistic processes for constructing meaning and fulfilling intentions. Readers and writers use their world knowledge and their knowledge of language, as well as their knowledge of written language conventions, to make meaning. Reading and writing are different from the sum of their parts and, in any case, the "parts" cannot be removed from the context of the whole without destroying the integrity of written language.

For example, a woman may be able to pronounce the French words on bilingual Canadian government forms, but if she cannot construct meaning from the French, she is not reading French. She is merely making what for her are meaningless sounds. Of course, an ardent behaviorist might argue that she should now focus on learning the meanings of the French words, and that this process could be task-analyzed and appropriate goals or objectives written, and so on. But again the meaning of a text is not the sum of the meanings of the individual words. Readers construct meaning based on a whole range of cognitive and sociolinguistic factors including, but certainly not restricted to, the meanings of individual words. Readers can only learn how this multitude of cognitive, social, and linguistic factors interact to affect meaning if they encounter words and word meanings within the context of whole texts and within meaningful, communicative contexts. Similar arguments can be made for writing. This still might not deter an especially ardent behaviorist, but we doubt that anything we say could.

Behavioral objectives are well motivated. They presume to ensure maximally efficient instruction by focusing on well-defined, easily achievable "building blocks" of learning. But they depend on a technology that does not exist. Precise descriptions of cognitive, social, and linguistic behavior, including reading and writing, are not possible and probably not desirable. Higher forms of human learning are not reducible to their component parts.

In addition, behavioral objectives trivialize learning, seriously underestimate the potential of learners, including students identified as learning disabled or remedial, and strip away the meaningfulness of what is presented to students. By stripping meaning from reading and writing, behaviorists deprive students of their most powerful vehicle and motivator for learning—making sense of their world. Certainly many students can learn the content of behavioral objectives that have been written for them, but what they learn in this way has little value for them in their lives outside of school. Poplin captures our feelings about behavioral objectives best when she states, "Anything you can put into a computer or analyze into behavioral objectives is not worth teaching" (Poplin, 1983, p. 10).

Our challenge is to offer an alternative to behavioral goals or objectives for teachers committed to holistic approaches to literacy learning but justifiably concerned with accountability and with fulfilling their legal responsibilities.

A Holistic Approach to Planning Instruction

Again, we believe that written goals and objectives and detailed instructional plans, especially for students who are struggling with school literacy, are sound practices. We object, however, to behavioral approaches to describing written language behavior and developing reading and writing objectives. As an alternative, we suggest three steps for planning written language instruction: 1) developing concise summaries of current reading and writing performance, 2) developing learner objectives; and 3) developing teaching goals. Of course, the development of useful goals and objectives emerges from a careful assessment of students' reading and writing development.

Developing Summary Statements

For purposes of discussion, we'll look at planning instruction for students new to your program. The first step in planning instruction tailored to the needs of an individual student is to write concise summaries of the student's current reading and writing development, based on the observations you've made, from which learner objectives can be produced. These summaries include brief statements describing what students do as readers and writers—statements of effective and ineffective processes and products. Some examples of summary statements for one student are presented in Figure 5-1.

Ideally, summary statements will be developed only as teachers have the opportunity to work with the student over several weeks, observing and talking with the student as he reads and writes and as he responds to reading and writing instruction. If teachers are compelled to develop an instructional plan after only initial evaluation sessions with a student, they should remember that the behaviors they have observed may not be representative. More reliable information about students' reading and writing performances will come only from daily observation of the students' reading and writing during instructional time.

No doubt some of our readers will be uncomfortable with terms like "usually," "typically," and "seldom," which we used in the summary statements. Those trained to write behavioral objectives have been taught that general terms like "typically" are imprecise and antithetical to good teaching practices. After all, how do you measure "typically"? How will you know if the student has progressed? Many would probably be tempted to translate the kind of general summary statements we're proposing into more precise, behavioral-sounding objectives. What's wrong, for example, with stating that "John's reading miscues do not make sense 76 percent of the time"?

This kind of quasibehavioral statement would be very misleading, however. As we noted earlier, students' reading and writing performances are variable and context dependent. A student may depend heavily on the sound and appearance of words when she reads her history book at school but focus much more on meaning when she is reading a Goosebumps story or *Anne of Green Gables*. So statements like "76 percent of her miscues do not make sense" imply a false precision. At other times, in other contexts, more (or fewer) of her miscues may make sense. On the other hand, words like "typically" and "seldom" are also signals that the teacher may be able to learn more about the student through careful observations and adjust instruction on the basis of these observations. The summary statement that "John's miscues are seldom corrected," for example, begs the question, "Under what circumstances are they corrected?" If there is a discernable pattern to his corrections, it indicates a possible strength that might be nurtured during instruction. In other words, the teacher can help John understand what he sometimes does well and help him do the same thing well in more contexts.

Reading miscue performance (and other aspects of reading and writing) will depend on a host of factors, including the text, students' background knowledge, their interests, and so on. The use of general descriptive statements is a recognition of reality, because reading and writing performance, like all higher forms of human learning, are variable and context dependent, and can only be described generally.

EXAMPLES OF SUMMARY STATEMENTS

John's reading miscues are typically graphophonically similar but do not make sense.

John's reading miscues are seldom corrected.

When John encounters a word he doesn't know, he often asks the teacher or another student to tell him the word.

John's oral retellings consist mostly of the random recall of a few facts.

John's oral retellings do not include any references to his own personal experiences with the topic of the text.

John rarely writes more than one or two sentences at a time.

John does not usually use capital letters or punctuation to mark sentence boundaries in his writing.

John's background knowledge does not include information about "classical" literature, i.e., common fairy tales, folk tales, and tall tales.

John's spelling depends heavily upon a letter-naming strategy, including those words he frequently sees during reading.

John doesn't initiate the reading or writing of texts outside of school; he does choose to read (but not write) during school "choice time."

When John chooses books to read, he frequently selects those recommended by classmates or previously read by the teacher.

Though John reads and writes far less than his classmates in the same length of time, he concentrates on the reading and writing for the established period of time.

John does not revise or edit as he writes.

John pays attention to students' writing during Author's Chair and offers general comments such as "I liked your story."

Until this year, John's reading instruction in the classroom and resource room has been skills-based. He has not been involved in writing extended text.

John's mother reports that she reads the newspaper and an occasional novel but that the father does not read at home.

FIG. 5-1 *Examples of summary statements*

Developing Learner Objectives

Once a student's current reading and writing performance has been described using summary statements, the next step in instructional planning is to think about how you want that reading and writing performance to change. Learner objectives refer to what teachers hope will happen as a result of their teaching interactions with students. Here, it is necessary to consider normally developing and proficient readers and writers so that goals and objectives reflect normal performance, attitudes, and so on.

Of course, the overriding objective of written language instruction is that students develop into lifelong readers and writers. This is the ultimate test of a reading and writing program. If students achieve a series of learner objectives but fail to use reading and writing in and out of school for their own purposes, the reading and writing program has not succeeded. Examples of learner objectives, based on the preceding summary statements, are presented in Figure 5-2.

Remember that learner objectives should be based on the summaries of a student's reading and writing behavior that you have prepared and on what you know about the course of reading and writing development, including children's "typical" performance. Your knowledge about development may preclude writing a learner objective for some summary statements. For example, because the teacher knows that fluent writing needs to precede the development of the conventional use of capitalization and punctuation, no learner objective was written to correspond with the summary statement on capitalization and punctuation. In other cases, the learner objective should take into account the "usual" course of development. Developmentally, students learn to add information in revision before they learn to subtract or reorganize information. Thus, the objective written for John regarding revision takes that into account.

The summaries of effective reading and writing (e.g., "he concentrates on the reading and writing . . .") do not require a corresponding learner objective unless you feel that you need to do something as a teacher to maintain or expand the behavior.

Developing Teaching Goals

The next step in instructional planning is developing teaching goals—the general steps the teacher expects to take to encourage the student's literacy development toward the learner objective. In other words, what will you do to help the student move from the current descriptions of reading and writing performance in the summary statement to the learner objectives you have established?

Teaching goals will include general statements about instructional strategies, suggested materials and resources, and so on. These goals represent an overall plan or a road map for literacy instruction. Some examples of teaching goals are presented in Figure 5-3. Again, they are related to the summary statements and learner objectives presented earlier.

As with learner objectives, it's sufficient to indicate just some of the teaching strategies and resources that will be used with students. It's unreasonable to be

EXAMPLES OF LEARNER OBJECTIVES

John will balance his use of the language systems more consistently while reading.

John will correct oral reading miscues that don't make sense more frequently.

John will rely on a variety of independent strategies when he comes to words he doesn't know.

John's oral retellings will include important information from the texts he has read, organized in a logical fashion.

John will make connections between what he reads and his own life, first at the teacher's initiation and then on his own.

John's writing will increase in length and fluency.

John will edit his writing to include capital letters and punctuation, especially those which mark sentence boundaries.

John will read a variety of classical literature.

John will use features of standard English in his spelling; he will begin to use correct spellings of the words he sees most frequently while reading.

John will initiate the reading and writing of texts outside of school; he will occasionally choose to write during school "choice time."

John will add information to his writing drafts when appropriate.

John's comments to fellow classmates during Author's Chair will reflect a more specific understanding of literary elements.

FIG. 5-2   *Examples of learner objectives*

expected to indicate all of the instructional strategies that will be used. However, these are the issues a teacher who works with John would attend to. It's also important to remember that teaching goals will change continually in response to students' ongoing development. Thus, it's best to consider teaching goals as a way to start out your journey with the student, keeping in mind that the student will reveal new roads as you make the journey together.

When writing teaching goals, remember to consider the importance of establishing a literate environment for students, and of adjusting instruction as necessary. Note the effort John's teacher has decided to make with regard to both his home and school environments. This will be a reminder, once again, to attend to the context in which the students learn, not just to attend to the students themselves.

Revision of Summaries, Learner Objectives, and Teaching Goals

Learner objectives and teaching goals make sense only if they're routinely reexamined and revised in light of the assessment information gathered as part of the

EXAMPLES OF TEACHING GOALS

I will help John learn to monitor whether the text is making sense to him as he reads.

I will help John discover meaning-based strategies for figuring out words.

I will help John identify miscues that don't make sense and discover strategies for self correcting those miscues.

When John asks for help with words, I will refer him to the chart of strategies for independently figuring out words that he has generated.

I will encourage John to participate in oral storytelling based on well-structured stories he has read.

I will use prereading strategies with John to encourage him to activate his background knowledge prior to reading.

I will schedule daily journal writing time for the entire class.

I will construct a thematic unit featuring classical literature for the entire class.

I will encourage John to think about how words look in print so that he begins to access visual information he has from reading.

I will talk with John's parents about establishing an inviting literacy environment for John at home and involve his mother in reading aloud to him. I will also establish a literacy environment at school that encourages more person-to-person writing, such as message boards or mailboxes.

I will arrange for others to conference with John about what he has written so that he learns what information can be added to his writing. I will help John learn how to add information to his writing.

I will help John discover what he might say in response to his classmates' writing during Author's Chair.

Once a week, I will review the anecdotal records I take on John to see if I am addressing and/or adjusting the learner objectives I've set out. I will also share one insight or accomplishment per week with John's resource teacher in hopes of influencing her instruction with him.

FIG. 5-3   *Examples of teaching goals*

students' daily reading and writing instruction. Thus, ongoing assessment is a necessity in instructional planning if instruction is to meet the needs of students and respond to what they are currently trying to learn and do.

As we said in the introduction to this chapter, assessment and instruction are intertwined. Teachers will need to spend a routine amount of time reviewing not only recorded assessment information but also summaries, learner objectives, and teaching goals, and then revising as needed. Evidence that learning is taking place will not be limited to what is observed with regard to the stated learner objectives. Teachers must be alert to other evidence that learning is taking place. Awareness of students' growth depends upon consistent and continual review of assessment data, summaries, learner objectives, and teaching goals. One way that resource teachers can make certain that they continually review and adjust assessment information and instructional plans is to schedule a daily review of a certain number of the total number of students seen. A classroom teacher can do likewise, perhaps with a more frequent review of the students who struggle most. Of course, it would be most useful if resource teachers and classroom teachers could review these materials (from both classrooms) and plan together on a regular basis.

Careful record keeping and close monitoring of goals or objectives is the only way teachers can respond flexibly to the needs and development of individual students. It isn't enough for teachers to teach the class and hope for the best with struggling readers and writers; that is a "shotgun" approach to teaching reading and writing. It fails to consider students' individual needs and development and is contrary to the basic principles of special and remedial education. Careful record keeping is also important for communicating with parents, who deserve a detailed account of their child's literacy development.

The Individual Education Plan: A Note to Special Educators

As any special educator in the United States is well aware, the main components of the individual education plan (IEP) include statements indicating students' current levels of functioning, short- and long-term instructional objectives, and some indication of how short- and long-term objectives will be evaluated. The format we've presented for developing written instructional plans was designed to be as IEP-like as possible. Our format includes summaries or statements of current reading and writing performance, and long-term learner objectives. The evaluation of progress toward objectives can be based on the various means of collecting and recording information discussed in the first chapter of this section: occasional performance samples, observations, interviews, and products collected in folders or portfolios.

Our format does not include short-term objectives for learners because we feel that short-term learner objectives are inconsistent with basic principles of holistic education. It's easy enough to state that some isolated skill (e.g., "Sally will pronounce all of the letters of the alphabet") will be learned by such and such a date, but more meaningful types of learning just don't work this way. It's not possible to predict the rate or precise course of higher forms of learning, including oral and written language, with any certainty.

For example, a teacher we know described the emergent writing development of one of her students for us. In September she observed that the student's writing was limited to several lines of unintelligible scribbling, which resembled cursive writing, written alternately right to left and then left to right. A few weeks later the teacher noted that the student had begun to write cursivelike lines only from left to right. After several more weeks, she noticed that letters were beginning to appear in the student's writing and, finally, that the student's name appeared among the letters. Certainly this student's writing showed development, but it's unlikely that the rate or the nature of this development could have been predicted.

Short-term behavioral objectives also imply that teachers are technicians. Presumably, task analysis and appropriate reinforcement techniques allow teachers to influence the rate and course of learning with a high level of success. Anyone who has observed the cognitive development of students knows that the rate of students' cognitive development is often uneven and unpredictable. It would make no sense to state that we expected a two-year-old to begin using adjectives within a month, and it makes no more sense to us to make similar short-term predictions for students' reading and writing development. We have set aside expectations of a gradual and incremental learning curve; we have observed that many students do not reveal their progress toward literacy in this way. In the place of writing short-term goals, daily and weekly planning should include reference to and sometimes adjustment of long-term learner objectives, as a way to keep the short-term or daily instructional plans heading in a direction that assists students in making progress toward achieving the learner objectives.

We have also made some compromises to make our planning format IEP-like. We aren't entirely comfortable with the format we've presented for writing learner objectives. There is a risk that teachers will unduly focus their attention on these objectives and fail to respond to what students are trying to do or notice other developments that may come about as a result of their teaching efforts. For example, Allen and Hansen talk about a boy who shared a piece of writing about whales that had only three lines of information (1986). A teacher who had written learner objectives like the ones for John about increasing the length of writing and adding information to writing might have responded to the boy's writing by calling attention to these things. In this case, the boy's friends asked him what he wanted to do next and he replied, "Write one on seals. This was the first time I used the card catalogue and I want to use it again tomorrow before I forget" (1986, p. 689). Obviously, this teacher needed to set aside her learner objectives in such a case and respond to the student's initiative even though it may have nothing to do with established learner objectives. The teacher needs to be open to the leads the student presents, and these leads do not always match predetermined learner objectives.

In general, we are confident that the format we have presented for planning instruction satisfies the basic components of the IEP and, more important, satisfies the spirit of the IEP, which holds that all students placed in special and remedial education programs should have individualized education plans tailored to their needs as learners. However, in some cases special education teachers (and even remedial teachers) may feel compelled to write short- and long-term behavioral objectives even though they are uncomfortable with behavioral approaches to teaching reading and writing. In this case, teachers should probably try to shape their goals and objectives into a behavioral format. For example, they might state something like "Johnny will write a story with thirty words by June 1" or "Mary will spontaneously correct 80 percent of any reading miscues that don't make sense by March 1." Given the conditional nature of these goals, they aren't very meaningful, but they will likely satisfy those administrators who insist on behavioral goals and objectives. (See Hill & Ruptic, 1994, for other examples.)

Gradual Release of Responsibility

In addition to using assessment to conduct long-term planning that results in summaries, learner objectives, and teaching goals, teachers use assessment information to consider how to plan lesson sequences that eventuate in student independence. Pearson and Gallagher's model of instruction, adapted in Figure 5-4, is useful in planning and adjusting instruction for students who are struggling to learn (1983). It is also useful in considering how to withdraw the teacher support given to LD and remedial readers as they gradually assume responsibility for using new language knowledge or strategies. The model is grounded in Vygotsky's developmental theory, which posits that learners can operate at a higher level of functioning with assistance or scaffolding (1986). With this assistance, children can operate in their "zone of proximal development," the area in which a student who cannot do something independently can do the task with assistance.

Since reading and writing rely on active construction of meaning, this model, which moves from 1) teacher demonstration or teacher-led discovery to 2) use that is supported by the teacher to 3) independent use, is important in planning and adjusting literacy instruction for struggling learners, especially those who suffer

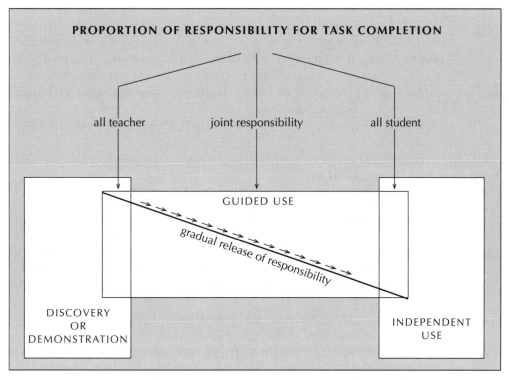

FIG. 5-4   *The gradual realease of responsibility model of instruction (adapted from Pearson & Gallagher, 1983)*

from "learned helplessness." This model allows teachers to demonstrate the active meaning-construction processes of reading and writing and ensure that students assume responsibility for constructing meaning for themselves. The model also helps teachers understand how they might "back up" or "back off" as their assessment information indicates and provide the level of instructional support needed to ensure both learning and eventual independence.

Clarifying the Goal for Independent Use

Although the model is meant to be read left to right, we want to begin our discussion with the right-hand side of the model, at "independent use," for it is at this point that the model connects with the previous discussion of using assessment information to serve instructional planning. A "fuzzy" notion of what teachers want students to be able to do independently is not sufficient to assist struggling readers and writers; teachers need to be clear and precise in defining the behaviors they want students to employ as independent users of the strategies or knowledge that will be taught. Further, the image of what students will be able to do must guide teachers' lessons as they gradually release responsibility to students; it is this image that keeps lessons focused unwaveringly on the end goal. The assessment data that you collect, the summaries and long-term learner objectives that you write will help you both form and hold onto a clear image of what you want students to be able to do as you guide them through a series of lessons designed to help students learn new strategies, knowledge, behaviors, and so on. This is true whether independent use is a long-term goal (becoming someone who chooses to read) or a relatively shorter-term goal (being able to use the appropriate form of *their/there/they're*) on the way to the ultimate goal of more skilled use of conventions in writing. By creating and holding this image of independent use in mind, teachers can effectively plan lessons that will allow them to achieve their instructional goals.

Discovery and Demonstration

Returning to the beginning of the model, a discovery or demonstration lesson(s) taught by the teacher, we can think about how the teacher might kick off a series of lessons that will result in independent use over time. In the initial lesson or lessons, the teacher initiates new learning in one of two ways: through demonstration or through teacher-led discovery. From our observations, demonstration is a seldom-used, but effective, method of teaching students various aspects of reading and writing. In the following chapters, we'll present many lessons in which teachers demonstrate reading and writing strategies such as predicting, self-correcting, revising, and spelling. Demonstrating a reading or writing strategy involves showing students how you use the reading/writing strategies as you read/write and talk aloud about what you are doing. At first, you may find it odd, and perhaps even difficult, to get in touch with what you usually do intuitively. And you may find it uncomfortable to talk about what you so naturally do as a reader or writer. But you'll find that the students learn from your demonstrations, even when you may not think you've demonstrated well. Over time, you will become both skilled and comfortable with demonstrating strategies you use in the process of reading and writing, and students will learn even more from your demonstrations.

Demonstration may also be used to teach students other aspects of reading and writing that we outlined in the previous chapter. For example, teachers can demonstrate how to consider the needs of an audience for a piece of writing—a social aspect of literacy. They can demonstrate how to go about locating information about favorite authors' lives—a literary aspect of literacy. They can demonstrate flexibility by doing such things as showing and talking with students about how they adjust speed of reading for various purposes. Of course, because demonstration requires talking about what you are showing students how to do, you are also constantly demonstrating how to be metacognitive about various aspects of literacy.

Another way to introduce students to aspects of literacy is through "discovery" lessons. Although these lessons do not involve students in discovery in the true sense of the word, they do help students uncover or discover how language works for themselves. Active student learning about how language works encourages understanding and learning on the student's part. The lessons may take longer to teach, but they are often more effective because they encourage students to discover and infer rules for themselves.

Lessons that help students discover information about literacy are often taught by comparing texts. The texts may be trade books, students' writings, your writing, or some combination of these materials or other texts. First an example of discovery regarding a literary aspect of literacy: If you want students to discover the characteristic of "threeness" in folktales, comparing a variety of folktales that feature "threes" will encourage students to discover this and other characteristics of folktales. An example of discovery regarding written conventions: If students are using a nonstandard grammatical construction (e.g., "me and John" instead of "John and I" as the subject), you might lift some of the sentences containing these constructions from their writing and have the students compare them with the way those same sentences would be written in books. On the basis of the grammatical patterns found in books, they will be able to generate the grammatical rule you want them to attend to in their own writing.

Comparison can also be useful for helping students discover strategies for dealing with traditional classroom tasks more effectively. For example, if students are struggling with sequencing worksheets that they are assigned, we might involve them in a lesson in which we ask them to sequence the statements on the worksheet before reading the passage, then to read the passage, and then to renumber the sequence where necessary (see Atwell and Rhodes, 1984, for more detail about this lesson). After the students experience success with sequencing in this way, we could have them compare the procedures they used in the lesson with those they usually follow in completing such worksheets. They might conclude that what was different in the lesson was that they guessed or predicted the sequence and then read to confirm/disconfirm their predictions, and, in the process, read much more actively. On the basis of such a lesson, teachers can help students think about other school situations in which predicting on the basis of the final task (e.g., statements to sequence, questions to answer, multiple-choice answers on tests) and then reading to confirm predictions will be useful.

Guided Use

Guided use follows demonstration or discovery. Guided use is done within the context of students' readings or writings, and is continually informed by assessment information gathered as you observe the students' performances during lessons. For example, if you've demonstrated how to translate story dialogue into play dialogue (The troll growled, "I'm coming to eat you up!" translated to Troll: I'm coming to eat you up!), the next step might include having students try it with your support, then work with each other under your supervision, translate dialogue alone with immediate feedback from you, and finally work independently. Of course, this sequence assumes that your observation of the students indicates that they are moving toward independence in being able to write play dialogue. Individual help and review of what was demonstrated or discovered may be fine in cases where teachers are able to work with few students, but it's more efficient to provide guided use in a group situation when a number of students have need for it.

Teachers in our classes who have considered and experimented with guided use have uncovered a general lesson sequence and aspects of instruction that they find useful to consider in carefully sequencing lessons for students who need a great deal of support to achieve independent use. (Other educators have undertaken this as well; see Reed, Hawkins & Roller, 1991, for another approach.) The teachers used the instructional aspects to sequence lessons that provided for repeated use of the aspect of literacy being highlighted, with each lesson in the sequence encouraging students to move toward greater independence. The general lesson sequence is outlined below with an example given about how to teach students to take notes from informational text. Of course, it is assumed that this sequence of lessons was preceded by at least one lesson in which the teacher demonstrated how she took notes from informational text.

- The teacher continues to demonstrate the new learning but encourages students to take over the demonstration and/or thinking aloud about it. For example, on an overhead projector in front of the class, the teacher might read informational material and write notes about it in her own words; as the teacher proceeds, students describe what she is doing, often referring to a chart labeled "How to Take Notes" that the students generated after watching the teacher's original demonstrations/think-alouds of note taking.

- As the students take over the demonstration and think-aloud, the teacher observes the students' use and provides feedback. The teacher offers help when needed, sometimes in the form of a question that directs students to observe something or think about what might come next. For example, as some students describe how others are taking notes from informational material, the teacher asks the students questions to help them better articulate the process.

- Students work together at using the new learning in small groups or pairs, with the teacher observing and providing feedback. For example, as pairs of students read informational material together and figure out what to record, the teacher asks questions to redirect their work and/or demonstrates again what she would do.

- Students use the new learning, knowing that they will reflect on the use of it in a self-assessment that is structured to guide their thinking. For example, after students have taken notes from informational material, they are asked to rate their performance and report the processes they used and/or difficulties they encountered and how they addressed those difficulties.

- Students use the new learning with the assistance of a written guide that provides structure for their thinking. For example, as students take notes in preparation for writing a report, they refer to the ideas they have generated about how to take notes on a chart ("How to Take Notes") hanging in the classroom.

The teachers in our university class also summarized various aspects of instruction that can be adjusted as indicated by assessment information in order to gradually release responsibility for new learning to students. These include:

- The degree to which the lessons are structured. Less structure increases student responsibility.

- The degree to which the students' responses are constrained. Less constraint on student response increases student responsibility.

- The number of students involved in the lesson: whole class, small groups, pairs, individuals. The fewer students in the group, the more individual student responsibility.

- Whether the lesson requires that the students recognize or produce something. Production requires more responsibility than recognition. (Example: It is easier to recognize a correct spelling than to produce it.)

- The degree to which the teacher or the student assesses success. Student assessment requires more student responsibility.

- The timing of teacher feedback, from immediate to delayed. The greater the delay in feedback, the more student responsibility.

One way to provide guided use for a group of students is by "lifting" their work. For example, if you've demonstrated how to proofread, you might then "lift" a student's composition (or a portion of it) and proofread it as a group or class. If you've helped students to discover the difference between *its* and *it's*, you can then "lift" sentences containing the words from students' papers and let students consider the use of the words in those sentences as a group. Other aspects of literacy can be treated in the same way. One second-grade teacher who wanted to help her students conduct better discussions about books had her students listen to and critique videotapes of their discussions. At first, she guided them in looking for what went well and not so well, and then she began to let them take over the process and suggest better ways to approach such discussions. Eventually, the children's discussions about books—a social aspect of literacy—improved.

"Lifting" students' writings, debriefing videotapes, or other methods of guiding use of a new learning in a public way, must be done with care so that students treat each other's work and presentations with respect. To help them establish respect for each other's work you need to make some things clear: first, that everyone's work will be considered by the group, including the teacher's; and second, that work does not get "lifted" or shown because it's poor but because there is potential in it that the group, working together, can help to achieve. Until students understand this, you might even remind them that if their work is "lifted" so the group can work on it, at least they won't have to do the work alone!

When we begin "lifting" or sharing student work in other ways, we discuss the above issues with students. In addition, we "lift" or share the work of several students at a time—a number of sentences from various student products that feature the aspect of literacy we wish to highlight, the work of those students who are respected by others, and work that is above that done by the students who perform least well. Using examples from students who are least likely to be threatened, we set the tone for the remainder of the year. Some teachers make it a point of not identifying written work that is used in lessons, but our preference is to acknowledge whose work it is for several reasons. We find that students make a game of trying to identify whose it is anyway, and if the class is sharing reading and writing frequently, it's likely that at least some students have seen, heard, and discussed the work already. We also think it's important to involve the student whose work is being discussed at a different level than the others. For example, if we've "lifted" sentences to work on substituting more interesting words for overused ones (see Chapter 11), we usually ask the writer to tell the rest of us which word of those suggested she will probably use in revising the composition.

Independent Use

Independent use of new learning isn't always straightforward, especially when what is being learned is complex. For example, learning to independently use *their*, *there*, and *they're* appropriately in context is far less complex than learning to write a report. When projects like writing a report are made up of multiple tasks and strategies that must be orchestrated to produce a single product like an effective report, each task and its related strategies may need to be taught separately. We've previously demonstrated one strategy—the note-taking portion of the larger task of writing a report.

Further, independent use of a new learning is not always fixed. Students who have learned to write a report independently when the topic is already very familiar to them, for example, may require teacher support (guided use) again when they are assigned to write a report about a topic that isn't based in their experiences. Assessment information may reveal that students require guided use in how to learn about unfamiliar topics and make them their own as part of the report writing process. When the topic was familiar to them, they did not need this help.

What is often helpful in moving toward independent use is that most students very much want to be independent, especially when they see the value of what is being taught. We have approached the teaching of aspects of literacy from a rather logical point of view in using the Gradual Release of Responsibility Model of Instruction, but it should not be forgotten that we need to engage students' hearts in the process of teaching. It is far easier to encourage movement toward independence when students see themselves as becoming increasingly capable of doing things that they believe have value in their lives. As one special education teacher commented, "Mostly, I ask myself, does this child feel good about himself as a reader, writer, learner? Does this child feel successful? Does this child see reading and writing as a joy, not a task? If I can answer yes to these questions, I know that the child is making progress, no matter how subtle" (Furnas, 1991, p. 7).

READING INSTRUCTION
A Focus on Struggling Readers

We treat reading and writing separately as a matter of convenience. We believe strongly that reading and writing instruction ought to be closely linked—a point we'll make often in the rest of this book. Throughout this section on reading instruction, for example, we present recommendations for involving students in writing in order to explore text; conversely, you will see that the writing section is heavily dependent on students' involvement in reading as students read their own and others' texts. We believe that students gain information from being involved in one process that provides them with the information and motivation to learn more about the other process.

The theoretical basis for the instruction recommended in this section is that people learn to read by having access to complete or whole language information in contexts that are meaningful to them. We do not, therefore, discuss prescribed curricula focusing on isolated skills and phonics instruction. On the other hand, having worked with struggling readers for many years, we are firm in our conviction that most struggling readers will not learn to read (or write) without *frequent, intensive, explicit* instruction designed to meet their needs as readers affectively, cognitively, and linguistically. Children who come to school from homes that do not value particular literacy practices may need to be convinced of their value through school instruction. Students who do not intuitively use effective reading strategies must learn them through school instruction. And children who have not developed the knowledge base required to use graphophonic, syntactic, and semantic cueing systems must learn it from teachers who can both build the knowledge and show them how to orchestrate that knowledge in the process of reading.

In the first chapter of this section, we discuss how teachers can create rich literacy-learning environments in their classrooms through physical, organizational, and interpersonal decisions. The remaining four chapters focus on lessons that can be done before, during, and after the reading of text. Chapter 7, on prereading instruction, focuses on teaching students to choose reading materials, helping them learn to establish purposes for reading, and on activating and increasing students' knowledge so they use it while reading. Two chapters address instructional strategies that can be used as students read text. Chapter 8 addresses strategies that assist students in building fluency as readers and that teach how to make sense of text while reading. Chapter 9 focuses on students' processing of words while reading; it includes lessons that assist students in learning to read words more effectively and lessons that help emergent readers build a knowledge base about the graphophonic cueing system. The final chapter of this section offers recommendations to encourage students to share and extend their comprehension of text after they have read texts or text sets. In addition, attention is given to helping students learn to answer questions and study text more effectively.

6 Environments That Facilitate Reading and Reading Development

In the previous chapter, we argued that teachers who engage students' hearts as readers will help students become successful, especially when the students have little history of success as readers. We begin our discussion of reading instruction with a global view of the environment in which it takes place. We address the type of environment that facilitates reading—an environment that encourages previously unsuccessful readers to believe that they can read, that they want to read more effectively and will put forth effort to do so, and that they will even choose to read, or at a minimum, no longer avoid it. None of these changes will occur overnight, but they will occur over time with close attention to the reading environment (addressed in this chapter) in combination with effective teaching of reading strategies (addressed in the remaining chapters of this section).

In this chapter, we will also attend to a large issue—how regular classroom teachers can meet the needs of struggling readers in their classrooms. Although the chapters that follow provide ideas for specific lessons for such readers, it is necessary to consider the context or the environment within which reading instruction occurs. Many struggling readers have Individual Educational Plans that must be implemented in the regular classroom, and all have instructional needs that are difficult to meet if the environment itself is not conducive to individualization of instruction. Engaging a large group of students in learning at the same time is a complex challenge for any teacher. Creating an environment that supports such efforts is a major and necessary first step.

As we stated in Chapter 3, we believe that students' past and current reading environments ought to be a paramount consideration in reading assessment and instruction. Just as we cannot limit our assessment to what is "in" the student, we cannot limit our attention to teaching reading strategies; this teaching takes place in a context that can either facilitate or negate the instruction. Just as certain home environments are likely to foster literacy development, certain classroom and school environments are much more likely to foster literacy development than others, especially for struggling readers. Literate classroom environments will encourage students to learn *how* to read as well as to *choose* what and how to read. Charlotte Huck states that readers are "children who *can* read, *will* read, and will *want* to read" (1976, p. 590, emphasis added).

What elements make up a reading environment? Certainly, reading materials are an important element, just as the area they are housed in plays an important role. These two things make up the physical environment. The organizational environment consists of the routines teachers use to create opportunities for students to engage with the reading materials. And then there is the interpersonal environment constructed by the people who orchestrate the routines, make the reading materials available, and ensure that the students make the most of both. In this chapter we focus on the physical and organizational environments, waiting for an extended discussion of the interpersonal environment until the final section of this book.

The Physical Environment

In order to convince students of the functionality and importance of literacy, and to ensure that they have reading materials that they *can* read, students need to be surrounded with print that invites them to read and write often, demonstrates that reading and writing are purposeful and worthwhile, and is readable for them. It is best to think about how to immerse students in print throughout a classroom and school, but at the least, a classroom library center should immerse students in print in inviting ways. When classrooms contain good library centers, children more often choose to read, spend a greater amount of time reading, have more positive attitudes toward reading, and exhibit higher levels of reading achievement (Applebee, Langer & Mullis, 1988).

A classroom library center is a comfortable place, set off from the rest of the classroom and stocked with well-displayed and -stored books and other reading materials, where students read (Huck, 1976; Shuman, 1982). Shuman recommends that library centers also include collections of taped stories (purchased or teacher-recorded) and a tape recorder (1982). In this age of computers, a computer that allows students to read books in CD-ROM format could have a place as part of the classroom library. In addition, we think such a center is more inviting if it's homelike. For example, a couch or bean bag chairs and stuffed animals (for younger children) and plants and artwork (for older students) can help to make the area inviting. Smaller special education or Title I classrooms can be conceived and arranged as library centers. According to a study of elementary classroom library centers (Fractor, Woodruff, Martinez, & Teale, 1993), key features of an excellent library center include:

- A stock of approximately eight books per student in the classroom
- An organizational scheme according to book categories
- A name for the area
- A space large enough to comfortably accommodate five students

- A space that offers privacy through partitions
- Front cover display of some of the books

To this list, we would add *books that are both readable and challenging for every student in the classroom*. Too often, we find ourselves in classrooms where the students who struggle the most with reading have few reading materials available to them that they can read or want to read. Without books that are inviting and that they can read, struggling readers will find few reasons or opportunities to read.

There are many other possibilities for displaying print and inviting students to interact with print. Classroom walls can be covered with prominent displays of written work or the written work of others. One teacher we know copied poems onto large sheets, illustrated them, and then displayed the poems in her room, often a half dozen or more poems at any one time. Some readers may be skeptical about the chances of interesting many students in poetry this way, so it's worth noting that the classroom in which this was done is an elementary learning disabilities resource room in the urban core of a large American city. This same classroom also displays posters advertising children's books, a written schedule of the activities for the upcoming month, the daily lunch menu, and a chart listing the poems each child has learned to read independently. A bulletin board features each student's picture and an accompanying autobiography. Written notices to students (from the teacher and other students) frequently appear on the blackboard. The key to this teacher's success in engaging the students in the displayed print is that she continually uses it or calls attention to it. The lunch menu is posted by the door and consulted as the students leave for lunch. The poetry charts are hung after students have learned to read and enjoy them. The print that is displayed is read because it is familiar, often loved, and functional.

As a note, we seldom see secondary classroom environments that immerse students in print. In fact, most are so sterile that it is not possible to determine what is taught there or who the classroom inhabitants are by visiting the classroom when it is empty. We challenge our readers who are secondary teachers to create print-rich environments in their schools, content-area classrooms and resource rooms—environments related to students' studies and activities, that display the products that they create as part of their studies and activities, and that invite the students to read, think, and talk about what is displayed.

The variety, quality, availability, and readability of reading materials plays a major role in whether teachers can engage students' hearts in reading. Variety is necessary to address the wide variety of students' needs, interests, and current reading abilities. Variety also helps students understand the many purposes for reading. High-quality material is important as well as material that is known to be popular with students; you'll need the more popular books to hook them in as you help them learn the value of higher-quality materials. (See Christian-Smith, 1988, for an example of this using teen romance novels.) In addition, the materials must be easily accessible. Reading development is not facilitated by a wide variety of quality materials that students can't easily access and/or check out. (We once visited a special education classroom where all the books were kept in a locked cabinet.)

Finally, students must be able to read the materials that are available if they are to learn to read more effectively; students learn to read by reading, and if few materials are at the level they can read, no progress will be made.

Selecting Reading Material

Teachers who have worked with students with learning disabilities and others who struggle as readers know that locating reading materials is not always easy. Too often, simplistic notions such as readability formulas are used to select books. Below we suggest some questions that can help you make decisions about reading materials for struggling readers (or any student, for that matter). We use the general term "reading materials" to signal that we're not just talking about books but about newspapers, magazines, the lyrics of songs found in compact discs, and so on. In the sections that follow, we will explore specific materials and make recommendations about titles and sources for other titles.

1. Were the materials written for authentic communicative purposes? Were the materials written to communicate a feeling, idea, information, or story, or were they written to teach or reinforce reading skills? Materials written for authentic communicative purposes are far more likely to invite repeated reading and the real construction of meaning.

2. Did the authors use natural language in writing the materials? Reading materials should contain language that is both natural and familiar to students (Gourley, 1984). It is much more difficult for students, especially learning disabled and remedial learners, to construct meaning from texts that use "unnatural" language (e.g., "The fat cat sat on the mat" or "See Spot run. Run, Spot, run"). Texts that use unnatural language make it very difficult for readers to use their knowledge of syntax and semantics while they read (Rhodes, 1979).

3. Are the materials relevant to the background experience of students? Students' experiences are an important factor in the selection of reading materials. If there is a serious mismatch between the information presented in a text and the background knowledge of the reader, it will be very difficult for the reader to construct meaning. A book may be the greatest children's book ever written, but if it doesn't reflect children's experiences, it may not be appropriate for them (Huck, 1976). However, this should not be taken to extremes. Books can also broaden students' backgrounds and beliefs when a teacher develops students' background knowledge and/or helps them understand how their experiences reflect a text.

4. Do the materials invite lengthy engagement in reading? Classroom environments should include some materials that invite lengthy engagement either because the text itself is lengthy or because the students like the text well enough to read it repeatedly. However, this is not an essential characteristic for all reading materials. Some excellent reading materials are naturally brief and may be read only once.

5. Do the materials encourage divergent responses? Reading materials that encourage a wide range of responses provide greater opportunity for students to talk about and extend the meaning that they have constructed from text.

6. What can the student learn about himself and/or the world as a result of reading the materials? It isn't necessary, or even desirable, that all reading material teach some value or provide information. However, much of what students read in school is unrelated to their everyday lives, especially if the student is from a low socioeconomic and/or minority ethnic group. Therefore, students may find little reason to read. Materials that students view as related to themselves and related to the world outside of school are likely to teach them about themselves and their world and thus invite reading. (See Singer, McNeil & Furse, 1984.)

7. Are the materials representative of out-of-school materials? Materials that are found in out-of-school settings often match and catch student interest and demonstrate that reading is meaningful and purposeful. Materials that are not found in out-of-school contexts may encourage the belief that reading is something useful only in the classroom.

8. Are the materials predictable? Reading materials that support the prediction of certain features of text are especially valuable for readers who aren't yet fluent or don't yet use effective reading strategies. (More about this concept will follow.)

9. Will the students learn something about the world from reading the materials? Too often, struggling readers are provided with "high interest, low vocabulary" reading materials that contain little or no content that will add to their knowledge base. The materials are not bad individually, but as a steady diet, they do not help the students learn anything new about the world. Predictable books or even "Easy to read" books that contain content are far better to select for students so that they can learn to read and learn new content simultaneously.

Although you will find the questions useful in selecting books for the classroom or even particular students, it's important that students are allowed to select many of their own reading materials. Even when the selection is not a good one in your eyes, the only way selection is learned is by doing it and reflecting on it. (You can encourage reflection by using some of the questions above to construct lessons that will help students become aware of what features are important to them in selecting books and what other features they might consider.) Although it is important that students spend the majority of their reading time engaged in text that they can read with some ease, students can and do learn from exploring texts that are beyond their reading capability, especially when they are interested in the topic, allowed to talk about what they are exploring, and can get help as they request it (Fielding & Roller, 1992). And, as you'll see later in this chapter, you can read material to students at a greater difficulty level than they themselves can read, and in the process, teach them a great deal about reading.

Trade Books and Paperbacks

Trade books (i.e., library books), including paperbacks, are the core of most reading programs that have a dual goal of teaching students to read and encouraging them to become lifelong readers. Trade books are especially likely to invite students to read because they are usually attractively packaged and written to be read, not to teach reading. Trade books include both picture books and chapter books. Including many titles of both in your classroom, no matter the age of students, allows for an enormous range of reading ability. There are many picture books that are very sophisticated and more suitable for older students than younger ones, even alphabet books (Chaney, 1993). For example, even adults find the picture books such as *Rose Blanche* (Innocenti, 1991) and *The Faithful Elephants* (Tsuchiya, 1988) moving and thought-provoking stories about war, or they find themselves reminiscing as they read *The Relatives Came* (Rylant, 1985). In addition, you can create an environment in which a wide range of picture books are acceptable in classrooms for older students by using some of these suggestions that are adapted from Fielding and Roller (1992):

- Modeling use and enjoyment of picture books. A fifth-grade teacher reads an age-appropriate picture book to her students daily, often as the basis for a writing minilesson. This helps them understand their choices as authors regarding topics, words, organizational features, how pictures and text relate, and so on. In addition, she often chooses books that represent the students' ethnic groups in the classroom because she finds that the illustrations convey as much as the text to the children about each other's backgrounds.

- Altering purposes for reading. An adult-literacy teacher has her students identify someone young in their family that they would like to read to. Once a picture book has been chosen for the child, the adult has a real reason to read and reread the book that is meant for a much younger person until they can take it home and proudly read it to the child. The same situation can be created in cross-age tutoring. Another way to alter purpose for reading picture books is to study the quality and variation of art in picture books (Short, 1993) or to have older students record books on tape for younger students (Robb, 1993).

- Making nonfiction picture books a part of the collection. A high school science teacher uses nonfiction picture books because they often provide a stunning amount of information about science topics and are well-researched. Good nonfiction picture books can be studied for quite some time and are inordinately useful as references for research projects or as models for students' own research writings, especially in science and social studies. Picture books can also be studied for their art; many even directly address the creation of art and being an artist. (See Short, 1993, for a listing.)

Classroom collections of trade books either should be very large or should change regularly. Including multiple copies of the same title allows several students to read the same book at the same time. Paperback book purchases make sizable classroom trade book collections and multiple copies affordable, and some students may actually prefer the paperback editions of books (Huck, 1976). Daniel Fader's "Hooked on Books" program, which depended heavily on paperback books, was successful with extremely reluctant adolescent readers (1976). Nonfiction books also often capture the interest of reluctant readers (Freeman & Person, 1992).

Classroom collections of trade books should include books that represent the lives of students who will read the books. There are many high-quality picture and chapter books now available that represent various ethnic groups and children from other countries. (See, for example, Norton, 1990; Aaron & Hutchison, 1993; the Jan. 1994 issue of *Book Links*.) In addition, consider special characteristics of the students you work with. For example, there are books about children with disabilities (Zvirin, 1994) and children who have had difficulty learning to read or who discover the magic of reading (Short & Pierce, 1993) that may be useful in particular settings. In addition, if your students have a first language other than English, locate good quality literature in their first languages as well. Good children's and adolescents' librarians can provide lists or resources to locate chapter and picture books that represent the variety of backgrounds, experiences, and characteristics students bring with them to school.

For teachers who are unfamiliar with children's literature, there are a number of useful resources available. First of all, many universities offer excellent courses on children's and adolescents' literature, and since special educators' training rarely includes such courses, they may benefit from additional course work in this area. If courses on children's literature are unavailable or inconvenient, school and public librarians are usually familiar with a wide array of children's and adolescents' literature, including nonfiction, and can offer suggestions. There are also a number of books about literature for children and young adults that are excellent resources for selecting and using children's and adolescents' literature (e.g., Cullinan, 1989; Donelson & Nilsen, 1989; Freeman & Person, 1992; Norton, 1991). Journals like *The Reading Teacher*, *Language Arts,* and the *English Journal* regularly feature reviews of children's and adolescents' literature. *The Horn Book* has long devoted its attention to literature reviews; newer on the scene but also excellent are *The New Advocate* and *Book Links*. Recommended books to use in content-area study are often available from professional organizations that support specific content areas. An annotated bibliography entitled *Notable Children's Trade Books in the Field of Social Studies*, for example, is published yearly by the National Council for the Social Studies. A number of books are also now available through publishing companies like Heinemann that list excellent children's literature to support learning in areas such as math and science (e.g., Whitin & Wilde, 1992; Saul & Jagusch, 1991). Parents and students themselves may also recommend titles of books that will likely appeal to the students in special and remedial programs.

Predictable Books

Books are predictable when they enable students to quickly and easily predict what the author is going to say and how the author is going to say it based upon their knowledge of the world. The following text characteristics, adapted from Rhodes (1981) and Atwell (1988), increase the likelihood that readers will be able to take advantage of the different types of knowledge they bring to the reading of a text:

- A good match between text content and reader's life experiences and concepts. Authors like Judy Blume, for example, are so popular because adolescents can easily identify with the characters and events in her books. The good match between the content of the text and students' experiences renders the books highly predictable.

- Rhythmical, repetitive, or cumulative patterns. The author repeats words, phrases, or themes in a pattern that can be discerned after only a few pages (McClure, 1985), or the author uses a pattern of successive addition. Bill Martin's (1970) *Brown Bear, Brown Bear, What Do You See?* is an example of a repetitive pattern: "Brown Bear, brown bear, what do you see? I see a redbird looking at me. Redbird, redbird, what do you see? I see a yellow duck looking at me." The old song *I Know an Old Lady* (who swallowed a fly) is an example of a cumulative pattern (Bonne & Mills, 1961).

- Familiar stories or story lines. Any text that is highly familiar to a student fits this category. Familiarity may arise from hearing or reading the text or a version of it repeatedly, or from experiencing it in other forms, such as an oral story, song, movie, or TV show. Examples include "The Three Little Pigs" and *Star Wars.*

- Familiar sequences. Eric Carle's (1969) *The Very Hungry Caterpillar* combines repetition with two familiar sequences, the days of the week and numbers: "On Monday he ate through one apple. But he was still hungry. On Tuesday he ate through two pears. But he was still hungry."

- Series books. Children and adolescents frequently get hooked on a character or character type and will read every book that features the character (or type). Examples include James Marshall's books featuring the hippopotamus friends, George and Martha, and C. S. Lewis's series, *Chronicles of Narnia.* It also includes the popular *Goosebump* books, *The BabySitters Club* series, and teen romance novels. (Teachers who find some of these series books objectionable might read Christian-Smith, 1988; Mackey, 1990; McGill-Franzen, 1993.)

- A good match between the text and illustrations. Good children's literature frequently contains effective and attractive illustrations. One benefit of these illustrations is that they allow readers to more easily predict meaning. For example, Mercer Mayer's (1975) *Just for You* features attractive illustrations that correspond closely to the text.

- Guessing books. These texts actually invite the reader to make choices, to become actively involved in the stories. *Choose Your Own Adventure* books are written in this manner for both older and younger students. Joke or riddle books and the *Encyclopedia Brown* series also invite this sort of interaction as do the *Ghostwriter* books and easier to read titles such as *Q is for Duck* (Elting & Folsom, 1980).

Highly predictable books, especially those that repeat language patterns, foster reading fluency in students, helping overcome the habit of struggling readers who sound out every word (McClure, 1985) or produce semantically unacceptable miscues. These books encourage students to use their knowledge of the world and of language in responding to text (Rhodes, 1981). In addition, students use the predictable aspects of books to develop word recognition knowledge while they are reading (Bridge, 1979). Predictable books can also be a valuable resource for children learning to write, since children frequently emulate the style, format, and conventions of authors they have read (Harwayne, 1992; Rhodes, 1981). Predictable books may be especially useful for students whose oral language is delayed (Rhodes & Shannon, 1982) and for students using nonstandard dialects (Tompkins & McGee, 1983).

Predictable books are most often trade books and found in libraries. However, many companies that produce books for schools are now republishing predictable books as "big books" (see below) or authoring their own.

"Big Books"

"Big books" are often trade books. The best are well known and highly predictable children's stories, which have been enlarged for the school market. Some are books that have been written specifically for school use. They may be fiction or nonfiction, and most of the nonfiction books contain a great deal of content about the world. These books are ideal for teachers reading to groups of young children since the large text makes it easy for many children to follow along. The novelty of "big books" may also be a special invitation for some children to read. Most publishers market packages that include "big books," a number of conventionally sized copies of the book, and a tape recording of the story. Students can watch the teacher read from the big book and then have the freedom to read their own copies or listen to the tape while reading along in their own books. Publishing companies such as The Wright Group, Rigby, and Scholastic are good places to search for big books and for information about how best to use them.

Song and Wordless Picture Books

Song picture books and wordless picture books are two specific examples of trade books that can be helpful for encouraging reading. Song picture books are particularly useful for some reluctant readers. Lamme presents a nice list of song picture books that includes lullabies, hymns, nursery rhymes, folk songs, and so on, and another more recent list of books with musical themes (Lamme, 1979, 1990). Newsom recommends the use of popular song lyrics and articles about rock singers and musicians to interest unmotivated readers (1979).

Wordless picture books are another vehicle for getting children interested in books. Although wordless picture books are usually associated with younger readers, McGee and Tompkins describe their use with older readers and provide a list of wordless picture books with special appeal for older readers (1983). Wordless picture books can be used to encourage prediction skills and writing fluency in both younger and older readers. They can also be used to generate language experience stories and repeated reading.

Textbooks

School textbooks can be a source of reading material for developing readers if texts, or portions of texts, are selected carefully. However, textbooks are seldom chosen by considering the kinds of complex questions we suggested for selected reading materials. Teachers should be very cautious about readability formulas that consider a restricted range of factors such as word difficulty and sentence length when selecting textbooks. Many texts that use controlled vocabulary and shorter sentences to achieve lower readability levels are choppy, disjointed, and difficult to read—especially some of the "high interest–low vocabulary" books and programmed readers written for the poorest readers (Gourley, 1984; Mason, 1981; Rhodes, 1979). For this reason, the National Council of Teachers of English and the International Reading Association issued a joint statement questioning the use and validity of readability formulas (K. Goodman, 1986).

Basal reading series are still the most commonly used reading textbooks at the elementary level (Goodman et al., 1988). A few basal reading series meet many of the selection criteria we outlined earlier and may be worth using as *one* source of reading material. (See Goodman et al., 1988, and Shannon & Goodman, 1994, for a critique of basal readers.) Teachers who don't feel confident about judging which basals might be worthwhile can consider our criteria along with criteria from sources such as university classes and the advice of librarians and colleagues. In general, teachers should avoid "Dick and Jane" type readers that employ unnatural language and are not predictable (Gourley, 1984; Rhodes, 1979). Also keep in mind that students will not learn to select good literature to read and may not even know it exists if basals are their major source of reading material.

One way to adapt textbooks (both basals and content-area texts) is to create "skinny books" (Watson, 1987). Teachers can cut out good and useful portions of old textbooks on particular topics or on themes being studied and bind them individually into "skinny books." For example, if some students are interested in reading about space, teachers might draw on a variety of sources including old magazines and textbooks containing articles, sections, or chapters on space, cut them out, and bind them using colored construction paper into small books with titles, authors, and so on. Because "skinny books" are short they have the advantage of being less intimidating to many students, especially readers who may lack confidence in their reading ability.

Student-Published Books and Nonbook Materials

A literate environment need not depend solely on commercially produced books. Student-produced books and a wide variety of nonbook materials also support students' literacy development. Students' own compositions, including dictated language experience stories, are one of the most useful sources of reading material. Compositions dictated or written by students are predictable because they are based on students' own experiences and language structures. Encouraging children to read their own compositions can result in better comprehension of materials written by others (Maya, 1979).

The audience for children's compositions is not, of course, limited to the children who authored them. It is increasingly popular for children to write and bind their own books, which can be placed in the classroom or school libraries where other students can check them out. From the standpoint of reading, this provides students with a rich source of interesting reading material. From the standpoint of writing, it provides students with audience response on the effectiveness and value of their own writing.

Classrooms can include a wide variety of nonbook materials to invite reading. Nonbook materials may be especially attractive to many students, and these materials are usually inexpensive and sometimes free (Shuman, 1982; Tolar, 1991). One very successful teacher we know devotes one day a week during her reading period to reading newspapers. The children sit in comfortable spots all over the classroom with hot chocolate or apple cider and day-old donut holes, looking every bit like a family settled down with the paper on a Sunday morning. This is an experience these students look forward to.

In addition to newspapers, think about using bus, air, and rail schedules; store catalogues; telephone directories; driver's license manuals; cookbooks; real estate catalogues; and labels from cans and empty food containers (Shuman, 1982). Everyday materials such as signs, advertisements, directions, recipes, posters, letters, magazines, and comics (Schoof, 1978) are also useful additions to reading centers. Publications such as the *National Enquirer* and *Sports Illustrated for Children*, because they are eye-catching and likely to appeal to the interests of teenagers, have been used successfully with unmotivated readers (LaSasso, 1983).

Many reluctant readers may also be attracted to shorter, less formidable reading materials such as jokes and jingles. Moe and Hopkins present a list of 150 short items including jokes, jingles, limericks, poems, proverbs, puns, puzzles, and riddles, which can be read quickly (1978). Poetry contained in books can be recopied on large charts or on single sheets of paper—presentations that are sometimes less forbidding to reluctant readers.

A literate classroom environment can include anything that children and adolescents are likely to read. The key is whether the materials are likely to interest students, not whether they interest teachers or parents or are judged by adults to be "fine literature." A case certainly can be made for not including materials that feature gratuitous sex or violence, but adults should generally let students' interests be their guide when they select reading materials, especially while students can still be characterized as reluctant readers. As students get hooked on reading, their interests in other reading material can be broadened through teacher read-alouds, book talks, and the like.

The Organizational Environment

Plentiful materials that students can read and that are available in a well-stocked classroom library center are a necessary element of a good reading environment. However, we need to also consider how to organize the available instructional time in such a way that students engage with the books and other reading materials and learn to read them more effectively. There are four basic elements in students' reading instruction. These elements constitute the foundation for the organizational environment that teachers create to assist readers, including readers who struggle.

Element 1: The teacher reads to the students as a reader (and as a writer).

Element 2: The teacher and the students share reading (and writing).

Element 3: Each student reads (and writes) independently.

Element 4: The teacher teaches students to read (and write) more effectively.

Below we discuss each of these elements, making reference to how these principles apply to writing as well as reading.

THE TEACHER READS TO THE STUDENTS AS A READER (AND AS A WRITER)

The less effective the readers, the more important it is for them to observe demonstrations (F. Smith, 1981) of others' reading and responding to reading, including their teachers. Like early readers whose parents or siblings read to them often, school-age students of any age also benefit from being read to frequently (Forester, 1977; Teale, 1978). Teachers who read to students help them understand the nature and purposes of reading and familiarize them with the patterns of written language which are often more complex than oral conversational language (Bass, Jurenka & Zirzow, 1981). In the process, teachers can also interest students in different types of literature and authors, encouraging them to discover the joys of reading good literature. Students' reading vocabularies, their reading comprehension, their reading interests, and the quality of their oral language have been shown to be positively affected when someone regularly reads to them (Huck, 1979; McCormick, 1977). Even secondary-level students enjoy and benefit from being read to. (See Evans, 1992, and Robb, 1993, for yearlong accounts of reading to seventh- and eighth-grade reluctant readers and Hennings, 1992, for an example of poetry reading.) Students from the lower ranges of reading achievement may benefit the most from being read to (McCormick, 1977). Reading to students is also an excellent vehicle for broadening students' experiences and may be an especially effective way to assist students who may not have had background experiences teachers feel are important. In addition, students can learn to reflect on literature in the context of listening to a teacher read (Hennings, 1992).

In a recent research study one of us conducted, we observed a fourth- and fifth-grade teacher whose read-aloud time was the centerpiece of her reading instruction (Clarke, Davis, Rhodes, & Baker, 1995). She gathered the students around her rocking chair twice a day. During one read-aloud each day, the students listened to literature (usually chapter books) and authors that the teacher wanted to introduce to them. On the basis of what they learned during this time, the students began to broaden their own reading choices. Once the teacher began to read or finished reading a book, it became a book that some students chose to reread on their own. The focus of the second read-aloud was to explore a writing technique used well by an author. The teacher typically utilized high-quality picture books, often by authors who represented the students' ethnic groups. The length of the books was more like the length of pieces her own students were writing. This read-aloud was followed by Writing Workshop in which students worked on their own pieces and could incorporate the literary techniques that were explored in the read-aloud sessions. These books were also often chosen by students for their own reading pleasure.

Hoffman, Roser and Battle offer a model of exemplary read-aloud time in a classroom (1993). The key factors of their model are outlined below and are similar to the practices of the teacher described above.

- Designate a legitimate time and place for daily read-aloud. The fourth- and fifth-grade teacher used her rocking chair as the gathering place—this signaled to students what was to happen and how they were expected to behave. She scheduled one session in the morning just before Writing Workshop and another after lunch so that students came to expect it daily. Almost nothing was allowed to interfere with these scheduled times and children complained if something did interfere.

- Select quality literature. The teacher always read quality literature, often talking to students about book awards, about what made books quality pieces of literature, about how she wanted to read books to them that they didn't yet choose for themselves so that they could discover the wonderful stories available to them, and so on. This allowed her to begin to shape students' choices and to worry less about the choices they sometimes made for themselves (like only the Goosebumps series). It is a good idea to include nonfiction as well as fiction in your choices of quality literature, especially when you are working with boys who are reluctant readers (Doiron, 1994).

- Choose literature related to other literature. The teacher frequently encouraged students to make connections across books she had read to them—connections by genre, theme, topic, literary technique, author, style, and so on. She encouraged connections to children's own writing as well as to published authors they had read together.

- Discuss literature in lively, invitational, thought-provoking ways. The teacher did this in a number of ways. She often approached the rocking chair with the book held close to her heart or hidden in some way, inviting immediate interest. She shared her own reactions to the author's content and technique; then she invited students to do the same, even in the midst of reading when it was appropriate to do so. Sometimes she would invite prereading discussion; for example, she asked the children to guess what they might find in a new book on the basis of what they discovered about the author in the last book they had read.

- Group students to maximize opportunities to respond. Hoffman, Roser and Battle recommend that teachers use smaller groups to facilitate more discussion of read-aloud time (1993). However, the teacher kept her class whole for discussions following the reading because she didn't want to miss the students' responses and the opportunity to push their thinking further.

- Offer a variety of response and extension opportunities. In the fourth- and fifth-grade classroom, extensions and responses most often occurred naturally in other parts of the day rather than as something specifically scheduled along with the read-aloud. Students often tried out literary techniques in Writing Workshop that they explored in read-aloud time, or they called the teacher's attention to the way another author they were reading used the same technique. Hennings offers many suggestions for this in K–9 classrooms (1992).

- Reread selected pieces. In the fourth- and fifth-grade classroom, students frequently choose to do this on their own, rereading a picture or chapter book the teacher had read to them. However, the teacher occasionally read the same picture book again or a portion of a chapter book for a different purpose, such as calling attention to a different feature of the book that related to something currently under study.

THE TEACHER AND THE STUDENTS SHARE READING (AND WRITING)   One way to share reading is during read-aloud times. However, there are many other ways for students (and teachers) to formally and informally share reading. Within each of these settings, teachers can provide for the individual needs of struggling readers through grouping that supports such readers or through individual or small group attention.

- Groups of students can read and discuss a single piece of literature, having "grand conversations" (Peterson & Eeds, 1990) about the book after or while it is read.

- Teachers and/or students can give book talks about books that they recommend for others to read, similar perhaps, to the format of the TV program *Reading Rainbow* on PBS.

- Teachers and students can keep reading logs about what they are reading. These writings may be used to enhance discussions of books. Or they might be exchanged for comment and questioning among readers.

- Students can engage in various presentations of books via drama, art, or music. Especially when the books are prominent in the presentation, this often encourages others to read the book.

- The teacher can conference as a fellow reader with students about books they are reading.

In addition, we have observed teachers having informal conversations with students that involve sharing the reading that they are doing. We frequently observed the teacher we previously described conversing with students about books during transitional times in the classroom, especially during bathroom breaks and on the way to lunch. We have also observed remedial and special education teachers having these informal conversations between students' classrooms and resource rooms. Informal conversations about reading are often instigated by students and most often occur in classrooms where books are very important and highly valued elements in the environment.

EACH STUDENT READS (AND WRITES) INDEPENDENTLY   In order to learn to do something well, we must have plentiful time to do what it is that needs to be learned. We cannot learn to sew clothes, build furniture, or conduct scientific investigations well by doing these things once a month or even a few minutes each day. We need frequent and sustained periods of time to figure out what to do and to stretch our capabilities. Likewise, students must have plentiful time to read independently if we expect them to become good readers. This is not a small point; Allington discovered that it is not unusual for poor readers to read text only six to seven minutes a day, alone or with others (1980). We cannot expect anyone to learn to read independently unless significantly more time than this is allocated to the reading of texts.

Independent reading can be scheduled by the teacher or chosen by the student during free time. Since few struggling readers choose to read (at least initially), it is very important that the teacher *schedule* time for independent reading. Independent reading does not necessarily require being alone to do the reading, but it must involve each student in independently processing and understanding text. Of course, if you can convince students of the worth of reading and they choose to engage in it on their own, the amount of independent reading they will do both in and out of school will increase significantly. The amount of reading that good readers choose to engage in is a significant factor in why they are as good as they are as readers.

Be sure to examine classroom management policies with regard to this element of reading instruction. For example, one of the authors' children who developed slowly as a reader kept telling his parents that he didn't get to read at school although the teacher had a clearly specified independent reading time on her daily schedule. When the situation was explored further, Lynn Rhodes and her husband discovered that the teacher's policy was that children who hadn't finished their seat work finished it during reading time. Since their son wasn't completing his seat work in the allotted time, he had very little actual opportunity to read. The practice of reading as a reward for finishing other work will always work to the disadvantage of struggling readers since these are the students most likely to need extra time to finish their work.

Independent reading typically occurs in one of two settings in classrooms. Whether it is labeled DEAR (Drop Everything and Read), SSR (Sustained Silent Reading) or by some other name, it is a block of time when everyone in the classroom or school (including adults) reads books. Once they have read their own books for a bit, this is an ideal time for teachers to listen to and assist struggling readers. Sometimes independent reading occurs as part of Reading Workshop, a routine that will be discussed in the next few pages.

THE TEACHER TEACHES STUDENTS TO READ (AND WRITE) MORE EFFECTIVELY

As we've said before, struggling readers will need frequent, intensive, and explicit instruction designed to meet their individual needs. Lessons that teach students to read more effectively should grow out of careful assessment of what students need to know in order to achieve goals or outcomes teachers and students have set. Lessons can be lengthy or they can be minilessons but whatever their length, they are designed to facilitate reading development by meeting the individual needs of students. The rest of the chapters in this section are devoted largely to lessons designed to assist students in becoming more effective readers.

Routines That Facilitate Reading Instruction

Predictable routines are helpful to both teachers and students, especially struggling students. Students are better supported when they know how the instructional time will be spent, what they can expect for assistance, and how they are expected to be-have as readers. Here we discuss two sample schedules or routines—one for emer-gent readers and one for readers who are able to process text independently. As we explore the two, we will particularly consider how struggling readers might partici-pate in the routines, how teachers can individualize instruction for students within these routines, and how the routines might be adapted for resource room situations.

EMERGENT READERS   The schedule that follows is recommended for use by K–1 teachers. The order of the activities is not important and, in fact, this particular schedule is dictated to some degree by the fact that the students arrive at school in the morning over a 15-minute period (due to bus schedules). Other teachers have similar constraints that indicate variations in the schedule. In addition, you will note that reading and writing are treated as relatively seamless processes. As we present each activity, we relate it to one or more of the four elements we listed earlier (p. 112) that support reading development:

Element 1: The teacher reads to the students as a reader (and as a writer).

Element 2: The teacher and the students share reading (and writing).

Element 3: Each student reads (and writes) independently.

Element 4: The teacher teaches students to read (and write) more effectively.

We'll also note how the teacher might utilize each portion of the routine to attend to the individual needs of students. The focus in this section is on the schedule it-self. In chapters that follow, more information will be provided regarding the con-tent of specific lessons such as attending to print lessons.

Independent Reading/Writing   As the children arrive at school individually or in groups, they put away their belongings and settle into reading books and/or writ-ing and drawing. The teacher confers with groups and individuals, recording as-sessment data via checklists and/or anecdotal records. During this time, the teacher focuses her attention on readers who struggle most, often following up on previously presented lessons. (Elements 1 and 4)

Tuning In   Once all the children have arrived and have had sufficient time to engage in independent reading and writing, the teacher calls them together. In addition to other opening routines (lunch count, and so on), the children engage in quick-paced choral readings of poetry, songs, finger plays, or chants, all of which are written on chart paper. Most often, this involves rereading text. Students who need greater support to attend to the print on the charts are often called on to point to the words with a pointer stick for the others. (Element 2)

New Story   The teacher reads a new piece of fiction or nonfiction to the children from a trade book or "big book." If the story is highly predictable, the children read along as they can. Students who have the hardest time attending during story reading are invited to sit next to the teacher or in a place where they have the best view of the book and the teacher. (Element 1; element 2 if the text is discussed)

Old Favorite   The teacher rereads a familiar text, perhaps calling attention to some aspect of the text that students have not previously noticed. If a "big book" is used, children who need the practice are asked to use a stick pointer as sections of the book are read in unison by the other students. Choosing the old favorite is a job in this classroom, one that rotates weekly. (Element 1; element 2 if text is discussed)

Attending to Print   The teacher conducts a lesson in which attention is paid to particular print features in text written by others (especially old favorites), text written by the teacher (News of the Day), and/or text written by children (children's writings). The intent of the lesson is to build children's knowledge about how print works for readers (and writers). Students who struggle most with learning to read sometimes have these lessons in groups that address assessed needs. When struggling readers participate with the whole class in attending to print lessons, the teacher asks them questions that are at their level of understanding. (Element 4)

Text Extensions   Children participate in writing, drama, art, movement, building, music, related reading, and other extensions related to literature or thematic units. If individuals or small groups are at work, the teacher confers with and/or participates with children, recording assessment information about what he learns. Again, this is an opportunity for the teacher to attend to individual needs in conferences or to group children so that struggling readers receive peer support. (Element 2; elements 3 and 4 depending on circumstances)

Sharing Time   Children share finished as well as in-process work and receive feedback on it from fellow students and the teacher. If possible, the teacher records assessment information that helps her plan new lessons. (Elements 2 and 4)

Students who are struggling can be accommodated in this schedule quite nicely. Whole-class efforts support individual efforts. For example, children can contribute as they are able during the whole-class reading of a poetry chart during tuning in. In small-group efforts such as text extensions and sharing time (when it is sharing of group-produced text extensions), they can be assisted by other students as they contribute to group projects and presentations. Independent work time, such as independent reading and writing, is flexible enough to accommodate a wide variety of abilities. During attending to print lessons, particular questions can be directed to students on the basis of assessed needs and attending to print lessons designed specifically to address selected students' needs can occur during independent reading time or text extensions time.

Special education and remedial reading teachers who work in resource rooms can utilize this schedule as the basis for all their instruction with students (see Zucker, 1993, as an example) or, if they have a short time period, they might consider engaging in similar sets of activities over a period of several days. In order to ensure that students who struggle are engaging in these activities, it also makes sense to explore with each classroom teacher which of these activities are featured and not featured in the regular classroom and to highlight those that are not in the resource room schedule. For example, it may not be as helpful to schedule a new story with students if they are getting at least one read-aloud session in their classroom each day. On the other hand, it may be helpful to know which books in the classroom are old favorites, so that you can utilize them for attending to print lessons when it is clear that is the kind of support the students need and are not getting enough of in their classroom. In other words, think about this schedule as one that you and the classroom teacher share. Together, you can plan how to provide more of what the struggling readers need.

INDEPENDENT READERS Probably the most commonly used whole language routine for older students who can independently read text is Reading Workshop. Reading Workshop is based on what readers do in the world outside of school: They "select their own reading material, read at their own pace, and talk to others about what they've read. (They) learn about reading by spending time reading, listening to others, and talking with others" (Hagerty, 1992). Reading Workshop is analogous to Writing Workshop in many ways. Again, the order of the activities is not important. Some teachers we know attempt to integrate reading and writing workshop while others keep them separate to assure themselves that students are spending sufficient time on both reading and writing. Again, as we present each activity, we will relate it to the four elements that support reading development (see p. 116), and we will highlight how teachers might attend to individual needs of students who struggle most as readers. More detailed information on the content of minilessons will be provided in subsequent chapters.

Teacher Read-Aloud The teacher reads the whole class a picture book or chapters from a chapter book, either fiction or nonfiction. Sometimes the teacher rereads text during this time. As the teacher asks questions, he does so on the basis of his understanding of individual student needs. For example, a student who needs to learn to summarize chapters may receive teacher support in summing up the previous day's chapter before the teacher begins reading. (Element 1)

Minilesson   The teacher presents a brief lesson, usually to the whole class. The lesson may be procedural (how to select "just right" books), literary (authors' leads), or it may address a reading strategy (how to figure out the meaning of difficult words in nonfiction text). The minilesson may be directly related to the teacher read-aloud for the day. Minilessons grow out of the teacher's daily assessment of students' needs; these lessons may be designed for the whole class, or for small groups of students who have similar needs. (Element 4)

Reading Time   Students read their books or other materials (e.g., newspapers). The books may be self-selected or small groups may be reading books the group or the teacher selected. The teacher reads for a short time and then confers with individuals or small groups, taking assessment information as she conducts conferences. This, of course, is an ideal time to work with students on individual needs they have as readers. (Element 3; elements 2 and/or 4 depending on teacher focus in conferences.)

Sharing/Response Time   The students think about, talk about, write about, and/or present the books they are reading or have read. Vehicles may include literature logs, literature discussions, book talks, written conversations, dramatization, and so on. The teacher records assessment information if possible. (Element 2)

Sometimes teachers refer to their reading time as Literature Circles, Literature Discussion Groups or Literature Groups (see Short & Pierce, 1990 and/or Peterson & Eeds, 1990) or Book Clubs (Raphael & McMahon, 1994), especially when students read common texts and spend a large portion of instructional time discussing them. Then the organizational label comes from the focus of instruction—talking about books.

When students self-select books for reading time and a wide range of books (picture books and chapter books) are acceptable reading in the classroom, struggling readers can be easily accommodated in this schedule. When students read group-selected books, struggling readers can be accommodated well if careful thought is given to the books they are to read and how supports might be created for their reading. If students are reading books that are thematically related (e.g., all historical fiction about the Revolutionary War), the struggling readers can read a somewhat easier, thematically related book and still contribute a great deal to the discussions. Remember, too, that struggling readers will put forth more effort if they are interested in reading something that is difficult. The key is to make sure that students actually read (as opposed to having someone read for them), especially if reading time is the only time you can address element 3, "Each student reads independently."

Just as is the case with the emergent reader schedule, special education and remedial reading teachers who work in resource rooms and have a shorter time period daily can engage students in the above set of activities over a couple of days. Again, it makes sense to explore with each classroom teacher which of these activities are featured and not featured in the regular classroom and to highlight those that are not in the instruction provided. Classroom teachers who use this type of schedule also find it easy to include resource teachers in an "in classroom" model during reading time and sharing/response time. In fact, it is even possible for selected students to have a different minilesson with the resource teacher if the one planned for the day does not suit all the students. At a minimum, resource teachers can read and confer with their students during reading time, working with the regular classroom teacher to design a supportive sharing/response time for the students with whom they work.

As a closing note, we want to mention special events as organizing features that can facilitate reading. For example, one of us has a son who talked about reading this year as he had never done before, all because of the build-up his teacher gave the upcoming "Reading Marathon," a schoolwide all-day reading event to which the children carted blankets, stuffed animals, snacks, and anything else that would make them comfortable with their books for the day. For several weeks, he created and re-created a stack of books for the day, convinced by the conversation at school that he would read more than one chapter book in a single day for the first time in his life. (And he did!) Children love novelties during the year, especially during the long months when there are no breaks from school—it's great when the novelty they look forward to means reading all day long! Reading novelties can also have themes such as the "Pig Out Week" where first graders read nothing all week but books that feature pigs as characters (Allen & Eisele, 1990).

Reading Across the Curriculum

We have treated reading thus far as a separate instructional entity. Of course, it can be, especially when teachers want to give plentiful attention to fiction, particular fictional genres and/or authors. However, reading is also a tool that is used—and learned—across the curriculum. That is, reading is used to learn in and about science, social studies, health, music, and other areas. Some teachers prefer to feature reading more as a tool for learning; when they do, they often organize their instruction through units that are referred to as "thematic" or "interdisciplinary" or by some other name. Some teachers do both—conduct reading instruction using one of the previously outlined routines or a variant while the rest of the curriculum is organized via a unit in which reading and writing play major roles in students' learning about a topic. Whether you organize your reading instruction one way or the other or both is dependent on your own preference and your instructional goals but also should take account of students' needs as readers.

Opportunities for reading can be provided any time during the day and in any academic area. Saul and Jagusch (1991), for example, provide a list of children's books that can be used to learn science concepts, Whitin and Wilde (1992) do the same for mathematics, and Tchudi (1993) edits a book in which K–college teachers tell their stories of how they integrate science/math and humanities through language. An excellent new resource for teachers, *Book Links*, provides an annotated bibliography of literature for a number of topics in each issue. (For example, the July 1994 issue included bibliographies of books in Spanish, on topics such as architecture, families and homes, drama and art, optics, puffins, related readings for an adolescent novel, information and books by two children's poets, and magazines for children.) Journals frequently contain sample units based on books such as a unit on the American Revolution (Johnson & Ebert, 1992). Nonacademic subjects also provide opportunities for reading and writing. Art teachers, for example, could encourage students to write text to accompany their projects, or they might read children's biographies of artists and craftspeople to their students. Physical education teachers might encourage students to read paperback books on sports and sports figures.

Although most resource teachers won't be directly responsible for teaching content-area subjects, art, music, or physical education, they may be able to influence other teachers to increase student involvement in reading. They can help teachers understand that students need to read frequently with support and to see reading as functional in their lives in order to become better readers. Teachers can use the Individual Education Plan, or its equivalent, to encourage more and wider reading throughout the school day. They can also let other teachers know how increased and supported opportunities to engage in reading can benefit their other students, including above-average readers. In addition they can show principals how promoting reading across the curriculum can reduce the reading problems in their school without detracting from learning in the content areas.

Some readers may feel that increasing the amount of reading in content-area classes increases the chances of failure for struggling readers. Until recently, most of us concerned with the education of learning disabled and Title I students, for example, have argued that teachers should adapt the curriculum in content-area classes so that less information was presented through text. Increasing students' background knowledge prior to the reading of a text through a variety of alternative modes of presentation will make reading much easier, as will alternative presentations such as films, field trips, film strips, class discussion, guest speakers, experiments, observations, simulations, trade books, and so on. Then textbooks can profitably be used as summaries of instruction instead of the only source of information (Stansell & DeFord, 1981). Allowing students to choose from alternative reading assignments is also helpful. Students may find historical novels, for example, an easier guide or a more engaging introduction to history than the content of history textbooks.

Although content-area teachers are in a particularly favorable position to demonstrate the value of reading as a tool for learning, some may be reluctant to make adaptations to accommodate the individual needs of students. These teachers may be much more flexible, however, if resource teachers express a willingness to work closely with them to help them modify their teaching practices, select a wider variety of materials, and more directly support students' learning in the content classroom. History teachers may suggest historical fiction for the resource room that will provide students with an alternative or supplementary view of material presented in history class. Or resource teachers may be able to locate some excellent picture books on the science or math concepts being introduced in content-area classrooms. In addition, volunteers can produce taped versions of content-area reading assignments for students to read along with in the resource room or at home.

INTEGRATED AND INTERDISCIPLINARY CURRICULUM   Integrated curricula integrate or merge two or more curricular areas but also retain the differences in the curricular areas. Teachers who are most vested in literacy tend to think of integrated curriculum as integrating reading, writing, and oral language with areas such as math, science, and/or social studies in order to provide real purposes and audiences for thinking and language use. Teachers using such units relate instruction across a variety of academic areas to a theme, an area of interest, or a topic (Hittleman, 1983).

Interdisciplinary curriculum is based on the notion that nature and our lives are whole, that "There are rocks and animals and stars, but it is human beings who decided to study those in separate fields called geology, biology, and astronomy" (Tchudi, 1991, p. 13). Thus, a classroom can operate with a vision of the universe as a whole and take advantage of the fact that "Little children so experience life in an integrated way that it will take more than a few weeks in school benches to knock this good stuff out of them. If we look at the learning of little children to discover what learning is really like, we discover that learning is *seeing connections*" (Peetoom, 1993). It is in this sense that interdisciplinary curriculum is different from integrated curriculum; integrated curriculum retains the disciplines as the organizing feature of a unit of study while interdisciplinary curriculum requires learners to explore issues, problems, and topics from different perspectives, including but not limited to the disciplinary perspectives that we adults like to take as geologists, astronomers, economists, lawyers, and so on.

Integrated or interdisciplinary units can be facilitated in students' regular elementary or secondary classrooms, within a special education classroom, in a Title I classroom, or across these classroom boundaries, providing resource room students more opportunity to learn more about the topic under study. Unit study has the potential to bring more continuity to resource room programs provided for remedial students and students with learning disabilities. Once a topic has been established, students understand the continuing nature of its study and begin to look forward to and plan for the day's activities. (This happens naturally because students help to shape their investigations and are in greater control of where they go next.) If the topic is well selected and the unit well implemented, students often become excited about learning more about the topic and take control of the direction of the unit and their own learning. They find themselves reading and writing for real reasons and come to revalue reading and writing as ways of exploring topics of interest to themselves. In addition, the broader curricular focus of integrated curriculum positively influences reading and writing development and academic achievement (Grant, Guthrie, Bennett, Rice & McGough, 1994; Singer, McNeil & Furse, 1984).

A teacher's development of integrated or interdisciplinary curriculum begins, of course, with the selection of a theme or topic. The theme or topic can be selected because it is a required curriculum topic, because the teacher knows that it will inspire students' interests and meet some of their needs, or because the students themselves have suggested the topic or revealed a great interest in it during another instructional experience. Some teachers prefer to develop thematic units around broad issues affecting the world (e.g., change, economic inequality, endangered species), while others prefer narrower topics (e.g., the Holocaust, weather, soil erosion). A broader issue frequently has the advantage of permitting more flexibility and creativity, as well as greater student ownership of the unit.

The concepts to be studied in an interdisciplinary unit are developed with the students' interests and needs in mind. Basically, the content the students will be exploring and learning must be identified. *Webbing* is a useful device for involving students in planning what they will study and learn about within a larger topic. The teacher may begin by leading a brainstorming discussion of subtopics and then represent them through the use of a web, showing the subtopics and their relationships to each other. Through webbing, the teacher and students can identify concepts for the unit. For a unit on endangered species, for example, related concepts might include "humans vs. animals" and "pollution." Webbing can also be used to encourage students to consider what they know and what they want to know. The subtopics or concepts may serve as the basis for dividing into small groups for special interest group study.

Organizing thematic units by concepts (e.g., pollution, things that live in water, ecology, and so on), instead of the common practice of organizing by curricular areas like science, math, social studies, serves to retain the integrity of the topic or theme. Organizing by curricular areas often forces connections to the theme that would not occur otherwise. If you are concerned about whether you have covered particular curricular areas sufficiently in your planning, you might review the concepts you have planned and categorize each to see if all the curricular areas you are concerned about are sufficiently covered, and if not, how you can teach other unrelated concepts outside the unit. (See Pappas, Kiefer & Levstik, 1990, pp. 54–57 as an example.) Or consider Tchudi's question: "It's very important to recall that in the field of education, 'coverage' has never worked all that well in the first place. We cover, but do they learn?" (1991, p. 49) Tchudi recommends planning with an interdisciplinary perspective by identifying issues or topics that encompass goals and objectives that are required in the curriculum or that teachers believe to be important. In these days when content standards are proliferating, interdisciplinary planning may begin where Tchudi suggests that it should—with a focus on what students are expected to learn.

In addition to identifying the concepts students will explore and learn, teachers must also identify what reading and writing instructional goals should—or could—be addressed within the unit. Certainly, plentiful opportunities for reading and writing can be included in the unit as well as lessons in which students extend their comprehension and composition abilities. Teachers' educational objectives for their students should be considered; it is often relatively simple to meet their reading and writing needs within the topic selected for study. Again, when it is not possible to naturally meet students' reading and writing needs within the unit, plan to teach students other aspects they need outside of the unit, rather than forcing the unit to carry everything that needs to be done.

Although teachers may need to assume the major responsibility for locating resources for studying the selected topic, students can also be involved in this aspect of the unit. Resources available for studying themes or topics are limited only by the imaginations of students and teachers. Information can be obtained from newspapers, magazines, trade books, encyclopedias, people in the community, government agencies, businesses, family members, guest lecturers, textbooks, films, tapes, museums, computers, and so on. Annotated bibliographies on selected themes or topics are available in many school and public libraries. Librarians can also help locate information on various topics, and computer searches of commercial databases (such as those available through CompuServe, Prodigy, The Source, or America Online) may be helpful. A number of book publishers have market databases on selected topics for the school market and magazines like *Book Links*, mentioned earlier, can also be useful.

Difficulty is the key issue a teacher needs to confront in gathering reading materials to support integrated curriculum. Although students will often deal with more difficult material than we might expect when they are interested in a topic, it's important that the majority of the materials gathered are easy enough for students to read if the unit is also designed to meet students' instructional needs in reading. If students are interested in a number of topics, keep this issue in mind in choosing which one they will study. If accessible reading material can be found for one unit but not another, choose the unit for which usable reading materials are readily available if reading development is a major goal.

As students study a topic, encourage them to assemble the materials they find on the topic in an organized way, not only for their own continued use but also for the use of other students in the future. Crocker recommends that students gather information on topics by building vertical files (1985). Here vast amounts of information on particular topics are brought together, classified, and filed alphabetically in cartons that can then be stored in the classroom or library. Electronic databases can be constructed in a similar manner. These are worthwhile projects by themselves since they require extensive reading, writing, organizing and, initially, a wide exploration of the topic. Of course, constructing lessons and activities to support students' learning of concepts and use of reading and writing is a major step in the development of a unit. If a unit is designed to examine economic inequality, for example, the teacher may decide to have students read several newspaper articles on the homeless and then generate questions to ask a representative from a local shelter for the homeless.

Planned lessons and activities should be considered as points of departure. Short & Burke suggest that units be "metaphorically written in pencil" (1991, p. 33). As the teacher and students live with and explore the ideas, lessons, and materials, they will generate new ideas and lessons, find some not worth pursuing, and adapt many others.

Teachers and students may base the unit around one or more shared experiences and/or culminate their study with some sort of project (Pigdon & Woolley, 1993). Again, there is no limit to the number of possibilities here. Shared experiences involve the use of a resource that is rich in information and plunge the students into new and deeper explorations. The resource may be a place (a homeless shelter), a guest speaker (a volunteer who works in the homeless shelter), a videotape or film (*The Grapes of Wrath* for a historical view of one kind of homelessness), observing a set of pictures, events, or beings, reading a powerful book like one of Joan Lowery Nixon's Orphan Train books, and so forth. Culminating projects could include making a movie, role playing, writing a TV script, creative dramatics, developing a newsletter, or some formal presentation (Norton, 1977). Burns and Swan describe a unit on food that included asking students to invent a new cereal and then develop an advertising campaign (1979). This campaign included writing slogans, designing billboards, designing and labeling the box, and so on. In another example, a unit on the study and exploration of classical and modern fairy tales by a class of fourth graders culminated in having students write their own fairy tales (Moss, 1982).

Thus far, we have presented the notion of integrated or interdisciplinary curriculum as if it were something a teacher must develop from scratch. In fact, teachers will find that many school districts have spent considerable time developing such units (though they will have various names) that contain much of what we have already talked about—lists of concepts students are to learn, resources, lessons, and so on. The missing element in the majority of these units is the infusion of reading and writing as tools for learning about the topic. In these cases, teachers need to think about the reading and writing goals they want to meet as part of the unit study and incorporate reading and writing opportunities and lessons into the unit in order to accomplish their literacy goals.

There are other places to look for prepared units. Mini-thematic units can often be found in well-written science or social studies textbooks and the bare bones of units are often suggested in topical bibliographies of children's literature. (As an example, see Pierce and Short, 1994, for a listing of books and a web of concepts for "environmental issues and actions.") Moss presents a number of thematic units that are based on the study of literature (1984). Even basal readers that group stories by theme contain the kernel of a unit that can be expanded. Finally it should be remembered that these and other integrated units are the *paper* curriculum, not the *enacted* curriculum that students actually experience. In using the paper curricula that are available, teachers will adapt them to their own needs and styles while considering the particular students with whom they are working (Lewis, 1982). In other words, the themes, activities, products, and goals of units change and come alive based on the needs and interests of particular students and cannot be implemented without considering them. Even if teachers develop a unit from scratch, they'll find that it changes when it is used with a different group of students.

INQUIRY CURRICULUM   Inquiry curricula derive from current views of learning, especially learning as a social process and learning as the construction of meaning. Teachers view their role in the inquiry curriculum as supporting learning or the students' constructions of meaning in a social context—the classroom, the school, and the world beyond. Harste compares integrated curriculum and inquiry curriculum:

In an integrated curriculum, teachers pick a topic and web what they might do in math, science, art, etc., depending on the objectives they see for the unit. In an inquiry, curriculum questions come from living. The disciplines are used to gain a perspective on these questions. Children see the disciplines as tools to be used in learning, not as subjects adults think they need to learn. As opposed to objectives, possibilities organize an inquiry curriculum. An inquiry curriculum assumes that kids are researchers, that they should be allowed to inquire, and they should be encouraged to go off in directions that may not be predetermined. Real inquiry has to have an openness about it so that people can go in directions and reach conclusions that are unforeseen. (Monson & Monson, 1994, p. 519)

Inquiry curricula are based on a student-centered view of instruction and on the idea that children learn through exploration, inquiry, and research into what is of interest to them. As in the case of interdisciplinary curriculum, a classroom of students study an issue or topic. However, the study is more fundamentally shaped by questions that students have about the topic—the study revolves around the process of inquiry. One of the teacher's roles is to help students examine the topic in a variety of ways, increasing students' abilities to conduct inquiry by utilizing various sign systems (e.g., music, math, language, art). Another role is to encourage students to find out about the topic from various curricular perspectives involving students in exploring the topic from the point of view of people who are historians, philosophers, mathematicians, physicists, and so on. Students can also make connections between fields of study such as the connections made between the processes of science and literacy (Casteel & Isom, 1994). (See Tchudi, 1991, p. 18 for a listing of fields or disciplines with which students could view any topic.)

In some ways, the teacher's roles in inquiry curriculum are like the roles that teachers play in interdisciplinary curriculum. The teacher locates, for example, reading materials and other resources for students and with students. However, the teacher understands and expects that the materials are as likely to spur new inquiry as they are to answer questions that students have. In effective implementation of interdisciplinary curriculum, the teacher is a participant learner. This is a *key* role that the teacher plays in implementing inquiry curriculum. Everyone in the classroom is an inquirer. Everyone, including the teacher, has a knowledge base and a set of skills to begin with and it is expected that both knowledge and skills will grow as the community inquires together about ideas of interest to individuals and to the group, united by an overarching issue or topic.

For more information about the theory and practice of inquiry curriculum, three books are helpful. One is *Whole language: Inquiring voices*, a book that invites you to interactively explore the theory behind inquiry curriculum and some examples of it (Watson, Burke & Harste, 1989). Another is *Creating curriculum: Teachers and students as a community of learners*, a book that presents the authoring cycle as an organizational vehicle for creating an inquiry curriculum (Short & Burke, 1991). In a third book, *Theme immersion: Inquiry-based curriculum in elementary and middle schools*, the authors provide information about teaching students research skills and give detailed examples of inquiry-based studies in first grade through eighth grade and special education classrooms (Manning, Manning & Long, 1994).

The Interpersonal Environment

The third element of environments that facilitate reading development is the interpersonal. Students who struggle most with school need people who care about them in school and people about whom they care. Even adolescents will put more effort into learning when people who care about them demonstrate the importance of learning and support them in their attempts to become effective and independent in school. By themselves, lots of books and well-planned routines and schedules cannot make someone a reader. Students need a teacher who can help them connect with and care about the materials, events, and other human beings in the school—a teacher who has faith in students' learning and who establishes trust by helping students use, acknowledge, and celebrate what they *can* do (Dudley-Marling, 1990). This aspect of the reading environment will be discussed at length in the final section of this book.

7

Before the Book Opens
Prereading Instruction

It's been said that reading begins even before a book is opened (Watson, 1978b). That is, even before we open a book we make some decisions about what we'll read and why. These purposes and decisions coincide and they vary; we choose one type of book or reading material for pleasure and another for information. In the first case, we read to enjoy and in the second, we read to gather knowledge. Before reading, we also have some expectations about what we'll find between the covers of the book. These expectations will vary with regard to content, language, and structure from text to text. If we've selected a book by an author we know well like Agatha Christie, for example, our expectations will be quite specific. We expect a mystery with both the characteristics of mysteries in general and of Agatha Christie mysteries in particular.

Prereading expectations or predictions guide our reading when we begin a book. These predictions are extremely important to the process of reading; good readers constantly confirm and disconfirm predictions they've made both before and during reading. The more knowledge readers already have, the more likely their predictions will be fulfilled and the easier they will find reading the book. It's clear both from our own experiences as readers and from research that the amount of background information possessed by a reader affects comprehension (Pearson, Hansen & Gordon, 1979). If you want to remind yourself of what it's like to read with inadequate knowledge, try to read about statistics or some other topic that you know little about. However, it's not enough simply to have the background knowledge—knowledge must also be activated in order for it to be helpful (Bransford & Johnson, 1972). Many students, especially struggling readers, do not spontaneously activate that knowledge.

There are four ways that teachers might help students prior to reading a text. Teachers can: 1) help students choose books well, 2) establish appropriate purposes for reading, 3) help activate the relevant background knowledge students already have, and 4) increase students' relevant knowledge prior to reading a text. One or more of these supports may be necessary, depending on the student and the context for reading. This chapter provides ideas for lessons in each of these areas.

Learning to Choose Reading Material

A "before reading" topic that effective literacy teachers often talk about and demonstrate to their students is how to choose appropriate reading material. You need to consider two types of information in teaching these kinds of lessons to students: 1) the information about reading materials that we introduced in the previous chapter, and 2) the strategies that readers like you use when they choose books to read.

Let's consider the second point—what strategies do you and other effective readers use to choose books to read? Here is what we do. We suggest you make your own list and compare it to ours.

- We choose books that friends recommend, especially when they have proven to be right about their recommendations in the past.

- We scan shelves of fiction and read blurbs of titles that attract our interest.

- We choose books by authors whose work we have enjoyed in the past.

- We look up topics in the library computer and scan books that have the Dewey decimal system number that corresponds.

- We join book clubs and choose books collaboratively with other members. Once a year, we even attend a book talk for book club members convened by a local bookstore.

- We read book reviews in the paper and save information about books that look great.

- In the newspaper or in bookstores, we look over the best-sellers' lists and displays.

In all of this, purpose focuses our choices and perceived difficulty (and potential interest) shapes our choices. For example, one of us belongs to a book club that reads only fiction, usually by female authors. Our purpose is to read things that please us and sometimes stretch our reading choices and to have an excuse to get together to talk, about the book and about anything else that occurs to us as the result of having read a common book. Even difficulty shapes our choices in the book club—one of the members pleaded at our last meeting for a thin book because she had too much going on in her life to read a longer one. Most of the time, adult readers do not consider difficulty in a conscious sense because it is a mute point for much of what they read. (However, think of the last time you had to read something like a manual that was supposed to teach you a new word processing program.)

Our point here is that we need to bring these real-life book selection strategies (and others you may think of) into the classroom and make them explicit, especially when students struggle with book selection. You may be using some of these strategies already without realizing the value of them or without helping students understand that these same strategies are those that they can use. For example, you or the librarian at your school may give book talks but do you also discuss with students how book talks also help *you* to choose books to read? Do you demonstrate how you go to the library, go to the fiction section, turn your head sideways and scan titles, choose some to read blurbs about (even on the basis of "thinness!"), and so forth? Students who do not choose to read often are unaware of such strategies and their lack of knowledge is often a barrier to selection of books.

One of the most effective literacy teachers we've ever known devotes considerable time and energy early in the school year to book selection strategies. On the first day of school, students choose their own books from her extensive classroom library and are expected to begin reading. Conversations about strategies for book selection begin immediately because many of her mostly low-income students are inexperienced at finding books they'll find interesting and readable. She deals with this problem in several ways: through minilessons in which she demonstrates and talks about the strategies she uses; in "on the fly" conversations whenever she sees a student selecting a new book; in regularly scheduled reading conferences; by inviting one student to tell another about a great book he is reading. Although the discussion about book selection strategies tapers off as children's awareness of good books and abilities to choose good books increases, it continues through the whole year in this classroom with more of an emphasis on learning about good books and authors. Just two weeks before the end of school, for example, she gave students a book talk about a group of twenty new books she had just purchased after attending a teachers' book talk sponsored by a local bookstore. Students worked very hard to finish reading the new books by the time they walked out the door on the last day!

Ross suggests that teachers elicit from students their criteria for a "good" book so that teachers can become more sensitive to what their students might enjoy (1978). Ross's students suggested the following criteria and their list may give you an idea about what your students might suggest:

- A topic interesting to me

- Easily readable, print not too small

- A book I've heard of before

- Main character my own age and sex

- A "now" setting, not the olden days

- Some pictures

- Paperback

- Action beginning on page one, not after pages of "dull stuff"

Ross also asked her students to share their strategies for choosing books with each other and their list looks a lot like our adult list. Once you've had discussions about book-selection criteria with your students, you can share with them strategies that you use that they haven't thought of—how to find another book by the same author, for instance. Their ideas included the following:

- Ask the librarian for a book in my interest area

- Look in the subject cards of the card catalogue

- Wander around, turning head sideways to read title

- If the book looks attractive, take it off shelf

- Flip through the pages to see if it looks easy enough

- Read the blurb about the book

Once you've become aware of your students' criteria for choosing books, you can keep your eyes open for books and other materials that fit those criteria. Share materials you find and encourage students to share books with each other as they discover them. Familiarity with a book or its author is a critical factor in its selection for reading (Ross, 1978): Aim to help your students be able to say, "Oh, I've heard of that book (author) before" about a large number of books and authors.

Besides finding books that are potentially enjoyable, students (and the teacher) also need to consider the level of difficulty of books, especially when reading is a struggle for students. Often, the only strategy taught by teachers for book selection is the "five finger method" where students read a potential book selection and put their finger down on each word they have difficulty with. (If they use all five fingers on one page, the book is probably too hard.) As we attempted to point out in the previous chapter's reference to readability formulas (of which the five finger method is an example), these methods are fairly simplistic and easily abused. In the context of helping students to select books using other strategies, this method is fine because it is leavened by other selection strategies and considerations. If you are going to teach the five finger method, teach it in tandem with other strategies or at least along with a question concerning comprehension (a far more important indicator of difficulty): "Do I REALLY understand what is happening in this book?" (Ohlhausen & Jespen, 1992). Needless to say, it is necessary for a child to read more than a page to answer this question.

In an excellent article on attending to difficulty in choosing books and on how to work as a teacher in a classroom where students select their own books to read, Ohlhausen and Jespen discuss "the Goldilocks strategy" for choosing books and talking about book choices (1992). They share lessons that the teacher (one of the authors) conducted to help students understand and utilize the differences between "too hard" (also referred to by some teachers as "on the hard side," "kinda hard," "challenge," and "dream" books), "just right" (also referred to as "workin' on"), and "too easy" (also referred to as "on the easy side," "kinda easy" or "vacation"). The teacher refers to her lessons as "the Goldilocks strategy" because she used the decisions that Goldilocks made several times in the folktale between three choices to highlight the choices regarding difficulty that students make in selecting books. In the process, the teacher shows how she demonstrates that all of us, including the teacher herself, sometimes read books that are "too hard," "too easy," or "just right." Ultimately, decisions about whether material is readable are best left to students, even if they make a number of mistakes in that regard. Hunt states:

> When the classroom atmosphere encourages self-selection, usual reading level performances become less meaningful. This author has watched many readers spend many rewarding moments with material which by any standard would be classified as too difficult. . . . If oral reading performances were required . . . performance would be catastrophic; the material would be classified as well beyond the frustration level. However, when [a student] has chosen the material to read because of personal interest, he can break many of the barriers. (1970, p. 148)

Establishing Purposes for Reading

It might be a useful exercise to stop reading for a few moments and write down what you have read in the last twenty-four hours. Write down everything, including grocery lists, signs, labels, notes, comics in the newspaper, and so on. When you've finished, go back and try to identify why you did the reading in each case.

When you selected a book or other reading material, you did so for a purpose and there are lots of reasons people read even if they aren't consciously aware of it at the time. These purposes are varied and include the use of records (Stubbs, 1982), the appreciation of art (as in a poem) (Applebee, Lehr & Auten, 1981), the exploration of ideas (Shaugnessy, 1977), diversion or enjoyment (Smith, 1983b), updating and applying knowledge (Blanton, Wood & Moorman, 1990), and so on. Some of us read habitually—anything that has print on it is scanned and then a purpose is formed if the reading becomes something more than scanning. Purposes also shift in reading. You may begin reading a novel only for enjoyment, for example, and suddenly realize that you are now reading to learn about the country in which the story is set—in fact, reading always involves readers in both aesthetic enjoyment and learning (see Rosenblatt, 1978).

Returning to your list, you'll notice that you are the one who established purposes for reading the items on your list in most cases. Occasionally, an author will suggest a purpose for your reading; sometimes an acquaintance, an employer, or a professor may ask you to read something for a specific purpose. Most often, however, adult readers establish their own purposes for reading.

Now consider who establishes the kind of reading and the reasons why children read in their classrooms. Perhaps you should also write these down for comparison. If your list is typical, you'll notice that students typically read for a limited number of purposes compared to the wide range of purposes for which most of us read in our daily lives. Given the limited reading purposes in school, students who take little advantage of reading outside of school often believe that reading, even of narrative material, is done solely to get information. Too often, reading is done only for the sake of reading—to practice reading skills. (There is nothing wrong with practice but it naturally occurs when students read for communicative purposes.) Teachers don't consciously encourage their students to read only for these purposes, but their actions demonstrate to children that reading is a matter of getting the words, facts, and skill exercises right (see Rosenblatt, 1978; F. Smith, 1981). Isn't most of the reading students do in many classrooms followed by exercises to see what they remember or by isolated skills work? Such exercises demonstrate to children that these are the purposes for reading. Teachers must consciously endeavor to demonstrate other purposes as a natural part of classroom life. Recalling our theoretical overview from the first chapter also indicates that limiting the purposes for which students read means that they will only learn to read for those purposes and not others.

You may also conclude from your list that teachers usually indicate the purposes for which students read. You might say to students, "Read to find out . . . ," a direct means of purpose setting. Or you might indirectly send a message that reading is "getting the words right" by immediately correcting students' oral reading miscues. In a review of purpose setting for classroom reading, Blanton, Wood and Moorman conclude that "most purpose setting seems to be primarily teacher-directed, perfunctory, and geared to having students locate and recall information. In such instances, readers are engaged in activities devoid of the rich elaborations, inferential thinking, and reasoning stimulated by good purpose setting (1990, p. 488)."

Shuman recommends that students and teachers keep Reading Activity Logs as a means of becoming aware of and demonstrating the various purposes of reading (1982). As an introductory activity, Shuman suggests that teachers generate a discussion leading to class definitions of reading. Teachers can ask students why they read, what they do when they read, and what they read (Page & Pinnel, 1979). Students are then given a length of time (a week, for example) during which to keep track of all their reading activities. At the conclusion of this week, students can share what they've read and why. For teachers of Title I students or students with learning disabilities who work with children individually or in small groups, we recommend persuading regular classroom teachers to try this activity in their classrooms when struggling readers are present. It's particularly useful for struggling readers to hear what good readers think about reading. Lessons like this go a long way toward helping students understand the multitude of purposes that exist for reading and their own role in setting those purposes.

This doesn't mean that teachers should never set purposes for reading. If teachers plan a focused (rather than open-ended) discussion following reading, it's a good idea to set a common purpose. Without it, students read for idiosyncratic reasons and may not have attended to ideas in the reading that pertain to the discussion. With a common purpose, readers are more likely to read with a common perspective. Teachers can also help students learn to attend to the purposes authors expect readers will be reading their work with—where these expectations typically occur in a text and how they are framed. Reading or listening for particular purposes often happens naturally in situations like Authors' Chair where authors explicitly ask their classmates to listen for a specific purpose.

Readers who are struggling may require explicit demonstrations of purpose setting and its impact on reading—in this case, teachers also need to set purposes. Teachers may need to think aloud as they set purposes for reading and, as they show students how their purposes guide their reading of the text, how it focuses their attention in the text, and how it molds their comprehension of the text. (See the next chapter for information about conducting lessons involving think-aloud.)

The ultimate instructional goal is to help students learn to set their own purposes for reading, especially when the reading selection is a personal choice or when the text invites a more open interpretation. On the way to this goal, teachers will need to help struggling readers understand the many purposes for reading, who might be involved in setting reading purposes, and how those purposes affect the process of reading and text comprehension.

Much of the remainder of this chapter contains lessons that directly affect students' purpose setting in reading. Other ideas for lessons may be found in Blanton, Wood, and Moorman (1990).

Activating Student Knowledge About Text

Since reading comprehension is dependent on making connections between what is in a text and what's in the reader's head, it's important to attend to helping students activate the knowledge they have (their schema) that's related to the text they are to read. Students' knowledge can be activated in a variety of ways—with and without the concurrent presence of the text that is to be read, with a variety of textual cues when the text is present, and with varying degrees of teacher direction or assistance. Although teacher direction and assistance is important and in some cases absolutely necessary, our focus here is on presenting lessons in which teacher direction and assistance may be withdrawn gradually as students develop independence in activating knowledge prior to reading. Research indicates that instruction is most effective when students are encouraged to apply strategies independently and to become actively involved in their own learning (Stephens, 1985). Reid and Hresko note that in most cases, teachers design the strategies that are taught to students (1981). Although struggling readers prove amenable to learning the strategies, knowing the strategy does not guarantee that it will be activated (Wong, 1985) or activated in appropriate settings (Deshler et al., 1984). We concur with Reid and Hresko that, although teacher involvement may be necessary in early instructional stages when a strategy is being learned, teachers must gradually replace their assistance with more and more student involvement, not only in using strategies but also in selecting the strategies that may be of use given the particular demands of the setting (1981).

Previewing the Topic

Teachers have long made it a practice to inform students of the topic of a text prior to reading in order to establish a purpose for reading the text. Basal reader teacher guides are infamous for suggesting exactly how this should be done, sometimes even providing the exact wording. Usually teachers are advised to give students some information from the text or related to it and then have students "read in order to find out." Beck, McCaslin, and McKeown found that these introductions to topic and purpose are misdirective, too narrow in scope, or divulge excess content (1981). Topic introductions may require that students read for information or ideas not contained in the text or that don't reflect the major ideas of the text. Revealing too much about the topic may leave readers with little motivation to read the text. Topic introductions contribute to another problem: increased student passivity. The teacher provides information and a purpose for reading. The teacher tells the students everything. The teacher does all the talking and the students listen (presumably).

One alternative to this sort of introduction is "already-know" time (Hampton, 1984) or **K-W-L** (Carr & Ogle, 1987), a strategy that involves students in thinking and talking to activate their own knowledge of the topic. Once teachers have presented the topic, they provide no further information but assume the role of discussion leader, drawing information out of the students and encouraging them to organize it. First, the teacher asks students to relate to the group what they already **K**now about the topic, then **W**hat they want to know, and finally, what they **L**earned after they have engaged in exploration of the topic.

One LD teacher who did this with three sixth graders on the topic of the United States wrote the students' already-know statements on large chart paper so everyone could observe as they were written. The following statements were generated by these students during their first brainstorming session:

- The national bird is the bald eagle.
- There are fifty states.
- There are many different kinds of people in the U.S.
- The U.S. is a country.
- There are billions and trillions of people in the U.S.
- The U.S. is a free country.
- There are thirteen white stripes on the flag.
- People come from all over the world to live in the U.S.
- The U.S. is in North America with Canada.
- The U.S. has a President as the head of the country.
- The U.S. has the Empire State Building and the Statue of Liberty.
- The U.S. has lots of beaches on the shores.
- The states have different things they're famous for.

Next students reread their statements and think of questions they have about the topic or what it is they want to learn. When one student isn't sure of the accuracy of an already-know statement, another may turn it into a question so its accuracy can be checked. The students' questions from the first brainstorming session were committed to large chart paper as follows. You'll notice that this was a lesson that was done prior to changes in Russia and its relationship to the United States.

- Why can the Russians come here and travel where they want? Why can't we travel where we want in Russia?

- How is life in the U.S. different from life in Russia or China or Africa?

- Is Africa like the U.S.A.—with states?

- Why do they call different parts of Denver by different names? (reference to all the suburbs)

- Why does the President say bad things about the Russians?

- How should they solve the nuclear war problem?

- Who's the President of the world?

- Why do they vote for President every year?

- Does the President have a boss?

On another day, these already-know statements and questions were categorized by students, a task that generated more statements and more questions. For example, the students developed a whole series of statements and questions about the flag, which revolved around its description, and questions about the origin of its colors and the number of stripes and stars. In addition, it was clear that the students had done some thinking about their statements and questions—they wanted to return to the content of several of them. The teacher took this opportunity to let students know they needed to gather more information about some of their statements and questions, including how often the President was elected.

As a result of engaging in this kind of categorization, students may develop a well-organized body of statements and questions that will, it's hoped, make it easier for them to organize the new knowledge they gain during reading. Most students, even older ones, have greater success with this task of organization if the statements and questions are printed on paper and cut apart so that they may be moved about on a desk or tabletop. Encourage students to share various ways of organizing statements and questions. There will be interesting differences that may generate more discussion and questions on the topic.

Langer's Pre-Reading Plan, or PReP, is a similar prereading strategy (1981, 1982). In PReP, the teacher begins, "Tell anything that comes to mind when you hear the word _____." The word (or phrase) is to represent or name the topic or issue the students will be reading about. Or, to get started, you might show the students a picture that represents the topic. As the students respond to the scene, the teacher writes their responses on the board.

When the associations with the word, phrase, or picture have been listed, the teacher asks, "What made you think of [naming each of the responses on the board in turn]?" This question encourages students' awareness of each other's associations, the genesis of these associations, and their usefulness given the topic about which they will be reading. This step helps students realize that they have information "in their heads" that they can link to a topic prior to reading. In the final step of PReP, the teacher asks students, "Based on our discussion, have you any new ideas about [the topic word, phrase, or picture]?" This step encourages students to talk about associations that have been elaborated or revised as a result of the discussion.

If a topic is controversial or likely to generate varying opinions or feelings, a debate might help students identify what they already know and believe. Once you've introduced a topic, ask students to write down their views, pro or con, about the topic. Let them share individual views in either a pro or con group, and then hold a debate based on their discussions. After students have read the text, they can compare and contrast their own views with the author's point of view. Of course, students' interpretations of the author's point of view will be affected by their individual opinions.

These lessons are useful not only as prereading activities for a single text but also for beginning an interdisciplinary or inquiry unit that uses a variety of texts and resources on one topic or issue. If students are about to begin a unit on insects or on folktales, they can begin by discussing what they already know or would like to know. Or if it is appropriate, they can begin by debating the topic.

Other prereading lessons have been successful in activating students' prior knowledge, but they are not as likely to develop student independence. For example, several researchers recommend providing a familiar example from students' lives of a theme, an event, or whatever is highlighted in the text. Gagne and Memory suggest this approach, which aims to encourage students to discover what an example has in common with a textual passage (1978). Au also recommends that teachers introduce content from students' experiences into discussions of reading texts, encouraging students to relate their experiences, and then helping students to link their experiences with text content after reading (1979).

Although researchers have shown that these lessons are successful in increasing comprehension, the lessons themselves are dependent on teachers' rather than students' activation of background knowledge. Even if such lessons may not lead to long-term independence in the use of a particular strategy, some instructional situations could benefit from their use. Long-term considerations such as independence in using a strategy may be less important when students require immediate comprehension support for a specific text, at least at the time. However, we recommend that teachers consider ways in which students can learn to activate their own knowledge prior to reading.

As students gain some facility using prereading strategies, encourage them to use these strategies independently, starting perhaps with the support of a small group, then a partner, and then on their own. The strategies used by students may be like those you've presented, or they may be generated by the students independently. From time to time during this move toward the independent use of strategies, review with students how they are activating their knowledge of a topic and why it's important to do so.

Book Introductions

When students are emergent readers or are in a situation where they must read text that's difficult for them, book introductions will help them activate and use a variety of information as they first read a text. Clay designs book introductions in such a way that emergent readers can read a story fluently and independently even at the first reading (1991). The teacher's introduction of the book serves as a scaffold for the child's first reading. This scaffold is created when the teacher and student rehearse responses together, because the teacher has modeled responses, because the child's background knowledge has been activated in relation to the story that is to be read, and because new knowledge needed to read the story has been introduced to the child. As Clay says, "This is not a case of telling the children what to expect. It is a process of drawing the children into the (reading) activity before passing control (for reading) to the children and pushing them gently towards problem-solving the whole first reading of the story for themselves" (1991, p. 265).

In a book introduction, the teacher briefly tells the students the title, topic, and characters unless the story is one that is likely to be recognized by students from the cover or a quick look at a few illustrations (e.g. a familiar folktale such as "The Three Pigs"). In that case, the teacher may elicit what the children know about the story. Clay (1991, pp. 266–267) suggests that the teacher engage in a conversational exchange by:

- Inviting response to the illustrations. The teacher may link these responses to other stories the children have read.

- Telling the students enough about the story that they have a framework for anticipating what will occur in the story.

- Inviting the children to relate experiences they've had to what they see in the illustrations or to what the teacher has told them about the story. This may alert the teacher to potential conceptual confusions that the children may have in reading the story and allow her to straighten them out in advance.

- Using story vocabulary or book language from the story in the discussion in order to introduce it and explore its meaning and sound with the children.

- Repeating interesting or unusual sentence patterns from the book that ready the children's ears and minds for the patterns.

In order to prepare for a story introduction, the teacher reads the text carefully and considers which elements will be familiar to children already and how she might elicit that information. In addition, she needs to consider which elements are going to be new or unusual and how she might conversationally supply the information that will support a fluent first reading of the story. The story introduction should take place as a conversational flow between the teacher and students resulting in the children understanding the story framework sufficiently to be able to direct much of their attention to detailed processing of the text.

Previewing Vocabulary

Teachers often introduce "new" vocabulary before asking students to read a new text. This introduction to vocabulary is intended to increase students' knowledge of the meanings of words they'll encounter when they read and their ability to recognize these "new" words. Teachers introduce vocabulary in a variety of ways, ranging from putting a word like *pay* on the board, changing the *p* to an *s*, and asking children to pronounce the revised word, to providing students with a paragraph that features the words in context and requiring them to figure out what the words are and what they mean from the context. Probably the most common procedures require students to look words up in a dictionary or glossary prior to reading or to read single sentences featuring the words.

We believe these lessons need rethinking. There are a number of assumptions behind lessons like these with which many teachers would not agree if they were consciously aware of them or if they had tested them. First, there is the assumption that students do not know the words that are to be introduced—that the words are not in their receptive oral vocabularies. How much time is spent teaching students what they already know? And what are we saying to the students who are unsure of their academic abilities when the subtle message they get in such lessons is that they don't know? We need to assume that struggling readers possess considerable knowledge that we can build on in our teaching (Blachowicz, 1991). These lessons also assume that students *need* the meanings of unfamiliar words in order to *understand* what they'll be reading.

Even when students don't know vocabulary that's to be introduced, its introduction may not be much help anyway. For most people, learning vocabulary won't help them cope with a book for which they have no background (like the passage from Steven Hawking we quoted in the first chapter). On the other hand, the natural introduction of new vocabulary in the context of a book introduction such as we previously discussed or in the context of hands-on activities (in upcoming pages) may assist students in reading and understanding text.

Again, these practices assume that students must be taught the words they don't know prior to reading. But when vocabulary is taken care of in this way, students don't develop independent strategies for word recognition or word meaning. Think of someone you know who has an extensive vocabulary—perhaps yourself. Almost invariably, these people do a lot of reading and they regularly encounter unfamiliar words, which they deal with *while* they are reading, not before reading. The same strategies proficient readers use to figure out new words can be learned by struggling readers (Blachowicz, 1991).

Yet another assumption is that the words suggested for introduction in teachers' guides are keys to understanding the text. Anyone who has examined the use of these words in the text itself and watched students struggle with other more important words that were not selected for introduction knows how wrong this assumption can be. A related assumption is that students will share publishers' or teachers' views on the importance of learning "new" vocabulary. But even the most fluent readers pay little attention to "new" vocabulary unless the word is crucial to understanding (it rarely is) or seen to be a useful or interesting word they might want to use themselves. It's doubtful anyone can tell readers, even struggling ones, which words they will find personally important.

Given what we know about reading processes and reading development, vocabulary instruction should focus on providing students with the tools they need for dealing with vocabulary as they read rather than focus on teaching particular words. If these instructional goals are realized, students will learn to deal effectively with new vocabulary in text and will have the tools to teach themselves the vocabulary they find relevant. Specifically, we recommend:

1. Helping students develop independent strategies for recognizing words and their meanings.

2. Helping students judge when individual words they encounter while reading are worth worrying about and when they are not.

3. Helping to develop students' insights about how words are used in text.

4. Encouraging students' interest in words.

We'd recommend few of the usual strategies for dealing with vocabulary prior to reading a text for the simple reason that they don't usually encourage the development of independent strategies for dealing with new vocabulary in the process of reading. The book introduction we discussed earlier provides students with a contextual understanding and preview of new vocabulary, but it is the teacher who decides what the children are likely to need to know. On the other hand, the two prereading strategies discussed below are directly connected with whole texts and involve student thinking and student talking rather than teacher telling.

The first prereading vocabulary lesson we discuss here is called *vocabulary prediction* and is easily adapted for use with almost any text, expository or narrative, at any grade level (M. Atwell & Rhodes, 1984). The following lesson was used with a group of remedial readers. The teacher chose five words from the fable *The Partridge and the Fox*, a basal reader story (Clymer & Martin, 1980). The teacher wrote each word across the top of the blackboard, leaving plenty of space to write children's definitions. The teacher read a word, provided thirty seconds of thinking time for a definition, and then wrote the children's definitions under the appropriate word. The children's responses were as shown in Figure 7–1.

The teacher then asked her students to read the story themselves. As they read, several exclaimed, "I found it! That's what it means!" After reading the story, the children discussed the events, and then attention returned to the children's prereading guesses. With each word in turn, the teacher inquired, "What does the word mean as it's used in the story?" and the group looked to see if one of their

WORDS WITH CHILDREN'S DEFINITIONS

Brush brush your teeth brush your hair brush the sidewalk brush the chalkboard eraser with a brush at the end brush your clothes off paintbrush brush by somebody	The children discussed "sweep" as an alternative to "brush the sidewalk," and "erase" as an alternative to "brush the chalkboard." "Brush by somebody" was dramatized by several children.
Spoke something on a branch that's sharp talk to somebody a spoke that's in bike tires spoke in a needle	A child who had severe language problems was a part of this group and volunteered the first and last guess. The others decided he meant "thorn" by the first guess; the last guess is probably in reference to "spike."
Preen touch practice test preen beef cut somebody pinch somebody	This was a new word to the children, and guessing had to be encouraged. The boy with language problems gave an answer that the group discovered meant "prime beef." "Practice test" no doubt came from the "pre" of "pretest."
Wish wish you had something you wanted make a wish wish something bad doesn't happen wishbone inside a chicken wishing well	Note the children's intuitive use of the word in a variety of grammatical functions. The "wishing well" response was followed by a story of how the child used to live by one.
Partridge the bird in the Christmas song the Partridge Family on TV a porch	Some marvelous responses from children who weren't expected to know this word! The last response is a guess from a child who was not familiar with the word.

FIG 7-1 *Words with children's definitions*

definitions matched. For *spoke, wish,* and *partridge,* the children quickly located the appropriate definitions, already on their prereading lists. *Brush,* on the other hand, was used differently in the story than anyone in the group had guessed, as a synonym for *bush.* Here is a child's response to that discovery:

Child: We forgot to put that one up [on the board]!
Teacher: Did you know it before?
Child: Yeah, I knew it before. It means like a bush.

Preen was a word for which students had to guess definitions prior to reading the story. When the teacher asked what *preen* meant in the story, three children took part in the exchange that followed:

Child: It means pretty feathers. [Child reads the sentence with the word in it.] "The partridge preened her feathers."
Second Child: It means like she feathered them down, like petted them.
Teacher: Have you ever seen a peacock preen its feathers?
Third Child: Yeah, they open them up so they're pretty.

We think you'll agree that this is an impressive lesson, especially for a group of remedial readers from an inner-city school, one of whom had language difficulties. It certainly reinforces what we said earlier about several of the assumptions we make in introducing vocabulary to children. These children not only had plenty of experiences to bring to bear on the vocabulary that was being given attention, but they solved for themselves the vocabulary they didn't know by reading the text and using the clues contained there.

Note that in this example the teacher didn't discuss grammatical functions with the children. She did note for herself, however, that these students had intuitive knowledge that many words can serve a variety of grammatical functions. Nor did she discuss with these young children the insights that many older students can consciously deal with: that words often have a number of meanings and that various meanings for a single word are sometimes related and sometimes not related. Further, this teacher didn't insist that children provide dictionary definitions. She accepted her students' strategy of using the word in a phrase or sentence or providing a function for the word to define words.

Teaching often grows spontaneously out of students' responses and should be considered the responsibility of everyone in the group. For example, it was the students who figured out that one boy with language difficulties meant "prime beef" when they asked him what he meant by "preen beef" and he described the purple markings on the side of meat. On the other hand, in another lesson, the teacher took the responsibility for clarifying a child's response. In response to *tide*, the children provided "sea tide," "detergent (Tide)," "tied shoes" and "tied in a race." As the teacher wrote the children's responses, she asked them to compare the spelling of *tied* with *tide* and then led a discussion on the difference between the words.

In general, a teacher should prepare this lesson by reading the text that students will read and then choosing between five and ten words that students may not know or words that have multiple meanings. The teacher can then ask students to give a definition for each word, either orally or in writing, without referring to any source other than their own knowledge, and guessing a definition for those they do not know. The group can share and discuss definitions for each word, focusing on the variety of definitions and the semantic similarities of some of the definitions, and if appropriate for the students, perhaps recognizing the various grammatical functions the definitions might play in the text. After reading the text, the teacher can ask students to reconsider the selected words, discussing how they knew what the word meant in the text, how or if the *post*reading definition related to any of the *pre*reading definitions, and perhaps, the grammatical function(s) the word performed in the text.

Blachowicz developed a related lesson for special needs students in a social studies class, based on similar assumptions about the place and use of vocabulary in reading instruction (1991). After choosing vocabulary from a social studies text, the teacher constructs a "knowledge rating sheet" on which each student indicates previous knowledge of each word: that he can define or use the word, that he has heard it before (but can't really define it), or that it is new or not known. After group sharing and discussion of individual responses, the students read the passage and then discussed the words again.

Though students may well learn new vocabulary items in these kinds of lessons, the main goals are to help them gain insight into how words work in our language, how they are used in text, and what clues can help them figure out their meanings. In the process of these lessons, the teacher demonstrates a belief that students already know a great deal about words and that they can figure out more. Such lessons are powerful for helping students learn how to figure out word meanings, but you may find that the direct attention given to words prior to reading the text interferes with text comprehension. This is far less likely, however, in content-area lessons like Blachowicz's where the vocabulary itself is conceptually related to the text meaning. In narrative lessons like "The Partridge and the Fox," students can reread the text after the vocabulary prediction lesson for greater comprehension.

Another prereading lesson for introducing vocabulary—*conceptually grounded vocabulary*—may be integrated with a number of other lessons presented in this book. As an example, consider the lesson in which students develop and share already-know statements and questions about a topic. As they share their statements and questions, they may use vocabulary not known by everyone in the group. The attention given to this vocabulary doesn't have to be formal—words do not have to be listed, defined, or tested. But if a student uses a word in a statement that may require some explanation or elaboration, encourage the student to explain or define the word: "Would you tell us what you mean by the term _____?" or "Tell us more about _____" is usually all that is needed. The same sorts of questions and discussions are integral to a number of other lessons that are presented in this chapter.

If you use a more formal approach to conceptually grounded vocabulary, you might also use the categorizing idea presented earlier in our discussion of K-W-L. Students will have used a great variety of vocabulary in their brainstorming, vocabulary that can be organized into categories or into a semantic web to reveal the relationships among the words. The categorization of vocabulary will generate further thinking and discussion about the meanings of the words used earlier. In fact, if the categories are referred to during and after reading, students will add new vocabulary as they integrate the words they've remembered or learned with the words they already know on their lists.

Once a prereading activity such as K-W-L has concluded, ask "Given the topic of the text, what words or terms would you expect the author to use?" Many struggling readers need direct questions like this in order to make the connection that the prereading activity and the knowledge it activated can be used to help them predict and confirm words in the text that may otherwise be difficult.

Other strategies for learning vocabulary will be presented in the chapters dealing with in-process and postreading instruction.

Previewing Text

A variety of textual features may be previewed as a prereading activity. Some teachers and researchers focus on engaging students in previewing a single text feature, while others encourage the use of several text features in combination. Which text features are appropriate for previewing depends on the nature of the text and what the student might find manageable and useful, given the purpose of the reading. Text features that may be previewed include:

- Illustrations

- Graphs

- Charts

- Titles and subtitles

- Chapter questions

- Introductory and summary paragraphs

- Whole text (using scanning)

- Relationship of chapter to other contents of book

- Dedications

Previewing any of these text features replaces the introduction of the topic by the teacher that we considered earlier. For example, once students have previewed the text in some way in order to discover the topic for themselves, they can generate what they already know about the topic and what they want to know—that is, a list of questions to be answered during reading (which provides purpose for their reading). An alternative is to have students generate a list of predictions on the basis of what they already know, of what they think the author will discuss, and what questions they think the author will attempt to answer in the text. With either alternative, keep in mind that conceptually grounded vocabulary development should also be a part of the lesson.

Here are some examples of the text-previewing questions you might ask to encourage students' questions and predictions:

- From looking at the title (or other text features), what do you think this will be about?

- What would you like to know about the title (or other text features)?

- What does this picture (or another text feature) make you wonder about?

- From looking at the subtitles (or other text features), what are some questions you expect the author to answer?

- Why do you suppose this graph (or other text feature) was used by the author?

Survey and *Size-up*, two more text-previewing strategies, require students to actively prepare to read (Schumaker et al., 1982). In *Survey*, students preview the introductory paragraph, the table of contents (to understand the relationship of the chapter to the rest of the book), and the chapter title and subtitles with a focus on chapter organization, illustrations, and summary paragraph. In *Size-up*, students preview the chapter questions—assuming there are chapter questions—and decide which answers they already know, read the chapter searching for clues to answers to the remaining questions, and recall as many ideas and facts as possible. In Schumaker's study, students with learning disabilities learned to use these two strategies independently as well as a third strategy, *Sort-out*, a postreading self-test over the chapter questions.

In a study of the use of text-previewing strategies, Wong and Jones found that secondary students who learned self-questioning, which included asking themselves why they were reading a passage prior to reading it, also improved comprehension scores (1982). In contrast, Idol-Maestras found that, although students with learning disabilities improved comprehension scores with a "teacher-guided probing technique" in which they previewed various aspects of the text, comprehension scores deteriorated once the teacher no longer assumed responsibility for implementing each step of the preview (1983). When the teacher, not the students, assumed responsibility for strategy implementation, students did not learn to implement the strategy for themselves. The contrast between the first two studies (Schumaker et al., 1982; Wong & Jones, 1982) and the Idol-Maestras study reinforces the idea that when students play a more active role in initiating and using a strategy, their comprehension is more likely to improve in general.

Even when instructional materials discourage text previewing, the procedures suggested for using the materials can be adjusted. For example, if a student is experiencing difficulty with a sequencing worksheet of the kind often found in basal reader programs, an adjustment in how the task is approached will usually pay big dividends. Instead of following the usual directions to first read the text and then put the statements that follow into the correct sequence, the student can activate the knowledge she needs to perform well on the task by attempting to put the statements in a logical sequence before reading the text, then reading the text, and finally reordering those statements that do not reflect the textual order. (See Atwell & Rhodes, 1984, for a more complete description of such a lesson.)

Increasing Student Knowledge About Text

We all occasionally find ourselves in reading situations in which we feel we know little, if anything, about the topic of the text. In these situations, we have two choices: to use what knowledge we have to begin to understand the topic or to rely on outside resources to build or activate related knowledge in order to help us begin to understand the topic. If we don't do one of these things for ourselves as readers, we risk reading the words on the page without comprehending the author's ideas.

In the same way, we may need to increase our students' knowledge about a topic and help them relate new knowledge to prior knowledge. For struggling readers, increasing knowledge is important not only from the standpoint of comprehension, but also for word recognition. Students whose word recognition abilities are largely dependent on a supportive context will find themselves in a double bind when they have little background knowledge to draw on while they are reading. They are unable to use the information they have constructed during the comprehension process, which might help in word recognition, and unable to recognize enough words to construct meaning.

Teachers frequently assume, especially in the way content-area classes are taught, that students increase their knowledge as a result of reading. Although this is often true, knowledge increases only if students have enough knowledge to attach new information to, and know that they do; if students activate that knowledge; and if the students' reading abilities permit them to deal effectively with the text. We've already shown that struggling readers frequently do not have either well-developed strategies for activating knowledge that might be used in understanding text or a well-developed ability to orchestrate cues in text. Adding a lack of information about the topic to these problems puts struggling readers in a situation they have no way of handling without outside help, usually from a teacher. This help needs to focus on building knowledge and then using it in reading the text.

What this argument implies is that text needs to be used more often, not as a major resource for learning new information but, as we said in the previous chapter, as a summary in a series of experiences designed to build students' knowledge about a topic (Stansell & DeFord, 1981). Many "tried and true" methods for increasing students' knowledge about a topic before they read about it have been suggested, methods that have been used by good content-area teachers for a long time. These lessons are, by necessity, teacher-directed although some involve students in directing some of their own learning once the teacher has provided initial instructional guidance. In the remaining sections of this chapter we will briefly review various lessons for increasing knowledge prior to reading.

"Hands-On" Exploration

If the topic permits, "hands-on" exploration, such as that which often occurs in science lab classes or in simulations in social studies classes, is an ideal way of increasing student knowledge prior to reading a text. Many of the recent studies of "excellence" in American schools have called for more active involvement of students in learning and have noted especially the importance of hands-on exploration in schools. Printed explanations cannot take the place of a student's individual discovery or direct observation of a fact, phenomenon, or feeling. In fact, active student observation and exploration makes an author's explanation come alive for students. Interdisciplinary units or inquiry units are typically built on this notion, especially when inquiry involves more than getting questions answered through reading.

An example: Students observe a small pulley in their classroom and operate the pulley a number of times, lifting objects of various sizes, weights, and shapes. As they do so, they learn the appropriate vocabulary, as it is used by the teacher, to discuss what is happening. They find and sketch pulleys in operation outside of school. As a result of these experiences, they are able to draw on a wealth of information when they read about pulleys in their science textbook.

Hands-on exploration is especially important when knowledge is insufficient to support students' reading efforts. Field trips often qualify as hands-on experience—visiting a petting zoo or a museum encourages students to touch and explore materials—but most hands-on activities can be done right in the classroom. Lots of ideas for hands-on activities can be found in social studies, science, health, and other textbook teachers' guides and in many trade books that feature active involvement of students in such things as science experiments.

Although teachers make the initial decisions about which learning situations will satisfy students' needs for additional information prior to reading, student exploration and observation offer many opportunities for student-directed learning as well. A teacher who is attentive to students' leads and notes their interests and spontaneous comments will be able to capitalize on these leads as students continue to explore the topic.

Using Alternative Presentation Modes

Students can also learn a great deal from teachers who present new information to students in a variety of alternative modes—CD-ROM, audiotapes, films, filmstrips, lectures, videotapes, picture files, records, slides, field trips, graphic organizers or overviews, or any combination of these. (See Rickelman & Henk, 1990, for sources for many of these materials.) Modes of presentation that provide students with more than one source of information are often the most successful; films and videotapes, for example, involve students in both hearing and seeing information simultaneously.

Teachers who view alternative materials such as film as less academic and thus not appropriate for school—except on an occasional and recreational basis—may be shortsighted. Good students, even as adults, find that they can learn a great deal from materials such as films, which they cannot learn, at least not in the same way, from books. If you took a language acquisition course in college, for example, you might have had the experience of seeing films of babies at various stages of language development. Such a phenomenon cannot be captured in the fullest sense in a book; observing it in action makes written accounts far more potent and comprehensible. Or think about what you can learn from seeing *Schindler's List* that you couldn't possibly learn from reading textbook accounts of the Holocaust.

The key to whether an experience like watching a film is academic in nature or not is what the teacher does with the experience and how well the film (or other alternative mode) serves to teach students concepts that have been identified as important. If teachers consider a film important and convey that sense to students, it will serve an academic purpose. And remember that if the film or other presentation mode is conceptually dense, you may need to use a prefilm activity to activate student knowledge, just as you would for a text.

The argument for using alternative presentation modes is even more potent for those students who find learning from text inherently difficult. The alternative modes should not take the place of reading the text itself if one of the educational goals for the student is more effective reading. But it's often helpful to students if you provide alternative presentations prior to reading so that they have more knowledge about the topic to bring to the text. Some students may become interested in reading a book as a result of seeing a film or viewing the book on CD-ROM. (See examples in Wepner, 1990, 1993.)

Even lectures, which are probably most like texts in their presentation of information (except that the information is conducted through the ears rather than the eyes), have been shown to be helpful to subsequent reading comprehension. Stevens, for example, provided tenth graders with a prereading lecture on the Texan War of 1836 in order to increase their background information and found that students' subsequent comprehension of the related text improved (1982).

Graphic organizers, structured overviews, and semantic maps are alternative modes of presentation especially useful in secondary settings that usually also involve an accompanying oral presentation or lecture. They are usually designed by a teacher (though one is sometimes found in students' texts) to provide a framework or structure for the concepts presented in a text. The organizer should graphically depict not only the important concepts but also the relationship of one concept to another.

Examples of these advanced organizers for text are provided in many secondary content-area reading/writing methods books. See, for example, DuPuis, Lee, Badaili and Askov, 1989; Readence, Bean and Baldwin, 1981; and Vacca and Vacca, 1993, for common organizational patterns of expository text—cause/effect, comparison/contrast, time order, simple listing, and problem/solution. Narrative text can also be graphically displayed using story structure or mapping (McConaughy, 1980). Once the organizer itself has been prepared, it should be orally presented by the teacher prior to students' reading of the text and referred to periodically both during and after reading.

Another sort of advanced organizer for narrative text has been suggested by Graves, Cook, and LaBerge, who provided remedial junior high readers with detailed and lengthy previews of difficult short stories they had been assigned to read (1983). The written previews began with information familiar to the students but also related to the theme or topic of the story. Questions designed to get students to activate and briefly discuss their own experiences were included with the information. A synopsis of the story up to the point of the story climax followed, describing the setting, the characters, the point of view, and the plot. The synopsis was connected to the preceding discussion of students' experiences. The entire preview session, including the reading and discussion, was teacher-led. Although students did not use the previews independently at any point during the study, they read the short stories independently.

Like some of the strategies presented earlier, these teacher-directed strategies are not likely to increase student independence in reading, but they are useful to consider given some of the circumstances in which struggling readers find themselves. A student's comprehension of a particular text does improve with prereading support. In spite of the fact that in these teacher-directed lessons it appears as if the teacher does a great deal of the text processing for the students, students' comprehension of the text, including material omitted from the previews, is significantly higher than when students are not provided with previews. (See Graves, Cook & LaBerge, 1983, for a discussion of this point.) Such lessons provide the immediate prereading support students need if they find themselves in a situation in which they are assigned difficult independent reading. Keep in mind, however, that support that leads toward long-term independence is far more powerful.

Related Reading

We conclude this discussion of building background knowledge for reading by taking you briefly back to a topic in the previous chapter. While it may seem odd to discuss the reading of related texts as a prereading activity, it's probably obvious to you that what you learn from reading one text can be used in understanding another text. What students learn from reading one text generates new background information they can then apply to another text (Crafton, 1983).

Careful structuring of related reading can be of real help to struggling readers, especially prior to reading the often dry and concept-dense textbooks that are central to many content-area classes. If, for example, you are aware that students will be studying the Revolutionary War in their social studies class in the near future, it would be helpful to provide them with easier and more interesting materials in advance of the textbook assignment. For a topic like the Revolutionary War on the secondary-school level, locate other expository and narrative pieces that are easier to read, involve students in exploring the ideas before reading their textbook assignments, and help the historical period come alive for them by using books such as *My Brother Sam Is Dead* (Collier & Collier, 1977) or *The Secret Soldier* (McGovern, 1975). (See the previous chapter and Chapter 10 for information about how to locate related readings, referred to there as "text sets.")

8

Reading Fluently and Making Sense of Text
In-Process Reading Instruction

R eaders generally spend more time actually reading text than they do talking about the text, either before or after reading. In response to this characteristic of reading, teachers generally spend most of their instructional time on in-process reading—listening to oral reading, waiting for students to finish silent reading, or working with individual students as others silently read. If that describes your instruction, we hope the chapters preceding and following this one will help you understand the importance of pre- and post-instructional reading activities to reading development and put in-process reading instruction in its place. Because in-process activity will continue to remain an important aspect of your reading instruction, however, this and the following chapters are devoted to instruction *during* the reading process.

From a sociopsycholinguistic standpoint, there are four goals for in-process reading instruction. Since students learn to read primarily by reading, our principal instructional goal is to encourage every student to read as much as possible. You may be tempted to use in-process strategies as listening strategies in which you read and students respond as if they had read. Although the strategies are valuable as listening strategies and may be introduced in that way, remember that the way students will learn to use the strategies in the process of reading is by reading, not listening.

The second goal of in-process reading instruction is the development of fluency. Rapid and smooth processing of text is influenced by attention to other aspects of reading such as comprehension strategies and strategies for dealing with words in text. However, there are some strategies that directly foster the development of fluency, and they will be addressed in the section "Developing Fluency in Reading" in this chapter.

A third goal of in-process reading instruction, one that is the foundation of all reading instruction, is to encourage comprehension. In a section of this chapter entitled "Making Sense of Text," we have included various strategy lessons, including a number focused on helping students increase their knowledge of text structure so that they can use this knowledge to facilitate comprehension.

The final goal of in-process instruction is to help students develop effective and efficient strategies for dealing with words in text, strategies they can use independently in the process of reading that contribute to the construction of meaning. We will address this goal in the next chapter of the text.

Before we turn to our discussion of in-process reading instruction, however, we need to restate a very important point: Reading instruction, including in-process reading instruction, cannot take the place of having students read texts. Although the instructional strategies in this and other chapters will increase reading effectiveness when used with students who have demonstrated a clear need for instructional assistance, they must not supplant students' opportunities for reading.

Oral Reading or Silent Reading?

Students read text either silently or orally; this is a decision that teachers make in planning and organizing in-process reading instruction. Professionals in the field of reading have been critical of oral reading practices for years (see, for example, Taubenheim & Christensen, 1978; Taylor & Connor, 1982; True, 1979) but these practices continue unabated in many classrooms. "Round robin" reading, with students taking turns orally reading the same text, is the most frequently observed reading activity in schools (Winkeljohann & Gallant, 1979). Our experience is that this is true even in Title I and learning disabilities classes. Teachers appear to prefer oral reading over silent reading and some students may also (Tovey, 1981). The younger the students or the less able they are as readers, the more likely it is that teachers will organize instruction so that students read orally rather than silently. Thus, the vast majority of a young child's or a struggling reader's time in reading may be spent in listening to others reading text aloud while waiting for a turn to read.

When viewed in light of the in-process reading instruction goals we outlined earlier, group oral reading is often not the best choice of reading modes. First, much of the round robin reading that is characteristic of reading instruction does not engender a great deal of reading on the part of the participants (Allington, 1980; Hoffman, 1981). In order to understand this, keep track of how much actual reading is done by individual students during round robin reading. Watch carefully—some students process little text unless it is their turn to read aloud in the group. The entire group may read a story, but individuals in a group may read only a page or two with struggling readers reading the least of all. Once you've made your observations, consider seriously whether that page or two of reading (which may be the only reading of text the student does all day) is enough if a student's reading is to develop.

Nor does round robin reading lend itself to the development of effective, efficient, and independent reading strategies. The typical feedback provided by teachers and other students to miscues produced during oral reading serves to reinforce the sort of reading observed in struggling readers, reading which does not make sense. We will discuss this topic in depth in the next chapter.

In addition, round robin reading, by focusing students' attention on correctly pronouncing words, often interferes with the most basic goal of in-process reading instruction—comprehension—especially for poor readers (Hoffman, 1981; Winkeljohann & Gallant, 1979). Some students do so much oral reading with corrections from others that it leads them to believe that correct word recognition is *the* goal of reading, even during silent reading.

If the amount and kind of oral reading that occurs in classrooms interferes with students' reading development, why does the practice persist? Apparently, oral reading persists because it has greater payoff for the teacher both from the standpoint of management and of gathering information about students' reading. These are both authentic needs of teachers; teachers do need to manage students effectively, and they do require information on students' reading. The question then becomes: How can the teachers' needs be met so that the reading needs of students can also be met? Ideas about collecting information can be found in our discussion of literacy assessment in Section II of this book. Other ideas about how to manage time during oral reading follow:

1. There are individual and group situations where oral reading has more purpose. Observations of oral reading can take place as students read scripts in preparation for Readers Theater or when they are preparing a story to be read orally to younger children.

2. You can listen to one student read while others are reading the same or different texts silently (Johns, 1982). The student may be asked to read aloud whatever part of the text she had just finished reading silently, the next part of the text to be read, or a part of the text she found interesting. In individual oral reading conferences such as this, you can help students discover or consolidate problem-solving strategies for word recognition.

3. If some or all of the students do not yet read silently, think about ways of allowing oral reading and doing it in such a way that the amount of reading can be increased substantially. For example, the students can be paired for oral reading, they can read along with a tape of the story, or they can simply read aloud to themselves.

4. As the students read silently, talk with individual students about what they are reading, using questions like those listed in Figure 8-1. In these comprehension-centered reading conferences, encourage students to talk about what they are reading several times during the process of reading—before, during, and after reading a text or part of a text.

5. Instead of using instructional time for in-process reading activities, you can use that time for prereading or postreading activities designed to enhance the meaning students construct during the process of reading. Of course, this means that students will spend some of their independent work time silently reading text.

6. Struggling readers *will* read silently on their own. Firmly establish expectations that the students will read and consider motivation for reading the text. Pre-

---

READING CONFERENCE QUESTIONS

What would you like to tell me about what you've read?

Do you have any confusions about what you've read?

What have you been wondering about as you read this?

How did you decide to read this?

What kinds of things have you been wrestling with as you read this? How have you solved the problem(s)?

If you had a chance to talk with this author, what would you talk with him/her about?

What do you plan to read next? Why?

Does this make you think of anything else you've read?

Why do you suppose the author gave this (book, article, etc.) this title?

What parts of this have you especially liked? Disliked?

Do you like this more or less than the last thing you read? Why?

Is there anybody else in our class who you think would enjoy reading this? Why?

Did you skip any parts of what you have read? What? Why?

What is the main thing the author is saying to you?

Why do you suppose the author began this the way s/he did?

Would you like to be one of the people in this? Who? Why?

What other texts by this author have you read? Are the other texts similar in any way to this one?

Does this text remind you of others you have read?

FIG 8-1   *Reading conference questions*

reading activities that assist reluctant readers in making a connection between the text, prior knowledge, and feelings are important. So are consistent postreading activities and discussions that firmly establish in students' minds that they must come prepared to postreading meetings. Be patient but firm in establishing such expectations. If a student arrives at a group meeting without having read the text, ask him to silently observe the activities of the rest of the group. Next time you assign independent silent reading, remind that student of your expectations and that you'd like him to be able to participate in the group's activities this time. If the activities are ones that students find interesting, it should not be long before they are prepared for them.

7. If you are teaching in a situation in which all the students read independently for a period of time, spend some of your time during individual conferences making anecdotal records about individuals' abilities, needs, and interests in reading. Such records are invaluable for planning instruction.

As Armbruster and Wilkinson note, simply having students read silently instead of orally may not result in an increase in reading engagement or comprehension (1991). Teachers also need to pay attention to what is done in the rest of the lesson, before and after reading occurs. Students who have established clear meaning-based purposes for reading and who know that postreading discussion will rely on their understanding of the text are more likely to utilize silent reading time well.

Developing Fluency in Reading

David (third grade) reads aloud to his teacher, faltering frequently, pleading with warm brown eyes for help at each difficult word.

Brian (ninth grade) reads aloud even more haltingly than David. Brian claims he cannot read silently and says his attention wanders almost immediately. Five minutes after beginning to silently read a brief paragraph in his history text, he is still trying.

Fluent reading is characterized by a rapid and smooth processing of text and an apparently effortless construction of meaning. No one is always a fluent reader; each of us can think of situations in which our reading was or could be less fluent. Thus we cannot set as a goal helping students to become fluent readers in all situations. Our goal instead must be to help them become fluent readers in an increasingly wider range of reading situations. We have contended that struggling readers often know and can do more than we give them credit for. This assertion is equally true with regard to fluent reading; that is, students are almost certainly fluent in some reading and writing situations. It's probably the case, however, that the range of situations in which they are fluent is so limited that you have not observed them to be fluent readers.

A lack of fluency in reading can be traced to several interrelated sources—the student's perception that reading is the correct recognition of words, the student's fear of taking risks in the process of reading, and the student's store of knowledge about reading as language. Proficient language users understand that written language exists to communicate meaning; less proficient language users typically believe that reading is done in order to practice written language forms such as word recognition skills (Harste & Burke, 1980). In the authors' experience, when fluent readers are asked what they would like to be able to do better as readers, they usually provide answers focused on meaning: "I need to understand more of what I read." On the other hand, less fluent students' answers to the same question are usually focused on words: "I want to know all the words" or "I want to be able to sound out all the words." If readers focus too heavily on individual letter/sound relationships or on the recognition of individual words, they cannot concurrently focus on the construction of meaning (F. Smith, 1982a). Closely tied to students' perceptions that the goal of reading is to read words correctly is the belief that the goal of this practice is perfection. Even adolescent students sometimes think that good readers know how to read/pronounce all words. They have no idea that readers must constantly take risks in their quest to construct meaning, risks that sometimes involve error.

Less fluent students' stores of information about reading as language also limit their fluency in reading situations. The instruction provided for less proficient readers commonly focuses on one aspect of the student's limited store of information about written language: graphophonics. Miscue research indicates, however, that proficient and nonproficient readers often do not differ in their use of graphophonics while reading; rather, they differ in their use of syntax and semantics in conjunction with graphophonics (Cambourne & Rousch, 1982; Y. Goodman, Watson & Burke, 1987; Pflaum & Bryan, 1982). In order to learn to use the language systems in an interrelated way, the student must be supported in reading whole texts, texts in which authors have used these language systems in an interrelated manner. This and the next chapter provide ideas for lessons that will increase the students' knowledge about reading as language.

Confronting Students' Perceptions About Reading

Before considering instructional strategies designed to engage students more frequently in fluent reading, we'll discuss some strategies that help students directly confront their perceptions and gain new insight about the nature of reading. Since students' perceptions about reading have an impact on reading performance (Harste & Burke, 1980), reading behavior may become more effective more quickly if misconceptions about the reading process are confronted at the same time that instructional strategies designed to increase fluency are instituted.

Questions like "What do you do when you come to something you don't know when you're reading?" often elicit profitable discussions, for example. Comments from good readers that they sometimes skip unknown words or that they ask someone to explain a concept that is difficult—perhaps as part of a group discussion about "What do you do when you. . . . ?"—may result in rethinking about the nature of reading on the part of poor readers. The rethinking can be further encouraged as the teacher agrees with the good readers' notions and shares examples of how she handled an unknown word she recently encountered. Similar questions and rethinking can also occur with regard to comprehension strategies.

It's not usually useful to hold discussions such as these with only poor readers; less proficient readers need to hear what proficient students do and think about during reading. By their very nature, resource room programs do not include proficient readers. Yet less fluent readers need proficient readers as models. If you decide to arrange for students to share and discuss reading strategies that they use, the meeting can take place in the students' regular classroom, perhaps with the classroom teacher and resource teacher using the "speak and chart" format for co-teaching a lesson. If less fluent readers don't volunteer much during the discussion, a teacher can review the session later in a small group, in their regular classroom or in the resource room, asking them what they learned and what they heard that surprised them.

A model of proficient reading that all students have access to is their teacher. This, of course, demands that teachers read with students frequently, showing them what they do and talking about it. When Dudley-Marling was a third-grade teacher, for example, he occasionally mentioned the difficulties he had when reading to his class and talked about how he might resolve these problems. If while reading to his class he came across a proper name he was unable to pronounce he typically commented, "I can't figure out what this name is and it doesn't really matter. I'll use a nickname I make up instead." Sometimes he also pointed out that the reading miscues he made (one of the girls in his class loved pointing out his miscues) usually didn't make any difference since they didn't affect the meaning of what he was reading. After a reading session with your students, you might engage them in a discussion about the word recognition or comprehension problems you or they encountered and brainstorm possible solutions for these problems with an eye to which solutions are more appropriate to the situation.

Teachers can use also demonstrations to help students gain new insights into the reading process. Some students, for example—even adolescents—don't understand what it is that people do when they read silently. In such cases, observation of good silent readers is in order, followed by discussion. You might begin by asking students to watch as you silently read a short passage. After you finish, ask them what they saw you do. You'll get answers like, "Your eyes moved quickly from one side to another," "Your lips didn't move," and "You moved around in your chair." Tell the students what the passage was about in some detail and ask them how they think you knew what it was about, that is, what else you must have been doing as you read that they couldn't see. Sometimes such discussions can encourage major insights such as: "Now I understand how people can read to themselves. They have to share it with their brains" (S. L. Smith, 1979, dedication).

You can also help the students change their perceptions of the reading process by sending them to interview other people about their reading. Each student might interview someone who really likes to read, for example, about what they read, why they think they like it so much, how they find time for it, when and where they read, and so on. Especially when students have no one in their lives who models such an enjoyment of reading, these individual interviews and the sharing and discussion sessions that follow them can be invaluable for helping them understand that there are perceptions about reading and its value very different from their own.

These are just a few examples of how we can directly confront students' perceptions of the reading process. As you help students examine long-held beliefs, remember that there is almost no strategy that a student uses (even avoidance!) that isn't appropriate in some settings. It may be appropriate to sound out a difficult name of a person if a student is reading a biography about the person. On the other hand, sounding a name out is probably an unproductive strategy if the student is reading fiction and has no reason to know exactly what the name is. The goal in helping students examine and rethink their perceptions about reading is not to rid the students of their usual strategies as much as it is to help them put these strategies into perspective, hurry along their awareness that other strategies and perceptions exist, and help them begin to understand which strategies will aid in their fluency, understanding, and enjoyment of reading in a wide variety of situations.

Instructional Strategies for Developing Reading Fluency

"Fluent reading depends on the ability to use the eyes as little as possible" (F. Smith, 1982a, p. 3). In turn, using the eyes as little as possible depends on the ability to predict the language and content of text. Thus, if we want to help a student become more fluent at reading any given text, we must attend to the match between text and reader. The match between reader's and author's thought and language may be addressed either by careful selection of readable or predictable material (see the previous chapter) or by activating or increasing the reader's knowledge of the text specifically and/or written language in general. Either increases the likelihood that students will be able to make more effective predictions in the process of reading text and thus read more fluently.

In the pages that follow, we present three techniques that can improve reading fluency by increasing readers' knowledge of both texts and written language in general. The first technique, assisted reading, provides students with a powerful model of fluent reading, and at the same time, increases students' knowledge of the text being read. The second technique, repeated reading, increases students' knowledge of a particular text as they repeatedly read the same text. The third technique, sustained silent reading, operates on the premise that the more we do something, the better we get at it. Thus, the more students read, the more they learn about reading, and the better they become at reading fluently. On the assumption that people learn to read by reading, all three techniques have the potential to increase students' general knowledge of written language. As students grow in their knowledge of written language, they can transfer to other texts what they have learned by fluently reading a single text.

Assisted reading, repeated reading, and sustained silent reading can be, and frequently are, used in concert with each other. If the reader with whom these techniques are to be used is not fluent in most reading situations, it's also important to carefully select highly predictable reading materials. The repeated reading of a highly predictable book may be the first situation in which you observe fluent reading in a particular student. Once students have experienced reading fluency and understand that reading should sound like language, then they can be helped to extend their reading fluency to more situations and a wider range of materials.

Oral reading fluency shouldn't be the primary goal for most students, however. Silent reading fluency is far more important. (There are occasional exceptions, such as the high school student with learning disabilities who desperately wants to participate in the drama club and must orally read from scripts.) Assisted reading must be done orally and repeated reading is often done orally because both the teacher and the student need to directly observe fluent reading for a time. Oral fluency instruction is intended, however, only as a way station to what is of real concern—increasing silent reading fluency.

ASSISTED READING   Assisted reading, often called the lap method, the neurological impress method, or shared reading, is the way many parents and children read books together. This technique—by providing students with a proficient model of fluent reading as well as support while reading texts that are sufficiently easy (Rasinski, 1989)—is a way for students to read books that interest them but are initially too difficult for them to read fluently by themselves. As an instructional technique assisted reading is particularly appropriate for severely disabled readers (Bos, 1982; Hollingsworth, 1978; Sears, Carpenter & Burstein, 1994).

Assisted reading is best done with a text, a whole story, or book that the student has already heard and enjoyed or one that the student is sure to enjoy and find predictable. If the student hasn't previously heard the text and requires a great deal of support, the instructional session can begin with the teacher reading the book to the student so that the student not only can hear a model of fluent reading but can also begin to build her knowledge of the text by hearing it read fluently. The student can be invited to read along with the teacher as the teacher reads the text a second time. Or, if the student needs less support or has heard the story before, the session can begin with the student being invited to read the text along with the teacher.

During the reading of the text, the teacher reads smoothly and evenly in order to provide a fluent model, lowering the volume of his voice slightly when it's clear that the student has control of the text, raising it slightly when the student falters. The reading of the text should not be interrupted; the goal is to experience the text through a shared reading of it. Discussion of individual words is usually unnecessary. When it is, the discussion should ordinarily wait until a reading of the entire text has been accomplished or a good stopping point has been reached so that the fluent reading of the text is not disrupted.

Several of those who have written about the assisted reading technique recommend that the student "read with her finger," pointing to words as she reads (Hollingsworth, 1970, 1978; Schneeberg, 1977). For students who are still learning voice-print match as emergent readers (Holdaway, 1979), such a recommendation is well worth following. However, students who can already track words with their eyes as they read them may find such a recommendation superfluous and, in fact, counter to the development of increased fluency.

There are several other ways to support assisted reading that don't rely as heavily on one-on-one interaction. One way is to conduct shared (Holdaway, 1979) or unison reading sessions in which pairs or groups of students read together, usually using a big book. Another is to read portions of a book to students and let them read other portions in between. (Students who decide to read along or reread a book the teacher reads during read-aloud time create this experience for themselves.) A third way is to have the student read along with a prerecorded tape of a text using headphones, perhaps, to reduce distraction (Chomsky, 1976, 1978)—multichannel wireless systems have the additional advantage of permitting the student to hear himself read aloud and the tape recording simultaneously (Hollingsworth, 1970). A fourth method is to use videos made from television programs captioned for the deaf. Televisions purchased after June 1993 have built-in circuitry to display captions with a push of a button. Some high-quality, high-interest programs for children, such as *Reading Rainbow* and *3-2-1 Contact*, permit educational taping for limited use (45-day limit and two presentations per teacher). A video recording may be stopped on a frame to allow rereading and discussion; it may be played with or without audio support and even on slower speed if suitable. (See Koskinen, Wilson, Gambrell & Neuman, 1993, for more information.)

Although there are excellent published tape recordings and corresponding books available to teachers and children, teacher- (or volunteer-) made tapes are often more valuable because the text selection, reading rate, cues provided, and length of reading can be better adjusted to meet a student's needs and interests (Carbo, 1981). It's possible to save yourself some time by recording your own reading the first time you read a text to a student or a group of students, thus producing a tape recording for students to use later. Students with significant learning disabilities in the U.S. may qualify for the "Talking Books" program of the Library Service for the Blind and Physically Handicapped, which makes available numerous books and accompanying tape recordings for home and classroom use by the qualifying student or the teacher of the qualifying student. Students in some areas may also be able to access the (expensive) Xerox/Kurzweil Personal Reader, an optical scanner that converts typewritten text into highly naturalistic speech (Rickelman & Henk, 1990).

In addition to the previous suggestions for conducting assisted reading, the following variations and recommendations are also useful in some instructional situations:

- Ask parents to do assisted reading with students, their own children or others, in the classroom or at home. Some parents may need to see you model the assisted reading technique and get feedback from you about their first few sessions; for others, it will be a natural.

- Have children read in pairs. You can read the book to both children, or a child who can read the book fluently can play the previously described role of teacher in assisted reading. (If you use assisted reading with younger students, this pairing and role playing will often occur spontaneously.)

- Arrange to have men record tapes too; the students, especially boys who need to be convinced that reading is worthwhile, can benefit from male reading models.

- Have teacher aides participate in assisted reading. Be sure to model the process for the aide and discuss your goals with her.

- Record only the first chapter for assisted reading if a book is quite long or record some but not all of the chapters. This is especially useful for secondary students who sometimes need a gentle assist in getting into a book or sticking with it (Carbo, 1981).

- Conduct shared reading sessions with a small group (five to six) of struggling readers or with struggling readers mixed into a larger class of students (Holdaway, 1979).

REPEATED READING   Repeated reading, another technique for increasing reading fluency, is frequently used in concert with assisted reading. Like assisted reading, repeated reading has been around at least since books have been written for children. Parents often tire of repeatedly reading their children's favorite books long before their children do. Repeated reading combines the principles of repetition with feedback, especially when students provide feedback to themselves about how their fluency is increasing as a text is repeatedly read (Rasinski, 1989).

Because a single assisted reading of a text is usually not enough for students to become fluent at reading the text, the teacher, like the parent, may need to be the lead voice in repeated readings. As the student approximates a fluent assisted reading of a text, the teacher may invite the student to read it alone. If the student falters at some point in the text, the teacher can briefly read along again, beginning with the phrase or sentence in which the student has encountered difficulty. Thus, the teacher uses the situation as an opportunity to provide a model of rereading that preserves the linguistic nature of text.

Several researchers, including Carbo (1978), Chomsky (1976, 1978), Hollingsworth (1970, 1978), and Samuels (1979), have reported significant gains in fluency and in other areas of reading ability in instructional programs that have combined assisted and repeated reading. (See Bos, 1982, and Moyer, 1982, for reviews of research in this area.) Gains were documented on texts that were read repeatedly as well as on the reading of new material. Some of these successful repeated reading programs utilized tape recordings of books. In such programs, students are asked to read along with a taped text of their choice repeatedly until they feel ready to read the text fluently to the teacher independent of the tape recording. In one such program, the teacher used a large number of texts at varying grade levels, each requiring a ten- to fifteen-minute reading/listening time (Carbo, 1978).

One resource teacher we know encouraged intermediate-grade students who were reading two or more years behind their assigned grade level to read the stories in their on-grade-level basal reader along with her tape recordings of the texts. The children's pride at being able to read the same material as their classmates was reward enough for the teacher to continue making tapes for them. When a text was too long, the teacher broke it into natural segments for recording and reading. Alternatively, Chomsky provided tape recordings of long stories and chapter books in their entirety and relied on the third-grade students she worked with to self-select portions of the text for rereading until they felt they were ready to read the whole text (1976, 1978). As the students worked on the text, Chomsky regularly listened to the students read the portions of the text that they had recently learned to read.

Several researchers have used assisted and repeated reading solely to improve students' word recognition (see Johnson, Johnson & Kerfoot, 1972, and Neill, 1980, for examples), a goal we don't support. Although the number of miscues ordinarily decreases as fluency increases in very poor readers, a decrease in semantically unacceptable miscues is a better goal than accuracy given what we know about the reading process of proficient readers. Together, an increase in reading speed and a decrease in semantically unacceptable miscues are good indicators that students are treating reading as language and have become more fluent.

Assisted or unassisted, young children do not often have to be prompted to repeatedly read enjoyable literature. One teacher we know can list at least a dozen trade books that students with learning disabilities in her class adopted as favorites and read innumerable times during the school year. The teacher tired of the stories, but the children never did. Nor do students of any age have to be prompted to repeatedly read text if they sense a gain in fluency (Chomsky, 1978; Moyer, 1982).

Lauritzen (1982) argues, and we agree, that speed- and error-charting motivators like those recommended by Samuels (1979) and others can be replaced with "motivation by appeal." When students do require external motivation to read texts repeatedly, establishing and varying real reading purposes and audiences may provide the necessary appeal. If students are taking part in a play, for example, they could read the play script repeatedly as a matter of course in preparation for the play. Many "natural" activities that call for the repeated reading of text can be used to advantage in school. Descriptions of some of these activities follow. Because some of these descriptions may not provide some readers sufficient information for implementation, references are included that give far more detailed information.

RADIO READING   Though developed as an instructional technique for content-area classes, radio reading can provide a reason for the repeated reading of any text, especially at the secondary level (Greene, 1979; also see J. Vacca, 1981). In small groups, students take turns reading a text or a portion of a text (such as a subtitled section of a science chapter) to the other students. Listeners do not have a copy of the text being read; their job is to listen to the reading as if they were listening to the radio. After reading the text, the reader invites discussion of what was read by asking listeners questions. The role of radio reader rotates until all in the group have had a turn. Repeated reading plays a role in the preparation of material to be read during radio reading. The readers quickly realize that they must read their material so that it can be understood by their listening audience. Repeated reading until fluency is achieved becomes necessary for listener comprehension.

READERS THEATRE   Students of all ages thoroughly enjoy the reading and rereading of scripts in Readers Theatre (Sloyer, 1982). Prepared scripts are available from Readers Theatre Script Service (PO Box 178333, San Diego, CA 92117), and scripts for plays such as those published by Plays, Inc., may be used in Readers Theatre as well. However, we recommend that students produce scripts themselves, perhaps from their favorite stories, fables, and folktales once they have experienced one script prepared by others. Even nonfiction books with and without narrative structures work well for adaptation to interesting scripts (Young & Vardell, 1993). Such an activity is not only an excellent reason for writing—it also prompts repeated reading of the original text as it is adapted to script form. (See Sloyer, 1982, for detailed instructions on helping students to write scripts.)

In preparation for a performance, students who are assigned script parts read and reread the script. Though props aren't necessary, a little time spent locating or making a few simple props adds to the fun. During the performance itself (other class members are a fine audience), students read the script again. Lines are not memorized as in plays; instead, each player reads from a script held in his hand. Students often request to read the same scripts many times, often exchanging roles, for the sheer enjoyment of it. Little do the students know the positive effect of all these repeated readings on their reading fluency.

CHORAL READING Choral reading is an interpretive reading of text, often poetry or songs, by a group of voices (Schiller, 1973). Schiller recommends that students themselves work on arranging the text for voices rather than depending on available arrangements, such as those found in choral reading collections by Rasmussen (1962) or Bryan (1971). Once students have experienced a prepared choral reading, such a recommendation is a valuable one since students must read a text repeatedly and understand it in order to decide how to prepare it for choral reading. Choral reading is valuable not only for increasing fluency but also for teaching students to read (Walley 1993) and for helping students learn English as a second language (McCauley & McCauley, 1992).

The Sounds of Language reading series (Martin & Brogan, 1972) is replete with texts suitable for choral reading as well as choral reading suggestions, especially the reader entitled *Sounds of a Distant Drum*. Shel Silverstein's collections of poetry, *Where the Sidewalk Ends* (1974) and *A Light in the Attic* (1981), contain possibilities for choral reading selections that will generate enthusiasm in students. A choral-reading arrangement of an old song is reprinted below (from Hess, 1968) in order to provide an idea of possible arrangement:

The Poor Old Woman

Solo 1: There was an old woman (say it on an ascending scale to discourage singsong) who swallowed a fly.

All: Oh, my! (Hands on face; act horrified.) Swallowed a fly? Poor old woman (tearfully), I think she'll die. (Shake heads mournfully.)

Solo 2: There was an old woman who swallowed a spider. Right down inside her (make an agonized face and bring hand down front of body to stomach) she swallowed a spider.

All: She swallowed the spider to kill the fly. Oh, my! (Same as first verse) Swallowed a fly? Poor old woman, I think she'll die.

Solo 3: There was an old woman who swallowed a bird. (Child chirps like a bird.) How absurd to swallow a bird (disgusted tone).

All: She swallowed the bird to kill the spider. She swallowed the spider to kill the fly. Oh, my! Swallowed a fly? Poor old woman, I think she'll die.

Solo 4: There was an old woman who swallowed a cat. (Sound of a cat mewing.) F-a-a-a-n-c-y that, she swallowed a cat.

All: She swallowed the cat to kill the bird. She swallowed the bird to kill the spider. She swallowed the spider to kill the fly. Oh, my! Swallowed a fly? Poor old woman, I think she'll die.

Solo 5: There was an old woman who swallowed a dog. (Sound of dog barking.) She went the whole hog! (Incredulous tone—accent on "whole.") She swallowed a dog.

All: She swallowed the dog to kill the cat. She swallowed the cat to kill the bird. She swallowed the bird to kill the spider. She swallowed the spider to kill the fly. Oh, my! Swallowed a fly? Poor old woman, I think she'll die.

Solo 6: There was an old woman who swallowed a cow. (Sound of cow bawling.) I don't know how (in a helpless voice, shaking head from side to side) she swallowed a cow.

All: She swallowed the cow to kill the dog. (Speak slowly at first but increase tempo faster and faster.) She swallowed the dog to kill the cat. She swallowed the cat to kill the bird. She swallowed the bird to kill the spider. She swallowed the spider to kill the fly. Oh, my! (Stop suddenly.) Swallowed a fly? (Shake heads mournfully.) Poor old woman, I think she'll die.

Solo 7: There was an old woman who swallowed a horse.

Solo 8: (idiotically): She died?

All: (turn toward last speaker, place hands on hips, speak in a disgusted tone): OF COURSE!

RECORDING BOOKS Older students will have a reason to read easy material repeatedly if they are asked to make tapes to be used for assisted reading by younger children. Have them listen to one of Bill Martin's Instant Reader tapes as a possible model for their own recordings. Possible audiences for the tapes include younger children in your school, or the closest elementary school, or children's wards in hospitals. Less expensive paperbacks of stories are best for recording so that the book may be sent along with the tape to the intended audience.

READING TO YOUNG CHILDREN Older students can also be persuaded to read easy material repeatedly if they are preparing to read to groups of kindergarten or first-grade children. In some cases, reading to youngsters at home is also good motivation for repeated reading. In Dudley-Marling's third grade his struggling readers were particularly motivated to repeatedly read texts in preparation for reading with their first-grade reading partners (Dudley-Marling, in press).

A DIFFERENT FORMAT Reading several different illustrated versions of the same text or the filmstrip format of a book often stimulates another reading of a text.

For example, *I Know an Old Lady Who Swallowed a Fly* appears in two different versions (Adams, 1973; Bonne & Mills, 1961) as well as in a filmstrip published by Weston Woods. Weston Woods is well known for its excellent reproductions of children's books in filmstrip format. Older children can have a wonderful time repeatedly reading a text in preparation for showing the filmstrip of it to a class.

EXPECTING REPEATED READINGS   Good literature often deserves at least two readings, and students deserve to find out what literature offers in the second (or third) reading. This notion is recognized in the Great Books program in which the text is read at least twice prior to story discussion. Instead of reading something new each class period, ask students to choose a text they've enjoyed in the past for a repeated reading.

SUSTAINED SILENT READING   As we said in the introduction to the discussion of reading fluency, the ultimate goal of the strategies presented here is to increase students' silent reading fluency. While hearing and experiencing fluent oral reading is frequently an important first step for the student who is a slow, halting reader, attention must also be given to the student's silent reading. After all, the vast majority of us spend our time reading silently, not orally.

Sustained silent reading (SSR) is a relatively simple technique that can be used to increase the amount of time students read silently. During regularly scheduled reading periods, students and their teachers independently read material of their own choice. Although a number of studies have been conducted on SSR programs for all ages and proficiency levels, results are often contradictory because of the vast differences in program implementation and the variety of tools used for measuring gains. Those who have reviewed these studies suggest that properly implemented SSR programs do enhance reading ability and encourage positive attitudes, and that much has been learned from programs that have failed (Bergland & Johns, 1983; Moore, Jones & Miller, 1980; Sadoski, 1980; Schaudt, 1983).

A successful SSR program requires thoughtful planning and implementation. Advance publicity about the program is recommended so that students perceive that their teachers value the program and approach it with enthusiasm. A wide variety of readable materials must be readily available for students to choose from, and scheduling decisions about when and how often sustained silent reading should occur must be made. We highly recommend daily sustained silent reading for all young readers, but especially for struggling readers whose reading development depends on frequent opportunities to read. It's generally recommended that SSR periods start out at about five minutes and gradually lengthen to a fifteen-minute minimum as the students begin to complain, "But I just got started!"

A number of those who have evaluated SSR programs suggest that the teacher establish particular procedures for sustained silent reading periods and firmly abide by them, at least until the program is well established (Bergland & Johns, 1983; Gambrell, 1978; McCracken, 1971; McCracken & McCracken, 1978). In approximate order of importance, here are the recommended procedures:

- All adults in the room are engrossed in reading and are not visibly distracted by minor disturbances. When SSR programs fail, it is usually because the teacher or teacher's aide was "watching" students or using the time to do something other than read. (This procedure can be relaxed once students no longer need to be convinced of the value of reading. At that point, teachers can use part of the reading time to read with individual students.)

- Each student in the room is reading. Most educators advocate silent reading, but others recommend that young or very poor readers be allowed to read in pairs and talk with each other about what they are reading (Hong, 1981).

- Each student has only one piece of reading material—a book, a magazine, a newspaper, and so forth. If the material proves unsatisfactory or if it is finished before the period is over, the student may quickly choose another. It may be useful for certain students to sit near the bookshelves so that traffic in the room is kept to a minimum.

- Students do not need to make records or reports. (If sustained silent reading time is the backbone of your reading program, you may want to have students keep records, however.) You will know that the periods have become effective when students begin to share spontaneously what they have been reading. If you occasionally share what you have read, students will often follow suit.

- If teachers use a timer to determine the end of the period, it keeps both the teacher and students from being clock watchers.

Several problems are commonly encountered when an SSR program is considered or initiated for students, especially poor readers. Struggling readers may have difficulty finding books they can and want to read; see the previous chapter for ideas about how to address that problem. Sometimes in whole school SSR programs, teachers dismiss the idea of an SSR program out of hand because they find it difficult to find room in the day for "just" reading. Often this is a matter of reconsidering instructional priorities. Several researchers have contended that reading is all too frequently overtaught, leaving few opportunities for students to use reading in fruitful ways (Moore, Jones & Miller, 1980; Norland, 1976). Allington adds that good readers become proficient in part because they are assigned greater amounts of silent reading and often read material that is easy for them, both inside and outside the school (1980). If poor readers are to learn to read, they must be extended the same opportunities. If you decide that providing time for students to read material of their choice is important, you may still face the problem of seeing students for only short periods of the day if you are a resource teacher. In such cases, one of the following suggestions may help:

- Ask students to come early, to find some reading material, and to engage in SSR until you finish with the students you are currently seeing. As soon as these students leave, find your own reading material and join the next group of students for the remainder of SSR.

- Arrange to have students' periods overlap; have first period students stay longer and second period students come earlier. Schedule SSR with all the students at once during the overlapping time.

- Encourage the entire school to schedule an SSR period at the same time. On a rotating basis, take your own reading material and silently read in the classrooms of the students you serve.

- Ask all your students to join you for SSR at a time during the day other than their regularly scheduled period. The first and last fifteen minutes of the day are frequently possible. Or think about using fifteen minutes of your planning or lunch period. It's a good way to find time for professional journals, a novel, or the daily newspaper.

When the SSR period begins, students should have already chosen reading material so that they can spend the period reading. Some students require help in thinking ahead about choosing materials. It might help to require students to choose something to read for the next SSR period at the end of each SSR period and to create a special shelf in the room to house their current reading materials. You might keep your own reading materials there too.

Another commonly encountered problem is the student who "can't" silently read. Even adolescent students sometimes make this claim and/or spend as much as ten minutes silently reading a brief paragraph. These students are usually less fluent oral readers who also need to be exposed to some of the oral reading fluency techniques discussed earlier in this chapter. In addition, students may benefit from discussions, such as those cited earlier, to develop insights about the nature of silent reading.

"Mumble reading" has been suggested by Cunningham as an intermediate step that is helpful for many students who have not learned to read silently (1978). In mumble reading, students are encouraged to participate in SSR periods by reading aloud softly. Bruinsma states that this sort of quiet reading aloud is visible subvocalization that should be expected of less proficient readers; it differs from the measurable subvocalization that takes place in all of us during both listening and silent reading only in that it is visible in poor readers (1980). Bruinsma also adds that subvocalization sometimes becomes visible even in proficient readers when they experience an increase in textual or environmental demands. Obviously, decreasing textual and environmental demands has the opposite effect. Students can silently read more easily when they have selected material that is highly predictable or familiar from past assisted and repeated reading encounters.

Making Sense of Text

The basic responsibility of readers during reading is to make sense of text by constructing meaning in the process of reading. Readers who focus on word recognition rather than on meaning do not make sense of text while they read, nor do those readers who process the words in a text without actively interacting with the ideas presented by the author.

Prereading activities such as those discussed in the previous chapter will certainly help some ineffective readers refocus their attention and more actively process the text, but those activities will be insufficient for others. Even though the prereading activity may be solidly focused on activating students' knowledge about the topic to be presented in the text, some students will not understand that they are to *use* that knowledge during reading. Others do not sustain their focus on meaning, even though they may begin with that focus.

Nor are postreading activities, like those we will explore in Chapter 10, always sufficient to help students focus on meaning. Meaning must be constructed during reading if meaning is to be extended after reading. If postreading activities constantly demonstrate to students that constructing meaning during reading is the goal of reading, some students will react by constructing meaning even though they may not have been observed to consistently do so in the past. Other students need additional assistance in the process of reading.

In the following section, we will discuss reading conferences as a means of assisting students in meaning construction, specific instructional strategies that help students learn to make sense of text, and various text features that help students make sense of text organization. All these things will help students make more sense of text during reading and know what to do for themselves when they encounter difficulty during reading.

Reading Conferences That Assist Students in Learning to Make Sense of Text

A reading conference is a meeting between a reader and someone who is interested in hearing the reader share what he has read, usually a teacher. Conferencing is an important instructional tool that may be used throughout the reading process. A reader may participate in a conference at any point in the reading process—before, during, or after reading the text. However, in this chapter, we will focus on reading conferences that occur as students are in the process of reading a text, especially conferences that serve to help students make sense of text as they are reading.

Conferencing is a natural part of teaching reading when conferences are viewed as processes by which readers may benefit from sharing and thinking about what is being read. Readers who have difficulty constructing meaning, whether in general or with a specific text, usually benefit from talking about the text and the problem with someone else. Students experiencing more difficulty require even more frequent conferencing. In general, the kinds of interactions you have with students help them find what they are interested in reading, set their own purposes for reading, develop and/or use strategies that help them better construct meaning, and provide them with someone to think with about their book.

As much as possible, it's good to leave the choice about the content of the reading conference in students' hands. How do you, as a teacher, help students retain ownership of the content of a reading conference? The most often repeated advice is by "letting children lead the way" (Cadieux, 1982). That may be an uncomfortable thought for teachers who like to be in control. But these teachers will feel more comfortable once they realize that letting students lead the way is simply responsive teaching, the kind of teaching done by teachers who individualize instruction effectively. You don't lose control by letting students take the lead; you gain by teaching them how to control themselves and their reading. Teachers' control simply takes a different form.

How do you know when a student has provided a "lead" for you to follow in a reading conference? Most students, especially struggling readers, don't march up to a teacher, specify a problem, and ask for assistance. Nor do they typically seek out others to talk with about books. But you can learn to spot students' leads, and you can encourage them to provide leads. One way to do this is by opening a conference with questions designed to get students talking about their reading. Broad questions like "How's the book coming?" or "What's happened (with your reading or in the book) since I last talked with you?" allow students to take more control of what they want to discuss than specific beginning questions about the content of the book.

To spot less direct leads, you'll need to fine-tune all your observational skills. When asking questions like "How's the book going?" you'll need to listen closely to what students say. The student's answer will provide information about what you should attend to in the conference. When the student's response is brief, like "Fine" or "Awful," you'll need to follow up in order to identify the lead—"What is it that's not going well (or going better than in your last book)?" Or you may find that a brief answer means "Don't disturb me right now—I'm reading." Whatever the case, follow the student's lead and attend to her focus.

Also, listen to what students say and watch what they do when you are nearby or in the middle of another conference. If you hear a student groan, "I don't get this!" or see a student sit back in his chair and say, "Hey, this is a great book!," that's a lead. A child who hides a favorite book under the rug is providing a lead. A simple "Why?" is in order and will provide you with useful information. A boy who is obviously struggling over something provides a lead as well—what can you do to help him define and solve his problem? Even students who aren't doing what we expect them to do provide leads. A girl who dawdles over a book without really reading it, for example, is providing you with a lead, either about general feelings toward reading or specific feelings about the book.

In addition to following students' leads, you may also want to follow up during reading conferences about lessons you have presented to students. If you have been presenting lessons on comprehension strategies, for example, you may want to follow up on the student's application of those strategies in her reading by asking questions such as "Have you noticed yourself using any of the comprehension strategies we've discussed?" or more specifically, "Did you find yourself creating a picture in your mind while you were reading today?" If your lessons have taken, you may find that students will take the lead here too by bringing up the relationship between what you have taught and how it applies to the reading they are doing.

During reading conferences it sometimes makes sense to ask specific but open-ended questions like those listed in Figure 8-1. (Note that most—but not all—of these questions are designed for conferences conducted while a student is reading a book.) When asking these or other questions, there are a few criteria that will help you assess whether the nature and quality of your questions yield responses that assure you that you're helping the student more effectively read a book. Ask yourself if your questions:

- Involve students in thinking about text, and in thinking about constructing meaning effectively?

- Involve students in uncovering connections between the text and their experiences, lives, thoughts, feelings, and attitudes?

- Involve students in real conversation with other readers (you and other students) about aspects of the text?

- Encourage readers to decide for themselves what was important about the text and how they can organize for others?

If students aren't responding as suggested by the above criteria, you might assess the nature of the questions you are asking as well as consider whether you are providing sufficient "wait time" for students (Gambrell, 1980; M. B. Rowe, 1974; 1986). Increasing wait time after asking a question to about five seconds has a number of positive effects: 1) Response length increases; 2) the number of unsolicited but appropriate responses increases, 3) student failure to respond decreases and confidence correspondingly increases, and 4) speculative thinking increases.

It may help students take the lead in conferences if you also work with them on generating questions as they read. Much has been written about encouraging students to ask their own questions in reading (Balajthy, 1984; Clark et al., 1984; Cohen, 1983; Kitagawa, 1982; Lindquist, 1982; Singer, 1978; Wong & Jones, 1982). Medway describes learners as "questioners"—"drawing conclusions, expressing surprise, speculating on implications, formulating hypotheses" (1981, p. 15). F. Smith, applying the same notion to reading, describes reading as a process of getting readers' questions answered (1982a). Children are skilled questioners long before they enter school. Our job is to encourage them to ask the kinds of questions that will facilitate their construction of meaning when they read.

Most of the time, informal encouragement will result in students asking each other and themselves questions that arise as a natural part of learning. Teacher-posed questions like "What did you want to find out as you were reading today?" or "What did you wonder about today?" help students uncover the questioning that naturally occurs during reading. Students also become more aware of this kind of reading-questioning if you demonstrate it yourself, often an easy behavior to incorporate into read-aloud time. Students who need greater support in this area may benefit from the use of strategies such as ReQuest (Manzo, 1969) or Reciprocal Teaching (Paliscar & Brown, 1984). Both strategies are discussed in the next portion of this chapter.

Some teachers we know become frustrated because they can't schedule more than one or two reading conferences in a time period. They become particularly concerned about not seeing their struggling readers enough. Since lengthy, individualized conferences are not possible (or even efficient) in many settings, we've outlined conferencing strategies and other types of conferences that you might consider that will allow you to conference with students more often and in a more focused fashion.

- Frequent, brief conferences are usually more effective than long and less frequent conferences, especially for struggling readers. Frequent conferences capture students' reading at various points in the process and provide a window into their thinking, their successes, and their difficulties. Short conferences have the advantage of focusing students' attention on one or two important and immediate aspects of reading rather than diffusing attention to other aspects that may not be as important or immediate. Because you are working within the student's "zone of proximal development," conferences are often quite intense (Vygotsky, 1986). The students (and you) can sustain that intensity for only a short period of time.

- One type of conference that can be very effective is the roving conference (Turbill, 1983). The teacher moves among students while they are either beginning or ending a period of reading, asking questions and taking mental or actual notes on students' progress in the material they are reading, noting who is having difficulties that need attention, and so on. Instead of sitting or kneeling down beside students (which signals a willingness to stay and talk), simply glance at each student's book and ask a quick question like, "How's it going?" or "Will you need some help today (or tomorrow)?" or "Do you want to talk about what you are reading today?" A roving conference should be treated as a fact-finding mission done to get a feel for how students in the class are currently operating and to identify those who need more attention than others.

- Groups can be convened whenever a number of students are reading the same text and could benefit from a discussion of it, or are encountering the same difficulties in their reading and need the same lesson.

- "Grand conversations" (Peterson & Eeds, 1990) or literature discussions held several times *as* students read a book can both sustain and extend a struggling reader's comprehension, especially of a longer book. (See Chapter 10 for more information.)

Strategy Lessons That Assist Students in Learning to Make Sense of Text

An effective way to teach students how to make sense of text is to demonstrate it yourself as you read through the use of *think-aloud* (Davey, 1983; Pitts, 1983). Teachers have frequent opportunities to read aloud to students—stories, excerpts from textbooks, newspaper articles, and so on. As they do so, they can think aloud about how they process texts—how they construct meaning, how they decide what's important to pay attention to and learn, how they relate information across sentences and paragraphs, how they deal with difficulties in making sense of the text, and so on. Hermann refers to this as the teaching of *strategic reasoning*—demonstrating the complex thinking processes that readers use to construct meaning (1992).

Some of the many think-alouds teachers might demonstrate are listed below, along with wording used by teachers we have observed thinking aloud. This list is by no means exhaustive; other strategies that you use as a proficient reader will become apparent to you as you think aloud while reading text to and with students.

- Use your own background knowledge: "Oh, I've ridden a horse before and I know just what the author means when he says the girl was 'saddle-sore.'"

- Create visual images in your mind: "It's as if I closed my eyes and saw what the author is talking about—(describe the scene)."

- Check predictions: "Hmmm—the author isn't having this character do what I thought he would do next. Remember, I thought he was going to . . ."

- Make an analogy: "This situation is like another one we've read about. . . ."

- Adjust reading rate: "I think I'll skim through this section—I don't think it pertains to what we want to find out."

- Determine what's important to understand from the text: "One way I decide what's important is to keep the subtitle of the section I'm reading in mind and think about how what I'm reading is related to the subtitle."

- Determine what's important to understand about the instructional situation: "The social studies teacher always wants people to be able to answer the questions at the end of the chapter, so I think I'll read them first so I know what information to look for."

- Use easier reading material: "I'm not sure I understand what this means and I know it's explained in this book over here, which is easier to read. I'll use the other book to learn what I want to know instead."

- Use sources other than books: "One way to learn about this is to keep reading this book, but the book is very hard to understand. Let's see if the librarian has a film or filmstrip that might help us."

- Reread: "You know, I don't think I was paying much attention when I read that last section. I'd better read it again."

- Read on: "I don't really understand what the author is talking about here. I hope she explains more in the next page or so."

After you have thought aloud as you read, ask students to help you list the strategies you used. Accept their way of describing the strategies and display the list somewhere in the classroom; keep adding to it and changing it until you and your students are satisfied that you have captured a set of strategies useful in making sense of text. You may also want to conduct some lessons to highlight a particular strategy. For example, some texts lend themselves especially well to having students visualize images of the action or scene described in the text (Clark et al., 1984; Miccinati, 1981; Rose, Cundick & Higbie, 1983). As students reveal what they have visualized during reading, they should discern differences between the images they have constructed, differences based on another strategy they are invoking—using background experience and information.

Encourage students to think aloud, to talk not only about what they have understood from the text but *how* they have understood it, and what they do to solve comprehension problems they may encounter (Baumann, Jones & Seifert-Kessel, 1993; Rose, Cundick & Higbie, 1983). This is often best done in a group situation. One student may, for example, read a paragraph and think aloud while others listen and do the same thing silently. Other members of the group can comment on the similarities and differences in the strategies they have used while reading silently. Then another student can continue with the next paragraph. In the beginning, most poor readers need to think aloud at the end of each paragraph or so (sometimes after even smaller chunks of text) if they are to internalize reading strategies and use them consistently. When students are able to read much longer segments or whole texts and relate the strategies they have used during reading, they have internalized the strategies well enough that they no longer need help in monitoring their own comprehension. Your long-term goal is for students to be able to use these strategies independently during silent reading; keep moving them in that direction. A well-defined series of ten lessons that focus students' think-alouds on comprehension strategies is outlined by Baumann, Jones and Seifert-Kessel in which they show how they used an analogy with what reporters do in order to teach students what they could do to make sense of text as readers (1993). Hermann also provides detailed examples of how she teaches what she refers to as "strategic reasoning" to students (1992).

Students may benefit from incorporating *comprehension rating* when they think aloud about text. Comprehension rating asks students to rate their own understanding of something they have read by signifying their degree of understanding—for example, "I didn't understand it very well" (Davey & Porter, 1982; Fitzgerald, 1983). Students may be asked to rate their comprehension of all or parts of a text. Comprehension rating will also help poor readers to be more effective with another "fix up" strategy—*learning to frame questions or requests for help* (K. S. Goodman, 1982). Students who rate their comprehension of a text and discuss the meaning they've constructed also find that they have to put into words what it is they don't understand and to specify what parts of the text are causing them difficulty. Requesting help is a social skill that requires knowing how to specify the difficulty clearly enough so that someone is able to supply appropriate assistance.

We recommend the preceding instructional strategies because they are most similar to the processes proficient readers use in making sense of text. There are, however, a number of other worthwhile ways to help students make sense of text during reading that may be useful in a variety of situations with some students. Some are completely dependent on teacher direction while others may eventually be used independently by students.

Teacher-dependent instructional strategies have one thing in common: The teacher prepares the text to direct students' attention to particular aspects of the text during reading. Of course, in this kind of lesson, students learn the content the teacher has highlighted. Although such strategies are useful in situations in which the sole focus of instruction is on helping students learn the content conveyed by the text, they may not help students learn how to deal more effectively with text.

An example of this sort of teacher-directed instructional strategy is the *Selective Reading Guide-O-Rama*, which is much like a study guide but has the additional feature of providing written suggestions about how to process the text (Cunningham & Shablak, 1975). The teacher determines what to direct students' attention to in the text and how to direct it. The written guide may ask the students to read a particular section (with identified page numbers) thoroughly and to list three major points made by the author, to skip another section, to read a summary before reading for supporting facts, and so on. Mateja and Wood showed how the Guide-O-Rama can be used with elementary materials, adding pictures for visual interest (1983). Maier found that using a similar oral procedure for narratives assisted students with learning disabilities in providing more organized and thorough retellings of stories (1980). A similar technique is the use of marginal notations or *glossing* (Richgels & Mateja, 1984). The teacher supplies marginal notes keyed to the text, which guide students to focus on particular content and help them discover what reading strategies are best used to read and learn the content. Richgels and Mateja illustrate sample lessons, which reveal how glossing can be demonstrated by teachers and eventually used independently by students (1984).

The *graphic organizer*, which we discussed as a prereading technique, can also be used during reading. Instead of providing all of the information in the organizer prior to reading, the teacher leaves some out. The location of blanks for the missing information clearly shows where it belongs and what its relationship is to the rest of the text (Mateja & Wood, 1983; Pearson & Spiro, 1980; Readence, Bean & Baldwin, 1981). As students read, they fill in the blanks with missing information. This encourages students to discern the structure of a text and the relationships between pieces of information in a text; it also helps them produce their own graphic organizers as they read in order to study and review important concepts. An alternative is to provide a graphic organizer that has only major labels on it—such as a Venn diagram with two characters from a novel or two groups being studied in social studies—and have students figure out the characteristics of each that are different and in common. Hadaway and Young provide several elementary level examples, including a Venn diagram with outer labels of "Greeks" and "Romans" and a label for the overlapping circles of "Greek influence on Rome (1994)."

An alternative to the graphic organizer, the *K-W-L* prereading strategy that was presented in the previous chapter, also involves students filling in missing information but leaves them more in control. While students are reading, they can refer to their categorized statements and questions, confirm or disconfirm what they know, answer questions, and generate new questions from their reading. Another strategy that builds on K-W-L and provides more structure for students' readings of text is *Inquiry charts*, also referred to as I-charts (Hoffman, 1992). Hoffman presents the strategy as one that helps students develop and apply critical thinking to reading situations. Although the strategy certainly has this potential, it basically serves as a way to help students actively engage in the process of reading in ways that we have already discussed—looking for answers to questions they or others have posed, generating new questions, and working to integrate prior knowledge and beliefs with information gained from reading. Like other "during reading" strategies, the strategy includes prereading and postreading phases as well. Hoffman provides an excellent example of an I-chart based on an exploration of Columbus in which the student used three sources to gather information about four questions that he had. (See Figure 8-2.) In his exploration, the student found conflicting views about Columbus's role as an explorer and even conflicting information about such seemingly unarguable facts as how many children Columbus had. Although the strategy could be used to support students' readings in different situations, it's particularly useful in the "inquiry curriculum" that we discussed in Chapter 6.

Other instructional strategies, like note taking and underlining, are probably familiar to most teachers. But teachers often expect students to take notes or underline important information without considering that they may need explicit instruction in these skills. Again, demonstrating what you do as a proficient note taker and underliner is an effective way to help students learn both strategies. For *note taking*, read a selection aloud to students and compose notes on the blackboard or on an overhead projector. Think aloud about the process as you take notes. Invite students to describe what your demonstration reveals and encourage them to decide what your note taking should focus on and why. Have pairs of students take turns reading a selection to each other while the listener takes notes. They can then discuss whether the notes capture the important points of the text and continue on to the next selection (Wood, 1983).

Underlining, another familiar strategy, is also useful for helping poor readers make more sense of text (Dyck & Cox, 1981; Poostay, 1984). To teach underlining (or highlighting), put the pages you will be reading on the overhead and, as you read, underline portions of the text you consider to be important. Talk about why you are underlining key words and phrases, why you may connect one underlined portion with another, why you are making notations in the margins, and so on. Then, using another selection, have everyone work together on underlining, talking aloud the whole time about what decisions are being made and why. Finally, move to having everyone underline the same selection independently and discuss the results. (Make sure the students understand that there are lots of right answers here.) Of course, lessons like these are most effective if you use materials the students are currently reading in their classes. You'll be helping students learn

GUIDING QUESTIONS

TOPIC Columbus	1. Why did Columbus sail?	2. What did he find?	3. What important things did he do when he got there?
WHAT WE KNOW	to prove the world was round	America	... not sure
SOURCES 1. *Meet Christopher Columbus.* de Kay New York: Random House, 1989	He was trying to find a new route to the Indies	He found friendly Indians... some pieces of gold... different islands. He found America	He named the islands. He claimed the land for Queen Isabella and King Ferdinand. He brought back gold for Isabella
2. *The World Book Encyclopedia* World Book Childcraft, Inc. 1979	to find riches... and a shorter route to the Indies. He wanted to be famous... to be known as a great sailor and explorer.	He found America. Indians... new islands.	He named the islands. He captured some Indians as slaves. He became the governor.
3. *Where do You Think You're Going Christopher Columbus?* Jean Fritz. New York: G.P. Putnam's Sons, 1980	Because he liked to travel and explore they said they would give a big reward for finding a new route to the Indies	He found Indians... Some small hunks of gold	He talked to the Indians. He asked for directions to the Palace of the Khan. He named the islands
SUMMARY	To find a new route to the Indies... He hoped to find riches and become famous as an explorer. He already knew the world was round.	He found America and the Indians living there. He found a little gold.	He claimed the new land for Spain. He named the islands. He met with the Indians. He took some back to Spain as slaves. He became Governor.

FIG 8-2   *Inquiry chart or I-chart (from Hoffman, 1992) (Part 1)*

4. How was Columbus regarded by others?	Other Interesting Facts & Figures	New Questions
He was a hero	He sailed in 1492 He was Spanish	Did he have a family?
At the beginning people regarded him as a normal person. Later when he got back, they thought he was a great man.	C.C. had asked the King of Portugal for ships. He was turned down. When he came back he landed in Portugal and was taken to the King. The King was mad that he didn't help him.	Whatever happened to his son?
He was an "understanding... dreamy" person. It sounds like he had a lot of friends	In other books I've read he wasn't very popular. He had 2 sons, not 1. Six brothers and a sister. He was born in Italy.	Whatever happened to his sons?
Before he went he was wealthy because he had married a rich woman. He was famous after he sailed, but a couple of years later, everyone forgot about him.	Columbus sounded greedy in this book. He said he saw land first and claimed the prize money. He claimed that all of this was God's work.	Was he really cruel to the Indians? Whatever happened to the slaves he brought back to Spain?
Before he sailed he was normal... a dreamer. After he came back he was famous and a hero. He seemed greedy. Everyone forgot about him after a while.	He claimed he was doing God's work. His family supported him. He tried to get money for his voyage from lots of people. He was born an Italian.	Find out more about his family and what happened to them. Was he cruel to the Indians? What happened to the slaves?

SOURCES

FIG 8-2 *Inquiry chart or I-chart (from Hoffman, 1992) (Part 2)*

176 ▪ *Reading Fluently and Making Sense of Text*

strategies that apply to many texts, but at the same time they'll be learning the content they need in their classes.

Several other strategies for making sense of text depend on a community of readers; that is, two or more students working together to make sense of text. As the teacher, you are in charge of the process until students can proceed independently and then you can act more as a participant or remove yourself. One of these strategies, radio reading, was explained previously (Greene, 1979). *Say something* is similar in some ways to radio reading (Harste, 1982). Working in pairs, students look through a text and decide whether they will read the text orally or silently and how often they will stop reading in order to discuss what they have read. After each person has read a paragraph or so, students stop reading and each one says something about what has been read. After reading through the entire selection and commenting in this way, the pair writes a summary of the selection, then shares and discusses the summary with other students.

Reciprocal teaching is a powerful strategy that encourages students to become aware of and take control of their reading and understanding of text (Palinscar & Brown, 1984). In reciprocal teaching, a different student in the group takes a turn at being the "teacher-student" each time the group meets. The steps that a small group of students uses during reciprocal teaching are:

1. The teacher-student for the day leads the group in deciding the amount of text to be read.

2. The group reads the agreed upon amount and waits silently, mentally preparing for a discussion based on the four components listed below.

3. The teacher-student leads a discussion of what was read using the four components to structure the conversation:

    a. *Clarify:* The teacher-student proposes a word or phrase for the group to clarify. Then she asks if anyone else has something that needs clarification.

    b. *Question:* The teacher-student asks a question, preferably one she doesn't know the answer to.

    c. *Summarize:* The teacher-student asks the group to summarize what was read.

    d. *Predict:* The teacher-student asks the group to predict what will happen next and then to support predictions with information from the text.

4. The teacher-student repeats the previous steps if there is sufficient time and more text to be read.

5. The teacher-student chooses the teacher-student for the next day.

6. If time permits, the group reflects on how the process worked and evaluates work together.

As children learn to engage in reciprocal teaching more effectively, continue to teach them from your seat as a participant in the group. In particular, increase the sophistication of each of the components and provide feedback on how you see students' effectiveness as readers increasing. For example, as students learn to ask questions that engage others in conversation, you can remind students that they used to ask questions that could be answered with a single word.

An adaptation of *ReQuest* is also suitable for helping students work together to make sense of text (Manzo, 1969). In pairs, students read a predetermined piece of text silently, close their books, and then question each other about what they have read. Fitzgerald recommends an alternate procedure in which students read part of the text in pairs, generating questions for a second pair of students (1983). Students continue this procedure until they've finished the text, finally exchanging questions with the second pair of students. Each pair then answers the other pair's questions. So that students learn to ask questions that are focused on important points, participate in the situation in order to demonstrate the sorts of questions that are worth asking. Encourage students to ask questions that connect ideas across sections of the text, especially if the selections they are reading are short. Refer to the previous criteria for good questions as a way to help them consider how to help themselves and others think about what they are reading.

One text feature that students will benefit from learning to pay attention to during reading is *chapter titles*. If you hold a conversation about chapter titles in a book you've read to the students during read-aloud time, they are more likely to utilize them in posing questions for each other when involved in ReQuest or reciprocal teaching lessons. Landes provided detailed information about how to begin such a conversation with an open-ended question such as "What do you think about this title?" and where the conversation might go from there, using each of the chapter titles in *Bridge to Terabithia* (Paterson, 1977) as examples (1989). Once students have experienced such a lesson, they are likely to appreciate the "gift of meaning" in chapter titles and use them in thinking about books and discussing them with others (Landes, 1989, p. 167). In addition, generating the names of chapter titles in books that separate chapters with only numbers becomes a likely avenue for rich talk as a book is read.

Increasing Knowledge of Text Structure

Making sense of text can be difficult for some readers because they don't understand how texts are globally structured or organized. To make sense of text, readers employ intuitively the structures and structural cues authors use to convey meaning in text, both narrative and expository.

Well-formed stories are governed by a story grammar or narrative structure. The story grammar includes those elements that researchers (Mandler & Johnson, 1977; Rumelhart, 1975; Stein & Glenn, 1979; Thorndyke, 1977) have found to be typical (stated or unstated) elements of stories:

1. A theme

2. A plot that contains episodes

3. Episodes that each contain a setting and a series of events

4. A setting that includes time, place, and character introduction

5. A series of events that each contain:

   a. An initiating event that reveals a goal or problem

   b. Attempts to achieve the goal or solve the problem

   c. Attainment of the goal or resolution of the problem

   d. Reactions of characters to the events

Children in kindergarten and first grade have been shown to use this basic story structure to comprehend stories they hear or read, to remember and recall stories, and to create new stories (Mandler & Johnson, 1977; Stein & Glenn, 1979). Basically, story grammar allows listeners and readers to comprehend or compose a story more easily because the story structure helps them "slot" and remember the particulars of the story. It should be noted that no one claims that five-year-olds can label or explain story grammar elements. Knowledge of story structure, like the majority of our other knowledge about language, is largely intuitive. It should not be surprising that attempts to teach story structure explicitly to students have had mixed but largely negative results (Dreher & Singer, 1980; Gordon, 1980; Gordon & Braun, 1980; Sebesta, Calder & Cleland, 1982). We agree with the argument that "if [story grammar] is to aid many children, that aid is likely to come from knowledgeable . . . teachers who act as intermediaries between the story grammar concept and children's use of it as an aid to comprehension" (Sebesta, Calder & Cleland, 1982, p. 184).

Compared to narrative structure, recognizing and using expository structure in texts is relatively sophisticated. Certainly narrative is more often a part of students' lives from the beginning—not only in the stories that are read to them, but also in retellings of family events, in TV cartoons, and so on. Researchers have concluded that, compared to proficient adult readers, more students demonstrate an insensitivity to expository text structure and do not use structure to understand and remember information even from well-structured expository or factual texts (Meyer, Brandt & Bluth, 1980; Taylor, 1980; Taylor & Samuels, 1983).

Expository texts employ a wide variety of structures. We have listed the dominant organizational structures below, along with descriptions and cues commonly used by authors. (The list is a combination of information from McGee & Richgels, 1985, and Vacca, 1981.)

1. Enumeration.

   Definition: listed bits of information (facts, propositions, events, ideas), sometimes qualified by criteria such as size or importance.

   Cues: *first, second, third, next, then, finally, to begin with, most important, also, in fact, for instance, for example*, and so on.

2. Time order.

   Definition: facts, events, or concepts in a chronological or time-ordered sequence.

   Cues: *on* (date), *not long after, now, as, before, after, when, since, during,* and so forth.

3. Comparison/Contrast.

   Definition: similarities and differences established among facts, people, events, concepts, etc.

   Cues: *however, but, as well as, on the other hand, not only . . . but also, either . . . or, while, although, unless, similarly, yet, different from, same as, alike, similar to, resemble,* and so on.

4. Cause/Effect.

   Definition: shows how facts, events, or concepts (effects) happen or come into being because of other facts, events, or concepts (causes).

   Cues: *because (of), since, therefore, consequently, as a result (of), this led to, so that, nevertheless, accordingly, if . . . then, thus, since, and so,* and so forth.

5. Problem/Solution.

   Definition: describes a problem and a solution and/or considered solutions.

   Cues: *problem, difficulty, solution,* and so on.

Teachers' uses of narrative and expository text structure research in constructing activities for students will help students use or further develop their intuitive knowledge of text structure. Reading professionals have written extensively about how teachers might take advantage of this research (see Beck & McKeown, 1981; Bruce, 1978; Fowler, 1982; Golden, 1984; Lewis, Wray & Rospigliosi, 1994; Marshall, 1983; McConaughy, 1980; McGee & Richgels, 1985; Meyer & Freedle, 1979; Moldofsky, 1983; Moss & Oden, 1983; Rand, 1984; Sadow, 1980; Whaley, 1981). Their instructional recommendations can be summarized as follows:

- Read to students. Students develop an intuitive knowledge of narrative and expository structure by hearing and reading well-formed stories and expository texts. Some reading materials designed for instructional purposes, e.g., primers, do not qualify as well-formed. If your students have little background in literature, begin with well-formed stories, such as the classic folk and fairy tales in which story structure is most salient, and expand to a wide range of narratives. Also read expository text to students often, including younger children.

- Encourage students to compare story elements across narratives and text structures across expository texts. With narrative material, compare new stories with past stories. Questions such as, "Does this story remind you of others we've read?" or "How does the boy's problem in this story differ from the boy's problem in the last story we read?," will encourage intertextual comparisons and, of course, discussion of story elements. A thematic unit based on a variety of narratives that feature a particular theme is helpful in encouraging students to make intertextual ties and discover story elements.

In expository text, students can compare different structures within the same context and the same structure in different contexts. Meyer and Freedle provide examples of the first (1979). They prepared three differently structured passages (compare/contrast, cause/effect, and enumeration) containing basically the same content. Students read all three passages and then discussed how the author organized or structured the information differently from one passage to another. Teachers can help students discover the differences, listing what students have observed for each of the passages on the board as they talk and encouraging them to generate a label to describe the overall organization.

Using the same teaching procedures, you can also provide students with several passages that feature the same structure but are concerned with different topics. You may wish to end this kind of lesson by referring to the label and the cues provided by researchers who have studied expository structures. However, do not insist that students use the labels researchers have invented; inventing their own labels may lead to greater understanding.

- Ask questions that lead students to notice and use various story elements or expository text structures. Here are some questions (from Marshall, 1983) you might ask during and after reading, for example, to help students focus on particular story elements:

Initiating event:

What is _____'s problem?

What does _____ have to try to do?

Attempts:

What did _____ do about _____?

What will _____ do now?

Resolution:

How did _____ solve the problem?

How did _____ achieve the goal?

What would you do to solve _____'s problem?

Here are some questions that can encourage students to attend to particular expository text structures:

As (after) you read, write down the similarities and differences the author reveals with regard to . . . (Comparison/contrast)

As (after) you read, jot down the problem the author discusses and list the solutions suggested. (Problem/solution)

Prereading discussions that establish a broad purpose for the students' reading will also help them key into important story elements or text structure: "Read to find out who the main characters are, what problems they are having, and how they solve those problems" or "Read to find out what steps are necessary in rotating tires on a car." Since your ultimate goal is to help students learn to set purposes for themselves, attempt to utilize their background knowledge about narrative structures or text features to generate purposes like these.

- Involve students in story retellings, summaries, storytelling, drama, role playing, or anything else that stimulates them to generate a story they have heard or read as a whole. In doing so, the students will work at generating a structure for the content. If students need guidance in such activities, scaffold the students' attempts by asking questions that will help them include and structure the story elements.

- Involve students in writing that encourages active thought about text structure, whether narrative or expository. Students can write narratives, both self-generated and based on literary patterns they have discovered in other stories. McGee and Richgels recommend a writing lesson in which students generate an expository text on the basis of a graphic organizer of a published expository text (1985). After the students have written their text, they compare it to the original, focusing especially on the expository structure and the cues they and the original author have used to create it. Many teachers assume that students can respond to writing tasks like "compare and contrast" without teaching students how to structure such a response, what cues might be beneficial to the reader, and so forth. Lessons like these not only increase students' abilities to use particular structures in essay exams or in assignments in content areas, they also increase their comprehension of expository structure during reading.

- Provide students with open-ended frames to fill in as the text is read a second time or after reading. Narrative frames can be designed to focus on setting, character analysis, plot, or other single or multiple story elements. Fowler offers several story frames as examples, including the following one, which focuses on story plot (1982):

    In this story, the problem starts when _____

    _____. After that, _____

    _____

    Next, _____

    _____. Then, _____

    _____.

The problem is finally solved when _____

_____. The story ends when

_____.

Expository frames can be designed to focus on the particular expository structure that has been used in the text being read. Here is an example of a frame used in reading a text with a problem/solution expository structure:

In this passage, the problem is defined as _____

_____.

The various solutions that have been suggested include _____

_____

_____ and _____.

The author believes that _____

is the best solution because _____

_____.

There are many ways to create expository frames that support students' attention to text structure. In an article which provides examples of frames for four commonly used expository structures and a sequence of lessons for teaching them, Armbruster, Anderson and Ostertag provide an alternative frame to the previous problem/solution frame (1989):

_____ had a problem because _____

_____.

Therefore, _____.

As a result, _____.

A frame can be helpful in focusing students' attention on story elements or expository structures but its format can also be constraining and thus frustrating to students. The frame can become less constraining if you have the students copy the frame onto a sheet of paper as they fill it in, allowing the students to determine the amount of space they need for their answers. Also, encourage students to delete or add to the frame if they find it necessary to do so to capture the essence of the text.

An alternative to frames is the use of charts, Venn diagrams, and the like. When a text features a discussion of the differences between two things such as sea turtles and land turtles, for example, a "differences" chart with two columns headed "sea turtles" and "land turtles" and rows that are labeled with the elements discussed in the text (e.g., size, habitat, food, and so on) will help students become more aware of the author's purpose and the structure the author used to fulfill that purpose. (See Cudd & Roberts, 1989, for this and several other examples completed by elementary students.)

Besides the global structures authors employ for narrative and expository texts, they also use many other textual cues to structure meaning across sentences and paragraphs. Some of these cues are found in almost every text, while others are specific to a particular kind of text. We take many of the cues for granted—using *a* instead of *the* when a new topic or character is introduced, using subtitles to capture the main idea of the succeeding paragraphs, that one topic must logically precede another, referring back to an already explored topic, and so on.

An interesting way to call students' attention to these structural cues is the puzzle strategy lesson (Kucer & Rhodes, 1986). Basically, students put back together a text that has been cut into pieces (usually paragraphs and subtitles, although a paragraph may also be cut into sentences in order to explore cues across sentences). As they work and after they've completed their work, students discuss reasons for the decisions they make during the task. These reasons, of course, are the cues the author used to structure the text as it was written. As students repeat this lesson with a number of texts, they'll discover a variety of cues that writers use to help their readers understand text (which they can use in their own writing to help readers understand text).

9

Making Sense of Words and Text Features
In-Process Reading Instruction

Probably the most obvious characteristic of poor readers is that they typically don't make sense of text in the process of reading. As we noted earlier, poor readers, relative to good readers, frequently produce semantically unacceptable miscues. And, since oral reading behavior correlates highly with comprehension (Beebe, 1980; Sears, Carpenter & Burstein, 1994), students who produce many semantically unacceptable miscues will have difficulty "making sense" in the process of reading. There are exceptions, however. Some students who produce poor quality miscues while reading orally are able to show—through retellings, written reports, or participation in book talks, for example—that they have constructed appropriate meanings but may not have felt the need to correct miscues for the benefit of those listening (D'Angelo, 1982). Since the goal of reading is fluent *silent* reading we're not particularly concerned with these students unless oral reading is a concern for them (e.g., embarrassment over oral reading). Here we're concerned with students who aren't making sense in the process of reading. We expect that, if these students can be helped to make sense, their overall comprehension will improve. It is these students that the strategies in the next section and elsewhere will benefit most (Y. Goodman & Burke, 1980; Johns, 1975; Maring, 1978).

Learning to Make Sense of Words in Text: Strategy Lessons

Readers who don't make sense when they read need to learn to recognize and repair any breakdown in sense making just as they would in their role as speakers and listeners. To help students learn to recognize breakdowns in meaning making we usually begin by asking them to identify which of a number of sentences don't make sense and why. The "why" helps the student focus on the word(s) creating the "nonsense" in the sentence. We used the following paragraph with a boy named Adam whose oral reading often resulted in nonsense.

> I like to kick my soccer donut. Almost every day after school, I go outside and kick it around. Sometimes I go over to my bear's house and ask him to play soccer with me. Sometimes I go over to the soccer field and kick it by myself.

It's important in such a lesson to have *the student* read the sentences or paragraph. Presumably, the child can already distinguish what makes sense from what doesn't when he is listening. What the child needs to learn is to apply the same active sense-making strategies to written language.

Once students have learned to apply what they know about sense making in oral language to written language, they need to learn how to repair these breakdowns in making sense. That is, they must learn which information they can use to help themselves make sense of words in the text and which strategies they can use when they find word identification difficult. Poor readers' information sources and strategies are usually limited; that is what makes them poor readers in the first place. These students typically rely on classmates or teachers for help or their own efforts to identify words by "sounding them out." They need to broaden their sources of information and the strategies they use to make sense of text.

Sources of Information

Through a series of lessons, Adam, for whom we wrote the soccer donut passage, discovered a number of new sources of information he then began to use (in addition to graphophonic information that was already his main source). In his own words, here is his list of new sources of information he began to use as he read:

1. Look at pictures. (illustrations)

2. See how long word is. (word length)

3. Think of what rhymes. (rhyme scheme)

4. It says the same thing over and over. (repeated structures)

5. Think about what I know. (background knowledge)

In order to arrive at this list, Adam participated in lessons that helped him discover what sources of information he could use while reading to make sense of words. We won't describe all the lessons that led to Adam's list of new information sources, but we'll describe one to illustrate the content and form of such lessons.

To help Adam discover that he should rely on his background knowledge while reading, we presented him with a list of words from a Mother Goose rhyme (e.g., *nimble, quick, candlestick*) that we thought would be difficult for him and asked him to read them. He could not. We then asked him to recite the "Jack Be Nimble" rhyme. After he recited the rhyme we gave him a written text of the rhyme and asked him to read it. After pointing out to him that he had just successfully read the three words he could not read a few minutes earlier, we asked him why he was now able to read them. After we talked about his discovery, Adam added "Think about what I know" to his list.

In a follow-up lesson, we asked Adam to tell us the story of "The Three Little Pigs," and we jotted down some of the words he used to tell the story:

- The first little pig.

- The big bad wolf.

- "I'll huff and I'll puff and I'll blow the house down."

- House of straw.

We showed Adam this list and asked him if he'd try to find these words in a book containing "The Three Little Pigs" story, which he was able to do. We then asked him to read the book, keeping in mind the words he knew would be there as he read.

Reading Strategies

We also helped Adam discover new reading strategies which included, in his words:

- It needs to make sense.

- Read it over again. (reread)

- Read the rest of the sentence.

- Read the rest of the paragraph.

Let's illustrate some lessons we did with Adam that helped him learn to "read the rest of the sentence" when he encountered a difficult word or realized that he wasn't making sense of the word. We presented Adam with sentences containing cloze blanks at a spot in each sentence where many possibilities could make sense. The information beyond the blank in the sentence was what Adam needed in order to decide which of many possibilities made sense within the context of the whole sentence. So that Adam couldn't possibly use the information beyond the blank at first, we covered up the remainder of the sentence and asked him to make at least three guesses that made sense. Thus, for the following sentence, we covered *in the pool* and he made a number of guesses, each of which was written below the blank.

Let's go _____ in the pool.

now

fishing

shopping

to the movies

After Adam had made his guesses, we uncovered the rest of the sentence and asked him to read the whole sentence and tell us if any of guesses still made sense.

After much giggling about his guesses, Adam indicated that *swimming* was the only response that still made any sense here. (If you're working with a student who lacks confidence, take care to help her understand that it's unlikely that she could come up with something that would make sense in a whole sentence like this when part of it is covered—there just isn't enough available information.)

As we worked with Adam we asked questions like "How did you figure out that *swimming* made sense for the blank?", "Is the information before or after the blank?", "What if you had come across a word here [pointing to the blank] and you didn't know what it was, where would you have found more information to figure out the word?", "Then what might you do if you come across a word or an idea you don't understand when you are reading?" Adam learned quickly that the information he needed to figure out words could sometimes be found beyond the word itself. To his list of strategies, Adam added "Read the rest of the sentence."

Although our lessons with Adam were conducted individually, they could just as easily have been conducted with a group of poor readers assuming we had similar instructional goals for each student. Groups of students offer lots of ideas to each other, often enriching the conversation about sources of information in reading and about strategies they use as readers.

Instructional Cloze

Once poor readers have learned about various sources of information as well as strategies like rereading and reading beyond the word, cloze may be an appropriate next step. Cloze passages require students to make decisions about which information sources and strategies are most appropriate in various situations. (See Jongsma, 1980, for a review of research on cloze instruction.) As students read and encounter the blanks in the passage, they use various sources of information and reading strategies to decide what word makes sense in the blank.

When we have observed cloze lessons in classrooms, students are usually given a cloze passage and asked to write what makes sense in the blanks, or they are provided with "maze" exercises in which they're asked to select the word for the blank that best makes sense from among several choices. It is our opinion that neither exercise is in the best interests of students if the goal is to improve their ability to make sense while reading. Reading requires automatic processing and reliance on the reader's own information sources. Writing the answers permits considered responses rather than the quick responses required in reading. Maze exercises not only permit a considered response, they also provide information instead of encouraging readers to use what they already know.

If the goal is to help students learn to make sense consistently as they read, we recommend *instructional cloze* procedures, which require that readers respond as they do when they read naturally in whole text without blanks. Readers should be provided with a cloze passage (a short but "whole" text at a level considered easy for them) and asked to read the passage silently and then aloud at a normal pace, filling in as many blanks as possible without slowing their rate. We often do this in group situations and ask students to read in unison, helping each other maintain a normal reading pace. Of course, when students encounter blanks, they often give a variety of responses. We think it's useful to just keep reading to the end of the passage and then to return to the beginning to discuss students' choices.

As the students recall their choices after unison reading, write their responses in the blanks on an overhead transparency of the cloze exercise so that everyone can refer to them. The discussion of choices for each blank should center on which sources of information students used to decide which word or phrase made sense in the blank, on the location of clues in relation to the blank, and on strategies necessary to make sense from the passage. In other words, when responses are considered after the exercise, the focus is once again on sources of information and reading strategies. Gradually, these discussions following the reading should have an impact on in-process reading behavior.

Sometimes students learn to respond effectively to cloze exercises but don't transfer the strategies and information they used to make sense to everyday reading situations. That is, the students know that they should make sense while reading and do make sense as long as there are blanks, but when they encounter difficulties in a typical text, they don't consistently choose to make sense, reverting instead to overuse of the graphophonic system. For example, if American students encounter an illustrated page from a British version of *Oh, A-Hunting We Will Go* that reads, "We'll catch a lamb and put him in a pram," they may only sound out the word *pram* rather than use the information from the illustration to substitute a word from their own background that makes more sense, like *stroller,* or to at least arrive at a meaning for the word that causes them difficulty.

Teachers can provide two kinds of assistance in situations such as these. The first kind of assistance can be given in any oral reading situation. For example, if the student settles for sounding out *pram* and has developed no meaning for it, cover the print so the student is forced to use the illustration instead of graphophonic cues and ask "What would make sense there?" If the student responds with a word or phrase that does make sense, ask him to read the sentence again, this time substituting the word or phrase that makes sense for the word in the text. After the student has finished reading, discuss the strategy, helping the student to understand that substituting a word that makes sense and continuing to read is preferable to getting stuck on sounding out or reading a word that doesn't make sense.

Substitution lessons may also help these students. Substitution passages are constructed in the same way as cloze exercises, and the lessons follow the same procedures as for instructional cloze. The difference is that, instead of replacing words with blanks, the original words are left in the text and simply underlined:

The brown bears, lean-flanked and rough-coated from their long winter's sleep, would amble down off the high snow fields and congregate along the spawning streams. There would be colossal battles for choice fishing sites; but once those were decided, the animals would all settle down to eating their fill every day as the returning salmon fought their way upstream to spawn. Herds of seals and sea lions would mass on jutting points of land and along rocky shores of islands to dip into the run for their annual feast. They would charge into the nets of seiners, ripping them to shreds, and spend hours searching for the opening to a fish trap, trying to get at the thousands of salmon inside. Eagles, hawks, crows, and foxes would vie with the brown bears, seals, and sea lions at every stream and sandbar. Over all would circle hordes of screaming gulls scouring land, sea, and beaches, cleaning up, to the last morsel, every crumb left by previous feeders. (Morey, 1965, 18–19)

In substitution lessons, students read at a normal pace and, when they encounter an underlined word, they substitute another word that does make sense. (Your demonstration of substitution is probably the best procedural explanation.) Don't tell the students to substitute a synonym. The processes of synonym substitution aren't the same as the processes readers use when they confront unknown words. Here we merely want students to learn that one way they can respond to a word they don't know in the text is by substituting another that makes sense even if it doesn't look like the word in the text.

This sort of lesson isn't designed to teach students to take a cavalier attitude toward authors' words. The goal is to help them understand that, when they must choose between substituting a word that looks like one in the text, but doesn't make sense, and substituting a word that makes sense, but does not look like the word in the text, they should always prefer sense to nonsense. Another payoff to lessons such as these is an introduction to new vocabulary in a way that allows students to use what they already know in coming to learn about new words, which is consistent with the guidelines for vocabulary instruction that were discussed in the previous chapter and by others (Blachowicz & Lee, 1991).

Of course, the point of all the lessons discussed here is to help students learn to use a wide variety of informational sources and strategies to solve problems with words as they read. As teachers read books with students, these lessons can be recalled and used in the process of solving word problems that students encounter as they do their everyday reading. The next section focuses on how teachers might assist students as they make miscues during reading.

Teacher Feedback to Miscues

When students substitute one word for another, skip a word, or even pause in their reading, teachers decide if and how to intervene. These interventions are based on a combination of factors such as teachers' beliefs about reading, their goals in general and in the particular reading situation, their knowledge of the student—and even on the reading context itself. Their interventions may also be affected by the amount of difficulty students experience when they are reading a too-difficult text (Roller, 1994). All these factors influence how teachers will respond when they hear a student miscue during oral reading.

To provide examples of the kinds of decisions teachers make when they hear students' miscues, we'll discuss two teachers' responses to the oral reading miscues of a girl named Florine, a third-grade child with learning disabilities. Florine moved to a new school—and a new LD class—midway through third grade—

which gave us an opportunity to observe two very different responses to Florine's oral reading miscues.

During the first half of the school year, Florine worked with a learning disabilities teacher whose literacy instruction drew on sociopsycholinguistic theory (see Chapter 1). In this classroom, Florine read children's literature with her teacher and wrote on a daily basis. The pattern of feedback when she read *Neat and Scruffy* (Gale, 1975) is consistent with other observed instances of her reading with the teacher (see Figure 9-1). Florine spoke a Southern Black dialect which is evident in some of her miscues.

As Florine read *Neat and Scruffy*, her teacher listened and enjoyed the story with her. (There is, we think, a difference between listening to a story and listening to a student read words.) The miscue marking of *T* denotes an intervention by the teacher and, in this reading event, there is only one *T* indicated because Florine's teacher believed (she told us so) that silence would permit Florine to assume responsibility for making sense of her own reading. We also believe that the teacher's silence provided Florine with an opportunity to take responsibility for processing and using textual cues and self-correcting when her miscues didn't make sense to her.

The teacher's single intervention during the reading of *Neat and Scruffy* occurred on line 13 when Florine paused for about ten seconds and then proceeded to try to sound out *short*. Only after giving Florine time to figure out the word on her own did the teacher provide a semantic (i.e., meaning-based) cue rather than a graphophonic cue (like *sh* or giving her the word). Note that the semantic cue the teacher provided was one outside the text, a reference to her own short hair. A cue that might have been more helpful to Florine's long-term reading development would have been a semantic prompt referring to the illustration as an informational source: "Florine, is there something in the picture that tells you what would make sense there?"

Although the teacher interrupted her listening of Florine's reading with only a single intervention, she took a more active role in providing miscue feedback when she started working with Florine at the beginning of the year. Then her miscues were often semantically unacceptable and were not self-corrected. The teacher used the sorts of lessons we presented earlier in these pages as well as semantic prompts (hints that call the reader's attention to text meaning) during oral reading in order to help Florine learn how to make sense of words.

When a dialect speaker is effectively processing text, as Florine is in reading *Neat and Scruffy*, dialect miscues often occur, a sign that the reader is using her language to construct meaning while reading. The construction, "One time was a man had neat hair" is a typical grammatical construction in Florine's oral language, and unlike many teachers who correct dialect miscues (Tovey, 1979), this LD teacher treated them as acceptable because they were evidence that Florine was using her own language patterns to process meaning.

Florine's new LD teacher responded very differently to Florine's oral reading miscues. In this example Florine read from a basal text, *A Risky Trip* (Richardson, 1976), in round robin fashion. The pattern of teacher feedback to miscues revealed

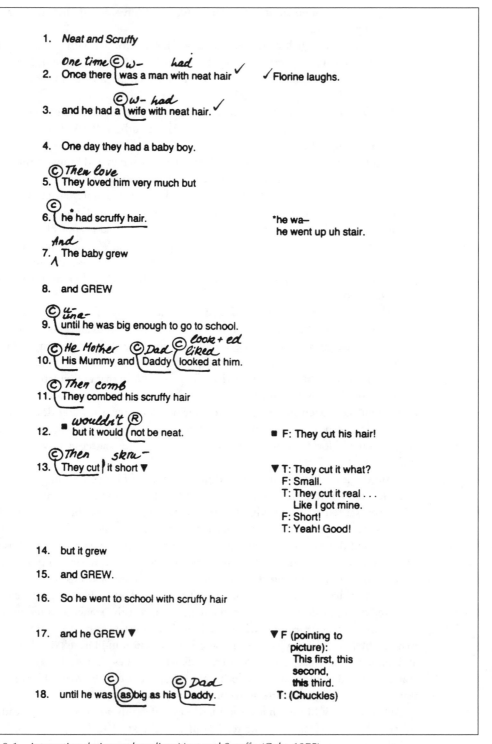

1. *Neat and Scruffy*

2. ~~One time~~ ©w— ~~had~~
   Once there | was a man with neat hair ✓   ✓Florine laughs.

3. ©w— had
   and he had a | wife with neat hair. ✓

4. One day they had a baby boy.

5. ©Then love
   They loved him very much but

6. ©
   he had scruffy hair.   *he wa—
                           he went up uh stair.

7. And
   ∧ The baby grew

8. and GREW

9. ©u— una—
   until he was big enough to go to school.

10. ©He Mother ©Dad ©look + ed liked
    His Mummy and | Daddy | looked at him.

11. ©Then comb
    They combed his scruffy hair

12. ■ wouldn't ®
    but it would | not be neat.   ■ F: They cut his hair!

13. ©Then skru—
    They cut | it short ▼   ▼ T: They cut it what?
                            F: Small.
                            T: They cut it real . . .
                               Like I got mine.
                            F: Short!
                            T: Yeah! Good!

14. but it grew

15. and GREW.

16. So he went to school with scruffy hair

17. and he GREW ▼   ▼ F (pointing to
                       picture):
                       This first, this
                       second,
                       this third.

18. © ©Dad
    until he was | as big as his | Daddy.   T: (Chuckles)

FIG 9-1   *Interaction during oral reading:* Neat and Scruffy *(Gale, 1975)*

in Figure 9-2 was consistent with our observations in other reading situations and with other students. As Florine read, the teacher responded to her miscues by giving Florine the correct word or an occasional graphophonic prompt (hints that call the reader's attention to sound-letter relationships). In general, the teacher assumed responsibility for identifying each miscue and correcting it rather than allowing or encouraging Florine to do so.

Even when Florine's miscues made sense, this teacher's responses indicated that precise word recognition was the important goal of reading. Note, for example, the feedback provided for the miscue *cat* in line 5001 (the teacher corrected the child by supplying *kitten*). A distraction in the classroom caused the teacher to miss the miscue of *the* for *a* in line 4006, but she corrected the same meaningful substitution in the following line. With less than a second between Florine's miscue and the teacher's feedback, Florine was unable to use what she had learned in the previous classroom about making sense of words while reading.

What's instructive about comparing Florine's readings in the first and second classrooms is the impact of the teachers' differing miscue feedback on Florine's processing of text. When Florine read the *Neat and Scruffy* passage earlier in the school year, she consistently produced semantically acceptable miscues or self-corrected those that were not. In other words, she used strategies other proficient readers use to construct meaning. She exhibited the sorts of reading behaviors, especially self-correction, that allow readers to teach themselves about reading in the process of reading.

Later in the same school year, on the other hand, Florine's miscues often did not make sense, and she no longer self-corrected miscues that resulted in "nonsense." The second semester videotapes of Florine reveal a child who had become dependent on someone else to determine whether texts made sense. When she encountered difficulty reading she no longer relied on her own resources. Instead, she stopped and physically looked toward her teacher. With a teacher who took over responsibility for Florine's reading and with a text chosen for its readability rather than its predictability, Florine no longer used the proficient reading strategies she had developed in the first classroom.

A particularly important line of reading research into helping students make sense of words during reading has to do with the feedback teachers provide to students' miscues. Miscue feedback research reveals a characteristic profile in teacher feedback to the miscues of poor readers; a profile much like the pattern of feedback that Florine's second teacher provided. Recommendations about the feedback that ought to be given to students during oral reading are like the feedback that Florine's first teacher provided. Interestingly, the feedback recommended for poor readers is characteristic of that which teachers frequently provide to good readers. Also of interest is that teachers provide the sort of feedback to good readers that encourages them to use a variety of informational sources and reading strategies, the topic of our previous section.

When we read with students, we favor assisted reading if the student is having a fair amount of difficulty constructing meaning; assisted reading keeps language whole and can be withdrawn as students are able to read the text on their

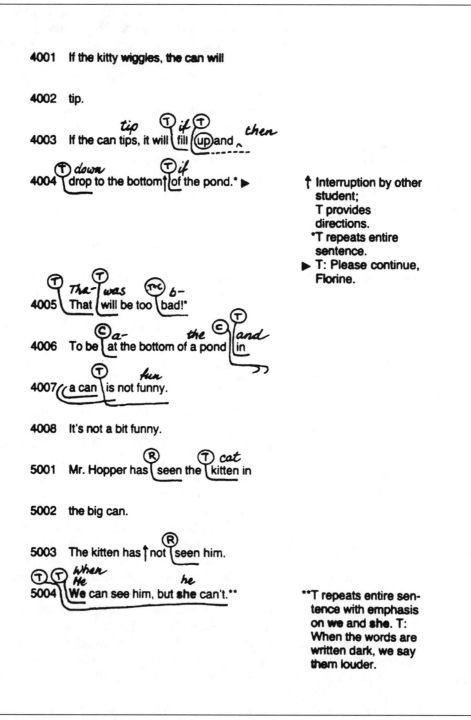

4001   If the kitty wiggles, the can will

4002   tip.

4003   If the can tips, it will fill up and *then*

4004   drop to the bottom of the pond.* ▶

↑ Interruption by other
  student;
  T provides
  directions.
*T repeats entire
  sentence.
▶ T: Please continue,
  Florine.

4005   That will be too bad!*

4006   To be at the bottom of a pond in

4007   a can is not funny.

4008   It's not a bit funny.

5001   Mr. Hopper has seen the kitten in

5002   the big can.

5003   The kitten has ↑ not seen him.

5004   We can see him, but she can't.**

**T repeats entire sen-
tence with emphasis
on we and she. T:
When the words are
written dark, we say
them louder.

FIG 9-2   *Interaction during oral reading: A Risky Trip (Richardson, 1970). The* T *marking represents the teacher's interventions.*

CHARACTERISTIC FEEDBACK	RECOMMENDED FEEDBACK
The teacher provides the student with the word that has caused the student difficulty and/or calls attention to graphophonic cues (Allington, 1980; Hoffman & Clements, 1984; Lass, 1984; McNaughton, 1981; Pflaum et al., 1980; Spiegel & Rogers, 1980).	The teacher accepts those miscues that do not greatly change the author's meaning (Hoffman, 1979; Hoffman & Clements, 1984; Recht, 1976). The teacher may comment positively about a miscue that reveals attention to meaning (Lass, 1984).
The teacher provides feedback immediately at the point of difficulty or miscue (Allington,1978; Hoffman & Clements, 1984). Wait time between miscue and feedback is less than three seconds (Hoffman & Clements, 1984).	When a miscue disrupts meaning, the teacher waits to intervene until the end of the paragraph or sentence (Hoffman, 1979; Hoffman & Clements, 1984; McNaughton, 1981) or until the student has finished reading.

FIG 9-3   *Characteristic feedback vs. recommended feedback*

own. It may also be the case that the student needs to read a text that is easier—that is, the text itself supports more effective use of reading strategies. If students are having little difficulty constructing meaning, we recommend teachers respond as Florine's first teacher did—listen and enjoy the story in silence. If some miscues require attention, teachers ought to call students' attention to them *following* the reading.

If occasional support is necessary because a student stops reading (as Florine did) or you make a judgment that a miscue has resulted in significant meaning change that the student is unlikely to correct, semantic text-based prompts like the following may be useful in supporting a student's reading:

SEMANTIC PROMPT	READING SITUATION
"Keep reading and see what makes sense there."	Useful if you see semantic cues ahead that will help the student.
"Did that sentence make sense? Read it again so it makes sense this time."	Useful when students continue to read with no sign that they have not understood.
"Is there a clue in what you've read so far (or in the picture) that tells you what would make sense there?"	Useful when textual cues (or picture clues) prior to the difficulty will help the student understand the meaning of the word.

FIG 9-4   *Semantic prompt and reading situation*

Like the lessons about information sources and reading strategies in the previous section, these sorts of prompts alert students to precisely what strategy they could use or what source of information they ought to attend to. Just as we suggested to use instructional cloze strategies to involve students in making choices from among informational sources and reading strategies, we recommend that miscue feedback move students toward greater independence in their selection of strategies and sources of information. With this in mind, you can gradually replace the semantic prompts in Figure 9-4 with assists like the two that follow, alerting students that something needs to be done yet putting them on the road to deciding independently which strategy and/or source of information is appropriate in the reading situation.

1. What can you do when it doesn't make sense?

2. What information might you use to figure out what makes sense there?

Retrospective Miscue Analysis and Reader-Selected Miscues

There are two other techniques that teachers can use to provide students with feedback to miscues: *retrospective miscue analysis* and *reader-selected miscues*. Unlike the instructional situation in the previous discussion, neither technique requires the teacher's presence when students read; both occur after reading has been completed by students.

In retrospective miscue analysis (RMA), the teacher asks students to record themselves reading text and lets them know that they, the teacher and the student, will be discussing what has been read (Costello, 1992; Goodman, Watson & Burke, 1987; Marek, 1989; Miller & Woodley, 1983). When the teacher joins the student following the reading, the student first retells what has been read. Then the teacher and student listen to the tape together and talk about six to ten miscues, focusing on those that reveal the student's reading strengths until the student understands that miscues are natural and the process becomes more comfortable. These questions (from Costello, 1992) are often used to direct the conversation about each miscue that is highlighted during the RMA session:

1. Does the miscue make sense?

2. In what way does it make sense? OR In what way doesn't it make sense?

3. Did you change it after you made the miscue?

4. Why do you think you made this miscue?

5. Think of as many possible reasons for this miscue as you can.

Costello has worked with middle school students in what she refers to as "collaborative retrospective miscue analysis" (1992). After group or whole class work in which students are taught about miscues and how they occur and lessons on effective and ineffective strategies that result in miscues, one student is taped reading aloud and his peers work together with the student to discuss the miscues, again using the kinds of questions listed above. As students work together, they usually become quite sophisticated in their understanding of miscues and the reading process, all of which they can draw on in their own independent reading. Costello's transcripts of the students working on their own without the teacher even present show that children learn to distinguish between miscues that need to be corrected and those that don't and to identify the sources of miscues.

Teachers can also provide assistance to students about miscues made during silent reading using an instructional strategy called "reader selected miscues" (Hoge, 1983; Watson, 1978). Students identify the miscues they've made during silent reading, and the teacher helps them resolve the miscues by focusing on strategies for identifying words and their meanings. For this procedure:

1. Prior to reading, students are provided with slips of paper or markers about the size of bookmarks.

2. As students read, they insert the markers in the page where they encounter difficulties or make miscues.

3. At the end of the reading period, students select three to five miscues for attention.

4. Students copy the sentences containing miscues onto the markers and underline the difficult words or phrases.

5. On the other side of the marker, students write their names, the page number from which the sentence was copied, and, if students are reading various texts, the title of the text.

Occasionally, when students are unable to identify their difficulties during reading, they need to be taught how to do so. We recommend that these students engage in lessons like those suggested in the first section of the chapter or that you utilize retrospective miscue analysis techniques, helping students learn to listen to taped reading in order to locate words and sentences that don't make sense.

Once you have collected the markers from the students, you can categorize them to determine common difficulties or patterns of difficulties across students. Instruction focuses on helping students identify options available to them when they have difficulties like those they've marked. That is, as the students read a number of sentences that reveal a similar difficulty, the class can discuss possible reading strategies or language information that might help in these and similar situations. The goal is to help students learn to select and use informational sources and reading strategies given the types of miscues they have identified, though learning specific new words and word meanings may occur in the process.

It is also occasionally useful to discuss miscues that students have either resolved for themselves or judged as less important to discuss than others. Students could, for example, be asked to mark and record words they didn't understand initially but came to understand as they read. These could be discussed using the reader-selected miscue procedures. Such discussions heighten student awareness of the positive strategies they do use and help them understand that all readers encounter difficulties that make little or no difference to their construction of meaning.

Reader-selected miscues is an instructional strategy with a number of features we believe are important in a lesson highlighting making sense of words in text. First, seeing patterns in their own miscues helps students understand that there are widely applicable strategies for making sense of words in text. Second, such a lesson focuses on students' needs. Students decide for themselves whether or not a miscue has caused a loss of meaning or whether they need assistance. Third, there is great potential for vocabulary development, vocabulary that the students themselves have identified as important to understanding the text. (See Stansell's reader-selected vocabulary procedure, 1987.) Revisiting new or unusual vocabulary following reading helps students develop their problem-solving abilities regarding vocabulary (Blachowicz & Lee, 1991). As teachers facilitate students' collaborative problem solving, the sense of a community of readers will continue to develop.

Learning Words and Other Text Features

There is a great deal of controversy over how to teach emergent readers. (For a recent sampling of views, see Adams, 1990; Goodman, 1993; Goswami & Bryant, 1990; Moustafa, 1993; Stahl, 1992; and Weaver, 1994.) The *commonsense* notion so popular in programs such as Hooked on Phonics is that children should begin with alphabetic recognition, learn the sounds associated with letters of the alphabet, learn to blend these in order to recognize words, then move from single word recognition to words in sentences and finally onto whole text (Mayher, 1990). This perspective is driven by adult logic, buttressed by behaviorist theory, that breaking learning into smaller "bits" makes learning easier. The problem is that this logic contradicts what we know from research about children's developmental learning, especially their learning of oral and written language.

Commonsense metaphors abound in education. Mayher cites these as the prevalent ones: "the learner as empty vessel to be filled with the content of education, the learner as maze runner who needs to master the basics of complex processes by learning them separately and in an appropriate sequence, the learner as sponge who absorbs information and squeezes it back out when appropriate, and the learner who practices through drills to develop good habits and avoid bad ones" (1990, p. 50). An analysis of most reading instruction today would reveal that it remains based on these commonsense notions about learning.

In this section, we will replace these "commonsense" notions about learning to read with "uncommonsense" ideas that are based on the study of *how children learn* to use oral and written language, rather than logical notions of *how they should be taught*. If we pay attention to how children learn as the basis for reading instruction, the following principles (adapted from Freppon & Dahl, 1991) become helpful guides, especially with regard to how teachers can support children's learning about the graphophonic system of written language. Learning graphophonics should be:

- *Learning centered:* Instead of using a predetermined sequence of information to organize graphophonic instruction, the teacher observes students' needs for information about print and takes advantage of the context and the need.

- *Learned in context:* Graphophonics is learned in whole language contexts—where students are reading and writing whole text that has communicative purpose.

- *Presented after foundational concepts are learned:* Until children understand that written language has communicative function and meaning to them, instruction focused on graphophonics does not make sense to them.

- *Meaning-based:* Instruction arises out of contexts in which children are using written language for purposes that have meaning for them.

- *Integrated with other written language concepts:* Learning about graphophonics occurs in settings in which students are likely to also be learning about other concepts of language at the same time. There is no need to separate or sequence the learning.

- *Learned through teacher demonstration:* During communicative events such as creating a new poem based on a charted poem that they can read, the teacher shows children how to think about graphophonics in spelling the new words they want to use to replace the old.

- *Learned through active involvement:* The teacher invites children into events where they have to figure out the puzzle of print for themselves. "What sounds do you hear in that word?"

- *Learning through multiple information sources:* The teacher provides many print experiences for the children and helps them connect the experiences. They also learn from each other, from repeatedly going back to familiar text, and from others.

In essence, these principles can be summarized as follows: Readers have language strengths they can rely on as they learn about the graphophonic system *if whole text is available to them* (Freepon & Dahl, 1991; Goodman, 1993; Mills, O'Keefe & Stephens, 1992; Nicholson, Bailey & McArthur, 1991). Whole texts embody graphophonic, syntactic, and semantic cues that permit emergent readers to use their already developed knowledge of language as they encounter the graphophonic system and other text features that they need to learn in order to become independent readers.

Unfortunately, many teachers assume that students cannot read whole text until they have achieved a certain level of mastery over phonics and word recognition. For students who have a great deal of difficulty learning about the graphophonic system in isolation, such an assumption is deadly. They may never read a whole text. When whole text is not available to students, they do not have the opportunity to learn how to orchestrate the graphophonic, syntactic, and semantic systems effectively during reading. And readers who have serious difficulty learning the graphophonic system can't learn to compensate for that difficulty because the syntactic and semantic cues that might support them are not available.

Here is an illustrative example. When fourteen-year-old Rich was referred for remedial help, we discovered that he could read only three words in the very simple story he was asked to read. When we read sentences to him from the text and asked him to reread the sentences, pointing to the words as he did so, we found that he had not even stabilized a voice–print match in reading. Rich was clearly still an emergent reader at the age of fourteen.

In investigating Rich's instructional history, we found that teachers had worked intensively with him for years, first struggling to teach him the alphabet and then teaching him sight words. When these strategies didn't work, a number of carefully structured phonics programs were used, one of which was still being used on a daily basis in his special education classroom. In our first meeting with him, Rich pleaded, "I want to learn to read. But please don't teach me the alphabet and the sounds again." When we asked if he had ever read a book, Rich looked at us in amazement and said, "How can I? I don't know any words."

Though Rich's case is certainly extreme because of his age, many younger students have experienced difficulty in learning the graphophonic system in isolation. As a result, they haven't had the opportunity to read whole texts, which has deprived them of the use of other language information in the process of reading.

Language information can be made available to students like these during assisted and repeated readings of predictable texts. However, teachers who use predictable texts (including dictated language experience stories) with emergent readers often report, "But the kids have just memorized the story!" Students may be aware of the same phenomenon; although Rich experienced great joy in reading a book for the first time on his own, he also reflected, "I'm just remembering it."

In these observations, teachers and students are identifying a real dilemma. On the one hand, ineffective readers often have experienced a lack of success learning the graphophonic system through isolated sound/letter and word instruction. On the other hand, some pay little or no attention to the graphophonic system when reading whole predictable text. Though the students feel a sense of satisfaction in being able to read a book independently, their learning of the graphophonic system cannot proceed satisfactorily if they do not attend to the graphophonic cues in the text.

Children who learn to read before they come to school often teach themselves by attending to graphophonic cues within stories they have memorized during parents' repeated readings. Undoubtedly, some poor readers will teach themselves in the same way once they have the opportunity to experience whole text. However, because of the passivity or resistance of many poor readers, teachers must frequently play an active role in drawing students' attention to the graphophonic cues.

The solution to this dilemma, helping students attend to the features of print or the graphophonic system within the context of whole texts and in settings that attend to the principles we cited previously, is the subject of this section. Our discussion begins with two instructional strategies, *pointing* and *graphophonic prediction check*, which can be used to draw students' attention to print features whether or not they have prior familiarity with the text that is being read. Then we will explore several instructional strategies that are dependent on student familiarity with the text that is being read during instruction.

Pointing

Pointing is useful in establishing a voice-print match for emerging readers. Children need to learn what words are and how they are represented in print. Although it would be nearly impossible to explain the concept of a word, it isn't difficult to demonstrate the concept so that children intuitively learn about the nature of words, word boundaries, and the directionality of print. As you read books to children, you simply point to the words as you read. In a group situation, this requires the use of "big books" or large print charts (published or teacher-made) so that all the children in the group can experience how the eyes (indicated through pointing) process print (indicated with the voice). Though pointing usually necessitates a bit of slowing down in oral reading, *avoid choppy, word-by-word reading*. At various points in their emergent reading, children learn different aspects of text features from observing teachers' demonstrations of the voice-print match. In the very same lesson, for example, some children may be learning that the English language is represented from left to right and top to bottom. Some may learn that a syllable does not necessarily make a word, a common hypothesis. Others may learn something they did not know about particular words. For example, a child who is observing the voice-print match of a sentence like "I've got to hurry home after school today" may realize for the first time that the spoken *gotta* is represented by two words in print.

Once students have established a basic voice-print match with familiar text, they should take over much of the pointing during reading. The student's behavior in pointing provides evaluative information for both the teacher and the child. For example, we observed a child in a classroom reading "Mary Had a Little Lamb," pointing to the text as she read. When she arrived at the line "And everywhere that Mary went," she pointed and read as follows:

(pointing) And everywhere that Mary went

(reading) And every where that Mary

Because the girl still had one word left to say and no words left to point to in the line, she knew something was wrong. The teacher, alert to an instructional opportunity, briefly introduced the notion of compound words, showing the girl how *every* and *where* were combined into a single word.

Pointing is often thought of as a bad habit and in some cases it is. However, for children who need to learn how language is represented in print, it is the only way teachers have of demonstrating that basic notion. It is also helpful for those children who find pointing the only way of keeping track of where they are in text.

For students who have a well-established sense of the voice-print match and can track print with their eyes, pointing is a bad habit. Revealing to students that grown-up readers do not point and reminding them not to point may solve the problem. However, pointing may be a symptom of an underlying problem, the student's belief that reading is a word-by-word process. In that case, you also need to address this underlying belief if pointing is to stop.

Graphophonic Prediction Check

Another technique to help students attend to graphophonic information is encouraging them to check predictions made on the basis of syntax and semantics against graphophonic cues in the text. In a first reading of a text, it is often easy to encourage such prediction checks.

For example, if children are reading *Did You Ever See?* (Einsel, 1962), every pair of pages in the book offers opportunities for prediction checks. One page reads, "Did you ever see a crow?" and the students in the class predicted that the paired page might say *blow, row, grow, hoe,* or *mow.* When the page was turned so that they could check their predictions, the students could tell from the picture that the author had chosen *row.* In order to call attention to the print cues, the teacher pointed to the word on the page and asked, "How else do you know this says *row*?" The children, of course, told the teacher that the word began with an *r.*

In familiar text, we've observed teachers encourage graphophonic prediction checks by placing Post-It notes over selected words in a big book or on a charted poem or song. As children read the sentence in which a word is covered, the teacher encourages them to think how the word looks or is spelled. Teachers who know their students' knowledge bases well can direct a series of questions to students in such a way that students with less knowledge are able to supply initial letters or just letters they hear while those with a more sophisticated knowledge base can fill the word out from there. The teacher writes their guesses on the Post-It and then removes it, placing it next to the actual text word so that the students can compare and complete the graphophonic prediction check.

The remaining instructional strategies in this chapter are most successful if students have experienced the text so many times that it is memorized, or almost so.

Sequencing Text Parts

One technique that directs attention to the features of print is usually perceived as a game by many students. They are provided with parts of a familiar text (sentences of a text or lines of a rhyme), one part to a "strip," and asked to put them in order or to sequence them in the way the author did.

When working with a group of students, the best materials to use for sequencing are precut tagboard sentence strips. The strips may be sequenced in a cardboard or plastic pocket chart, or lightweight magnet strips may be fastened on the back of each sentence strip for use on the blackboard. The size of the print on the sentence strips should permit everyone in the group to view the print easily. Sentence strips are available with preprinted lines, and when these lines are used, the writing is large enough for a whole class of students to see the words easily.

If students need a great deal of teacher support in attending to print features, the teacher may begin by asking the students, "What is the first sentence/line we need to look for?," and once the children have located a strip (correctly or incorrectly), "How do you know that says, '(whatever the sentence is)'?" The session can continue in the same way with the teacher asking what sentence ought to come next and inquiring about what features helped the children choose the strip.

As students suggest the features they are attending to, the teacher may reinforce their choices and call attention to others. If students' choice of a strip is incorrect, it's usually possible to reinforce the feature that the child was attending to and then call attention to another feature that makes the difference between the correct and incorrect choice. For example, if the children are sequencing lines from "One Two, Buckle My Shoe," and the child chooses "Seven, eight" instead of "Shut the door" and tells you that he found the strip with the letter *s* at the beginning, you can put the two strips next to each other and say something like, "Yes, you are right. This strip does have *s* at the beginning, but so does this one. How do you know which one says 'Shut the door'?" Or if the child's choice was correct in the first place, you might put the "Seven, eight" strip next to the correct one and ask, "Why did you choose this one instead of that one?"

Cut and paste worksheets are another way of engaging children independently in the same sequencing activity. The worksheet reproduced in Figure 9-5 was used with children who were highly familiar with *The Great Big Enormous Turnip* (Tolstoy, 1968). Rather than using the lengthy whole text, note that only the portion representing the important repeated sequence was used.

Here are several other related ideas:

- If the tagboard sentence strips are laminated, they last a very long time and may be left for children's independent use in a learning center. One teacher we know has about a dozen sequencing sets, each for a different predictable book or piece of poetry. The learning center is a frequent choice of her struggling readers.

- Small desk sets of sentence strips can also be made and laminated for repeated use by individual students. They can be stored in envelopes labeled with the name of the book from which the sentences were taken.

- Not all texts are useful for this sequencing activity, even when they are predictable. Bill Martin's sequence for *Brown Bear, Brown Bear* (Martin, 1970), for example, could be almost entirely rearranged without affecting the sense of the story. (On the other hand, we've observed students mix the sequence up for their friends to read, a great way to encourage attention to print.) Generally, try to locate books that have a logical sequence, one that wouldn't make sense or would sound odd if it were rearranged.

Matching

There are various matching activities that also help children attend to the print of a familiar text. Begin the lesson by rereading or perhaps sequencing a familiar text.

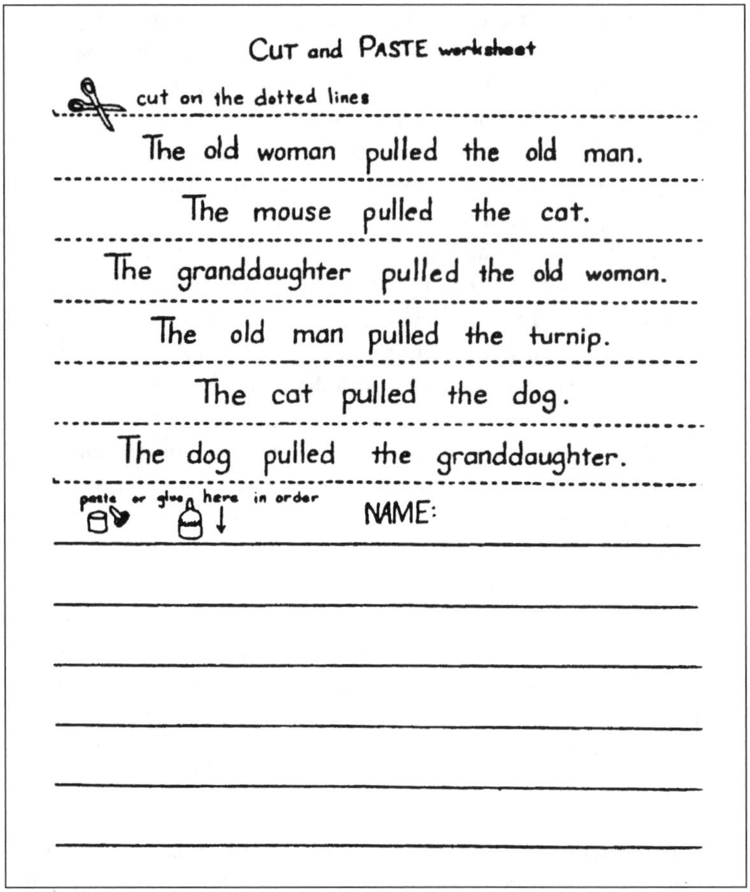

FIG 9-5 *Cut and paste worksheet*

Then pass out individual word cards to the children with important words from the selected text. For "Jack Be Nimble," you might pass out *Jack, jump, candlestick, nimble,* and *quick.* Each child in turn brings a card to the pocket chart and puts it in the pocket, covering up the matching word. If the child knows the word, she can then tell what it is; if not, she can read (while pointing) the verse from the beginning up to the word in order to discover what it is.

Games

A number of the techniques for calling attention to print can be incorporated into games. For example, *matching* is the basis of games such as Bingo and Concentration. Both games, however, are difficult for children unless they already have a fairly good knowledge of the print features of the text. Here are some examples of how the games may be prepared and played:

- Cloze sentences can be the basis for either a Bingo or a Concentration game. In a Bingo game for *The Great Big Enormous Turnip,* a square containing the sentence "The old _____ pulled the old woman" could be marked if the caller called *man*. In a Concentration game, the cloze sentence (The old _____ pulled the old woman.) and the cloze response (man) would be the matches.

- Bingo cards may be prepared with phrases or sentences from text children have read. For example, bingo cards could contain sentences and phrases from "The Three Little Pigs," such as "Little pig, little pig, let me come in" and "The first little pig." Cards for the person who is the caller could include matching sentences and phrases, such as "What the wolf said when he knocked on the pigs' door" and "The pig who made a house of straw." The same ideas can be used to construct a game of Concentration.

Other board games or games based on TV game shows can also be constructed, both to call students' attention to print and to extend their comprehension of literature. When you have an old board game you're about to dispose of or have a favorite game, consider how you might adapt it to encourage students to attend to text in their stories, poetry or songs. Encourage students to devise their own games as well (Mills, O'Keefe & Stephens, 1992).

Regenerating a Text

Engaging children in making a copy of a text is another activity that is helpful in calling children's attention to the way print is used in a familiar book. The activity can be very engrossing and will result in a text students can call their own, especially important in situations where students have few or no books in their homes.

The page reproduced in Figure 9-6 (DiMartini, 1987) is one of the pages of a Mother Goose collection that was regenerated by second- and third-grade students with learning disabilities. In regenerating the rhyme, the students filled in the blanks with the missing words; some retrieved a book of Mother Goose rhymes from the classroom library shelves, others copied from a chart showing the rhyme, and still others relied on their own knowledge of the spellings. The day after these books were completed and taken home, there were many stories about how they were read to brothers, sisters, and cousins during the previous evening.

Other teachers we know have engaged students in regenerating a single text such as a song they've learned in the classroom. Once the children have completed the text by filling in the blanks, they take the song sheet home and gather signatures on the back of the song sheet from people to whom they have read or sung the song.

Innovating on an Author's Structure

Instead of—or in addition to—regenerating texts using an author's original words, call students' attention to print by having them use an author's original structure to create new texts. Many predictable books, songs (Mateja, 1982), poetry, and the like are suitable for creating a new version of an original text.

BAA, BAA BLACK SHEEP

NAME ______________________

Fill in the blanks with a word that makes sense.

Baa, baa ______________ sheep,

have you any ______________?

Yes, sir, yes, sir, three bags full;

one for ______________,

and one for ______________,

and one for the little boy

who lives down the ______________.

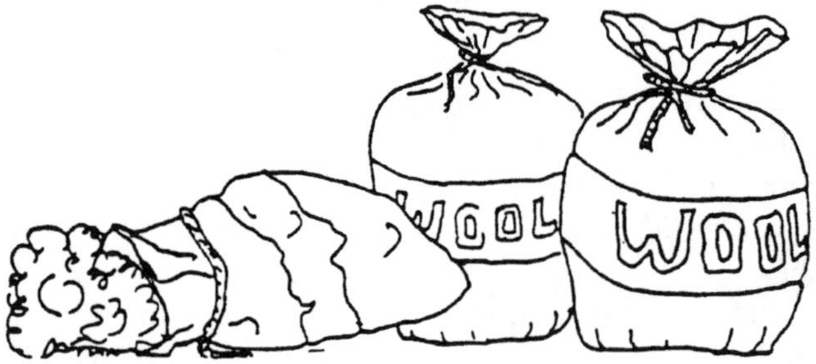

FIG 9-6 *Page from Mother Goose collection (DiMartini, 1987)*

A group of students with learning disabilities, for example, innovated on the structure of *Brown Bear* and dictated pages to their teacher for an illustrated Christmas version. The first page said, "Santa Claus, Santa Claus, what do you see?" and the last page, "We see presents under the tree!" As each page was dictated, the teacher involved the children in learning about the graphophonic system by asking them to spell some of the words borrowed from the book and by asking for the beginning letters in some of the words that were different from those in the book.

As another example, the worksheet reproduced in Figure 9-7 is an extension for *Q Is for Duck* (Elting & Folsom, 1980), a marvelous book to use with children who need to attend to graphophonic cues. This worksheet borrows the author's original structure and substitutes words that most students enjoy: *monsters*, *dinosaurs*, and the like. By the end of the worksheet the child is choosing all the words.

Using the author's structure to produce a new text is valuable not only for children who are learning about the graphophonic system but also for children

```
Name _____

_____ is for Monster.  Why?
Because _____
_____

_____ is for Dinosaur.  Why?
Because _____
_____

_____ is for Gorilla.  Why?
Because _____
_____

_____ is for Teacher.  Why?
Because _____
_____

_____ is for _____ Why?
Because _____
_____
```

FIG 9-7   *Extension for* Q Is for Duck *(Rhodes, 1985; Elting & Folsom, 1980)*

who are learning about other features of print. For instance, two fourth-grade girls who were writing another version of *Fire! Fire! Said Mrs. McGuire* (Martin, 1970) referred to the original text to figure out how to use quotation marks in the version they worked out:

> "Snow! Snow!" said Ms. Low. "Where? Where?" said Mr. Glare. "Up there!" said Mrs. Pear. "In the sky!" said Mr. Li. "Get the Shovel!" said Mrs. Lovel. "Scoop it up!" said Mr. Lup.

Writing

Regenerating a text and innovating on an author's structure both involve students in writing. In particular, the activities focus student attention on how to represent words in text. In general, writing is an excellent way to get children involved in attending to print. The old adage "I do and I understand" is of assistance in considering the relationship between writing and reading. Children who write begin to pay greater attention to the way authors spell words. When writing does not generate greater interest in how words are spelled (sometimes the case among struggling readers), teachers can work with small groups and individuals during writing time to focus more attention on how authors spell words in books. In the instructional routine for Reading Recovery, the portion of the lesson where students write a sentence related to the text they have read serves this purpose. This portion of the lesson is based on Clay's theory about how writing affects reading: "Early writing serves to organize the visual analysis for print, and to strengthen important memoric strategies" (Clay, 1982, p. 210). The information on spelling instruction in this book will also help you understand how to generate this attention in students who need such a boost.

Reading Alternate Versions of a Text

Often, different versions of children's text exist in literature, especially when the text is a folktale, fairy tale, rhyme, song, tall tale, fable, or some other literary gem that has been passed on for years. Sometimes there are major differences between versions and sometimes only minor ones. For emergent readers, those versions that feature minor differences in wording are most suitable. When students read the second text, they should find that they can handle it as well as the first version because both are so similar. Finding the differences between the versions and wondering about them is intriguing. Some book pairs with minor variations, which students may enjoy exploring, include:

P. Adams. *There Was an Old Lady Who Swallowed a Fly*. New York: Grosset & Dunlap, 1973.

R. Boone and A. Mills. *I Know an Old Lady*. New York: Rand McNally, 1961.

S. Kellogg. *There Was an Old Woman*. New York: Parents' Magazine Press, 1974.

N. B. Westcott. *I Know an Old Lady Who Swallowed a Fly*. Boston: Little, Brown, 1980.

B. S. de Regniers. *Catch a Little Fox*. New York: Seabury Press, 1970.

J. Langstaff. *Oh, A-Hunting We Will Go*. New York: Atheneum, 1974.

R. Quackenbush. *Go Tell Aunt Rhody*. Philadelphia: J. B. Lippincott, 1973.

Aliki. *Go Tell Aunt Rhody*. New York: Macmillan, 1974.

Older emergent readers also enjoy exploring different versions of texts and speculating about the reasons for the variations. For this purpose, folktales such as "The Three Bears" and "The Billy Goats Gruff" are easy to find in many versions. Your students may want to predict which version might be more popular with younger children and find out whether they are right by reading various versions to young children, leading them in a discussion of the versions, and taking a vote on their favorites.

10 *Sharing and Extending Text*
Postreading Instruction

Postreading instruction follows the reading of some text, a story, a poem, or some other kind of reading material. Typically, postreading activities include a discussion of what's been read. These discussions—which could be characterized as a "test" of students' comprehension (Crafton, 1982)—often follow a pattern: the teacher asks a question ("Mary, what did he do then?"); a student replies ("He went back to his house."); the teacher evaluates the students' response ("Are you sure? Tom . . . ?") (Buttery & Powell, 1978; Kitagawa, 1982; Lehr, 1984). Worksheets also figure prominently in traditional approaches to postreading instruction. From our perspective, however, these sorts of activities encourage a narrow view of the purposes and processes of reading. In particular, they require students to read for someone else's purposes. The underlying assumption is that students' roles as readers is to reproduce meaning using the text as a template.

In this chapter, we discuss postreading instructional strategies that encourage the sharing and extending of comprehension as an alternative to the traditional comprehension-testing activities that dominate most postreading instruction. We suggest a variety of ways to engage students in thinking about the text after reading. Many of the activities will be familiar; they're frequently referred to as *enrichment* activities, the sorts of activities that are done "if there's time." It's our position, however, that sharing and extending comprehension with a community of readers is basic to improving reading comprehension, including what are considered lower "levels" of comprehension. Ryan and Torrance, for example, improved the abilities of the poor readers in a seventh-grade class 7.5 months for every month of instruction by engaging them in activities such as writing new endings for stories, writing plays, and making dioramas (1967). Sharing and extending activities deserve to be thought of as central to reading instruction rather than enrichment.

Much of what we'll recommend depends on the development of a community of readers who share their understanding of texts with each other. The readers with whom you work may not have any sense of community at first, but sharing and extending activities, and time, will help to develop a community of readers. Once that sense of a community develops, the sharing and extending of comprehension begins to grow more from the students' own purposes and less from teachers' assignments.

Helping students better understand what they've read and integrate what they've read with what they already know is the general goal of postreading instruction and, from our perspective, this is the meaning of reading comprehension. To achieve this general goal, we consider three more specific goals for students as a way to plan postreading instruction:

1. Students reflect on what it is that they've learned or experienced (and what they haven't learned or experienced) in reading a text.

2. Students extend their comprehension of the text by rethinking the text.

3. Students relate texts not only to their lives but also to other texts they have read, seen, or heard.

We will address these goals, often in an integrated way, throughout this chapter. The first and major section of the chapter presents instructional strategies designed to help students share and extend their comprehension of a *single text* and, in the process, become a community of readers. In the second section, we discuss how these same instructional strategies can be used productively with *multiple texts or text sets*. Finally, we'll discuss situations in which students must comprehend text for someone else's purposes; in particular, when they must prepare for some school assignment, such as an end-of-the-chapter assignment or a test.

Sharing and Extending a Text

As you read this chapter and this portion of the chapter in particular, we recommend that you reconceptualize your role as a teacher so that you and your students come together as a community of readers (see Chapter 6) who share your understandings of text. Students' comprehension of text will change as they talk with others about their understanding and insights about a text. An adult who takes the role of fellow reader/comprehender can add another, often more sophisticated, point of view to such discussions. Unless teachers share their insights about the text as participants in the discussion, students will view the situation as a test of their comprehension, especially if their teachers adopt the traditional role of teacher-asking-questions-about-the-text. Thus, in the following lessons, think about responding as participants—as a reader does to the text, preferably in the same manner in which you have asked the student to respond. In other words, if you have asked the student to sketch a response to the text, you should sketch a response as well. Try consistently to assume the role of another reader in a community of readers. Your participation will contribute to both the development of the community and students' knowledge about the nature of text and proficient reading.

Oral Sharing and Extending

Certainly the most common way of sharing and extending comprehension is by means of talk about a text. However, the usual pattern of teacher question, student answer, teacher evaluation must be broken in order to help students approach postreading activity as a time in which their meaning of text is further enriched rather than as a time when their understanding of the text will be tested. The alternative is built on a transactional theory (Rosenblatt, 1978) and often referred to as "reader response" (Karolides, 1992).

In the years since we wrote the first edition of this book, interest in implementing transactional theory in the classroom has increased significantly, often taking the form of literature group discussions, also called Literature Circles, Literature Studies, Book Clubs, or other terms that reflect the response of readers to literature. In essence, students who are reading a piece of literature gather after they've read the literature (if it is a brief piece) or several times in the process of reading the literature and have what Peterson and Eeds refer to as "grand conversations" about the book (1990). Grand conversations happen in classrooms where good literature prevails and the precious commodity of time is allotted for students to dialogue about literature and other text they've read. Peterson and Eeds suggest two "simple" rules for promoting effective dialogue:

> The first (rule) is to respect the interpretations of others and help in their development whenever possible. It is not necessary to adopt other interpretations, but everyone must be obliged to listen to them and give them full consideration. The second rule is that participants—teachers or students—must not enter the dialogue with a plot in mind. Spontaneity is essential. It is the immediacy of the responding, and the listening, that moves participants to insights that cannot be realized through solitary thinking. (Peterson & Eeds, 1990, p. 22)

Peterson and Eeds note that teachers can prepare for dialogue or discussion by considering the possibilities for interpretation that are likely to arise, but that it's important for teachers to maintain an open stance to what happens in the course of the dialogue and to new ideas about the text as well (1990). (See Eeds & Peterson, 1991, for examples of what teachers learn during dialogue with students.) Their book as well as Short and Pierce's book, *Talking About Books* (1990), contain many examples of elementary and middle school students in dialogue with each other over both narrative and informational books.

Based on a synthesis of much of the research done in the National Research Center on Literature Teaching and Learning, Langer (1994) suggests some general instructional guidelines that are useful for teachers attempting to shift from "testing for content" models of interacting with students about a text to a transactional or reader response model:

1. Use class meetings as a time for students to explore possibilities and develop understandings as opposed to recounting already acquired meanings (what they remember) and teaching what they've left out.

2. Keep students' understandings at the center of focus. Always begin with their initial impressions. This will validate their own attempts to understand and is the most productive place for them to begin to build and refine meaning.

3. Instruction, the help that moves beyond students' initial impressions, involves scaffolding their ideas, guiding them in ways to hear each other—to discuss and think. Teachers need to be listeners, responders, and helpers rather than information-givers.

4. Encourage wonderings and hunches even more than absolutes. They are part of the process of understanding literature. Whenever possible, ask questions that tap students' knowledge. Pick up on what they say rather than following your own agenda or the sequence of the piece you are reading.

5. Encourage students to develop their own well-formed interpretations and gain vision from others. There is more than one way to interpret any piece of literature.

6. Remember that questioning, probing, and leaving room for future possible interpretations is at the heart of critical thinking in literature. Teachers as well as students need to be open to possible meanings; in literary experiences there are no preconceived ends or final inviolable interpretations.

7. Provide scaffolds that help students learn to listen and speak to one another and to think about their own developing understandings.

8. Help students engage in more mature literary discussions by eliciting their own responses, asking for clarification, inviting participation, and guiding them in sustaining the discussion.

9. Help students think in more mature ways by guiding them to focus their concerns; shape the points they wish to make; link their ideas with what they have already discussed, read, or experienced; think about their issues in more complex ways (Langer, 1994, pp. 207–208).

There are many instructional features that can be varied and explored as teachers implement reader response in the classroom, including the text, the degree of structure provided to students, and the teacher's role. Leal, for example, found that informational storybooks (e.g. a narrative like *How to Dig a Hole to the Other Side of the World* (McNulty, 1979) that contains scientific information) had great potential to enhance student discussion when children worked with peers in literature-sharing groups (1993). Goldenberg identified specific instructional elements and conversational elements that characterize what he refers to as "instructional conversations" (1993). These elements may provide some teachers with a basis for examining their own progress in leading discussions of literature and other texts. For teachers who want to move from teacher-led to peer-led literature discussions, Wiencek and O'Flahavan (1994) offer useful suggestions (see Almasi, 1995, for research evidence supporting these practices). Other teachers provide examples of how to assist students who do not participate in the group dialogue about books and how to assist students when it appears that their book talk is not what the teacher hoped for (Gilles, Dickenson, McBride & VanDover, 1994; Roller & Beed, 1994).

When implementing literature discussions with struggling readers, you may find, like Wollman-Bonilla, that struggling readers do not discuss books as freely and effectively as more effective readers (1994). In such cases, you'll need to consider how to build trust among students (Close, 1990), how to demonstrate what you mean by grand conversations (perhaps by consciously forming groups that include both good and struggling readers as done in a study by Goatley, Brock & Raphael, 1995), how to "talk about talk" (Heath, 1983)—directly providing instruction about how to initiate and sustain dialogue about books, and how to establish discussion structures that will initially support students.

Asking students to formulate questions based on their reading—questions to which they would like to hear everyone else respond—is one way to provide more structure for children's discussions (Kitagawa, 1982; Singer, 1978). At first, the questions may be the sort that only require single, short, text-based answers. Formulating your own questions along with students will give you an opportunity to demonstrate the questioning process (see the reading conference questions in Chapter 8) and encourage more open-ended discussion. However, students may also need explicit instruction to help them learn to ask productive questions. You might, for example, have students decide on a set of questions that are most likely to involve them in grand conversations about the book. If you want to help students consider the nature of their questions with the goal of improving them, hold a debriefing session on questions at the conclusion of the discussion. Ask "Which questions made us think the most? Why?" or "Could some of the questions be changed to make us think about the relationship of what we read to our own experiences? How?"

Another structural support is for each participant (including the teacher) to write one interesting, important, or confusing thing about the book, share that with the rest of the group, and invite the group to comment on it or to "say something" (Harste, 1982). Or you might ask students to jot down questions or points of agreement and disagreement with the author, share one or more of these with the rest of the group, and invite reaction from the group (Burke, 1982). If the reading selection stimulates a debate, the points of agreement and disagreement might be used to establish pro and con debate panels (Brenneman, 1985). Some teachers have found a way to help students metacognitively consider their talk in these situations by referring to discussion starters (such as identifying an important thing or a question) as a "seed" (Villaume et al., 1994). "More effective seeds" for discussion grow into lots of discussion while "less effective seeds" result in very little discussion.

Another way to engage students in oral sharing and extending, especially of expository material, is to return to the already-know (K-W-L) statements, questions, and predictions generated during prereading instruction. Guide students' attention back to the prereading lesson and encourage them to reflect on what was discussed before the reading in light of their reading. When their questions aren't answered by their reading of the text, encourage students to consider why. In your role as participant, you can offer suggestions about why the answers haven't been found as well. When predictions aren't borne out, encourage students to think about why. Ask students to compare their prereading discussion with what they learned from the text; be sure to share what you have learned so they can see you in a role as a learner too. Help them learn to listen well to each other and to relate one idea to another by demonstrating these skills yourself and by asking questions such as, "Tony, how did what you just said relate to what Ann said earlier?" or "You know, what you just said makes me think about . . ."

Oral retelling of texts, because students must compose retellings in their own words, also provides them with opportunities to extend their understanding of a text's meaning (Brown & Cambourne, 1987; Y. Goodman, 1982). Although you'll need to be careful that the retelling doesn't feel like a test for an individual when all the students have read the same text, a retelling may be used to *initiate* the sharing and extending of a single text. After one student has completed a retelling to which everyone else has listened (including the teacher for purposes of assessment), the rest of the group (including the teacher) might write questions for the student. Some questions can encourage students to expand on something that was only mentioned in the retelling, others can encourage the student to reflect on feelings or attitudes toward some part of what was retold, and still other questions can encourage relating the text to other texts the group has read. In turn, the student being questioned is free to turn the question back to the questioner, e.g., "I've told you what I think about what Jefferson did. What do you think?"

Text dramatization is another way of orally sharing and extending students' comprehension of text (Flynn & Carr, 1994; Heinig, 1992; Hendersen & Shanker, 1978; Micinatti & Phelps, 1980; Miller & Mason, 1983; Vawter & Vancil, 1980). For the purposes of sharing and extending comprehension, dramatization need not become a theatrical production. Informal, quickly devised dramatization is less time-consuming and often equally effective in achieving sharing and extending. Martinez, for example, describes how spontaneous, child-initiated, dramatic story reenactments in a low-socioeconomic kindergarten classroom contributed to children's knowledge of literature and their interpretation of it (1993). Flynn and Carr show how "teaching-in-role" can engage students in thinking about text from very different perspectives without what Carr used to consider the "painful, time-consuming preparations" of doing drama in the classroom (1994). They provide an extended example of how a teacher assumed the role of the mother in *Lon Po Po* (Young, 1990) and engaged the students in thinking about the story as the mother's children. However, students can also benefit from lengthier interactions with books as Wolf shows in her description of how three "labeled" boys prepared a Readers Theatre production of a scene from *Tikki Tikki Tembo* (Mosel, 1968) over a period of time (1993). She notes that it was in their *talk* and negotiation with each other over how to portray a scene from the book that the boys came to be "capable interpreters of text" (Wolf, 1993, p. 545).

Dramatization can take a variety of forms—spontaneous story reenactments, Readers Theatre, role playing, putting on a play, acting out mime, creating a flannel board story. Different students might decide to dramatize different parts of the same text. Instead of sticking close to the original text, they might try recasting it in the form of a monologue or dialogue in which students take different points of view (Bixby et al., 1983; Edwards, 1991). Students might, for example, dramatize the troll talking to himself about how he might capture the largest billy goat or about what the troll might do to amuse himself while he waits for the billy goats to cross his bridge (Heinig, 1992). Reading a book that takes an alternative point of view such as *The True Story of the Three Little Pigs* (Scieszka, 1989) will help students understand what it means to adopt a character's point of view in other stories. As students engage in activities such as these, encourage them to think about what they've experienced by dramatizing the text, why they chose to dramatize particular portions of text over other portions, problems they encountered in carrying out the dramatization, and what they might do differently next time.

Written Sharing and Extending

All that we've said about the theory and practice of oral sharing and extending can be applied to written sharing and extending. Writing, which by its very nature is reflective, can play a role in extending the comprehension of text (Hennings, 1982; Squire, 1983; Stotsky, 1983). Some researchers argue that writing has greater potential to stimulate thinking about text than talk does (Atwell, 1987). When Atwell began her exploration of dialogue journals in her classroom, she noted: "I suspected kids' written responses to books would go deeper than their talk; that writing would give them time to consider their thinking and that thoughts captured would spark new insights" (1987, p. 165). Moving from text that's been read, to reflecting on text in writing requires interpretation, even if the reader chooses to write a summary of the text. As students write summaries of what they've read (Taylor, 1984), for example, they learn to make decisions about what's important to represent in a summary and to represent the content, both of which require interpretation. This is why no two students will write the same summary even if they've read the same text.

Although writing alone has the potential to extend students' comprehension of a text, sharing students' writings about literature has even greater potential for extending comprehension. Sharing the written text with others moves individual writers beyond their interpretation and introduces others' interpretations into the mix. As you will see in this section, sharing of writing can be done through reading others' interpretations or it can be done orally, combining written and oral reader response.

Just as literature circles or discussions have received a great deal of attention in the reader response literature, so have literature response journals—also known as "literary journals," "reading logs," and "dialogue journals," depending on the nature of the written response. We will attempt to summarize what has been learned by researchers (who are often teachers in their own classrooms) about how to support students' interpretations of literature in writing, the relationship between written response and oral, how teachers can look for patterns of response in students' writings about literature as a way to consider what students need to learn, and how teachers and students can respond to students' literature responses. And although we will use the term "literature" throughout this section for the sake of expediency, teachers can do all of what is discussed here with a wide variety of text and media. (See Parsons, 1990, for the use of response journals to respond to film, television, rock videos, advertising, newspapers, and magazines.)

In order to figure out how to support students' responses to literature in writing, it's helpful to consider what researchers have observed about the patterns of students' responses in literary journals. The list that follows is a compilation of response categories that two researchers (Dekker, 1991; Hancock, 1992, 1993) have uncovered as they categorized the responses that students made to literature when writing regularly about what they read:

Personal meaning-making: Responses that reveal that students are constructing meaning for themselves from their reading of text.

Retelling: Summarizing what has happened in the story, usually in the first part of the story (Barone, 1990).

Making inferences: Insights regarding the feelings, thoughts, and motives of story characters.

Prediction and validation: Speculation about what is going to happen as the story unfolds.

Expressing wonder or confusion: Questions or wonderings about what is happening in the story.

Personal experience: Connections made between something in the book and the reader's life.

Philosophical reflection: The reader's reflections on personal values and convictions that the story stirs.

Character and plot involvement: Interactions with or reactions to the characters and story elements.

Character interaction: Empathetic involvement with a character.

Character assessment: Judgments about the actions or values of a character measured against the reader's personal standards.

Story evaluation: Personal involvement or reaction to the story as a whole with no rationale (simple evaluation) or to specific elements of the story such as location, events, or time (but not character) with rationale.

Literary evaluation or criticism: Acknowledgment of personal literary tastes or connections between the current story and other stories.

Categories that have arisen from the study of children's responses to literature response journals are useful to teachers as they analyze their students' responses; they help teachers determine how students are currently responding and what other types of responses might occur with teacher support. The types of responses that students make to literature are dependent on factors such as the students' ages and developmental capabilities, where they are in the book (e.g. at the beginning of the book, more summaries of information can be expected), how they perceive the task of journal writing (as a test of what they've remembered or as an opportunity to reflect), and even the students' ease with the process of writing.

Teachers have developed a variety of ways of supporting students in light of these factors. Some simply give students time to learn to dig deeper in their responses to literature (not only over the course of the school year but also each time the reader begins a new book) while others begin by providing supports such as prompts that are gradually withdrawn. Some provide supports for children's thinking by recommending a particular format such as a double-entry journal (Barone, 1990) where students copy or paraphrase a quote from the book on one side and comment on the quote on the other side. Others provide frequent written responses back to the reader-responder (Atwell, 1987; Barone, 1990; Farris, 1989; Hancock, 1993); still others establish situations in which children respond to each other or engage in written conversation with each other about a book they are reading (Close, 1990; Dekker, 1991; Hancock, 1993). Some teachers recommend open-ended prompts as a way to either start children in response journals or support them in moving beyond the responses that they have been making (Angletti, 1991; Farris, 1989; Kelly, 1990). Some contend, because the journal is private, that written response should be viewed as a precursor to literature discussion groups (Dekker, 1991; Hancock, 1993; Kirby & Liner, 1981) while others view discussion as a precursor to learning to respond effectively in writing (Kelly, 1990). What seems to matter most is that the teacher carefully consider the nature of students' responses to literature in light of her standards for literature response and what factors might be attended to when the teacher would like students to respond to literature in more sophisticated ways. It's the teacher's knowledge of the range of possible responses, knowledge of her students, and understanding of how the context affects literature response that will work together to positively affect how students share and extend their comprehension through writing in literature response journals.

Another interesting way to assist students in extending their comprehension of text through writing is to involve them in innovating on the author's text or text structure. If, for example, students have just read a historical novel, they might write a newspaper piece that reports the events in the book like a newspaper columnist. Readers Theatre, mentioned earlier because it also involves oral interpretation, is another example of innovating on the author's text. For example, a group of Title I second and third graders who had just read a story called *The Missing Necklace* (Moore, 1971) were dictating the story as a script when they came across these sentences: "Mrs. Pig wanted her friends to come to a picnic lunch. She called and asked them" (p. 2). Because a script naturally demands more conversation between characters than a story does, the children decided to represent the two original sentences in their script as follows:

Narrator: Mrs. Pig wanted to have her friends come over to have a picnic.
Mrs. Pig: Will you come to my picnic, chipmunk?
Chipmunk: Yes, I will be there.
Mrs. Pig: Do you want to come to my picnic lunch, sheep?

Sheep: Yes, Mrs. Pig, I'll be right over!

Mrs. Pig: Hello, turtles, will you come to my picnic lunch?

Turtles: Yes, we'll be right over, Mrs. Pig.

Mrs. Pig: Cat, will you come to my picnic lunch?

Cat: I'll be right over, Mrs. Pig.

This might not seem like much of an accomplishment, but in order to dictate this portion of the script to the teacher, the children had to recall all the characters that attended the picnic and had to be phoned, and then create the conversations Mrs. Pig might have had with each of them. The discussion that the children engaged in as they made decisions about how to write the script engaged them in textual interpretation and extended their comprehension of this scene in the story.

Adding to a text and writing an alternative version are other ways to innovate on an author's story and to share and extend comprehension of texts. Creating new text demands that students consider what the author has written so that the new text "fits" with the old. Some software packages provide a playful way for children to explore ways to innovate on published stories by authors they love. (For examples, see Wepner, 1993.) While most struggling readers will find writing texts in which the new *content* is consistent with the author's challenging enough, some will also benefit from the additional challenge of trying to emulate the author's *style*. Invite these students to write new text so that readers will not be able to differentiate between their work and that of the original author.

Students can write a new section to fit into a text they've already read, a new episode to add to a story, a stanza to add to a poem, more information to include in an expository piece, and so on. One of our favorite "innovating on the author's text" activities is to engage students in writing their own ending to a story before they've read the author's ending. This lesson works best as part of a week-long learning center activity. First, select a story that has a point near the end where a variety of predictions about the story's ending can be made. (One we like to use with secondary students is Thurber's short story "Unicorn in the Garden"; our prediction point is just as the police and psychiatrist arrive.) Make a copy of the story with the ending cut off at the prediction point you've selected and place it in the learning center. You might leave the story at the center on Monday and give students until Thursday to read it and write an ending. Students can put their endings in a folder with a warning sign on the cover: "Do not read until you have written your own ending!" On Friday, students share their endings orally and discuss the similarities and differences across endings, what sorts of things led them to end the story in the way they did, and so on. When students read the author's ending, it usually inspires further discussion. Sometimes students prefer one of their endings to the author's.

When students share and talk about the writing in which they have innovated on the author's text, the discussion often takes them far from the original text. When that happens, it's helpful to end the discussion with a question that brings students back to the original text, e.g., "What do you understand better in this text (or about what this author did to create the text) as a result of our discussion?"

Sharing and Extending Through Graphic Representation and Visual Art

Visual art (drawing, painting, clay sculpture, dioramas, and the like) has long been used in many classrooms to represent what students have learned from an experience, including from reading a text. Some teachers specialize in creative ways of engaging students in visually representing what they have learned from reading. Students usually enjoy such projects and benefit from them personally, especially when visual art is a favored means of expression for a particular student (often the case with struggling readers). However, visual art can be considered as a way for students, even for those not artistically inclined, to construct meaning for themselves and to extend meaning about text.

One of us asked a class of fourth and fifth graders, for example, to sketch any scene they wanted to from *The Sign of the Beaver* (Speare, 1983), a book that had been the read-aloud (and one of the students' choices for independent reading) in the classroom for a couple of weeks. After the students and the teacher completed their sketches (with many of us returning to the story to reread the scene we decided upon), we organized the sketches into the sequence in which the events/scenes had occurred in the story, temporarily taping them to a free wall in the classroom. In the process of doing sketches, we constructed new meanings for ourselves by virtue of making decisions about what scene to represent, and details to include in the scene both from memory of the story and from returning to read the appropriate portion of the story.

The next portion of the lesson served to extend everyone's comprehension of the text, including the teacher's. The class began with a lively discussion of "what we noticed" about the scenes that were taped to the wall. About one fifth of the sketches were of Matt being stung by bees as he tried to steal honey from a beehive in a tree (with all of these representing different points in the event), while the next most represented scene was of Matt's rifle being stolen. The discussion ranged from why so many people had drawn the bee-stinging scene (for many it was the compelling initial event of the entire story), to why some scenes were not represented at all, to the fact that the sketches of Matt's rifle being stolen were actually a representation of the readers' images of what had happened since the event was not described in the book. As we talked about what we noticed for almost an hour as a whole class, the students and teacher returned again and again to the book, reading portions of it aloud to connect the author's words with the readers' visual images in these sketches.

We've involved students of all ages in sketching after reading both narrative and expository materials (even texts about how to study) with impressive results. In this lesson, students spend far more time sharing and extending their comprehension of the text than in producing the sketches. Talk that encourages students to share and extend comprehension can occur after sketching, as it did in the previous example, or it can occur in the process of producing the sketch. In a sketch-to-stretch (Siegel, 1984) lesson, Whitin observed four of her seventh-grade students working in a group together to decide on a visual representation of *Summer of the*

Monkeys (Rawls, 1976) that they would then present to the whole class for discussion (1994). During the collaborative decision-making that resulted in the visual representation they presented to the class, the four extended each other's comprehension of the story. Further extension of their comprehension occurred during the discussion that followed presentation of their sketches to the class.

Although we must personally confess a lack of expertise with visual art other than informal uses of it as we've shown above, others who have a good foundation in visual art have recommended the study of artists and their work as a powerful means of helping students become more effective readers and writers. Ann Alejandro tells a compelling story of her work in a poor rural area of Texas with second and third graders in which she involved them in exploring well-known (but not to the children) art works and their painters. In her classroom, she used art to help students learn to see and observe, noting that "when we analyze the small components of paintings—dots, circles, curved lines, straight lines, texture, angles, genre or media, use of color, mood, atmosphere, and even conflict of character or plot—we use thought processes similar to (readers who analyze) components of text (in order to comprehend)" (Alejandro, 1994, p. 13). This teacher used the lure and beauty of paintings to help children learn the processes of analysis and critique as well as to understand how they could and did use those same skills in the processes of reading and writing. Although her focus was on longer-term learning, Alejandro also indicated the standardized test scores of her students showed remarkable gains in spite of her refusal to drill them on specific reading and test-taking skills.

Instructional strategies that involve the graphic representation of text are also useful in helping students construct and share meaning, extending their comprehension of text in the process. Mapping (Davidson, 1982) or webbing (Freedman & Reynolds, 1980; Gold, 1984; Swaby, 1984) is an instructional strategy that combines writing and graphic representation. Students are asked to recall the major points of an expository text or some of the elements of a narrative text and to organize these graphically to represent their relationship. Essentially, this is a postreading, student-produced graphic organizer much like the graphic organizer that teachers present to students prior to reading. Students often go beyond the major points or elements of the text and add less significant ones, mapping them so that their relationships to each other and to the major points in the text are also apparent.

Johnson and Louis provide many suggestions for graphic representation that students enjoy such as literary sociograms, plot profiles, story maps, and literary report cards (1987). We have had very successful discussions with students on the basis of literary sociograms. Small groups of students who have read the same book create labeled construction paper circles to represent each character in a book, even using the size of the circle to represent the character's importance to the story. They then arrange these circles on a sheet of paper (the arrangement itself engenders conversation about character relationships), drawing and labeling relationship arrows to show how they think characters were related to each other. As children become accustomed to this strategy, they can experiment with many variations such as using distance between circles (representing the emotional connection of characters to each other), the directionality of arrows (one way only or both ways), the use of solid and broken lines (representing stated or inferred relationships), and so forth. When we have used this instructional strategy with students, we have experienced what Johnson and Louis describe: "The resulting diagrams are often childishly wobbly and apparently disorganized, but they are always accompanied by the most elegant rationales. The creators of sociograms know exactly why they arranged the characters in a particular fashion" (Johnson & Louis, 1987, p. 97).

Sharing and Extending Through Games

Games are another way to engage students in sharing and extending their comprehension of reading materials. For example, you may wish to consider developing board games based on a work of children's or adolescents' literature (Harste, Burke & DeFord, 1976; Keeler, 1993; J. Morris, 1987). Game cards and game boards can be designed to invite students to share and extend their comprehension of a book. Game boards and cards can also be developed to reinforce students' learning of content-area concepts from their textbooks or from nonfiction works (Strom, 1980).

Once students have read a number of books, you might consider different sorts of games, similar to some TV game shows or based on favorite childhood games. Johnson and Louis (1987) show how to use childhood games such as Mastermind and Twenty Questions with pieces of literature while Kettel (1981) suggests a quiz show in which students on opposing teams field questions or clues developed from each book or piece of reading material. Whichever team first signals that it can provide the appropriate title for the clue or answer the question, and does so correctly, earns points. Once students have experienced this game format, they may come up with other formats—Concentration or Jeopardy, for example.

Although participation in games like these may help students share and extend their comprehension of text, they will benefit even more if they participate in preparing the games (J. Morris, 1987; Nichols, 1978). If you work with a number of different groups of students during the day, you might consider having one group make up a game for another. Remember, it is often the process of creating something like a game that generates the "grand conversation" about the book, even more than the playing of the game.

Sharing and Extending Text Sets

In most classrooms postreading activities involve a single text, but Henry notes that this represents "a preoccupation with the skills that are entailed in reading the work (text) singly without relating it to other works" (1974, p. 1). As a result of the focus on single texts, students "are cut off from connecting larger ideas that are revealed across texts. Their role, as they have learned, is to stay within the boundaries of a single text" (Hartman & Hartman, 1993, p. 202).

Although the ability to comprehend a single text is important, relating information across texts may be more important for developing students' knowledge and comprehension. In this section, we'll present lessons that go beyond single texts and encourage students to relate one text to another, to share and extend comprehension through comparison, contrast, and synthesis across texts. Even in a single text lesson, you can encourage children to relate the text to other texts they have read in the past through questions like, "Does this story remind you of others we have read?"

Text sets are multiple texts—some combination of books, poetry, newspaper articles, scripts, and so on—related in a way that encourages students to compare and contrast the texts or to synthesize information from all of them. More broadly conceived, text sets can also include material other than written texts—films, filmstrips, records, and the like. The texts may be alternative versions of the same story, examples of the same genre (e.g., fairy tales or "how and why" stories), or texts that feature a similar structure, or the same character, theme (sibling rivalry, honor), plot, or topic. Text sets are almost always a natural feature of thematic units. We describe various types of texts sets in the following pages and suggest ways to use them in order to encourage sharing and extending of comprehension.

Crafton recommends that students who are studying in a content area read a variety of texts related to a topic, what she refers to as "conceptually related texts" (1983). In the study of vaccines in a science class, for example, students may read different texts to answer the same question: "What are the successes and problems with vaccines?" In reading to answer these questions, students may read a variety of expository texts, encyclopedias, nonfiction trade books, biographies of scientists involved in vaccine research, recent magazine articles, transcripts of TV documentaries, newspaper articles, and so on. Many topics lend themselves to a combination of expository and narrative texts in the same text set. (See Heine, 1991; McClure, 1985; Moss, 1978, for examples.)

Sharing genre-related texts extends the meaning of individual texts and understanding of the genre itself. For example, Moss recommends that students read, compare, and contrast fairy tales or folktales in order to discover common characteristics (1982, 1984). Kimmelman recommends that folktales be grouped into text sets according to the specific sort of plot that underlies the folktale (1981). One of our favorite genres of text sets is "how and why" stories, which abound in children's literature. Some of the books that might be included in a "how and why" text set include:

V. Aardema. *Why Mosquitoes Buzz in People's Ears*. New York: Dial Press, 1975.

B. Elkin. *Why the Sun Was Late*. New York: Parents' Magazine Press, 1966.

M. Hirsh. *How the World Got Its Color*. New York: Crown, 1972.

R. Kipling. *How the Camel Got His Hump*. New York: Spoken Arts, 1976.

R. Kipling. *How the Leopard Got His Spots*. New York: Walker, 1973.

R. Kipling. *How the Rhinoceros Got His Skin*. New York: Walker, 1973.

D. McKee. *The Day the Tide Went Out*. New York: Abelard-Schuman, 1976.

Informational pieces can be grouped into text sets in much the same way. For example, we cut out the "Far-out Facts" columns from several years of *World* magazine to use as a text set. Individual students read a single column and shared what they had learned with the group, relating the content of one column to another where appropriate. After all of the columns had been read over a number of days, students categorized the columns (Far-out Facts about Insects, Far-out Facts about Plants, and so on)—a task that involved them in another discussion of content— and pasted them by category into a book that became part of the classroom library.

Another type of text set features works with similar structures. A structure may be quite apparent, such as the highly cumulative or repetitive structure found in predictable books, or it may be less obvious, such as a compare/contrast or problem/solution structure found in expository materials.

Yet another type of text set features the same characters or people. Even as adults, we seek out reading material that features characters we have met and liked in other books. How many of us, having read *Clan of the Cave Bear* (Auel, 1980), couldn't wait to meet the heroine again in *Valley of the Horses* (Auel, 1982)? Authors write series stories featuring the same characters for all age groups. Beverly Cleary's Ramona and James Marshall's hippos, George and Martha, are among many characters who reappear in books.

Many students also enjoy discussing different versions of the same story. Students frequently find it interesting to compare the movie and book version of a story (Duncan, 1993), such as *Where the Red Fern Grows* (Rawls, 1974) or *The Outsiders* (Hinton, 1980), or a Readers Theatre version of a folktale with the picture book version (Barchers, 1993). It's especially easy to find different versions of traditional folktales. The versions can be surprisingly different, and the differences often lead to interesting discussion and writing. In the text sets listed below, for example, there are two versions of *The Miller, His Son, and the Donkey*, one told in standard English and the other in dialect. In the *Jack and the Beanstalk* text set, one of the texts is a modern-day version of the tale.

M. Calhoun. *Old Man Whickutt's Donkey*. New York: Parents' Magazine Press, 1975.

R. Duvoisin, illus. *The Miller, His Son, and the Donkey*. New York: McGraw-Hill, 1962.

R. Briggs. *Jim and the Beanstalk*. New York: Coward, McCann, & Geoghegan, 1970.

L. B. Cauley. *Jack and the Beanstalk*. New York: G. P. Putnam, 1983.

W. de la Mare. *Jack and the Beanstalk*. New York: Alfred A. Knopf, 1959.

B. S. DeRegniers. *Jack the Giant-Killer*, 1987.

J. Jacobs. *Jack and the Beanstalk*. New York: Henry Z. Walck, 1975.

S. Kellogg. *Jack and the Beanstalk*. New York: Morrow Junior Books, 1991.

Similarly, expository text sets can feature different accounts of famous (or infamous) people. Comparing biographies of the same person is always interesting and presents the readers with some critical reading opportunities, especially if an autobiography is also available. For readers who require shorter texts, you might try comparing pieces on a contemporary figure from *Time, People, National Enquirer,* and the newspaper for the same effect.

A text set that students often find fascinating is an author text set. This is an easy text set for teachers to gather. There are many materials that allow teachers to locate interesting information about the author's life that will further extend students' understandings of the author's books. Some authors have entire books that document their lives such as *Bill Peet, An Autobiography* (Peet, 1989), *Homesick: My Own Story* (Fritz, 1982), and *Laura Ingalls Wilder: Growing Up in the Little House* (Giff, 1987). Some magazines, such as *Teaching K–8*, do monthly features of a children's author or illustrator that teachers can collect and file for their use. In addition, there are a great many quality interviews of authors and illustrators on audio and videotape, often available inexpensively from children's or adolescents' book clubs. Numerous books are available for teachers about authors and illustrators that assist in planning for author study (for example, Asher, 1987; Cummings, 1992; McElmeel, 1988; Kiefer, 1991; Roginski, 1985; Zinsser, 1990). In addition, librarians can help you learn about and use excellent references such as *Something About the Author* (Commire, since 1971).

Students always enjoy reading a body of work by a favorite author or illustrator such as Eric Carle, Walter Dean Myers, Cynthia Rylant, Chris Van Allsburg, Jerry Pinkney, Katherine Paterson, Allen Say, Steven Kellogg, Byrd Baylor, or Cynthia Voigt (to name just a few!). They can uncover the similarities of the work, how the work has changed over time, the themes of the author, how the books are based on the author's experiences, and so on. Even very young children will generate surprising insights about books as a result of comparing and contrasting books written or illustrated by the same author or illustrator. Probably nothing serves better to help authors become real people than author studies.

Using an example of a theme-based text set, Cassidy describes one way to organize text sets for students (1984). In his example, a fifth-grade teacher placed three stories illustrating courage in a manila folder and wrote *Courage* on the outside of the folder. The first story, "Nobody's Better Off Dead" by Quentin Reynolds, is the true story of a basketball star who, because of an accident, must fight to live and then regain the use of his limbs. Another story, "High Above Niagara's Waters," taken from an old basal reader and made into a "skinny book," is about a man who walked a tightrope above Niagara Falls. The third story, "The Old Demon" by Pearl Buck, concerns a woman who sacrifices her life by releasing the "old demon river" from its dam to stop a Japanese military advance.

The teacher printed questions on the inside of the manila folder to encourage students to synthesize what they had read:

What is your definition of the term *courage* that encompasses all of the individuals in these stories? Tell how each fits the definition.

Of the three individuals, who was the most courageous? List at least three reasons for your decision.

Cassidy notes that, although the teacher used this folder with all her students, she adapted the activity for her struggling readers by reading the two more difficult selections to them and having them read the third. If you are working exclusively with struggling readers, try to find materials that are within the students' reading capabilities.

You can help students interact with text sets in a number of different ways. Individual students can read/see/hear several texts in a set and compare/contrast or synthesize information from the texts. Or individual students in a group can each take responsibility for one of the texts in a set and share what was read/seen/heard with other students in the group, comparing/contrasting and synthesizing information as a group.

You can formalize sharing of text sets by using a strategy called "jigsaw" (Aronson, 1978). If you have nine students in the group and three related texts, divide the students into groups A, B, and C. Each group receives a different but related text from the text set; each individual in a group receives the same text to read and become an expert on. After the students have each read a text, they meet together in the A, B, and C groups to clarify and extend comprehension with others who have read the same text. Then the groups reorganize so that there is an A, B, and C person in each group; each individual teaches the others about what he read and discussed. The second group is also responsible for tying the information together into a whole.

Students who need support in identifying important information in expository material or in synthesizing that information across texts may find data charts (Crocker, 1983; McKenzie, 1979) or I-charts (Hoffman, 1992) useful. (See Chapter 8 for specific information on I-charts.) Charts are applicable not only to reading expository material but also to reading narrative material when you want students to focus their attention on comparing story elements. Many of the lessons we have already reviewed for single texts are also suitable for use with text sets. Some oral discussion and dramatization ideas, writing follow-ups, art, mapping, and game ideas can be used with multiple texts. Though you'll be able to generate other ideas by reviewing earlier sections of this chapter with text sets in mind, here are a few to get started:

Consider a chapter in a book to be a text and the whole book to be a text set. Smith suggests that if each student reads a single chapter, and the students then retell the chapters in order, the students can "read a book in an hour," an idea that should be especially appealing for reluctant readers (1978). A related idea may encourage students to finish reading a book on their own: Several students read and retell the first several chapters; interested students can finish the book on their own.

Using the structural characteristics or the genre characteristics of a text set, students can write another text. For instance, once students have experienced the Jack and the Beanstalk text set, which includes a modern-day version of the tale, they may be interested in constructing modern-day versions of other folktales or fairy tales. Each student's new text may be rightfully considered to be a part of the original text set. Sipe's sixth graders identified a number of ways to transform stories such as changing the style of writing, the setting, the point of view, and so on (1993).

Using dramatization, students can carry on a dialogue based on a similarity they have discovered across stories. For example: Students acting as Snow White and Sleeping Beauty can compare how they met their princes.

An interesting Readers' Theatre script can be created if students use parts of series of books featuring the same character. For example, one Ramona Quimby adventure might be selected from each of Beverly Cleary's Ramona books and rewritten into a script.

The literature quiz show (discussed previously, p. 221) could be tailored to a particular text set. For example, a quiz show could be prepared for Lloyd Alexander's *Prydain Chronicles*.

The references we recommended in our discussion of integrated or inquiry units are also useful in identifying text sets for your students. In addition, rely on a good children's librarian for help, especially if you have identified a couple of texts and want to add others to round out the text set. Another way to locate text sets is to look for ready-made sets, with texts already grouped by the publisher. Basal readers, for example, frequently feature stories that can be grouped simply by rearranging the order in which they are read. What you will have to add are the activities and questions that help students relate one text in the set to another.

There are several references below that we have found to be very useful in identifying text sets for use with students. There are many other references that children's librarians can help you identify in order to locate books in specific categories such as American history, topics in poetry, various ethnic groups, etc.

Kathy Short and Kathryn Pierce's *Reading Teacher* column, "Children's Books," which was published from September of 1993 through May of 1995. These are sophisticated text sets, built around large concepts such as contemporary social and political issues, environmental issues and actions, and living in harmony.

Book Links, a monthly magazine published by the American Library Association. Each journal includes at least two text sets. Some text sets are published in a series of journals such as the "Dateline USA" series of text sets, with each one focused on a different era. Other articles feature authors and are useful in organizing author study text sets.

Children's Books in Print: Subject Guide (yearly) is a comprehensive subject index for children's books that are in print.

The Bookfinder (Dreyer, published since 1977) is a series of references that list children's books by topic or theme.

A to Zoo: Subject Access to Children's Picture Books (Lima & Lima; look for most recent edition) lists picture books by subject.

Learning to Answer (and Ask) Questions

Teachers often assume that students who have problems in answering questions at the end of a text or completing worksheets have had difficulty comprehending the text or have read carelessly. But it may be that these students simply don't know how to go about answering questions. Students who don't understand question asking and answering may experience difficulty in school because questions are such a prominent feature in teachers' instruction and assessment.

In summarizing key research on answering questions, Armbruster notes that answering a question involves three steps: 1) interpreting the question or figuring out what information is required by the question, 2) locating the required information or identifying the sources of the information, and 3) formulating an appropriate answer or deciding what information is necessary and sufficient to answer the question well (1992).

Interpreting the Question

As sophisticated readers, we don't realize that questions are often difficult for struggling readers to understand. The same question can be asked a multitude of ways, questions that are quite different from one another can appear the same on the surface, and questions are often ambiguous, requiring the reader to understand the intent of a question-asker or the intent of an evaluator. Armbruster (1992, p. 724) provides excellent examples of each of these problems with question interpretation:

> *The same question, asked a multitude of ways:* What caused the Boston Massacre? Why did the Boston Massacre occur? How did British tariffs result in the Boston Massacre? Explain the Boston Massacre. Trace the events that led to the Boston Massacre. Explain how the British tariffs and the Boston Massacre are related.

> *Different questions that appear to request the same kind of information on the surface:* Who were the candidates for U.S. President in the election of 1848? Who were the abolitionists?

> *Ambiguous questions:* What is photosynthesis? (This could be asking for a definition or an explanation of the process.)

In order to help students learn how to interpret questions, teachers can model their own interpretations through the use of think-alouds (see Chapter 8), rephrase questions in several different ways so that students can understand that rephrasing is possible, and students themselves can be encouraged to rephrase questions in different ways. As teachers, we also need to become sensitive to the fact that when a question is not answered the way we expected, we may be most helpful to students by first letting them know that they may have interpreted the question in a reasonable way (if this is the case). Then we can help them consider alternative interpretations of the question, perhaps offering them another opportunity to answer the question when it is important to do so (such as on a product that is graded). Sometimes the difference between students who do well on assignments and tests and those who don't is simply their ability to interpret questions and the intent of the questioner, not their underlying knowledge.

Locating Information to Answer Questions

A taxonomy developed by Pearson and Johnson is based on a robust view of reading comprehension as an interaction or transaction between reader and text (1978). Instead of labeling questions (as is the case with the oft-cited Bloom's taxonomy), Pearson and Johnson propose three different kinds of *question-answer relationships*:

> *Textually explicit:* In order to answer the question, the student reads or points to the appropriate information in the text.
>
> *Textually implicit:* In order to answer the question, the student integrates information across sentences in the text by making inferences or generating connections that the author left unstated.
>
> *Scriptally implicit:* In order to answer the question, the student uses prior knowledge that is relevant to the text and/or question.

Raphael and others (Hahn, 1985; Raphael, 1982, 1986; Raphael & McKinney, 1983; Raphael & Pearson, 1982, Raphael & Wonnacott, 1981) have developed this taxonomy into an instructional strategy entitled Question-Answer Relationships (QAR). QAR lessons are designed to help students, including learning disabled students, understand how to answer questions more effectively (Simmonds, 1992). The instructional strategy focuses on locating the required information or identifying the sources of the information needed to answer the question (step two as outlined above by Armbruster).

Using the Pearson and Johnson taxonomy, Raphael labels question-answer relationships (QARs) that may help students understand the potential sources of information useful in generating answers to questions. The QARs are "Right There," "Think and Search" (or "Putting It Together"), "The Author and You," and "On My Own" and are defined as shown in Figure 10-1 (from Raphael, 1986).

Raphael recommends the following steps for QAR lessons. Note how the lessons are set up to gradually release responsibility to students so that they can answer questions both effectively and independently.

1. Introduce the QAR concept. Students may first be introduced only to the first level of the QARs, "In the Book" and "In My Head." Once students understand the two basic categories, introduce the subdivisions of each category, perhaps presenting the explanations on an overhead. On short passages, demonstrate how you answer questions by showing the students where you found the answers and labeling each QAR as it is demonstrated.

IN THE BOOK QARS	IN MY HEAD QARS
Right There The answer is in the text, usually easy to find. The words used to make up the question and words used to answer the question are Right There in the same sentence.	**Author and You** The answer is *not* in the story. You need to think about what you already know, what the author tells you in the text, and how it fits together.
Think and Search (Putting It Together) The answer is in the story, but you need to put together different story parts to find it. Words for the question and words for the answer are not found in the same sentence. They come from different parts of the text.	**On My Own** The answer is not in the story. You can even answer the question without reading the story. You need to use your own experience.

FIG 10-1   *Question-Answer Relationships (QARs) (Raphael, 1986)*

2. Provide students with short passages to read and discuss as a group. Following the reading of the passage, solicit answers to questions. Rather than focusing on the correctness of the answers, help students focus on the information source for the answers by asking questions, such as "How do you know the answer was _____? Can you prove it in any way? Does the text tell you the answer? If not, how do you know it?" and so on.

3. As you continue with QAR lessons, provide students with increasingly longer passages and an increasing number of questions. As they gain experience, they should progress from group to individual responses and from total teacher guidance and feedback to independent use. The end goal is to help students use QAR information independently to deal more effectively with everyday instructional materials and with a wide range of materials.

With struggling readers, we recommend that teachers include other related information in these lessons as it is needed. For example, it comes as a shock to many struggling readers that students who succeed in answering questions often read the questions they are expected to answer before they read the text in situations such as standardized tests or end-of-chapter questions. It's an easy task to incorporate that feature into any QAR lesson, along with your demonstrations of how to go about answering questions.

If you are a resource teacher, you can help your students be more successful back in their regular classrooms by helping them use QAR information to analyze each classroom teacher's questions and expected responses, as well as the textbook's questions and expected responses. Some teachers and some textbooks avoid

"Right There" questions, while others are very dependent on those sorts of questions in both daily work and tests. Students who are aware of what QARs are likely in each class are better able to meet the expectations of that class. Students who perform poorly on an exam or assignment can often be helped to understand how to perform better in the future by learning to recognize the predominant types of questions and answers.

Formulating an Answer

After a question has been interpreted and the source of the information that answers the question has been located, students must also learn to formulate an appropriate answer. Like question interpretation, this is best taught by a teacher who demonstrates how she answers questions by deciding which information is necessary to answer the question well. Again, helping students learn to formulate an appropriate answer can be done as the teacher demonstrates *thinking aloud* about the underlying thinking process. As with other tasks that you want students to be able to do independently, consider how to sequence lessons that move from group to individual responses to questions, and from total teacher guidance and feedback to independent question answering.

It may also be useful to examine your own questions (or the questions of other teachers and publishers) when students do not formulate answers as you hope or expect. For example, you might consider the following:

Can your questions be reworded so that they more clearly invite the sort of responses you anticipated? Or at least a wider variety of responses?

Do the students' responses provide clues to their need for greater background knowledge (or that you need to activate their background knowledge)? (It's easy to think the information needed to answer the question is in the text when it is really in your own background knowledge but not that of the students.)

Are their responses actually indicative that they need instruction in some specific comprehension strategy?

Do your follow-up questions to the main question encourage students to clarify responses, expand on them (Ruddell, 1978), generalize from them about how to respond to these kinds of questions in the future (Riley, 1979), or connect one reader's response with another?

Beyond assisting students in formulating the content of answers to questions, be alert for other information that struggling readers need to know in order to complete a task well and to be successful in classroom settings. For instance, in the middle of such lessons, we have found it necessary to help students learn that they can spell the words in their answers far more successfully by looking back to the text for spellings. And, as is the case with question interpretation, students need to consider what it is that the evaluator wants in answers to questions. For example, students typically answer questions that occur in oral conversation without restating the question in the answer. Yet, many teachers expect students to answer questions in complete statements or sentences. For these teachers, it is not only content that is being evaluated, but also the form in which the students provide the content. Students who learn to ask or observe what their teachers' standards are will be better able to meet the expectations of that class. Students who perform poorly on an exam or assignment can often be helped to understand how to perform better in the future by analyzing the teacher's preferences beyond content.

Questioning the Author

Another approach that may help students comprehend text more effectively after reading is to use an instructional strategy called "Questioning the Author" (McKeown, Beck & Worthy, 1993). This strategy calls for students to take a critical and active stance in relationship to the text by questioning the author about what he is trying to get across and about whether he has made ideas sufficiently clear for the reader. Instead of answering someone else's questions, students are encouraged to ask a series of questions that assume that the author is a person who has attempted to get ideas across and may not have done the best job in the world doing so. In a classroom where students not only read but also compose, the questions will not be unfamiliar since they spring from the same concerns that readers have during Author's Circle as they provide feedback to student-writers. In essence, the teacher is asking the students to treat the writer of a textbook as someone who also had to make the same writing decisions they do about content and how to present it. The initial questions that students ask after reading a text are:

What is the author trying to tell me?

Why is the author trying to tell me that?

Is that said clearly?

In the process of asking these questions, students often identify their comprehension confusions and discover comprehension problems. At this point, they ask another set of questions that are designed to get them to rethink the author's ideas and put those ideas in what they consider to be clearer language:

How could the author have said the ideas in a clearer way?

What would I say instead?

McKeown, Beck & Worthy note that students transform the author's ideas into their own in the process of asking and answering these questions, just what successful comprehenders do as they read text (1993). The fourth-grade teacher who worked with the researchers to implement this strategy in the classroom reported to them that she saw significant differences in the readers who struggled most with regard to the amount of thinking about text and their involvement in discussion.

Study Reading

Studying as a general topic is outside the scope of this book. We would, however, like to address briefly what's been referred to as *study reading*: the "careful and deliberate reading in order to understand and remember both details and major ideas presented in a text" (Friedman & Rowls, 1980, p. 241). Study reading is usually done by students to prepare themselves to take a test. Study reading strategies help students identify the major ideas and important supporting details in the text and then organize that information so that they can more easily commit it to memory. Additionally, students learn that effective study reading is different from cramming.

One strategy that helps students identify and organize important written information is the post organizer (Robinson, 1983; Vacca, 1981). The post organizer is essentially the same as the graphic organizer and uses mapping or webbing. Sometimes a teacher supplies students with a list of the concepts and vocabulary to be learned (especially for tests) and, in such cases, the students organize the information that the teacher has supplied.

If identification of the major ideas and supporting details has been entirely left up to the students, the important concepts, ideas, and vocabulary can be identified with teachers' guidance through group brainstorming. If you are assisting students in doing this in the role of resource teacher, have students check the brainstormed list with the content-area teacher so that the students are clear about what they should study. Also help students keep in mind what types of information the teacher typically requires to be remembered (see the QAR discussion) as they identify important information.

Group effort is also useful for organizing ideas and details once they've been identified either in a brainstorming session or by a teacher. Students will have an easier time organizing ideas if they write their ideas or details on a card or a scrap of paper. In small groups or individually, ask students to organize their information by sorting the slips of paper into appropriate categories. Encourage students to use the text when they need an explanation of an idea or detail or need to review the relationship of one idea to another. As they finish, ask them to compare how they've organized information with other students. It's perfectly natural that one student's way of organizing will differ from another's; the key is whether the students can defend their arrangement of ideas and whether they will find them useful, given their study goals. If you have also organized the important ideas, share your arrangement of information with the students as well so they can see one way an experienced reader/learner thinks about the information.

Once students have arranged the information in a way that is useful for study, they should copy the information as they have arranged it onto a sheet of paper so that it is handy for studying. The information can be used as students refer back to the text and reread portions of it, and as they question themselves and each other about the information in the organizer, or as you conduct "fake pop quizzes" (Readence, Bean & Baldwin, 1981). As we noted in our earlier discussion of games, students will benefit more from such quizzes if they have a hand in making up the questions or quiz items.

If you are assisting students in the role of a resource teacher, be prepared to assist students through the post-organizer process of study reading well in advance of when they will need to have learned the information, especially if this is the first time students have used the process. As students are assigned chapters or portions of chapters in a content-area class for which they need your support as a resource teacher, begin to work on post organizers for each chapter. Once an organizer has been completed (a lengthy process at first), it is better to spend a small amount of time on review activities stemming from the organizer every day than to cram them into a day or two.

Before we end our discussion of study reading, we'd like to say a few words about a well-known and widely discussed instructional strategy for study reading, SQ3R and all its variations. SQ3R is solidly based on what is known about how proficient readers study and learn from text when they must commit the meaning of the text to memory. The steps in the instructional strategy are:

Survey: The student previews the reading material in order to determine the overall content and organization.

Question: The student establishes a purpose for reading by reviewing the questions posed by the teacher or publisher, or by changing the headings and subheadings to questions.

Read: The reader reads in order to answer the questions s/he raised in the previous step.

Recite: The student closes the book and attempts to answer the questions that were raised.

Review: At a later time, the student again attempts to answer the questions that were raised.

SQ3R originated years ago as a study reading strategy for college students (Robinson, 1961). Since then, it's been recommended in virtually every secondary content-area reading textbook published. Certainly many of the recommendations we have made in this and other chapters are consistent with the theoretical basis of SQ3R and engage students in similar steps, albeit not in a single instructional strategy.

Vacca has stated that, unless they are mature readers, secondary students have a difficult time using SQ3R independently (1981). It certainly can be expected that struggling readers will experience difficulty using SQ3R independently. This does not mean that it isn't a worthwhile instructional strategy for struggling readers, but it does mean that they can't be expected to use it without teacher support with some or all of the steps on the way to learning to use it independently. Like some of the other instructional strategies we have discussed, including the post organizer, SQ3R requires guidance through the process, guidance which is well worth the time when an important instructional goal is learning the content of a text.

WRITING INSTRUCTION
A Focus on Struggling Writers

Writers always begin with an intention. A writer may write to recount a series of events, to tell an entertaining story, to make a record of something, to give directions, or just to chat with a friend. For student writers these purposes are sometimes secondary to fulfilling the intentions of teachers. Students tell stories, write essays, record notes, and so on because their teachers require it. Whenever people write, and whatever their intentions, they both *compose*—that is, they make choices about topics, content, and language—and they *transcribe*—that is, they encode their meaning(s) using the conventions of spelling, punctuation, handwriting, and grammatical usage. Frank Smith observed that transcription is what a secretary does when he "does not have the bother of actually thinking of the words" (1982b, p. 21).

The "task of dealing with the multifaceted demands of writing has been described as a 'juggling act' " (Lapp & Flood, 1993, p. 254) in which composition and transcription compete for the attention of the writer (F. Smith, 1982b). If writers fix their attention on composition, concentrating on ideas and language choices to the neglect of transcription, for example, we might expect misspellings, fragmented sentences, missing punctuation, and illegible handwriting. Conversely, writers whose attention is focused on conventions like spelling and punctuation may lose sight of their intentions, their ideas, or the needs of their audience.

Proficient writers are able to achieve a balance between the competing demands of composition and transcription, having learned that concerns with transcription are secondary to purpose, topic, audience, and content—at least in early drafts. Struggling writers, however, tend to focus their attention on aspects of transcription, especially spelling and handwriting, to the detriment of their primary intention to communicate, to inform, to entertain, and so on. In extreme cases their fixation on print conventions may lead struggling writers to avoid writing altogether. Certainly these students must improve their knowledge and use of the conventions of print, but they must also learn to put transcription in perspective. Spelling, handwriting, and punctuation are important courtesies to the reader (Wilde, 1992), but they must not be allowed to distract writers from their intentions.

In this chapter, we'll discuss the process of composing a piece of writing including such issues as topic selection, audience, voice, language choices, and revision within the format of the writing workshop (e.g., Atwell, 1987; Calkins & Harwayne, 1991; Calkins, 1994; Graves, 1994 ; Harwayne, 1992). In the next chapter we'll take up spelling, punctuation, usage, and (briefly) handwriting, again in the context of the writing workshop.

11

Writing Instruction
The Writing Workshop

When the students in Mr. Reid's third-grade class returned from lunch recess they hung up their coats, picked up their pencils and writing folders, and sat on the carpet. The writing workshop began with the usual minilesson. Since many of his students weren't including many details in their writing, today's writing period began with a brief lesson focused on adding details to make their writing more interesting. Mr. Reid shared a piece of his own writing which lacked specific details. "Last weekend we went camping at Presque Isle Provincial Park. We went swimming, hiking, and rode our bikes. We had a great time but we decided to come home early." He asked his students what they thought of this piece of writing and everyone agreed that they wanted to know more, and there was a general discussion about the kinds of details the class was interested in knowing more about. Mr. Reid concluded this five-minute lesson by offering students some advice on how they might go about adding details to their writing.

The students then returned to their tables to spend the next 40 minutes working on their writing. Rachel and Crystal resumed work on a collaborative piece about Crystal's brother. Sally continued working on a poem she'd begun the previous day. Margaret celebrated her friendship with Colleen by beginning a piece called "My Friend, Colleen." Philip sought feedback on his latest mystery by reading what he'd written so far to Adam. Rebecca and Tara exchanged notes with each other while Edward used the computer to respond to some E-mail messages he'd received the day before. Several students jotted notes in their writer's notebooks. A few others stared at the blank sheets of paper in front of them, unable to think of anything to write about.

Mr. Reid spent his time meeting individually with students. He asked Dan how the story about his baby brother was going and what direction he expected it to take. He asked Carole Ann, who was using dialogue in a story for the first time, to look around for books in the classroom that used dialogue to see how commercial authors used quotation marks. He helped Stanley and Patrick look back through their writer's notebooks for possible writing topics. He suggested to Sandie that she try rewriting her piece about her "nosey sister" as a poem, perhaps using Shel Silverstein, her favorite poet, as a model. After he helped Adeeb identify a writing topic, Mr. Reid insisted that he write "at least a half a page" before the end of the writing period. He suggested to Aman, who was ready to edit a piece of writing, that he would help Aman with misspelled words after he circled all the words he wasn't sure how to spell. Finally, Mr. Reid helped Anne use the computer to put a finished piece of writing into "publishable" form.

Mr. Reid then asked his students to bring their writing to the carpet and, for the next five minutes, several students shared pieces of writing with their classmates, who responded by focusing on parts of peers' writing that they particularly enjoyed. Catherine, for example, responded to Crystal's poem saying, "The way you talked about your sister made me laugh. It reminded me of my brother. . . ."

Another day Mr. Reid might have had a longer minilesson. A genre study on poetry, for example, led to a twenty-minute discussion of the way a particular poet used language to evoke feelings of sadness. Some days he might have had longer writing conferences with fewer students. And there were days when no one had any writing to share, in which case he sometimes asked students to share writing-in-progress or, alternatively, he might read a trade book to his class. Some things never changed, however. Students knew that the basic structure of the writing workshop in Mr. Reid's class did not vary—minilesson, writing/conferencing, sharing. More important, students knew that they would have *at least* forty-five minutes each day to write and to discuss the craft of writing.

Writing workshop is based upon the assumption that student writers, like published, commercial authors, need predictable, concentrated amounts of time to write, preferably each day (Atwell, 1987; Calkins, 1986, 1994; Graves, 1983, 1994; Murray, 1990). Writing workshop provides opportunities for students to discover the power of writing to make a difference in their lives. Students also learn that writing is a craft requiring hard work, dedication, and patience. Within the structure of the writing workshop students write on a variety of topics of personal interest to them with the active support and direction of teachers who immerse their students in literature (Atwell, 1989; Harwayne, 1992) and provide *explicit* instruction in the craft of writing.

Writing workshop is also informed by the belief that there are processes by which writers, including novice writers, transform their intentions into effective written texts (Graves, 1983; Calkins, 1994). Sometimes writers actively explore a range of ideas before settling on a writing topic. At this stage writers may welcome opportunities to talk about their ideas with teachers or fellow students. Writers may also spend concentrated amounts of time writing and rewriting pieces with the aim of sharing with wider audiences (e.g., publishing). Teachers' support must be responsive to both writers' intentions and to where students are in the process of writing. It makes little sense to spend a lot of time teaching students about the use of quotation marks, for example, when their writing does not yet include dialogue. Similarly, we wouldn't want to talk to students about brainstorming when they're at the stage of revising their work.

"Writing process" teachers do not—or, at least, should not—teach students *a* unitary writing process. (We are well aware, however, that this happens all too often.) "Prewrite, write, revise, and publish" describes what *some* writers do *some* of the time, not what all writers do all of the time or even most of the time (Donald Murray's collection of quotations of commercial writers talking about their craft demonstrates the range of ways writers think about the *process* of writing [1990]). Sometimes writers write as a means of discovering a topic. Other writers revise *as* they write, not after they've written (Lapp & Flood, 1993). And much writing (e.g., grocery lists, notes and letters, diaries) is neither revised nor published. Teaching informed by research on the writing process attempts to respond to process*es* used by writers as they work to fulfill various intentions. Writing process advocates seek to make teachers sensitive and responsive to what writers do, not to force student writers into particular processes.

Assigned topics and story-starters rarely have a place in the writing workshop. First of all, ALL children, including students in remedial and special education programs, have important and interesting things to say (Thorne, 1993). They don't need teachers to *give* them something to say. The tendency to push, lure, motivate, or bribe students to write is based on our own experiences with writing in school and, for most of us, writing was a dreaded activity (Calkins, 1994). Research indicates, however, that students are more likely to commit the time and effort to revise their work if they are personally invested in their writing (e.g., Dudley-Marling & Oppenheimer, 1995; Graves, 1983). In the writing workshop students learn from their teachers, their classmates, and commercial authors the skills and strategies writers use to write effectively, that is, writing that *works* by fulfilling writers' intentions.

Finally, we believe that the writing workshop is particularly congenial to the needs of struggling writers, including remedial students and students with learning disabilities and the teachers who work with these children (Schwartz & MacArthur, 1990; Zaraguzo & Vaughn, 1992). Writing workshop provides a space where students with very different levels of proficiency can work side by side and teachers have the freedom to offer support and direction that responds to the specific needs of individual students (Calkins, 1994). Writing workshops also provide a structure within which regular classroom teachers and special or remedial teachers can work more closely together in support of struggling writers. Special and remedial teachers could, for example, provide students with additional support for a particular piece of writing within either the regular classroom or the resource room.

In the rest of this chapter we will discuss the writing workshop from the perspective of *what students do* by examining the range of processes writers use and *what teachers do* in support of these processes by looking at the structures of the writing workshop.

What Students Do: A Writing Process

In this section we briefly discuss what writers may do in the process of writing. The various processes we describe here are adapted from Calkins (1994). Again, we want to be clear that there isn't *a* process that describes what writers need to do or what teachers should teach them to do. Rather, a sensitivity to the writing process can help teachers respond to what students are trying to do with their writing.

Rehearse

Lucy Calkins observed that it isn't true that writers live more significant lives than nonwriters, only that they are in the habit of "*finding* the significance that there is in their lives" (1994, p. 7). She adds: "Just as photographers are always seeing potential pictures, so too, writers see potential stories and poems and essays everywhere and gather them in entries and jotted notes" (1994, p. 23). As Neil Simon put it, a writer is "that person at a cocktail party standing in the corner and watching" (in Murray, 1990, p. 21). Writers are in the habit of finding the extraordinary in the ordinary.

The best way to develop the "wide-awakeness" (Greene, 1978) that is so fundamental to writers is to write often (Calkins, 1994). People who write regularly are always on the lookout for an interesting idea, a new word, a useful quote, or a turn of phrase. Many writers keep notebooks in which they can keep a record of their thoughts and observations. Writer's notebooks encourage student writers to look at the world as a writer and are, therefore, increasingly an important part of many writing programs (Calkins & Harwayne, 1991; Calkins, 1994). Talk is also a means by which writers develop ideas that may or may not emerge in future writing. Sometime writers discover ideas *by writing*. Edward Albee said, "I write to find out what I'm thinking about" (in Murray, 1990, p. 4).

Rehearsal isn't as much of a *stage* (i.e., something that writers always do) in the writing process—the time for brainstorming activities, for example—as it is a stance or a gaze. Children who write learn to see the world *as writers*. Developing writers benefit from classrooms where there are opportunities for students to write and to talk about their ideas and the craft of writing. Writers also draw inspiration from the writing and ideas of others. Students who read widely and listen to the ideas of their classmates will never be short of inspiration. This writerly gaze is nurtured by establishing "an atmosphere of graciousness and care and respect in our classrooms" (Calkins, 1994, p. 31). Too often school teaches children that what they have to say is not important, which leads to the common refrain, "I don't have anything to write about." Respect is especially important for struggling writers whose experience has taught them that they have little worth saying. To view the world as writers they must believe that they have something important to say—something which all children believed before they walked into a classroom for the first time.

Draft

Drafting is the process by which writers translate their intentions into text. At this stage writers often focus on getting their thoughts down on paper as fast as they can, confident in the transience of the words on the page. They can always return to what they've written and change it, but if they don't have a record of their thoughts they are likely to forget them. Other writers prefer to "think it out" first before they commit their ideas to paper, fearful that words on paper will take on a terrible permanence. (We wonder if this isn't an issue with writers for whom getting the words onto the page in the first place is often a struggle.) The novelist John Irving says that he spends up to a year working out a story in his head before he puts anything on paper that looks remotely like narrative and then he writes a draft as quickly as he can (this may take him another year).

Drafting text involves writers in various decisions about content, word choice, language structures, register, organization, and so on which must take account of their purpose and intended audience. Persuasive writing, for example, may suggest the need for particular vocabulary and language structures although these decisions will also be affected by the audience to be persuaded (e.g., children versus adults). Some of these decisions may be worked out before writers begin writing (i.e., putting words on the page), while others will be attended to in the process of writing, and some may be postponed until when, and if, the piece is revised.

Whatever the decisions with which writers are faced, drafting requires concentrated blocks of time for writing, reflecting, and, perhaps, talking. It is very difficult, for example, for students to get back into a piece of writing if they only are given fifteen to twenty minutes for writing. Sometimes it takes five to ten minutes just for student writers to reorient themselves to a piece. Writers also need space that is considerate to their need to stand back and reflect or, in some cases, get away from their writing for a while. Students may hit a snag that requires that they stop writing for a time in order to think or seek advice from a classmate. Teachers cannot expect that students will always have "pen to paper." Most of the time we spent writing this book, for example, was spent reading, planning, and talking and not with our fingers on the keyboard.

Writers also need to learn patience, which for student writers means teachers who are also patient. Kurt Vonnegut makes the point humorously. He says, "novelists . . . have, on the average, about the same IQs as the cosmetic consultants at Bloomingdale's department store. Our power is patience" (in Murray, 1990, p. 65). The Muse cannot be rushed. It is difficult to write on demand and unrealistic to expect any writer to churn out a new piece of writing every day or even every week (although our expectations may be different for emerging writers). This doesn't mean that teachers can't tell students that it's time to finish one piece and move on to something else. They can. It's just that we need to be at least as considerate of student writers' needs for time as we would be for commercial writers (who rarely write more than a couple of pages a day). For this, student writers need to discover the value of hard work and patience, as well as having the support of teachers who have faith in their potential as writers.

Revise

Drafting implies that writers will return to a piece of writing once, twice, or any numbers of times to shape—and reshape—it into something more effective (or, perhaps, different). But writers do not return to every piece of writing. Many kinds of writing—notes, letters, lists, and so forth—don't usually call for multiple drafts. And sometimes writers give up on a piece of writing. So a draft isn't always a "draft." Sometimes, however, the words on the page are to the writer what a lump of clay is to a sculptor. The sculptor shapes, smooths, adds, and removes clay as she works toward some vision of what she imagines the thing will be. At other times the shaping molds the vision. Writers do the same by adding and replacing words, deleting sentences or paragraphs, moving bits of text here and there, and, sometimes, throwing it all away and starting over. And, like the sculptor, the writer's vision of a piece of writing may emerge through re-visioning a text (Calkins, 1994).

Revision isn't easy. Like drafting it takes time and patience, but it can be the most satisfying part of writing for any writer. However, because revision is difficult, writers have to care enough to revise their work. It has to be worth their effort. To care about their work children have to have some investment in their writing. They must have some measure of control over purpose, topic, and content. The evidence indicates that many student writers, having little investment in their writing to begin with, do little revision at all (Dudley-Marling & Oppenheimer, 1995). As Donald Graves (1983) puts it, "When people own a place, they look after it. When it belongs to someone else, they couldn't care less" (in Calkins, 1986, p. 23). To look after their writing students have to care and, to care, it has to "belong" to them.

Caring may be a necessary condition for writing, but it isn't enough. Writers have to learn how to revise their work. Teaching students the strategies writers use to revise their work (i.e., adding, deleting, replacing, and moving text) is the responsibility of teachers. Minilessons, conferencing, and immersing students in literature are the strategies teachers use to teach the skills of revision. (These skills will be taken up in the next section.) However, teachers not only want students to learn *to* revise, they want them to learn *from* revision. As some children move forward as writers they may not learn anything from their writing; however, "the importance of *revision* isn't the succession of drafts but the act of 'revision,' using words as a lens for reseeing the emerging subject. When children merely add on and on and on, when they do not stop to hear and see what their writing is saying, they don't experience the potential power of revision" (Calkins, 1994, p. 129) Revision offers writers a lens on the writing process.

Edit

When sculptors are satisfied with the shape of their creations they will likely attend to finishing details like trimming, firing, glazing, and cleaning as final steps in preparation for sharing their work with an audience. Similarly, when writers are satisfied with the shape of work they intend to share with an audience—even an audience of one as in the case of letters—they will use editing as a means of putting a finishing touch on their work. Writers edit their work by repairing misspellings, adding missing punctuation or words, deleting multiple occurrences of words (e.g., *the the*), checking tenses and number agreement, and, in the case of handwritten text, perhaps recopying text to make it readable. Unlike sculptors, writers can draw on a variety of supports to edit their work, including people who offer to proofread their work and computer programs that check their spelling and grammar.

Like revision, editing is something writers learn to do. Effective writing teachers teach their students about the strategies other writers use to edit their work as a means of preparing it to share with an audience.

Share

Writers typically share their work with an audience. Letters are mailed, poems read to girlfriends or boyfriends, notes passed, notices posted, leaflets distributed, E-mail sent, essays turned in, forms submitted, and so on. In most cases writers are able to fulfill their intentions only by sharing their writing with an audience. If the writer's intention is to persuade, for example, the writing must be shared with the person(s) to be persuaded. Similarly, if the goal is to entertain, as in the case of a poem, a story, or a play, the writing must be read by a wider audience. Sometimes writers write for themselves, but it is still likely they will return to these pieces of writing (e.g., diary, journal, grocery list, reminder, and so forth) at some point in the future and, in this way, become an audience for their own writing.

Simply put: *writing is a communicative act*—except in school, perhaps, where too often the primary purpose for writing is to demonstrate competence to teachers. For their part, teachers (usually) do not respond to students' writings as audience, but as evaluators. The criterion by which teachers evaluate students' written works isn't whether they are entertained or persuaded, but whether students' writings contain elements of persuasion or entertainment. An eighth-grade teacher we observed who assigned his students the task of writing letters to the editor evaluated students' writings solely on the basis of the presence or absence of certain stylistic elements (e.g., argument and counter-argument) and not whether the teacher found the arguments persuasive or not (Dudley-Marling & Oppenheimer, 1995). In general, when teachers act as evaluators they compromise their role as authentic audiences, and students' communicative intentions become secondary to pleasing teachers.

A fundamental assumption underpinning writing process pedagogy (e.g., Graves, 1983, 1994; Calkins, 1994) is that students should write to fulfill *their* intentions. From the perspective of teachers, "We cannot teach writing well unless we trust that there are real, human reasons to write" (Calkins, 1994, p. 12). Students can only write for their intentions, however, if they share their writing with audiences who respond to those intentions. Therefore, in writing process classrooms "Children's greeting cards are mailed, their letters answered, their stories read aloud, their plays performed, their recipes followed, their songs sung, their posters and notices hung, their poems chanted and given as gifts and learned by heart" (Calkins, 1994, p. 70). This does not mean, however, an abdication of teachers' responsibilities nor does it mean that teachers can *never* tell students what to do (something about which we'll say more later). Effective writing teachers actively and directly teach students the skills they need to fulfill their communicative intentions. If students' writings aren't persuasive, teachers help students learn the skills of persuasion. If their stories aren't entertaining, perhaps because they're poorly organized, teachers teach students how to better organize their writing. But the best way for students to learn that their writing isn't persuasive or entertaining is to get the response of an interested audience.

What Teachers Do: Elements of the Writing Workshop

In this section we describe elements of the writing workshop—predictability, immersion in literature, minilessons, conferencing, and sharing—as a means of discussing the nature of teacher support within the structure of the writing workshop.

Creating an Environment for Writing

Writers need regular times for writing. Professional writer Flannery O'Connor observes: "Every morning between 9 and 12 I go to my room and sit before a piece of paper. Many times I just sit for three hours with no ideas coming to me. But I know one thing: If an idea does come between 9 and 12, I am there ready for it" (in Murray, 1990). Ideally, student writers are given time to write every day, but, if this isn't possible, the writing schedule should at least be predictable—writing every Monday, Wednesday, and Friday, for example. A predictable writing time encourages students to write, or at least think about writing at home and at school, between writing workshops. A student who knows he will be starting a new piece of writing the next day at school may, for example, be alert to possible writing topics outside the classroom. Students who know that, on Thursday, they'll be returning to a piece-of-writing-in-progress may give considerable thought outside the writing workshop to developing some detail, adding a character, describing a setting, or making an argument. Some may even write between writing workshops. Students who do not know when to expect writing—as in the case of a resource room teacher who treats writing as an occasional diversion—are denied opportunities to learn to think like a writer and see the world as writers see it.

Writers also need access to the tools of writing—pens, pencils, markers, crayons, erasers, lined and unlined paper, note pads, book-binding materials, staplers, Scotch tape, typewriters, word processors, and so on. Clever teachers also invite writing by leaving writing materials in places students are likely to use them, by encyclopedias and dictionaries, for example. Surrounding students with good literature and the writing of classmates also invites writing.

Students need good places to write, including places where students can talk about their writing without distracting their classmates and places to write where they won't be distracted. We have visited many classrooms where teachers have set aside quiet places for writing (maybe in the hall) and places for talking about writing (e.g., a table designated as an editing table or a conference center).

Writers also need concentrated blocks of time for writing, teacher-directed lessons, conferencing, and sharing. Twenty- or thirty-minute writing blocks leave student writers little time to write at all—much less share or conference—after they've gathered together their writing materials and reoriented themselves to a piece of writing. If we expect that writers need time to write, reflect, share, and discuss then they'll need lots of time for this. For this reason two or three sixty- to ninety-minute writing blocks per week are preferable to twenty to thirty writing periods each day. In general, "The most important thing . . . is that we do not abbreviate the writing workshop so that it lasts only as long as our children's attention for writing lasts. One of our major goals at this point is to encourage children to say more, to sustain their work longer, to approach a text expecting it to be more detailed, and all of this means that we need to give children more time for writing than they know what to do with" (Calkins, 1994, p. 115).

Time is especially important for struggling writers who often need more time for the physical act of getting the words onto the page as well as the development of their ideas. Yet writing in the context of resource room programs, in which students spend much of their time just going to and from the resource room, may give struggling students little time for actually writing. Competition between reading and writing may also deny students many opportunities to write in resource room settings. These realities support the model of remedial and learning disabilities teachers working to support struggling writers within the regular classroom (see Chapter 13) or, alternatively, students coming to resource rooms for longer, if fewer, reading and writing sessions.

Immersing Students in Literature

PBS recently broadcast a ten-part series on the history of rock 'n' roll. Over and over again vocalists and musicians talked about how they learned their craft by listening to the records of other artists. British rockers learned about the blues by listening to Black American blues artists. Several generations of guitarists learned to play the guitar by listening to Jimi Hendrix. Future record producers learned their craft from Phil Specter records. Little Richard, Elvis, and Jerry Lee Lewis taught countless rock 'n' rollers how to perform. Learning to perform (or produce) music by listening to records and the radio stands in sharp contrast to the way many students are taught to write. How often have any of us seen, for example, teachers give formulas for writing cinquain, haiku, acrostics, sonnets, and limericks which students were expected to follow? On other occasions we've observed teachers direct students to follow simple models for rhyming poems. Less often we see teachers and students learn about poetry by reading, discussing, and studying the poetry of Robert Frost, Langston Hughes, Carl Sandburg, e. e. cummings, Eloise Greenfield, Cynthia Rylant, or Karla Kuskin. But is it possible to learn the power and craft of poetry from any place other than reading poetry? We cannot imagine that musicians could learn their craft without hearing music, and we don't think students can learn to write poetry without reading it and hearing it read. The best teachers of poetry are poets themselves, although we expect good teachers will draw students' attention to the topics and techniques of various poets. The alternative is the probability that our students will learn about poetry from commercial rhymes, jingles, and pop songs. (As we were writing this chapter one of us attended a wedding where a syrupy, vapid poem read and written by a friend of the bride showed just these influences.) Of course, these arguments apply to the writing of any genre, not just poetry.

An effective writing program immerses students in good literature, using literature to support what students are trying to do and encouraging them to try new things. "Teachers . . . know that if you want to attract children to the joys of a writing workshop, you must prepare fertile ground and do what the experts suggest: 'Bathe, immerse, soak, drench your students in good literature' " (Harwayne, 1992, p. 1). Fictional narratives teach students about the use of leads, plot, and character development. Biography teaches our students about expanding details and the need for research. From reading essays and editorials, students learn how to construct concise arguments. Poems teach children about words and language. Teachers can also draw on literary resources during minilessons and conferences to help teach students about the writer's craft. But, as Shelley Harwayne puts it: "Students need to value listening to good literature, talking about good literature, and owning good literature before they are asked to have a good lead or to use surprising details . . . We can use literature to help students view reading and writing as lifetime pleasures and to nurture their own images of good writing" (1992, p. 3). It comes as no surprise to us that great writing teachers (and fine writers) like Nancie Atwell, Lucy Calkins, and Shelley Harwayne share a love of literature. How could it be otherwise?

Conducting Minilessons

It's common for writing workshops to begin with a minilesson, although we have known some teachers who preferred minilessons at the end of the writing period. Whenever they are conducted minilessons are a "forum for making a suggestion to the whole class—raising a concern, exploring an issue, modelling a technique, [or] reinforcing a strategy" (Calkins, 1994, p. 193). Ideally, minilessons teach *into* our students' intentions (Calkins, 1994), perhaps developing skills our students are ready to use (e.g., punctuation, developing leads, adding details, and so forth) or challenging students to tackle new genres or techniques. Minilessons would not, however, normally be used to teach a predetermined list of skills without reference to what students are actually doing with their writing.

Here we'll illustrate minilessons by discussing several kinds of minilessons including minilessons that discuss procedures for writing workshop, help students discover writing topics, demonstrate writing processes, involve students in "writerly conversations," confront students' beliefs about writing, and offer students explicit instruction in writing skills, strategies, and techniques (Calkins, 1994).

DISCUSSING PROCEDURES FOR WRITING WORKSHOP The minilesson is a good place to discuss writing workshop procedures (Calkins, 1986, 1994). Students need to know, for example, whether, or when, they're free to move around the room during writing workshop. In some classes students may be asked to stay in their seats for some portion of the writing period before being allowed to move about the room in order to conference or share their writing. In other classes students may be free to move about the classroom any time as long as they continue to focus on their writing. In Dudley-Marling's third grade the students and teacher discussed how to solve a problem at the beginning of writing workshops. Too often students were taking up to fifteen minutes to get down to writing. Finally, it was agreed that the first ten minutes of every writing period would be a quiet time in the hopes that this would enable students to return to their writing more quickly. (It worked.) Minilessons can also be used to discuss other procedural issues such as: Where do we keep our writing tools? How can we move to the carpet quickly for Authors' Chair without a lot of disruptions? How can we plan an authors' celebration? (Calkins, 1994).

In general, minilessons are a good time to discuss the range of policies and procedures needed to keep writing workshops running smoothly. The nature of these policies and procedures will vary according to such things as class size, the availability of space, and school policies. We also would expect very different procedures in regular classrooms and in resource rooms, where minilessons may not always be practical.

HELPING STUDENTS DISCOVER WRITING TOPICS   The first day of writing workshop in Ms. Carter's class began like this. Ms. Carter gathered her second graders around her on the carpet and told her students the story about the day a stray cat "adopted" her family when she was seven years old. The most observant of her children noticed that Ms. Carter's eyes grew moist when she reached the part of her story when, after three or four months, the cat left to adopt another family. After she finished her story she asked her students to take a couple of minutes to think of their own stories which she asked them to share with another student. A few shared their stories with the entire class. Finally, Ms. Carter gave each student a blank sheet of paper and asked her students to return to their tables and put the stories they'd just told their friends in writing. In this extended minilesson (adapted from Nancie Atwell, 1987), Marion Carter helped her students discover writing topics by sharing a story she knew would resonate with her second graders.

When Dudley-Marling taught third grade, he continued to share with his students pieces of writing drawn from his experience as a means of suggesting genres and topics to his class. He emphasized everyday stories which he hoped would overcome the reluctance of some of his students to tell stories that came from their everyday experiences, which they were quick to dismiss as "not interesting." For example, the following story about getting locked out of his father's house inspired a number of stories about parents losing car keys, being locked out of the house, and, in one case, being locked *in* the bathroom.

Bees and Keys

We'd driven all day in the car and we got there around dinner-time. My dad wasn't there when we arrived, but he'd left us a note telling us that there were steaks in the refrigerator for us to cook on the grill. We had a wonderful feast on the deck. Then some wasps came around and Chris closed the door to the house. As soon as she started to close the door I said, "Don't . . ." But it was too late. We were locked out. The car keys and our shoes were locked in the house and then it started to rain. Finally, we gathered up the courage to go to a neighbor's house and phoned my dad. Within 15 minutes his secretary came by with a spare key. All was well—until I, still barefooted, stepped on a wasp. By then I just wanted to go home.

In general, Dudley-Marling discovered that stories about a trip to the grocery store, a childhood pet, or getting locked out his father's house encouraged students to draw on similar experiences for their writing. Once, however, he forgot the value of the commonplace and shared with his class a story about a transcontinental bike trip he'd taken several years before. That day Dudley-Marling found John, one of his third graders, staring at the blank page in front of him explaining that he'd "never done anything like a bike ride in the mountains."

Brainstorming is another strategy some teachers use from time to time during writing workshop to help students identify the range of topics they might write about. In one third-grade class the students generated the following list of topics which their teachers posted in a prominent place.

Possible Writing Topics

hockey	pets	dinosaurs
soccer	planet	Santa Claus
baseball	nature	swimming
Olympics	Canada	golf
football	books	animals
government	lacrosse	things you did
volleyball	other people	stories
basketball	places	things you know about
beauty salon	family	skating
tennis	TV shows	our class

An alternative version of brainstorming is to ask students to generate a list of topics from what they've been reading or books that have been read to them. A second-grade class responded to this challenge by generating the following list of topics.

giants	postmen	pigs
spiders	jokes	news
wolves	frogs	monsters
people	ghosts	kids
lighthouses	friends	turtles
moms	dads	snowsuits

sisters	detectives	mysteries
comic characters	brothers	princesses
grandparents	caterpillars	cats
plums	dinosaurs	sad things

One teacher we know routinely asked her students "What memories does this book wake up in your head?" after she read to them, offering another opportunity to use literature to suggest writing topics to students.

Brainstorming may also help move students who are stuck on a topic (we all know students who write endlessly about superheroes, friends, hockey, or pets, for example) or encourage students to try out a new genre. One weakness of writing programs in many whole language classrooms is the heavy emphasis on personal narratives and story writing to the near exclusion of other genres like poetry, biography, essay writing, and so on. Expanding the range of genres within which children write increases the chances that they will discover their voices as writers. (Author Ann Rice says that it wasn't until she started writing stories about supernatural characters set in New Orleans that she found her voice as a writer.) Students will not learn the techniques of writing in various genres unless they actually write in those genres. You don't learn much about writing nonfiction, for example, if you only write fiction.

The risk of brainstorming is that some students may limit their topic choice to topics on the "official" list. Therefore, sometimes it's better to use brainstorming with individual students or groups of students who are having difficulty finding something to write about. Some teachers encourage students to keep lists of possible writing topics inside their writing folders. Often these teachers will ask students to add to their list of prospective topics when interesting ideas appear in students' talk or writings.

Some teachers succumb to the temptation to give students writing topics, arguing that some students, especially students for whom writing is a struggle, don't have anything to write about, perhaps because they haven't had as many experiences as other children. Some teachers also argue that assigned writing topics or story-starters get students down to writing more quickly. We believe teachers should reject these arguments and, instead, use the kinds of strategies we've suggested to help students identify their own writing topics. As we've said before, all children come to school with a rich set of experiences they can draw upon in their writing. The assumption that some children have more or less experience is the (unconscious) privileging of some experiences (e.g., middle-class) over others. Moreover, students' best writings arise out of their own experiences (Graves, 1983), and students who select their own topics learn how to choose writing topics independently. Children who are regularly given writing topics by their teachers learn to write to their teachers' intentions. Students who select their own topics are also more likely to achieve significant growth in the information they present about topics, in the organization of information, and in the use of conventions (Graves, 1983).

In general, the use of assigned topics and story-starters may be most destructive for students for whom writing is a struggle since these practices risk diminishing these students' already low confidence in their ability to write anything people would be interested in reading.

DEMONSTRATING WRITING PROCESSES   Another kind of minilesson demonstrates some of the strategies and techniques writers use and the decisions they make in the process of writing. One way to demonstrate some of the decisions writers make is to write in front of students. In the following example a fourth-grade teacher began a minilesson by telling her class that she wanted to write a story about a boy returning to a cabin to warm up before resuming his search for friends lost in a snow storm. She began by writing the following sentence at the top of the chart paper: "The boy walked into the room." Then she asked her class what kind of information they thought she should include. Her students suggested the following questions:

- What's the boy's name?
- How did he get to the room?
- What was he wearing?
- What was he doing?
- Why did he come into the room?
- How old is he?
- Where does he live?
- What does he look like?
- What is he like?
- What school does he go to?
- How big is the room? What does it look like?
- Whose room is it?
- Why did he go into the room?

The teacher then wrote the following passage in front of her students, talking aloud about some of the decisions she was making and sometimes responding to her students' comments about what she was writing.

Tom [a name one of her students suggested] pushed open the door and dragged what he thought were his legs into the room ["We'll have him come into the room to warm up."]. It took almost all his energy to loosen his icy shoelaces and remove his frozen boots. He [first she wrote "had lost the" then said, "no let me change that" as she crossed out these words] could no longer feel his toes so he was almost surprised to see they were still there. [first wrote "Then" and then crossed this out] He took off his snow-encrusted cap and too-thin jacket before walking across the room. Cautiously, [she said, "I want to show that he was so cold the heat from the fire almost hurt] he moved closer to the fire letting the [she started to write "flames" and then asked her class what they thought. One of the students suggested "heat" would sound better] heat warm his face. ["Let's make this an adventure."] Then his mind turned toward his friends who were still out there—somewhere. He'd have to resume his search for them soon, but for now . . . [Then she talked about why she chose to use an ellipsis to end this passage.]

Minilessons can also be a good place to demonstrate the process of revision. Dudley-Marling began a minilesson on revision by sharing the following piece of writing about a childhood treasure with his class. He then revised the piece as his class watched, explaining the symbols he was using and the bases for various decisions he was making as he went (e.g., "This doesn't sound very interesting" or "I don't need to say this," and so on).

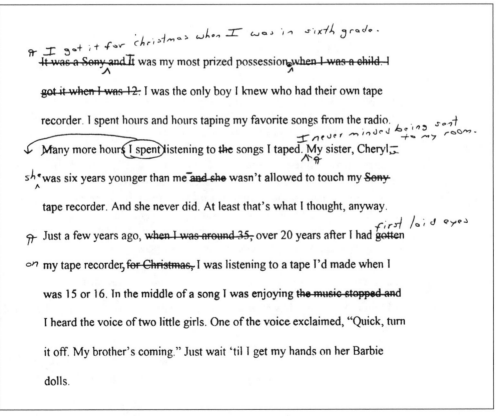

FIG 11-1   "My sister and the Sony"

Similar lessons can be used to demonstrate a variety of revision strategies including:

- Cutting and taping or stapling to reorganize portions of text.

- Drawing arrows to places where additions could be made (e.g., margins).

- Using codes to denote where additions coded the same way fit into text.

- Crossing out words, lines, whole blocks of text.

- Using carets to insert information.

- Numbering to reorder paragraphs.

- Writing on one side of the paper.

- Writing on every other line.

- Leaving large margins for additions.

- Any other revision strategy you use as an author.

- Moving, deleting, and inserting text with a word processor.

We can also use minilessons to share revision strategies we have observed students themselves using. If, for example, we observe a student using Post-Its to insert text we can use the minilesson for the student to share her revision strategy with the rest of the class.

Other minilessons illustrate the processes of editing, drafting, writing leads, adding details, and so on. In the following minilesson Dudley-Marling shared with his class a piece he'd written about a trip to a carnival when he was fourteen as a means of demonstrating the process by which some writers select appropriate leads (i.e., introductory lines) for their pieces by first generating and then choosing among a number of alternatives. He confessed that he didn't like the way it began (his students agreed that the beginning wasn't very interesting) so he told his students that what he thought he might do was write several different leads (explaining to his class what this meant) and ask them to help him choose the best beginning for his story. He generated the following list of possibilities:

1. I'd worked all day for that money—and it was gone in less than 30 minutes.

2. My mouth was already watering thinking about the cotton candy and candied apples.

3. The carnival was coming to town and I didn't have any money.

4. It was over 30 years ago and it was the last time I ever gambled. Now I won't even buy a lottery ticket.

5. I spent over an hour hiding in my closet crying my eyes out. I was fourteen and I thought it was the worst day of my life.

What followed was a ten-minute discussion of the merits of each of these leads and the importance of leads in general. Other minilessons demonstrate what writers might do when they get stuck (e.g., just get something down because you can always revise it), how they handle words they don't know how to spell (e.g., maybe just try a spelling followed by a question mark), choosing among alternate conclusions, revising as they write, and so on. It is important not only to illustrate the kinds of decisions writers make, but to talk about how writers might go about making these decisions.

INVOLVING STUDENTS IN WRITERLY CONVERSATIONS   Developing writers, like experienced writers (even commercial authors), benefit from opportunities to talk about the craft of writing. By situating these conversations within the writing workshop (i.e., minilessons) we help students make the connection between talking about writing and the physical act of putting pen to paper.

One kind of writerly conversation is to talk about the work of commercial authors, perhaps as part of genre studies or explorations of the work of particular authors. Students and teachers can discuss the techniques of various writers, where commercial authors get their ideas, how they go about writing and revising their work, and so on. Some of these lessons may depend on teachers doing a little research, but more often these discussions are based on students' responses to the work of commercial authors. To get students to talk about commercial authors' uses of technique, for example, Shelley Harwayne (1992) asked students questions like:

- Do you think the author wrote her story to be funny on purpose or do you think that's just the way it turned out?

- Could you ever imagine using this same kind of humor in your writing?

- What techniques might you borrow from this author?

Arguably, talking about the work of commercially published authors is a key to students developing into effective, lifelong writers. It is within these writerly conversations that authors like Katherine Patterson, Lois Lowry, E. B. White, Beverly Cleary, Robert Cormier, Tomie de Paola, Jack Prelutsky, Maurice Sendak, Shel Silverstein, Robert Munch, Eric Carle, and so many others *teach* our students how to write.

Writerly conversations can also be a place for students to share their own perspectives on writing. For example:

- Where do they look for ideas when they can't think of anything to write about?

- What do they do when they're stuck? (Calkins, 1994)

- To whom do they turn (or what strategies do they use) when they are uncertain about the spelling of a word?

- Where and when do they like to write (and why)?

- How is writing at home different from writing at school? (Calkins, 1994)

- What have they learned about writing recently?

Talking about the craft of writing this way enables students to learn from each other and from commercial authors by reading like writers (Smith, 1982b).

CONFRONTING STUDENT BELIEFS ABOUT WRITING   Many struggling writers are reluctant to write at all, in which case whole class or small group minilessons can be used to confront students' beliefs about writing. For example, a fifth-grade teacher we know found that it took three months for her less able writers to reach an acceptable level of writing fluency. No matter how many times she told her students that she didn't want them to worry about spelling and neatness, that their ideas mattered most in initial drafts, her students wouldn't take risks and continued to do "safe" writing. Only gradually did her students stop writing about things they were sure they could spell; only gradually did they stop balking at frequent writing.

The following year the same teacher was faced with a new class of unconvinced fifth graders reputed to have low self-concepts and a reputation for dreadful academic performance and behavior. This time she decided to enlist the help of the previous year's fifth graders to talk with her new class about what they had learned about writing when they were in fifth grade. She constructed a series of open-ended statements for each group to respond to in writing.

For previous students:

1. When my teacher first told us we were all authors, I . . .

2. At first when I was given a writing assignment, I . . .

3. When I first found out I was expected to write a book, I . . .

4. If I were advising other kids about writing, I would tell them . . .

5. I felt much better about writing once I realized . . .

6. I first realized that I could really write when . . .

7. For me, the least enjoyable part of writing was . . .

8. The most valuable thing I learned from writing was . . .

For current students:

1. When my teacher tells us that she knows we are all authors, I . . .

2. When my teacher gives us a writing assignment, I . . .

3. When I saw the books from last year's fifth graders, I . . .

4. If I could ask another student one question about learning to write well, I would ask . . .

5. What scares me about the whole idea of writing is . . .

6. Writing would be a lot easier if I knew more about . . .

7. The best part about making a book would be . . .

8. What makes writing good is . . . (Clyde, 1981)

Then the teacher arranged to have the two classes meet during the time usually set aside for minilessons so that they could exchange their ideas about writing. Hearing their older peers discuss their previous year's experiences—how these experiences had affected their perceptions about themselves as authors and resulted in new insights into the writing process—seemed to help the current students react much more quickly to the teacher's instructional strategies for increasing writing fluency. The fifth graders in the second class wrote fluently by mid-October, in spite of their reputation.

Questions from the writing interview (see Chapter 4) are also useful for initiating discussions about students' beliefs. The question, "When you are writing and you have a problem (or get stuck) what do you do?" might elicit comments from acknowledged writers that they too encounter problems when they write. This "news" will often come as a great surprise to many struggling writers who imagine that encountering problems when they write is what makes them poor writers.

TEACHING WRITING STRATEGIES AND TECHNIQUES   Minilessons can also be a place for occasional teacher-directed lessons on various writing skills such as learning to provide details by including more specific information, making language choices, organizing writing into paragraphs, and so on. The following lesson, for example, was designed to help students learn how specifics contribute to effective writing. The teacher began by finding a text that contained specifics (see Figure 11-2) which, for purposes of comparison, she rewrote in more general terms. She asked her students to read and compare each version of the text, focusing on details the authors used that were not included in the more general version she had written and how the details helped readers. A follow-up to this discussion might have students attempt to locate places in a piece of recent writing where they could have incorporated more details. Another lesson might show students how specifics can sometimes be overdone.

Another lesson for illustrating the importance of including specifics requires students to write directions for making a peanut butter sandwich (Murray, 1968; Yoakley, 1974) for readers who have never made a peanut butter sandwich before. Once students have finished writing their directions, the fun begins as directions are read aloud and followed to the letter. When students watch the teacher trying to put peanut butter on an invisible piece of bread because the bread wasn't mentioned in the directions, they quickly see where they need to revise their writing. Of course, this activity can easily be adapted to a number of other situations. It is

SPECIFICS	GENERAL MEANING
Bumpty, bounce. Bumpty, bounce. Stanleigh ran into a field a field of flowers. Swish, swish. Swish, swish.	Stanleigh ran into a field.
He found a tall flower. He pulled the blossom down so he could see it better. He put his nose into its yellow center. Ummmm. It smelled sweet.	He found a flower and smelled it.
For a long time Stanleigh lay on his back in the grasses and flowers. Then he heard a noise. Bubbly, gurgle. Bubbly, gurgle. Rolling over, he ran, looking for the sound. Soon he smelled water. The bubbly gurgle sound was water.	He found water.
Stanleigh put his paws in the water. The water was cool, and it moved. The water in his dish just sat there.	He touched the water.

FIG 11-2 *Specifics and general meaning:* But Not Stanleigh *(Steiner, 1980)*

also interesting to have students share examples of incomplete or inexplicit instructions they come across outside of school (instructions for assembling a model car, for example).

Sometimes writers choose topics for which they lack sufficient information, in which case they need to spend some time gathering specifics by observing, researching, or otherwise learning more about the subject. Vergason suggests an observation assignment to gather specifics to write about one person (1974). Students are asked to select a person to observe and then surreptitiously observe that person over a five-day period, capturing a variety of moods and situations by using all their senses, noting mannerisms, and recording quotes that are typical or provide insights into the person's attitudes, opinions, and speech patterns. Of course, when students discuss or write about the person they've observed, they should protect the person's identity.

Another kind of teacher-directed minilesson focuses on helping students organize their writing into paragraphs, a decision that befuddles many novice writers (and even some more experienced writers). Paragraphs alert readers to topic changes, but they do not stand alone. Paragraphs must relate to texts as a whole and to other paragraphs in terms of an overall coherent structure. Writers don't write paragraphs as much as they use them to organize their writing out of consideration of the needs of readers.

Students need to learn about the nature of paragraphs and how paragraphs function within texts. This isn't the same, however, as teaching students "formulas" for writing paragraphs. Even a quick perusal of commercial fiction, for example, demonstrates that most paragraphs do not include a topic sentence, several sentences expanding the topic, and a summary sentence. Authors may place topic sentences in the middle of paragraphs and sometimes paragraphs go on for pages. And what do we make of one-sentence paragraphs? It's not surprising that most of us would despair just thinking about trying to explain the precise form and function of paragraphs within texts, even to secondary students. Instead of looking for paragraphing formulas we should look to provide students with experiences that increase their intuitive knowledge about the function and structure of paragraphs. The primary source of that information is students' reading. However, there are minilessons that can draw students' attention to paragraphs.

The puzzle strategy described in Chapter 8, for example, can be used in a whole class or small group minilesson. As students work together to order the paragraphs of a text in some logical way, they will have to consider the kinds of choices authors make about paragraphs: which paragraphs are gathered under which subtitle, how paragraph topics are related to each other, how authors use transitions between paragraphs, and so on.

The same strategy can be used to help students get a feel for the choices authors make in arranging sentences into paragraphs. Several paragraphs that make sense out of context can be selected from a text and written separately on strips of tagboard arranged on the blackboard in a random fashion. As students work together to put the sentences into some kind of order (and there may be several possible orderings that make sense), they'll discuss some of the decisions they'll make when they compose and revise their own work. Additionally, by ordering sentences within each paragraph students may begin to develop an intuitive sense of how sentences are related to each other within paragraphs.

The puzzle strategy can also be used with students' own compositions as a means of encouraging students to explore alternate arrangements of sentences and paragraphs within their work.

When writers compose sentences—and paragraphs—they also make decisions about vocabulary and sentence structure. Since these choices are made within the context of whole texts, instruction in sentence structure and vocabulary use should also occur within the context of whole texts. The practice of teaching grammar as an end in itself, for example, has not been found to have any effect on students' speaking or writing. To the degree that the teaching of grammar steals time away from students actually writing, it may interfere with writing development (*Language Arts*, 1986, p. 103). There is little reason to believe that isolated vocabulary instruction will be any more effective (Dudley-Marling & Searle, 1991). Minilessons using *sentence expansion*, *word substitution*, and *sentence combining* can, however, help some students understand choices available to them at the sentence and word level.

Preparing a minilesson using sentence expansion begins by identifying sentences in students' writings that have the potential to be expanded. In a Title I class, for example, we lifted one sentence from each student's composition which we wrote on the board. Where we thought words or phrases could be added to the sentences, we inserted a caret and asked students to suggest how sentences could be expanded. The students supplied a number of ideas for expansion, which we wrote on the board above the caret. Then the students who wrote the sentences were asked to indicate which words or phrases they preferred from among those suggested, keeping in mind clarity, how the new sentence "sounded," and the original context.

Another day we again asked students to discuss different sentences lifted from their writing, this time focusing on places where their ideas could be expanded. Finally, we asked students to locate sentences that could be expanded in their own compositions, to expand those sentences, and then to share their revisions with their classmates. In time many students in this class used sentence expansion as a technique for spontaneously revising their writing.

Similar techniques can be used to deal with the tendency of many students to overuse words like *pretty, nice, happy,* or slang terms like *cool, awesome,* or *excellent.* In this minilesson, teachers write sentences with these words on the board—explaining where the examples came from—and invite students both to offer alternative wording and to discuss why varied vocabulary may be desirable.

Students may also overuse "placeholder" phrases in their writing. A typical example, "I like . . . because . . . ," comes from a writing sample written by a boy named Jeremy after a trip to a museum:

> I liked that Cheetah because it pulled up that deer. I liked the zbra because uve his shrips. [I liked the zebra because of his stripes.] I liked the Tyrranasaurus Rex because of his sharp teeth and he's a meat eater and that's why I like him. I liked the gold at the musem because it is shiny. I liked the saber tooth tiger when he was going to jump on the dinosaur.

To help Jeremy and several other students whose writing was marked by the repetition of stock phrases his teacher prepared a small group minilesson. She wrote Jeremy's piece on an overhead. First, she and her students offered their impressions of Jeremy's piece. Then the teacher used small strips of paper to cover up all occurrences of "I like" and "because." Next, the teacher wrote her own alternatives to the

"I like . . . because . . ." pattern. As an alternative to Jeremy's wording she suggested: "The saber tooth tiger was going to jump on the dinosaur. The zebra had stripes." She then asked students to suggest their own variations. On different days she constructed similar lessons using examples lifted from other students' writings.

Students can also learn about the language choices available to them through sentence combining (Nutter & Safran, 1983, 1984; see S. L. Stotsky, 1974, for a review of research). For a whole-class or small-group minilesson a teacher might lift several sentences from a student's writing, put the sentences on the overhead or blackboard, and then ask students to suggest ways to combine these sentences into a single sentence. (Obviously this lesson requires that students have some sense for a sentence.) Combinations of the following sentences, "My dog's name is Patches. He likes to play with me. He likes to chase tennis balls," might include:

My dog Patches likes to play with me and chase the tennis ball.

Patches, my dog, likes to chase the tennis ball and play with me.

My dog Patches likes to play with me, especially when I throw the tennis ball for him.

When I want to play catch I can always count on Patches to play with me.

Moffett suggests that "The learner must hear and read many sentence constructions that would not initially come to his mind. But he needs to try out the forms he takes in" (1968, p. 168). Students can use sentence combining to try out various sentence forms. We don't recommend commercially developed exercises, however. First, students need to understand that sentence combining is a language choice, not an exercise. Through playing around with various sentence combinations, students learn that it's their choice whether the sentences should be combined, and if they are to be combined, how to combine them. It's only through comparing various combinations of the same sentences that students can sense the subtle changes in meaning caused by the various sentence combinations and the effect of those changes in meaning on the composition itself. Moffett says, "Only a comparison of sentence alternatives—in the context of what the author is trying to accomplish—will teach judgment" (1968, p. 177).

In general, teacher-directed minilessons can help develop students' understandings of various writing strategies and techniques, but we must be careful not to overuse teacher-directed lessons, which can discourage students—especially students for whom writing is a struggle—from relying on their own resources in the process of writing. It is also important to construct teacher-directed lessons that respond to the specific needs of the whole class (for whole-class minilessons) or groups of students (for small-group minilessons).

Finally, "Understanding good writing requires more than a minilesson. Ideas need to be studied deeply. We can't teach an idea by teaching one minilesson and adding that idea to a student checklist or classroom poster. There can't be a bumper sticker that says, 'Do it with details' " (Harwayne, 1992, p. 278). Conferences are places for following up on the content of minilessons and helping students make connections between minilessons and their own writing.

Conferences

Children's development as writers depends on frequent, sustained periods of writing time as well as the active support and direction of their teachers. Minilessons respond to the general instructional needs of groups of students, while writing conferences are places where teachers can focus on the specific needs of individual students. Teachers who conference with individual students, or groups of students, while the rest of the class is engaged in writing are able to respond to individual writer's needs for frequent, intense, explicit, and individualized instruction. In this section we discuss several types of writing conferences of particular interest to teachers of struggling writers.

Nothing ensures talk so much as the presence of an interested listener, and one of the goals of a writing conference is to *listen* to what students have to say. Writing conferences "should be natural . . . full of good listening and honest reactions" (Calkins, 1986, p. 132). Teachers who ask students to "Tell me about your piece" or "How's it going?" focus on the content of students' writings while acknowledging students' control over their writing. Some teachers, for example, encourage students to put aside their writing and just talk about what they've written. Other teachers ask students to read what they've written. In either case, teachers deliberately avoid words or actions that risk taking control of students' writings. This caution is especially important for remedial students and students with learning disabilities, for example, since it is likely these students already have doubts that they have anything worthwhile to say. This all requires considerable patience on the part of teachers who may feel remiss if they don't provide students with direct, immediate feedback on the quality of their writing. But, however successful in the short term, this sort of instruction can seriously affect students' long-term development into confident, fluent, independent writers.

Listening to students' writing does not mean, however, concealing our honest reactions. We don't do students any favors if we pretend we understand them when we don't. Listeners work with speakers to avoid communicative breakdown by signaling the need for clarification if it should be necessary. An honest response to a student who says his piece is about "that funny thing that happened to my dad the other night" can reasonably include a request for more details. The student who keeps talking about "he" over and over again should be asked to clarify who "he" is. It's also fair to confess to the student who goes on and on, supplying an infinite number of details, that we're getting confused. The honest response of a listener is natural and usually welcome. What is not helpful—at least at this stage—is strictly evaluative response that focuses on the form of students' writing rather than what students have to say. This stance can discourage developing writers from taking risks and signals to the student that, whatever we may say to the contrary, students should write to please their teachers.

Another kind of writing conference responds to specific problems students are experiencing. Despite our best efforts to help students discover interesting writing topics, for example, some students may continue to complain, "I don't have anything to write about." (We wonder how often this really means: "I want personal attention from my teacher.") The following conference helped a third-grade girl named Roya find a topic she was interested in writing about.

Teacher: What's the problem?

Roya: I have nothing to write about.

Teacher: [Joking] The problem is when you have a dull, uninteresting life—

Roya: Yeah, there's nothing to write about, especially when you have a brother. [But] when you have a brother there's so much you can write about. You can write about what a pain he is.

Lila: [Who has been listening] You *do* have a brother. Why don't you write about what a pain he is and stuff?

Teacher: Actually, you might have something there. I think Lila is right. That is exactly the kind of thing you could write about. Those kinds of stories are funny sometimes.

Roya: Trust me, they are. Once we went to the church when we were coming to Toronto from Montreal. On the way we went to the church with my aunt and everything. There was a cross and Jesus was on it and my brother goes "Who is that?" My dad said, "Jesus." And my brother said, "Tell him to come down." It was just a statue of him.

Soon several students who overheard this conversation joined in and told stories about their brothers and sisters and, over the next several weeks, the students in this class wrote and published many sibling stories. Of course, helping students identify writing topics isn't always this easy.

Other teachers help students identify possible writing topics by asking them to look through their writers' notebooks (see Calkins, 1994) or previous writings they've done. Teachers who routinely ask students to keep a list of possible writing topics, perhaps on the inside of their writers' notebooks or writings folders, can always suggest students take a look at their list of topics. Some teachers draw on literature as a resource for writing topics by asking students to talk about the kinds of books they like to read and why. A student who is particularly interested in mysteries, for example, might be challenged to try his own hand at mystery writing.

Other students may have an idea of what they'd like to write about but have difficulty getting it on paper (often an issue for remedial students and students with learning disabilities who may worry about handwriting, spelling, and punctuation). It can be helpful to ask these students to talk about their ideas while the teacher makes notes on what he hears. Giving students back their words in writing (Harwayne, 1992) gives students something concrete to get started on and provides the security of spelling words of which they may be uncertain.

It is not unreasonable, however, for teachers to finally insist that students pick a writing topic and even direct students to write at least a half page or even a page before the end of the writing period. Students should be able to exercise significant control over certain aspects of their writing, but it is fair to remind our students that *not writing* isn't an option during the writing workshop (Harwayne, 1992). Of course, some students may still resist and, for these students, teachers may have to use various strategies to improve students' writing fluency.

One strategy for increasing a student's writing fluency that teachers can use during conferencing time is the *written conversation* (Burke, in Crafton et al., 1980). In written conversations, two people "talk" to each other about topics of interest to both of them—on paper. The written conversation between fifteen-year-old Brian, a student with learning disabilities, and his teacher is presented in Figure 11-3.

The conversation begins with a question about a recent trip to the Epcot Center in Disney World. Note the open-ended nature of the teacher's questions to Brian, which encouraged Brian to make relatively lengthy responses.

As they wrote this conversation, Brian and his teacher sat near each other, passing the paper back and forth when they were ready for the other person's response. The nature of the activity encouraged Brian to focus on ideas and to write rapidly so that he could respond quickly to his teacher's conversation with him.

Some students' writing is unreadable. Others cannot read what teachers write during a written conversation. For these students, oral language support must be added to what is a silent activity for most students. Brian's teacher, for example, couldn't read part of one of his responses to her and when she couldn't, she asked him to read it to her.

An entire written conversation could be carried on in the same way, with the writer first writing and then reading aloud what she has written before she passes the paper on. Young children and very delayed readers/writers learn a great deal about the relationships between oral and written language in this way, just as they do from language experience dictation. A number of variations on the written conversation technique are possible. Some of the following variations may better suit your students or provide occasional alternatives to written conversation between you and students:

- We have observed a teacher carrying on written conversations with several children at a time, all seated at a round table. Only infrequently did a child have to wait for a response from the teacher.

- Once students understand the nature of written conversation, they may want to carry one on with each other. Students in your class may be paired for written conversation, or older and/or more proficient writers may be paired with your students.

- If students seem to enjoy written conversations with each other, you might consider legitimatizing notes in the classroom or formalize written conversations by setting up a post office in the classroom.

- Written conversation may be carried on using microcomputers. Students can send and respond to electronic mail.

- You and the student may assume other identities as you carry on a written conversation. For example, a third-grade learning disabled student showed up in

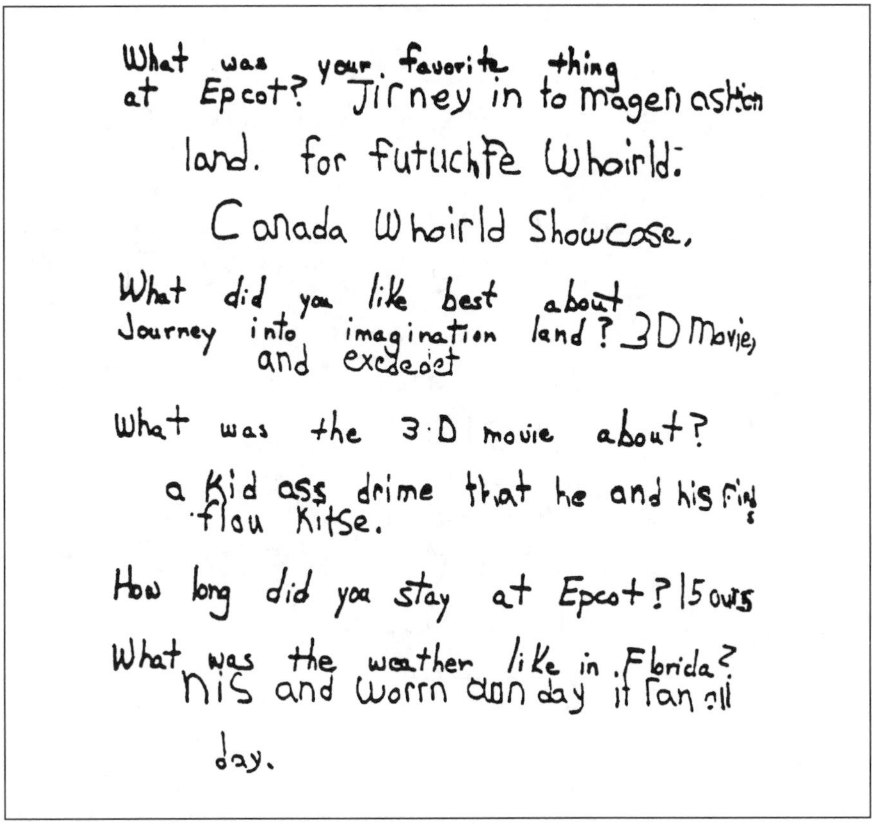

What was your favorite thing
at Epcot? Jirney in to magen ashin
land. for futuchfe Whoirld.
Canada Whoirld Showcase.
What did you like best about
Journey into imagination land? 3D Movie,
and excdeoet
What was the 3·D movie about?
a kid ass drime that he and his fin
flou kitse.
How long did you stay at Epcot? 15 ours
What was the weather like in Florida?
nis and worrn don day it ran all
day.

FIG 11-3   *A written conversation*

class one day with two pocket-size rubber gorillas. Instead of taking the gorilla figures away, the teacher made them a part of the instruction by involving the child (as a gorilla named Ligo) and herself (as a gorilla named Mushka) in a written language conversation and adventure. (see Figure 11-4)

Writing conferences are also places to offer students *tips*, sometimes building on instruction begun in minilessons. Students who need additional information for their writing, for example, can be directed to the appropriate resources. Students whose writing indicates a need for a lesson on punctuation or adding details will benefit from focused, individual lessons. Other students may benefit from advice on organization, leads, sentence structure, word choice, conclusions, character development, revision, and so on. Sometimes teachers direct students to particular authors so students can learn from them about word choice, details, style, and organization (Harwayne, 1992).

Writing conferences can also respond to the needs of struggling writers for tools, techniques, or strategies for dealing with particular kinds of writing including writing assignments in other classes (for example, the case of a student

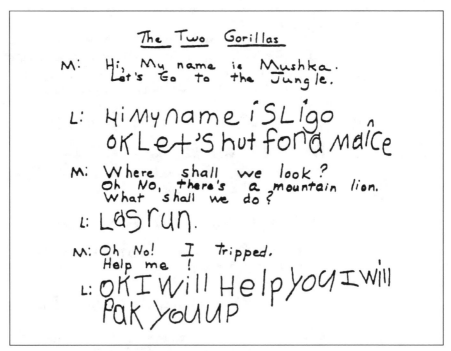

FIG 11-4 *A written conversation: Ligo and Mushka*

bringing a writing assignment to the resource room which has been assigned by the regular classroom teacher). Many students, including remedial students and students with learning disabilities, have difficulty, for example, doing research and organizing information into reports. They may need to be taught a process that includes generating questions to be addressed, gathering information, answering questions, and organizing information into their reports. One useful technique for teaching students how to write reports is the data chart (Crocker, 1983b; McKenzie, 1979). A data chart for a report on insects might look something like the one shown in Figure 11-5.

We recommend that teachers construct data charts with students rather than for them and this might be done in individual conferences or small-group mini-lessons. Construction of the chart itself ought to be part of the report-writing process. If, for example, students are asked to write a report about insects, perhaps in another class, we begin by having them tell us what they understand the assignment to be, giving special attention to those things the teacher has specified should be discussed. Each aspect should be turned into a question and entered by the student in a column of the chart. (See the first three columns on the chart as examples.) Any other questions students want to answer in their report (see the last two columns on the chart as examples) should be entered as well. Then we show the students the function of the horizontal columns. Note that students will often have background information that can be recorded in the *me* column. Or they may be able to make direct observations and record those observations in the *me* column.

	What is the habitat of _____?	What eats _____?	What does _____ eat?	What does _____ look like?	How does _____ harm/help man?
Me					
Source #1					
Source #2					
Summary					

FIG 11-5 *Data chart for insects*

The *sources* columns should be filled in with the names of the books, magazine articles, videos, encyclopedias, and similar sources they have used to locate information. Encourage students to verify information by consulting additional sources. Sometimes they'll locate conflicting information; more often, they'll simply find more information. The summary column encourages students to synthesize the information from all their sources and forms the basis for the report itself.

Students may find that each column lends itself to a paragraph in the report if enough details have been gathered. Writing paragraphs on separate index cards and moving them around may help students explore various ways of organizing their reports. A useful strategy lesson for more sophisticated writers at this point would be to help students create transitions between the paragraphs that need them.

Writing conferences are also places to "nudge" students into new challenges (Atwell, 1987). As a means of encouraging the development of students' writing styles, it might be useful to request a student to imitate the style of a commercial author. Harwayne, for example, asked a student to rewrite what he'd written about his father in a style similar to the way a particular commercial author had written about her father (1992). Or students might be challenged to rewrite stories as poems or plays as a means of getting them to explore different genres. To learn more about revision strategies a student might be asked to rework a confused section—the ending, the title, the lead, part of the text—take a long draft and make it shorter, experiment with different leads, or imagine a different purpose or audience for a piece of writing and then reorient the piece accordingly (Calkins, 1994). Similarly, if a teacher discovered that some of her students were writing drafts that were all about the same length, she might recommend that the students circle sections of their papers that could be expanded with more detail and then turn the sentences into paragraphs.

Many teachers also have editing or "prepublication" conferences with students to discuss "nearly final" drafts of writing they expect to share with a wider audience. (Again, not every piece of writing will be shared and, therefore, not all require editing.) In these conferences teachers might ask the students to take another look at their writing, circling words they're uncertain how to spell and, perhaps, indicating places where they think punctuation might be missing. They might also be asked to mark any places where their piece doesn't "sound" right (i.e., inappropriate syntax). This might, in turn, provide an occasion for a brief lesson on spelling, punctuation, or grammar. Teachers might also act as copy editors and make their own corrections. We talk more about this in the following chapter.

So far we have focused our discussion on conferences between teachers and students, but peer conferences are also valuable. The models presented during minilessons and individual conferences can enable students to provide useful response and feedback to each other at every stage of the writing process. Many teachers take up the issue of learning to provide appropriate, supportive response to each other's writing in minilessons. In some classes students are always free to seek out the response of a classmate to their writing.

One way to regularly organize feedback from peers and to encourage revision is "Authors' Circle" (Burke, 1985). As Carolyn Burke describes it, Authors' Circle involves the following steps:

1. Gather together a group of students, usually three or four, each with a piece of writing "in process." The teacher should join the group regularly, at least in the beginning, and as a member of the group, should share writing from time to time as well.

2. One person begins by reading her writing aloud to the other group members. It's the job of the others to listen as well as possible.

3. Each listener in the group "receives" the writing by telling what he liked best about the piece. Students need to be helped to make specific comments as they receive writing. As one of the group, the teacher also receives the writing and in so doing, demonstrates receiving.

4. A group member asks the author, "What (part) did you like best about your piece of writing?" and the author replies to the question.

Conferencing is, from the teacher's perspective, the key to an effective writing workshop, but it may be the most difficult skill to acquire. Learning to conference effectively requires experience. Teachers cannot learn to conference "by the numbers" and we should be wary of conferencing formulas. There are good questions, but there are no magic questions that serve *all* teachers with *all* students on *all* occasions. To learn from their experience, however, teachers must regularly reflect on what they're doing in conferences. We know some teachers who regularly tape their writing conferences and then listen to these tapes in order to take a more careful look at what they're doing.

While we must all learn how to conference with our students, we do believe that there are several prerequisites for successful conferencing. First of all, teachers need time to conference. Writing programs that limit students to fifteen or twenty minutes for writing also limit teachers' opportunities to conference with their students. Successful conferences also depend on regular evaluation and record keeping. We can't effectively support our students if we don't know what they're doing. It is also important to keep conferences relatively brief. Sometimes long conferences may be called for but, in general, ten- to fifteen-minute conferences deny other students the attention they need. (Of course, longer conferences may be possible in a resource room setting.) However, a two-minute conference every day adds up to a ten-minute conference by the end of the week (Susan Stires, pers. com. 1993). Keeping conferences brief and taking advantage of the possibility of peer conferencing enables teachers to better meet the range of individual needs of their students.

Encouraging Students to Share Their Writing

In our experience most students write to and for their teachers. Students who write primarily for their teachers, however, learn mainly to anticipate teacher response to their writing. If teacher response focuses on elements of style, students will likely concentrate on style. Pretending to write for other audiences, as in the case of students who are asked to write newspaper editorials or letters to politicians, makes little difference if students know (and they *do* know) that their teacher will be the only person reading their writing. Therefore, within the context of the writing workshop students are encouraged to share their writing both as a means of obtaining helpful feedback—as in the case of Authors' Circle—and to fulfill their communicative intentions. Since audience affects both the form and content of writing, students are encouraged to write for a wide range of audiences. Writing for audiences separated from them by time, space, and familiarity, for example, is the only way students can learn to anticipate the needs of distant readers.

The following list of potential audiences (adapted from Kirby & Liner, 1981, pp. 134–35) includes audiences who are well known to students and share their physical and social worlds and unknown audiences whose background knowledge and experience differ markedly from those of our students.

Peers

- in class
- in other schools
- generalized peers (children of the world)
- in other classes (e.g., students' books placed in the school library)
- pen pals (including electronic mail)
- in the school newspaper
- famous peers

Teachers

- classroom teacher (e.g., notes, letters that position teacher as an audience and not an evaluator)
- resource room teacher
- other teachers (former teachers, specialist teachers, and so forth)

Wider-known Audiences

- parents
- neighbors
- parents' friends
- principal
- relatives

Unknown Audiences

- newspaper editor (i.e., letters to the editor)
- athletes
- information sources (e.g., travel agencies, consulates, and so forth)
- heroes

- TV and movie personalities
- citizen groups
- authors
- corporations
- governmental bodies and officials

We believe it is worthwhile to encourage students to write for different audiences or, alternatively, to share their work with a wider audience. We would, however, discourage the practice of routinely assigning audiences to student writers since designating audience can affect the purpose for which students write. Still, asking students to revise a piece of writing as a means of sharing with another audience can alert students to the relationship of content, form, and audience.

Probably the most accessible audience for students' writing is the other students in the classroom. One way many teachers take advantage of this audience is by establishing an *Author's Chair* (Graves & Hansen, 1983), a special chair from which students and teachers read trade books and "finished" pieces of students' writing. Typically, students read a piece of writing, written by themselves or a commercial author, and the other students "receive" it (Graves, 1983) by indicating what they liked about the piece and, perhaps, sharing their own "reading" of the piece (e.g., "I really found your story about your family's escape from Iran interesting. I liked the part at the end when you surprised us by telling that your mother was going to have a baby.") Listeners are also invited to ask questions of the author, ranging from "How did you come up with the idea for this story?" to "I don't understand what you meant when you said . . ."

The same procedure is followed when trade books are read from the Author's Chair—students receive the writing and then ask questions. Since the author is not present, however, the class must speculate on how they imagine the author might respond to their questions. It is hoped that the routine of Author's Chair will influence students to internalize the questions they hear and use them as a guide to revising their writing. As Graves and Hansen put it, a student learns to respond to his or her own work "with a sense of what the class will ask when he or she reads the piece from the author's chair" (1983, p. 182).

Probably the most widely used means for sharing and celebrating students' writings is *publication*. Publication takes many forms: a bound book featuring a piece of writing or, alternatively, the collected works of a group of students, perhaps on a common theme or topic; a piece in the class or school newspaper; a wall display in the classroom at eye level so it can easily be read by everyone; submission to a children's newspaper or magazine; dittoed or Xeroxed copies distributed to the whole class. Directions for binding books can be found in lots of places and many schools now have bookbinding machines. Some teachers set up a *Publication Table* in their classrooms containing materials often used for publishing students' work including: a word processor (or typewriter); good paper; markers or crayons; bookbinding materials (e.g., pre-cut tagboard for covers, construction paper, yarn, staplers, and so forth) and directions; and so on.

Publishing students' works celebrates their accomplishments, confirms their status as authors, and provides personal reasons for students to edit and revise their work (Dudley-Marling, 1995). In general, there is an expectation that only "finished" work will be published, that is, work that has been carefully revised, proofread, and edited. Teachers may take on the role of copy editors for students for whom spelling, punctuation, and proofreading are particularly difficult. Publication is especially valuable for developing writers, including struggling writers who are often reluctant to revise and share their work.

Finally, although publication is an important part of the writing workshop, not every piece of students' writing needs to be published. Publication should be reserved for those pieces of writing students care most about, the pieces they are most willing to "look after" as Donald Graves puts it (in Calkins, 1986, p. 23). An overemphasis on publication can give students the message that every piece of writing is equally worthwhile, discourage students from tackling genres that do not lend themselves to publication (e.g., letters), and overburden teachers. A writing program without publication, however, will always be incomplete.

12

Transcription
Choices and Instruction

Language is a code whereby ideas about the world are represented through a *conventional* system of *arbitrary* signals for communication.

Bloom & Lahey, 1978, p. 4 (emphasis added)

Effective communication between readers and writers depends on a number of shared understandings about language use including a tacit agreement about how various written language conventions (spelling, punctuation, grammatical usage) will be used to represent meaning (F. Smith, 1982b; Tierney & LaZansky, 1980). Readers, for example, have certain expectations about the significance of letters and letter sequences, letter clusters (i.e., words), upper- and lowercase letters, punctuation, and the ordering of words of which writers need to be mindful. Although a complete disregard for written language conventions will result in communicative breakdown, readers are able to deal with some degree of ambiguity. Most readers, for example, could cope with a text without punctuation even though this might require more effort and risk some misunderstanding. Poor handwriting and unconventional spellings will also tax the efforts of readers. Some writers (e.g., e. e. cummings) deliberately flout writing conventions as a playful way of conveying certain meanings, but it usually requires more effort and sophistication on the part of readers to *get* these meanings. In general, the predictable use of writing conventions will always make reading easier. Therefore, the appropriate use of written language conventions—and what counts as appropriate is a function of context, purpose, genre, and so on—may be seen as a courtesy to readers (Wilde, 1992).

Of course, writers also have a stake in fulfilling the expectations of readers. As we have argued throughout this text, learning to write is a matter of learning to use written language forms to fulfill a variety of intentions in a range of social and cultural settings. Writers who do not learn to represent their meanings in conventional ways will not fulfill their intentions or, perhaps worse, they risk being misunderstood. Learning to use written language conventions appropriately is important and cannot be taken for granted. Our experience indicates, for example, that students identified as having writing problems most often have difficulties with spelling and punctuation. Misspelling "is still the single most egregious evidence of supposed illiteracy in the eyes of the general public and employers" (Wilde, 1992,

p. 56) and whole language teachers do not take writing conventions for granted despite claims to the contrary (e.g., Schevermann et al., 1994). Good whole language teachers provide students with explicit support and direction in the use of written language conventions. The intensity of this support depends on the needs of the student, but we expect that most struggling writers will require considerable assistance and instruction from their teachers.

In this chapter we take up the teaching of writing conventions within the context of the writing workshop. The writing conventions we will discuss here include spelling, punctuation (including capitalization), handwriting, and grammatical usage.

Spelling

Not too long ago at a conference for learning disability professionals in Buffalo, a physician presented several examples of misspellings he had gathered from children with whom he was working. These included spellings like "chran" (for *train*), "jrif" (for *drive*), "rad" (for *red*), "yet" (for *went*), and "feh" (for *fish*). Dr. Disability (not his real name) concluded that these "illogical, deviant" spellings supported his diagnosis that these children were "dyslexic." The problem with this analysis, however, is that substitutions like *H* for *sh*, *J/G* for *dr*, *Y* for *W*, and so on are common among letter name spellers (see the discussion of letter name spellers in Chapter 4). They represent sophisticated hypotheses about English orthography (e.g., *Y* is closer to the initial sound in *went* than *W*) and phonology (the child who produced "chran" for *train* was sensitive to the fact that most of us pronounce train "*ch*rain," not *train*) (Temple, Nathan, & Burris, 1993).

Spelling is a cognitive, developmental process (Frith, 1980; E. Henderson & Beers, 1980) that involves basic knowledge of orthographic rules and the strategic application of those rules in the process of writing (Gerber & Hall, 1981; Wilde, 1992). By and large, the research indicates that children's spelling "errors" represent developmental attempts to use orthographic information in a strategic and logical fashion (Read, 1975; E. Henderson & Beers, 1980). This same pattern holds true for remedial students and students with learning disabilities, contrary to the assertions of Dr. Disability. Learning disabled and remedial students tend to make more spelling errors—Graham & Voth (1990) found that students with learning disabilities made two to four times as many spelling errors as their normally achieving peers—but the quality of their errors closely resembles the development of younger, normally achieving students (Bookman, 1983; Gerber & Hall, 1981; Gerber, 1984; Holmes & Peper, 1977; Invernizzi & Worthy, 1989; Nelson, 1980). Invernizzi & Worthy conclude:

> The[se] findings are congruent with the theory of developmental word knowledge and support the position that learning disabled and normally achieving children acquire specific aspects of English orthography in highly similar progressions. (1989, p. 173)

In general, poor spellers tend to sound out words phoneme by phoneme while good spellers use a range of knowledge and strategies to spell words (Hughes & Searle, in press). Poor spellers also seem to be less aware that there are a number of systems at work in spelling (e.g., meaning and sound systems) and less able to generate alternative spellings or make choices among alternate spellings (D. Searle, personal communication, July 6, 1995, regarding the study that he and Margaret Hughes are conducting on the spelling development of three groups of children they followed from kindergarten through sixth grade).

These findings have important instructional implications. If the spelling patterns of learning disabled and remedial students are not atypical then these students do not need unique instruction. They may, however, require more instruction, more intense instruction, and more individual instruction compared to their normally achieving peers (Wilde, 1992).

Our discussion of spelling instruction is based on several important assumptions. First, since spelling is a cognitive process, "Learning to spell requires the active, hypothesis-testing involvement of the learner" (Zutell, 1978, p. 849). Therefore, teachers should encourage students to take responsibility for spelling during writing. If students request help, a consistent reply of "Spell it the best you can" and the acceptance of students' efforts will usually assure students' active involvement. Conversely, teachers who regularly spell words for their students or use strategies like "Write the first letter and draw a blank for the rest of the word" relieve students of responsibility for developing their own hypotheses about English orthography and learning their own strategies for spelling unknown words.

Another assumption underlying our approach to spelling instruction is that, contrary to popular belief, learning to spell is not just a matter of memorizing the spelling of words (Beers & Beers, 1977; Wilde, 1992). The lists of spelling words featured in commercial spelling programs suggest that memorization is the principal means by which children learn how to spell. However, if memorizing weekly spelling words were the only way children learned to spell, few adults would know how to spell more than four or five thousand words, a reasonable estimate of the number of words children will encounter in weekly spelling lessons over six to eight years of schooling. In reality, adults can correctly spell far more than four or five thousand words (Wilde, 1992). By taking advantage of the regularities of English orthography children and adults are able to spell many words they've never seen before. Good spellers use a variety of knowledge and strategies to spell words. Therefore, although memorization may have a place in a spelling curriculum, spelling instruction must include much more than lists of spelling words.

"Spelling is for writing" is another belief underpinning our approach to spelling instruction (Graves, 1977, p. 90). We believe that students learn a great deal about spelling as they interact with print (Gentry & Henderson, 1978; Lancaster, Nelson & Morris, 1982; Zutell, 1978). Therefore, spelling instruction must be embedded in a broader program of literacy instruction which offers students frequent opportunities to engage in meaningful reading and writing (Harris, Graham, &

Freeman, 1988; Zaragoza & Vaughn, 1992; Wilde, 1992). Wilde observes that "reading may be the single best avenue to good spelling" (1992, p. 79).

Finally, we believe that the principal goal of spelling instruction for struggling spellers is to provide the necessary support and direction to help them expand their orthographic knowledge and the range of strategies they use when trying to spell unknown words. It is important to remember that this knowledge will develop little by little (Wilde, 1992). Students' spelling development cannot be judged simply in terms of the number of words they spell correctly, although this is important. In general, we would be satisfied to see students' spellings reflect a more sophisticated knowledge of English orthography. A student whose spellings begin to include more sounds or incorporate more features of conventional English orthography, for example, has made significant progress whether or not she spells more words correctly. Similarly, a student who uses a wider range of print resources to spell unknown words is showing improvement regardless of his performance on weekly spelling tests.

The instructional strategies we present in this section for expanding students' orthographic knowledge are organized according to the continuum of spelling development we presented in Chapter 4. Our recommendations for letter name spellers, for example, support students learning to use conventional features of English orthography to represent the sounds they hear (e.g., -tion for "shun," -er for "rr," and so on). A note of caution here. The developmental stages of spelling we presented in Chapter 4 provide only a *general* sense of the knowledge and strategies students use in the process of spelling. A letter name speller, for example, may sometimes use the strategies of a phonemic speller to spell unknown words or a transitional speller may revert to the strategies of a letter name speller. And, of course, even a prephonemic speller may spell some words correctly. Our goal is to increase the orthographic knowledge of students and move them gradually toward correct spelling. We do not expect, however, that all students will move through a lockstep sequence of developmental stages. Some may, but many will not (D. Searle, personal communication, July 6, 1995). So our goal for struggling spellers is to increase their knowledge and the range of spelling strategies they use, not to move them to the next "stage" of spelling development as though these were discrete stages through which everyone must "pass." Talking about stages does, however, enable us to describe generally students' progress as spellers between the time they make their first marks on the page and when most of their spellings are conventional. It is also a convenient way to organize a discussion of spelling instruction. We begin, then, with a discussion of instruction keyed to the needs of prephonemic spellers.

Instruction for Prephonemic Spellers

Developing spellers need to discover that there is a regular and systematic relationship between the sounds of oral language and the conventional symbols of written language. Teachers who repeatedly read books aloud to their students—especially when they turn the book so students can observe the print as it is read—help develop this insight; students will begin to notice that every time their teachers read the same book/page line, it is read the same way. For the benefit of struggling readers and writers, teachers may make the connection between voice and print explicit by pointing to words as they read.

The use of language experience stories also encourages struggling spellers to discover the correspondence between oral and written language. A teacher who was providing extra support to a first grader named Tommy discovered that Tommy's teacher had placed him in a pre-primer because she didn't believe that Tommy could read until he learned the alphabet, something he was having trouble learning. The next time the special teacher met with Tommy, she brought along a series of Snoopy pictures cut from newspaper comic strips. Each picture featured Snoopy doing something different. The teacher then asked Tommy to paste the pictures in a booklet, one on a page, leaving room for the teacher to write Tommy's description of the pictures. She gave Tommy time to look over the pictures and then asked him which one he wanted to paste on the first page of his booklet. When he'd finished pasting the pictures in his booklet he dictated to his teacher a description of what Snoopy was doing on each page. On each page Tommy's teacher wrote, "He's digging," "He's reading," "He's sitting on his dog house," and so on according to his dictation. After a few pages, Tommy stopped the teacher and said, "There's something suspicious about this!" and pointed out that the *He's* looked the same on all the pages.

Some struggling spellers have the requisite orthographic knowledge, but don't use it when they spell (Gerber, 1984; Gerber & Hall, 1981). If you ask a prephonemic speller what letter *dog* begins with, she may be able to tell you, but if she writes something about her dog, you may not see a corresponding *d* in her writing. One way to approach this problem is to sit beside the student as she begins to write and ask what she intends to write about. After listening, ask her what the first thing is that she wants to say. Begin with the first word, say it out loud, and work with the student to identify as many sounds in the words as she can. The following example is illustrative.

Teacher: Lila, what would you like to write about today?
Lila: I don't know.
Teacher: Did you do anything interesting last night?
Lila: I don't know. I guess so.
Teacher: What did you do?
Lila: I went to the mall with my mom.
Teacher: Well, why don't you write about that. What could you say about going to the mall?
Lila: Last night me and my mom went shopping at the mall.
Teacher: Let's start with last. L-ast. L-ast. What sounds do you hear?
Lila: L?
Teacher: Sure, L. Go ahead and write L. What other sounds do you hear? l-aa-st.

Lila: S.

Teacher: OK (Lila writes *s*). Do you hear any other sounds? Las–T.

Lila: T. (writes *t*)

Teacher: Great.

Some students, like Lila, may be able to isolate only a few sounds; others may only be able to identify the initial sound. In any case, expect students to write down only those sounds they can isolate. Do this for just a couple of minutes, perhaps for the span of a single sentence. Stop by the student's desk again the next day and do the same thing. When you see the student representing sounds with letters on her own, you know the lesson has taken and that the student is now capable of learning a great deal about representing sound/letter relationships on her own.

Another way to help developing spellers learn to use their graphophonic knowledge during writing is to engage them in a written conversation. We observed a resource teacher use this technique to help Joseph, a second grader who tended to represent words with random strings of letters. Because Joseph had revealed a knowledge of graphophonics during instruction, his teacher worked with him to draw on this knowledge while he was writing.

A visiting teacher educator began a written conversation with Joseph by writing, "Hi! What is your name?" She then read what she'd written aloud, pointing to each word as she did so. Joseph looked up and said, "I don't know how to write 'My name is Joseph.' " The visitor then helped him write "My name" as Lila's teacher did, asking him what word he wanted to write first, what sounds he heard as they said the word together, and so on. Joseph knew how to spell *is* and his own name so he was able to complete the sentence on his own.

Next the visitor asked Joseph if he wanted to ask her a question. Joseph grabbed the pen but then his enthusiasm turned to dismay, saying that he didn't know how to write "What's your name?" Joseph's new friend read and pointed to the first line of the conversation again, saying that there was probably something there that might help him. Joseph's eyes lit up and he immediately set to work copying the first line, even adding the "Hi!" He learned his lesson well enough that he had no trouble locating *have* and *brothers* from the previous line or in copying "Do you have any. . ." later in the conversation. The visitor helped Joseph listen to the sound of *daughters* in order to help him write it. By now, Joseph was feeling so successful that even after the visitor left, he asked his regular teacher, who had been observing, more questions. Note that Joseph corrected the conventional spelling of *daughter* by finding it in an earlier part of the conversation. (See Figure 12-1.)

Joseph's story isn't unusual. Children often don't use the orthographic knowledge they possess, perhaps because they lack the requisite strategies. The teacher who worked with Joseph helped him discover that he could use his knowledge about print by relying on two strategies—using the print in his environment (in this case, in the written conversation) and listening to and representing the sounds

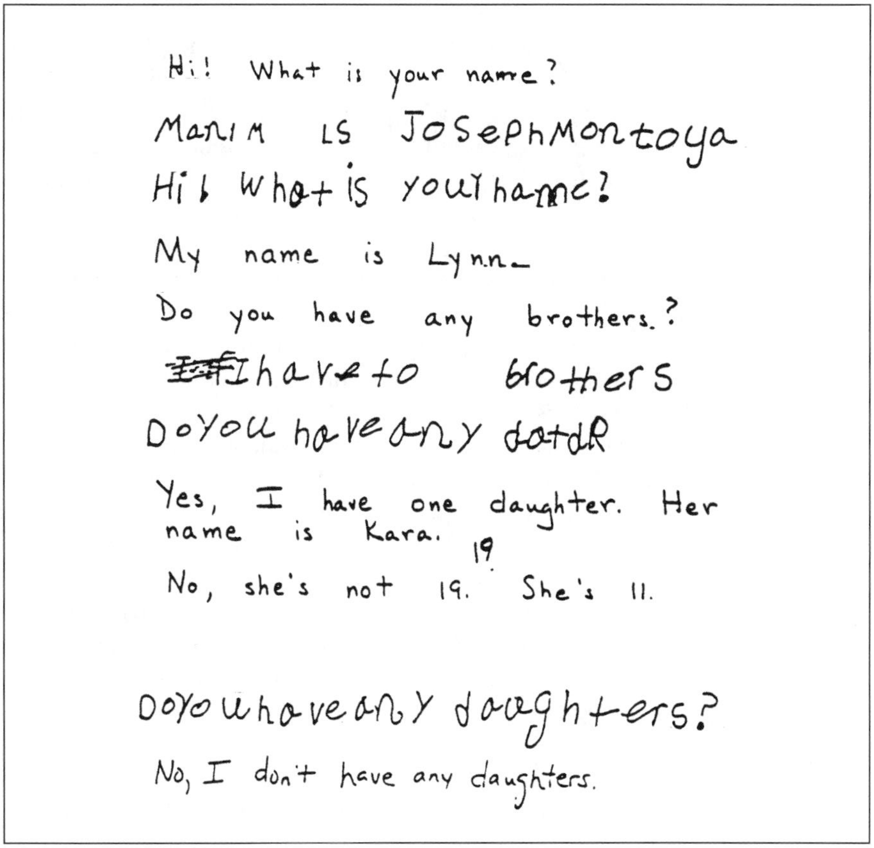

Hi! What is your name?

Marim is JosephMontoya

Hi! What is your hame?

My name is Lynn

Do you have any brothers?

~~I~~ I have to brothers

Do you have any datdR

Yes, I have one daughter. Her name is Kara.

No, she's not 19. She's 11.

Do you have any daughters?

No, I don't have any daughters.

FIG 12-1   *Joseph's written conversation*

in words. In a single lesson, Joseph began to use strategies more typical of phonemic spellers.

Instruction for Phonemic Spellers

Students who predominantly use the strategies of phonemic spellers benefit from instructional strategies similar to those for prephonemic spellers. The goal here, however, is to help students learn to represent more sounds until they are able to represent all of the sounds in most words (i.e., look more like letter name spellers). (We would also expect that phonemic spellers will begin to spell some frequently occurring words conventionally.) As students begin to represent some sounds, the teacher can help them listen for other sounds as well. The teacher can demonstrate how he listens to one syllable in a word at a time, and then to the sounds in each syllable, inviting students to listen along and represent all the sounds they hear. In the case of Lila, who wrote grandma as "gamoow," for instance, the teacher might say something like this:

Teacher: Let's listen to the sounds you hear in the first part—grand, GRR-and. What are the first sounds you hear in GRR—and [drawing the word out like a rubber band and slightly emphasizing the beginning]? Write down the sounds that you hear. That's right, g, r. Listen. Do you hear any other sounds in gr-a-nd [again drawing the word out and slightly emphasizing the *nd* sound on the end]? A, OK. N, that's fine. How about the second part of the word. What sounds do you hear in *ma*? M, yes. AW, that's fine.

Again, *brief* but frequent lessons are more helpful than longer, less frequent lessons. Lila's lesson on *grandma* was probably sufficient for most students, though some students may benefit from support for another word or two as part of the same lesson. Also, watch to see if students begin to syllabicate where necessary and draw out the sounds of the words as they write independently. As students get better at analyzing words independently, you might simply stop by their desks and suggest, "See if you can think about how this word sounds again and, if you can, add to your spelling of it." Also reinforce the student's increasing representation of sounds by saying such things as, "When you listened to that word, look at all the sounds you heard. You know just how to do it" (Giacobbe, 1986).

Be careful not to give students more information than they can handle. Be satisfied with "granmaw" or even "gama" at this point. Don't say things like "I know you may not hear it but there's a *d* after the *n* in *grandma*" (although you might say this with a more sophisticated speller). Overloading students with information can risk their confidence.

This process can be incorporated into group instruction by involving students in a bit of spelling instruction while you record their language experience dictations. As you write students' dictations, ask them to help you with the spelling of sounds that you know might push students a little further. For example, if you have students who are regularly capturing the first and last letters of words and you'd like them to start listening for middle letters, you can encourage them to think about a few middle letters as you write. As you record, for example, "Today we saw one squirrel at the park," you could ask students to listen to the middle part of *squirrel*. When they suggest letters that they've heard (for example, *r*), simply spell the word conventionally and, as you are doing so, say, "Yes, there is an *r* in the middle of the word *squirrel*," pointing to the *r* as you do so. It's easy to individualize instruction by involving particular students in spelling appropriate to their needs. If the group contains students who are only representing the first sound of a word, they may benefit from being asked to think about how words end rather than about midword letter/sound relationships.

Whole class or small group minilessons can also be used to encourage students to represent more sounds as they spell. Ms. Jackson, a first-grade teacher, often asks her class for words they'd like to learn how to spell and the whole class works together to represent as many sounds as they can. The same technique can be used during the dictation of a whole-class language experience story or writing the daily news. Similar lessons can be done with small groups of developing spellers in older grades.

Although our primary goal for students using the strategies of phonemic spellers is to help them represent more and more sounds as they spell, there may be times when we can draw these students' attention to conventional spelling. If, in the above dictation, you asked the group to help you spell *one*, it's likely phonemic spellers will suggest that *one* begins with *y*. In such cases, we find it best simply to say, "That is how you could spell it in your writing, but it's actually written this way." Then write the word quickly and move on.

In group lessons students who don't know some of the sound/letter relationships will learn them from those who do as they help you construct dictations on paper. However, be careful not to overdo your attention to sound/letter relationships during dictations; keep everyone's attention focused on meaning construction.

Instruction for Letter Name Spellers

Letter name spellers tend to rely on their ability to analyze and sound out words when they spell unknown words. Compared to more developed spellers, however, they are less likely to take advantage of the conventions of English orthography when they spell. Most letter name spellers would not, for example, use silent *e*'s (e.g., hat*e*) or vowel combinations (e.g., m*ea*t or m*ee*t) to represent long vowel sounds since these sounds are represented by the names of letters. In general, children begin to learn the conventions of English orthography—that is, the differences between their letter name spelling and standard spelling—by reading. Research indicates that students will not move from letter name to transitional spelling without demonstrating "the ability to orally read unfamiliar, age-appropriate material with expression and comprehension in a one-to-one reading situation" (Hughes & Searle, 1992, p. 15). Therefore, a program of instruction for letter name spellers must include immersing students in an environment rich in print and opportunities for reading. (See Chapter 6.)

Although fluent reading is a necessary condition for spelling development at this stage, it is not a sufficient one (Hughes & Searle, 1991). Many students, especially struggling readers and writers, will require the explicit support and direction of their teachers as they learn to incorporate the visual information encountered in reading into their expanding hypotheses about English orthography. Students will require reassurance from their teachers as they discover the differences between their spellings and the standard spellings they encounter in books. Some students, dissatisfied with their approximate spellings and anxious to spell words right (Bissex, 1980), may become reluctant to write anything at all. Third-grader Charles, for example, resisted writing any word he could not spell conventionally—and, therefore, wrote very little.

Students' discomfort with their letter name spellings, emerging from an increasingly sophisticated knowledge of English orthography, is a sign of growth. These students may, however, need some encouragement to continue to write fluently. Teachers need to reassure them that their spelling will become more conventional with time and continued reading and writing. Teachers need to help students assess the progress they've already made as spellers, perhaps by looking over old writing samples. It's important at this stage to reinforce the notion that communicating ideas is more important than perfect spelling. Spelling can be attended to when—and if—the writing is edited. (We'll talk more about editing and other spelling strategies later in this chapter.) It's also important to acknowledge evidence of students' spelling development. When Lila spelled brother "bruthr" (previously she had spelled it "bruddr") her teacher made a point of bringing this to the attention of the whole class during Authors' Circle.

The instruction you provide at this point also needs to draw students' attention to the visual information contained in conventional spellings. When a letter name speller requests help with spelling or when you decide to provide help, tell her to "think about what the word looks like in books." This contrasts with the advice given to phonemic or prephonemic spellers to write down the sounds they hear. If you provide the student with a conventional spelling in place of an unconventional spelling, you might point out, "That's the way it sounds but it's not the way it looks" (Bissex, 1980). You can respond in the same way as you continue to involve students in the recording of language experience dictations. At this point, if some students have not discovered some conventions—that the first sound of *chewing gum* is represented by *ch* rather than the *h* that letter name spellers often use, for example—involve them in spelling words featuring that letter sequence as it is naturally used during language experience.

Students who rely on a letter name strategy may also benefit from whole class, small group, and individual minilessons that focus explicitly on conventional representations of particular sounds. Mr. Marling asked his third graders, for example, to list words beginning with the *ch* sound (e.g., *church, chain, children* . . .). This gave him the opportunity to inform students that the beginning *ch* sound is represented by *ch*, not *h*. This particular minilesson raised another issue when a student suggested *train* as an example of a word beginning with the *ch* sound. Now Mr. Marling was able to explain that, however it may sound to us, words like *train, try, truck*, and so on are spelled *tr*, not *h* or *ch*. Similar minilessons may be constructed for other sounds, but it is best to design lessons that respond to the real needs of students. There is no reason, for example, to conduct a lesson on conventional representations of the *f* sound if this isn't an issue for the students in your class. Nor does it make much sense to conduct a whole class lesson if this is only an issue for one or two students (in which case individual or small group instruction would make more sense).

Again, explicit instruction is useful for developing spellers at this stage, but they must also have frequent opportunities to read and write if they are going to learn standard spellings.

Instruction for Transitional Spellers

Instruction for transitional spellers aims to increase students' expanding knowledge of the regularities of English orthography and the pool of words they can spell correctly. There are a number of word games that students will enjoy that may increase their knowledge of possible letter sequences, the relationships between words, and so on. Though these games are not related to students' writings, they do rely on students' vocabularies and encourage students' understandings of how spelling works. Keep the games in perspective, however. They cannot take the place of frequent reading and writing for developing spelling.

Hangman is a familiar spelling game that demands that students think about such things as what could come before and after certain letters, what letter sequences are likely, and so on. Boggle, Spill and Spell, Scrabble, and Word Mastermind (see Marino, 1981) are others that will help students think about words and consider various possibilities and relationships. We recommend that you sometimes sit alongside students and encourage them to verbalize their thinking as they play. If you find that the students are not using strategic thinking about letter sequences to play a game (see Marino, 1981 for examples), you may want to play the game also so that you can think aloud as a means of demonstrating the strategies you use and the graphophonic knowledge you possess. Do this with a light touch—you don't want to take the fun out of playing games by transforming them into academic exercises.

Students who have learned the visual patterns of spelling and who spell frequently used words correctly still may not have discovered that words with similar meanings tend to have similar spellings (e.g., *sign, signal*). Reading widely, writing more, and studying word derivations are helpful to these students who may also be helped simply by your calling attention to base words and affixes as needed when they edit their writing. Teacher-led minilessons that draw students' attention to the relationship of words like *theater* and *theatrical*, *sign* and *signal*, *nation* and *national*, and so on can also be useful. Some students may need teachers to draw students' attention to the fact that plural markers (*s*) and past tense markers (e.g., *ed*) are spelled similarly despite differences in pronunciation (e.g., *pigs, cups; raked, purred, traded*).

Another instructional strategy is to collect unconventional spellings from students' work over a period of time and categorize the errors, listing the conventional spelling next to each unconventional spelling (Ganschow, 1981; Marino, 1981). Invite students to consider words that belong to the same category and hypothesize the rule. In this way, students can revise their current rules in a situation in which the need to do so is personally relevant. For example, we observed a teacher who decided to help her students understand the differences between *their*, *there*, and *they're*—words that she had observed her students misspelling and misusing in their writing. First, she collected sentences from her students' writings in which these words were used correctly and incorrectly; then she grouped them together according to how the particular word *ought* to be spelled. To keep students from being distracted by other words, she corrected other misspellings in the sentences she'd selected.

Then she gave each student a copy of the sentences and told them that the sentences underneath the word *there* all had the word *there* in it, sometimes spelled correctly and sometimes spelled another way. She said the same about the sentences listed under *their* and *they're*. Students were then asked to read each sentence and to correct the spelling if necessary to match the word under which the sentence was grouped. Then each student was asked to talk with another student about how the word was used in each category. In other words, students themselves were asked to infer the rule for why the word was spelled the way it was in each of the three sets of sentences. The students then shared their findings and became involved in thinking of ways to remember which spelling was connected to which function or meaning. Some of what the students discussed follows:

there

1. Defined as "a place," "a direction."

2. Noted that *here* was in *there*.

3. Since *here* was also "a place or direction," and was in *there*, that was a way to remember the spelling of *there*.

their

1. Defined as "a group that had something or owned something."

2. Noted that *their* was followed by a noun while *there* wasn't.

3. Tried to figure out how to remember that the spelling was *ei* and not *ie* and noted that all three words began with *the*, including *their*.

they're

1. Stands for "they are."

2. Noted that if they substituted *they are* for *they're* and it made sense, then the word must be the short (contracted) form of *they are*.

It's probably best to encourage students to generate their own wording for these and for any other rules you feel it's necessary for them to learn in this manner. If students themselves are actively involved in figuring out the rule, they will understand it better than if they merely try to memorize a rule.

Probably the most common method for teaching standard spellings is to ask students to memorize lists of words, usually within the context of commercial spelling programs. We recommend that commercial spelling programs be avoided since they rarely address the needs of individual students. Spelling lists may be effective, however, if they adhere to three principles: *individualization, limited quantity,* and *limited time* (Wilde, 1992).

Rather than using spelling lists generated by publishers (or even teachers), we think it makes more sense to develop personal spelling lists that emerge from students' own writings and interests (Graham & Voth, 1990; Schwartz & MacArthur, 1990; Wilde, 1992). Students could be asked to indicate words they'd like to learn to spell, perhaps (with the help of their teachers if needed) identifying words they often use in their writing that they consistently misspell. Third-grader Lila often wrote about her brother but didn't know how to spell *brother,* so this would be a likely word for her personal spelling list.

There is general agreement that asking struggling spellers to memorize fifteen to twenty unrelated words each week overwhelms and frustrates them (e.g., Graham & Voth, 1990; McNaughton, Hughes, & Clark, 1994). It is more sensible to ask students to learn five to six words at a time, perhaps using a strategy in which students:

1. say the word

2. write and say the word

3. check the word

4. trace and say the word

5. write the word from memory and check

6. repeat the first five steps (Graham & Voth, 1990, p. 450)

Students should be encouraged to decide for themselves, however, the precise strategies they use to learn the words on their spelling list.

Another strategy for dealing with spelling lists is to tape a small index card containing a student's spelling words at the upper right-hand corner of his desk. If the student has no desk, the card may be attached to his writing folder and pulled out each time the student writes. Writing the word(s) on a card is an appropriate time for a quick lesson in which the student's spelling of each word is compared with the conventional spelling by the student. Thus, *often* is placed next to the student's spelling "ofen" and the student might say something like, "There's a *t* in it. You can't hear the *t.* I could remember the *t* if I pronounce it "off+ten" when I write it."

We work with index cards rather informally; that is, students know which words are on their card, and each time they use one of them in writing, they use the card to copy the word or to check their spelling. We tell students that once they no longer have to look at the card to write or check a word, it's time to replace the word with another one (and to have another quick comparison lesson). Thus, the student is always learning five or six words. Emphasize the student's responsibility in knowing when to tell the teacher that she's ready for a new word. A list of all of the words the student has learned during the year provides a record of learning for both the teacher and the student.

It may be useful for some students to take regular, informal spelling tests. For example, students could pair off and quickly test one another on words from their personal index cards. Or students might be regularly tested on high-frequency words displayed on a room chart for everyone's reference. (Make sure that the students understand that the words on the chart are those they use regularly and naturally in their writing.) Such tests are not meant to be graded, and in fact, it's recommended that the words to be tested remain in view during the test to assure success (Marino, 1981). These tests should take no more than five minutes and are especially effective if students self-correct their own tests (Wilde, 1992). In general, the test is a means of engaging students once again to think about words and how they work.

In summary, although the use of spelling lists may have a place in a spelling program, we should not rely too heavily on memorizing spelling words. Memorization is only one aspect of learning to spell. Good spellers also have extensive knowledge about the workings of English orthography and strategies for dealing with words they don't know how to spell.

What Do You Do When You Don't Know How to Spell a Word?

Even the best speller cannot spell all the words in the dictionary, but good spellers have a range of strategies for locating or generating correct spellings. If we are unsure how to spell a particular word we might, for example, use the spelling checker built into our word processor. If the spelling checker didn't "know" the word, we'd probably consult a dictionary. In the case of certain technical terms that didn't appear in our dictionary we'd likely check other sources (books, journal articles). In any case, we probably wouldn't worry much about spelling the word correctly until we'd finished the text. It is highly unlikely we would interrupt the flow of our text to look up the spelling of a word.

Good spellers have a range of strategies for dealing with words they don't know how to spell. Poor spellers, on the other hand, often don't have much sense of what to do when they don't know how to spell a word beyond asking the teacher or another student (D. Searle, personal communication, July 6, 1995). Therefore, in addition to increasing students' knowledge about English orthography, spelling instruction for struggling spellers must help them broaden the strategies they use to cope with unknown spellings when they're writing. We suggest the following strategies for dealing with unknown spellings: placeholder spelling; use of human resources; use of text resources; and proofreading (Wilde, 1992).

PLACEHOLDER SPELLING   Some children are convinced that, since they cannot spell correctly, they cannot write. For some students this means they only write words they can spell and, as a result, write very little if at all. Other students spend much of their writing time thinking of easy-to-spell synonyms for the hard-to-spell words. In the case of those students who have minor fluency problems caused by their synonym-hunting tactics, it's usually helpful to sit with them individually while they write, and as they finish writing each phrase or sentence ask, "What are you going to say next?" Then help them commit to paper the words they used to express their ideas orally, no matter how difficult they are to spell. If students ask for help with any of the words, tell them they should do the best they can, as quickly as they can. A session or two in which you help a student write down the words as best he can will usually convince even a particularly stubborn student that you mean what you say—spelling is important only in final drafts.

Sometimes it's helpful to suggest that students underline or otherwise mark words they would like to give more attention to later. If they can mark words quickly as they write, the marking needn't interfere with fluency. If, on the other hand, marking appears to cause interruption in the flow of writing, they should wait to do it until after they have finished writing the piece.

One of the major recommendations that Graves makes for children who are overly concerned with conventions is to find ways to heighten the importance of meaning in their writing (1983). One procedure he suggests not only heightens the importance of information, but also provides natural spelling support to students. Graves suggests that you have a short two- to three-minute conference with the student about the topic she has elected to explore. As she talks, you play secretary, recording some of the informational words and phrases the student uses in discussing the topic with you. When the conference ends, hand your conference notes to the student, saying "If you'd like to use some of the words you were just speaking, here they are" (Graves, 1983, p. 208).

More drastic measures may be necessary for students who won't write at all or write very little. A learning disabilities teacher in Denver had five students whose fluency did not increase for several months in the beginning of the school year, even though she involved them in daily writing with a stated and demonstrated focus on ideas rather than on conventions. One day, in despair, she gathered these students around a table, giving each paper and pencil. She told the children that she was going to tell them something about herself, a sentence with some very hard-to-spell words, and that they must write down exactly what she said on their papers. She said, "I am going to go to Hawaii for a vacation," and asked which words were very hard to spell. Although almost all words were difficult for these children to spell correctly, they immediately picked out *Hawaii* and *vacation*. The teacher told everyone to write down what she told them and they did. She praised attempts that included orthographic features of the words as well as the strategies they were using to produce those features. Some of her comments were "I see you are saying the word to yourself to see what sound comes next," and "Great! *Vacation* does have a *v* sound at the beginning." Then in turn, each of the five children thought of some news about himself for everyone to write with "hard words" in it.

This session, with each child writing all six sentences, lasted about half an hour. Since the children seemed to leave the session with positive feelings, the teacher repeated it the next day. One of the children asked the teacher on the third day if they could do some more "hardest word" sentences. The teacher told the child that she could write as many sentences and stories as she could think of with all the hardest words in the world! Following these lessons this group of students had little trouble quickly "inventing" spellings for what they wanted to say.

USING HUMAN RESOURCES   Asking another student for help is a natural spelling strategy (Wilde, 1992). In some cases students may even work together to create a reasonable spelling. Still, asking someone else may not always be helpful for struggling spellers who are able to spell few words correctly. Regularly asking for help with spelling can threaten the writing fluency of the poor speller and the students from whom help is being requested. Third-grader Charles, for example, made a nuisance of himself with his constant requests for spelling help. Charles was encouraged by his teacher to rely on placeholder spellings and then seek the assistance of his peers at the editing stage. In general, students should be encouraged to help each other, but they also have to learn to rely on their own resources (e.g., placeholder spelling).

USING TEXT RESOURCES   The most commonly used print resource is a dictionary. However, most students need help learning how to use dictionaries and, even then, dictionaries are most useful to students whose spellings closely resemble standard spelling. Dictionaries aren't the only useful text resource and, in general, a print-rich environment provides lots of support to developing spellers. First-grade teacher Jane Murphy wrote high-frequency words on index cards and then taped the cards on wall space above the blackboards. She numbered each card and then, when a student was uncertain how to spell one of these words, she directed his attention to the cards ("Check number 23."). Other classrooms include charts of vocabulary words compiled by the class related to content-area units, picture and rhyming dictionaries, thesauruses, well-illustrated reference books, commercial charts and posters related to content-area units, globe, maps, atlases, and lots of books. Some teachers have found personal spelling dictionaries, in which teachers help students keep a list of words they've had to look up (Schevermann et al., 1990). The *Bad Speller's Dictionary* (Krevisky & Linfield, 1974), a small pocket dictionary in which students may find common misspellings of words followed by their correct spelling and dictionaries used by secretaries to look up frequently misspelled words may also be helpful.

Electronic spelling checkers can also be helpful to many students. They are an increasingly common resource for checking spelling. Some of these merely "flag" students' spelling miscues, leaving it to them to generate alternative spellings, or both signal misspellings *and* offer possible spellings of the target word. These are only useful for students whose spellings are reasonably close to the correct spelling (i.e., transitional spellers). Even young students with learning disabilities appear to have little difficulty learning to use spelling checkers with appropriate instruction (Dalton et al., 1990). Spelling checkers still require some decision making on the part of the student, although some word processors automatically correct misspellings of common words like *the* or *to*. Though useful, they will never be a panacea and some schools simply cannot afford them.

As with human resources, text resources must not be allowed to interfere with students' writing fluency. Students must learn not only how to use these various resources but when to use them, that is, after they have "gotten it down."

PROOFREADING   Sandra Wilde observes that "building a strong proofreading component into spelling curriculum is one of the most important ways to develop writers who can autonomously produce writing that's spelled well enough to meet society's often extremely high standards" (1992, p. 115). So once students begin using transitional spellings it's important that they learn to edit their work for spelling.

It's helpful to begin by asking students to circle those words in their writing they're unsure of, those that "don't look right." (Notice how visual attention is invoked.) Once students are able to identify their spelling miscues they can be encouraged to use various human or textual resources to correct their spelling. Alternatively, when students decide that a word doesn't look right, you might ask them to rewrite the word a number of different ways and then decide which spelling looks the best. (Note again how attention is directed to visual information.)

Once students can locate their spelling errors, decide what they can handle in editing with relative ease yet still be challenged to learn. You might, for example, ask some students (those with less visual information) to find three of the underlined words in books or somewhere else and then correct them. Other students (who have more visual information) can use the "write it several ways and see what looks best" strategy. Don't ask students to fully edit for spelling unless there is an audience who will be reading their writing. Even then, if the amount of spelling that needs to be corrected is potentially overwhelming, have them do part of it; then you, another person, or a computer program can assist with or simply correct the rest.

Unusual Spelling Difficulties

Occasionally you'll encounter students with unusual spelling problems. John, for example, was a seventh grader whose spelling rendered his writing unreadable. His mother had enrolled him in our university Reading and Writing Center for help. The following piece of John's was based upon the popular children's book *Where the Red Fern Grows* (Rawls, 1974).

> dele is a huert. he wons a dog. he like to huot in the uoads. I thing he is nete.
> I Ithe to hoint. I like dogs to he will a dog
> (Billy is a hunter. He wants a dog. He likes to hunt in the woods. I think he is
> neat. I like to hunt. I like dogs too. He will get a dog.)

John had been in a learning disabilities classroom since first grade and none of our usual approaches to spelling seemed to help. When the teacher who had been assigned to John at the university helped him sound out words, he'd spell *hunter* as "hunert." Asking him to study the conventional spelling of the word and then to reproduce it from visual memory didn't work either, nor did the strategy of writing it down several different ways. But John could read his own writing immediately after writing it and could underline most of the words he had spelled unconventionally. This was especially surprising since John's teachers described him as a "nonreader." (We later discovered that John could comprehend difficult text as long as he read it silently.)

Every week, John's university teacher involved him in writing down his assignments, something the boy's mother was quite happy to follow through on at home. John wrote the following list of assignments one week, giving some indication of how poor his spelling was, especially when his heart was not in the writing.

rede p 135 (read to p. 135)
thing a blte the soide (think about the story)
blkah polhe book (bring poetry book)

John's teacher regularly recopied the assignments so that his mother could read them. One week she invited John to help by telling him, "I'm going to write down your assignments now. You help me with the spelling as I write. What does *assignments* start with?" The boy answered *a* and then, as the teacher wrote the *a*, he spelled out the remainder of the word—*assignments*. To the amazement of his teacher John proceeded to spell orally the majority of the other words he had just spelled incorrectly in his written list of assignments, and the ones that were orally spelled incorrectly were far closer to the conventional spelling than his original written spellings had been. This pattern was confirmed in future lessons. John could spell many words orally, but the moment he put a pencil in his hand his spelling ability disappeared.

It occurred to us that there might be a way to help John cope with his difficulty. Relying on the knowledge that John could read what he'd written, we began to involve him in self-correcting spelling after he had completed his original drafts following this routine: 1) He read the first word in the sentence, 2) he spelled it aloud, and 3) as he spelled each letter aloud, he wrote the letter. He continued the same routine with the next word and so on.

This was slow but it worked rather well, though some days were better than others. Eventually, John spontaneously began doing some oral spelling while writing his first drafts. For example, here's the original draft he wrote when he had completed his reading of *Where the Red Fern Grows*:

The red Fern lencht is that a Inend boy and flre wer walking and frzze to died. and in the summer thay find the ren Fern grow by dobies. The ren Fern mene that the dobies. of Billy dogs well allways de ther. Billy fledl dete win he know he's dogs spernt wood de ther for afer.

After he had finished his first draft, John edited the writing using the routine he had been taught and produced the following:

The red fern legend is that an Indian boy and girl were walking and froze to death. In the summer they found the red fern growing by their bodies. The red fern means that the bodies of Billy's dogs will alway's be there. Billy felt better when he knew his dog's spirit would be there forever.

In editing his draft, John was given help changing *find* to *found* (a grammatical problem), changing "dobies" to *bodies* in both places where he used it (a reversal problem), and changing "allways" to *always*, his only remaining spelling problem. It was his idea to look up the spelling of *legend* in the book.

John had essentially learned to translate what he had written through an aural mode that was working, making his pen follow what he spelled aloud. His feelings about what he had experienced and learned during the semester of individual help were summed up when he wrote, and then rewrote, the following:

1. redeing the red fren help me de cusdes I did think I codk:

1. reading the red fern helped me becaise I didn't know I could read it.

(John's ability here to proofread and correct his spelling challenges the observation by John's teacher at school that he was a "nonreader.")

2. I that I wodt have to ride off lafsh card dut in stude I ride a dook.

2. I thought I would have to read flash cards instead I read a dook.

(Indicating that John was aware of the differences between his past and current instructional experiences.)

3. spelling help me. I ride didnd now

3. spelling helped me because of writing on paper I read better now because of writing.

(The teacher asked John to add some information explaining "why" when he rewrote. Note John's intuitive sense of the connection between reading and writing development.)

4. spelling out and wting out the wake and pot in senoch

4. spelling out loud helped me and wting out the words and putting in sentences

(Here John is referring to the breakthrough we made in how to help him cope with his spelling.)

John's story supports our experience that the needs of poor spellers are not always easily met. Our experience with John also reveals how important instructional observations are, as is as being able to formulate creative ways to help such students.

Punctuation

"Punctuation, including capitalization, has to do with how we use written language to represent information other than the words themselves: grammatical divisions like sentences and clauses, meaning like exclamations and proper names, instructions to the reader, and so on" (Wilde, 1992, p. 119). As a means of carrying meaning, the appropriate use of punctuation is critically important to the writer's purpose. Writers who cannot use punctuation appropriately risk confusing or misleading their readers. Yet even well-educated adults may have difficulty with the use of punctuation marks like commas, colons, and semicolons. This indicates the importance of directly addressing punctuation within a writing program, although it is doubtful that the explicit teaching of punctuation rules will be very effective. We'll say more about this later.

Learning to punctuate, like learning to spell, is developmental. "Children's hypotheses about punctuation grow out of their experience with written language and evolve over time" (Wilde, 1992, p. 119). Cordeiro, Giacobbe, and Cazden, for example, found that first graders' hypotheses about periods ranged from: periods should be placed after each syllable, after each word, at the end of each line, at the end of the page or writing, or at the end of phrases (1983). All of these hypotheses make some sense. It is easy to see, for example, how first graders exposed to basal readers might think that periods go at the end of every line or even every word.

We might also expect that students' understandings and uses of punctuation will be gradual and, as with much learning, children will often overgeneralize developing concepts. Most of us have seen writing like the first grader's story in Figure 12-2, in which the child's discovery of apostrophes is being explored and is overgeneralized. This phenomenon should be expected of all students, including remedial students and students with learning disabilities. Punctuation should be taught as students' writings indicate the need for it. For example, once students begin using dialogue in their story writing, teach them quotation marks.

The teaching of punctuation should be embedded in a regular program of reading and writing. Students who read regularly are able to see how commercial authors use punctuation. Teachers of developing readers and writers may also draw students' attention to punctuation in texts. We observed a resource room teacher who read a big book to her class and then, pointing to periods in the text, asked, "Does anyone know what these dots are called? . . . Yes, they're called periods. Does anyone know why authors use periods?" Some teachers select particular texts to highlight particular uses of punctuation. Wilde, for example, suggests that books like *The Day Jimmy's Boa Ate the Wash* (Noble, 1980), which makes extensive use of dialogue, are excellent tools for exploring the use of quotation marks (1992). Teachers might also challenge their students to a comma hunt or a capital letter hunt as they pay particular attention to how commas or uppercase letters are used in various texts.

Students are also much more likely to learn how to use punctuation if instruction is linked to their needs as writers. For example, Lynn, a third-grade teacher, listened as Michael read the story he had written, which included dialogue for the first time. However, because he didn't use quotation marks or attribute dialogue to speakers (e.g., ". . . he said"), she was confused about who was saying what to whom and she said so. She suggested to Michael that they look at some books to see how commercial authors used quotation marks. She also suggested that Michael read his story out loud to see if he thought there was any need to specify who was doing the speaking in his story. As a result of this five-minute lesson, Michael made the revisions needed to make his story comprehensible.

Calkins is among those who have found that young writers who have frequent opportunities to *use* punctuation in their writing gain a better understanding of punctuation than students who are *taught* rules of punctuation outside the context of writing (1983). Our experience also indicates that children (and adults),

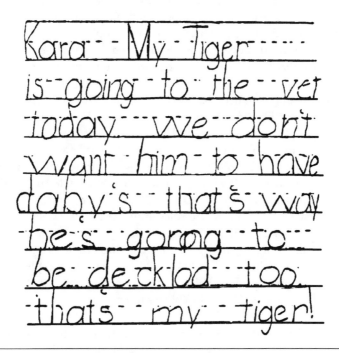

FIG 12-2   *Discovery of apostrophes*

including children with learning disabilities, need to learn about punctuation within a writing program that provides them with frequent opportunities to write for a variety of purposes and audiences (Zaraguzo & Vaughn, 1992).

Within the context of students' writing instruction, teachers' lessons on punctuation can be quite explicit. Punctuation is often taught during editing conferences, for example, when students are finalizing a piece of writing for an audience. Here the teacher may demonstrate the use of an aspect of punctuation, perhaps providing an explanation. Some aspects of punctuation may require a functional explanation. Cordeiro, Giacobbe, and Cazden (1983), for example, demonstrated the use of a possessive apostrophe while saying,

> When something *belongs* to someone else, we put one of these little marks (showing as she speaks). We call that an "apostrophe" and we add the *s*. That lets the reader know that "my friend's house" (pointing to the child's text) means that the house belongs to your friend; it doesn't mean "lots of friends." (p. 326)

Cordeiro et al. used a similar strategy to explain the use of quotation marks during an editing conference.

> Someone is talking on this page. If we could hear her talking, what would she say? (Student reads.) Well, we have some marks that we put around the words people say, before the first word and after the last. . . . (1983, p. 327)

Teaching rules of punctuation isn't always so straightforward, however. The rule for using periods, for example, is difficult to state precisely. The usual advice to "put a period where you hear your voice drop" doesn't always work. When many Canadians tell stories, for example, they end their sentences with rising intonation (a signal that the narrative is to continue, we think). The advice to "put a period when you 'hear' a long pause" doesn't work either since speakers often pause longer within sentences than between them (F. Smith, 1982b, p. 154). More formal explanations like, "A sentence contains a noun/subject and a verb" don't explain why "Stop!" is a sentence and "The dog is" is not.

The incredible complexity of grammatical rules for sentences and clauses suggests that we ought to aim for developing in our students an intuitive understanding of punctuation. If we want students to explicitly learn *the rules* of punctuation we are probably better off encouraging students to verbalize their own rules rather than having them memorize rules from a textbook (Wilde, 1992). Talking about teaching punctuation, Wilde suggests that it's better "to help students develop instincts about punctuation with a rule serving in some cases to describe those instincts more coherently" (1992, p. 123). Elaine, for example, was a young student who was quite confused about the use of periods, placing them almost at random within her stories (Wilde, 1992). Her teacher

> sat down with her and read one of her [Elaine's] stories out loud, asking her where she thought the sentences ended. Elaine was able to respond correctly, based on her general knowledge of language. Rather than giving her the rule for using periods, her teacher asked her just to listen in the future to where she thought the sentences ended, and from that point on, Elaine's use of periods was close to perfect. (Wilde, 1992, p. 123)

Whole class minilessons can also be used to develop students' intuitions about punctuation. Ms. Timmins, a primary learning disabilities teacher, often worked with small groups of struggling students in their regular classrooms. One day we observed her working with four third-grade students who were having difficulty using periods. She shared a piece of her own writing with them (punctuation removed) and together they discussed where they thought periods should go. She then suggested each student take another look at the piece of writing they were working on to see where they thought the periods should go.

As students increase their intuitive knowledge of punctuation, they can assume greater responsibility for editing their own writing. If a student continues to need a great deal of guidance in editing, the teacher may say, "Read this sentence and see where a period (comma, and so forth) might help your readers." A student who needs less guidance might be asked to read the same sentence and see what punctuation might be added. Students who need less guidance may be asked to reread their pieces and check the punctuation independently. As we stressed in our discussion of editing for spelling, students should be given more and more responsibility for editing for punctuation but not be overwhelmed. Balance your expectations against a student's ability to meet them.

Punctuation can also be addressed as teachers "lift" pieces of writing and use them to work on punctuation by comparing conventional and unconventional punctuation. For example, a secondary LD teacher whose students had written letters to obtain information for a social studies project observed that a number of the students had not capitalized words of personal address, such as *Mr.*, *Dr.*, *Ms.* The teacher constructed two columns, one in which the students' writing was featured (dr. Smith) and one in which conventional writing was featured (Dr. Smith). The students were asked to compare the two columns, to verbalize what they had learned, and then to use that information to edit their letters for this convention.

Some very difficult punctuation concepts seem best addressed by comparison. Students usually have difficulty understanding that direct speech is marked with quotation marks while indirect speech is not. In such cases, a comparison of direct and indirect speech sometimes eliminates the confusion. Examples like the following may be taken from familiar books or students' writing:

Mom said that she was going to the store.
Mom said, "I'm going to the store."

If students don't use the punctuation they know during editing, it may be that they don't know how to proofread for punctuation. In such cases, a group of students may benefit from proofreading a "lifted" piece of writing. Any student's writing may be used; placing it on an overhead is best because you can more easily help students focus on the particulars under discussion. Demonstrate how you go about proofreading for punctuation and then involve the students. Help them understand that you ignore other problems like spelling when you are proofreading for punctuation, that you read one sentence at a time and check for "sentence sense" before checking for punctuation within and between sentences. If you also find yourself teaching students about aspects of punctuation that haven't come up before, such as capitalizing and underlining book titles, teach these lessons quickly so that the focus remains on proofreading, using knowledge they have rather than developing new knowledge.

You might also involve students in "lifting" examples of punctuation from their environment. For example, if you do a comparison lesson between *its* and *it's* (where a semantic difference is signaled by punctuation), an interesting follow-up is to suggest that students find examples of the use of these words and "lift" them for sharing with the class. Students will find the convention misused everywhere— grocery store signs, garage sale signs, movie billboards, and perhaps even the school newspaper. This sort of follow-up will cement students' learning.

Learning to punctuate, like learning to spell, never ends as long as we read and write. How many of us, for example, are certain about how to use semicolons? Also, like spelling, punctuation rules are continually evolving and may vary depending on which set of style rules is consulted. And the use of dashes as punctuation marks seems to be in flux. We might expect, however, that students, especially students for whom school is a struggle, will find it nearly impossible to learn how to use punctuation if they do not have regular opportunities to read and write throughout their school careers.

Usage

Traditional grammar instruction, with its emphasis on classifying parts of speech and diagramming sentences, has not been found to have much effect on students' writing (Braddock, Lloyd-Jones, & Schoere, 1963; Cleary & Lund, 1993; Moffet, 1968; Wolfram, 1995). In 1986 the National Council of Teachers of English went so far as to resolve that "isolated grammar and usage exercises not supported by theory and research is a *deterrent* to the improvement of students' speaking and writing" (emphasis added) (*Language Arts*, 1986, p. 103). Still, the formal study of grammar remains a continuing tradition in many language arts programs (Wolfram, 1995).

Teachers are legitimately concerned about students' grammatical usage, especially in their writing. Students who are unable, or unwilling, to demonstrate mastery of standard English in their writing may be denied certain academic and economic rewards. Some students struggle with the rules of standard English usage because of oral language difficulties. These students should be referred to a speech and language pathologist. Other students struggle with the differences between the informal language style they use among themselves and the more formal kinds of writing preferred by schools and most other institutions. Often this discrepancy is related to dialectical differences (i.e., differences between the dialects spoken by students and those preferred by the schools). Dialectical differences can be troubling to schools but they are just differences, not deficiencies. Standard English is the standard because it is preferred by the people who use it (who also happen to be in charge of the schools) and not because it meets some higher standard for "correctness." Forms such as "I don't have no . . ." or "He be sick" are no less complex than "I don't have any" or "He is sick." From this perspective the issue isn't correct grammar, but appropriate usage, that is, learning to use the written language forms and conventions preferred by the schools and other institutions. In the long term we may wish to work against the linguistic prejudices that devalue certain dialects and the people who use them (Smitherman, 1995). In the short term, however, we may do well to help our students expand the range of language styles and forms they use to include the language of wider communication (Delpit, 1988; Smitherman, 1995).

If the issue is a dialectical mismatch between students and the school we should not expect students to adopt standard English as *their* English (Smitherman, 1995). We may, however, wish to engage them in a study of language and dialect awareness as a means of helping them learn how to use standard English forms in contexts where they are expected. Language awareness programs also challenge students to consider why some dialects are preferred over others. (Walt Wolfram has written extensively on dialects and dialect awareness programs. See especially Wolfram, 1995, and Wolfram & Christian, 1989.) Addressing standard English within the context of language awareness may overcome some students' resistance to standard English based upon threats to their identity.

Usage problems are also common among students (and adults) who speak and write standard English. Some of the more common problems include:

- Use of pronouns: How many of us would say "The teacher is I" (correct usage) rather than "The teacher is me" (incorrect usage)?

- Subject-verb agreement: "Each of the girls has money," not "Each of the girls have money."

- Inconsistent verb tenses within a piece of writing.

- Dangling modifiers: "Exhausted and feeling ill, I went to bed," not "Exhausted and feeling ill, the bed felt good when I climbed in."

Literature is a powerful tool for developing students' awareness and use of standard English (Cullinan, Jaggar & Strickland, 1974). Those who hear literature read and read literature independently learn more about both standard and non-standard uses of language (Chomsky, 1972). Repeated read-alongs of books that feature certain standard usages, read primarily for pleasure, also have the secondary advantage of repeatedly engaging students in producing standard usage (Tompkins & McGee, 1983). In addition, retelling, storytelling, dramatization, and writing a new story using the book as a model all encourage students in the repeated use of standard English as a natural part of instruction (Strickland, 1972). Reading books that feature dialect (e.g., Faulkner, Toni Morrison) offers opportunities to discuss both standard and non-standard varieties of English.

Instruction in language usage can take the form of teacher demonstration, comparison, and/or "lifting." But before we provide instructional examples, we need to consider how a teacher decides which usage problems or differences to focus on in instruction.

Since language usage differs from region to region, school to school, class to class, and student to student, teachers need to begin by surveying the usage differences and problems that exist among students, through observation of writing and speech (Pooley, 1974). The list does not have to be exhaustive. Instead, it should feature those usage problems or differences that appear most often and that are most likely to stigmatize students or brand them as "uneducated." Obscure or pedantic usage problems should not be targeted for instruction; our rule is that if we hear or see well-educated adults frequently using the same grammatical forms, the usage problem is probably not worth instructional time. Temple and Gillet recommend that the list contain no more than ten to fifteen goals for usage to be addressed over the course of a school year. For many students who struggle with reading and writing, even this may be too much, so adjust your goals accordingly (1984).

How you refer to students' usages during instruction is important. Avoid "wrong," "nonstandard," "incorrect," or other terms that carry negative evaluation. We prefer to talk with students about "book language" and "home language" when we discuss usage in writing. However, do not demand that students *replace* their home language with book or TV language or even encourage it. Language use is closely tied to students' identities and we should never ask students to compromise their cultural or social identities. Instead, our goal should be to *add* standard usage (i.e., the language of wider communication as Geneva Smitherman (1995) calls it) to students' language repertoires so that they may choose the usage appropriate to the situation. Since there is general agreement that formal writing features standard usage (although much writing is not formal), we prefer to help students with usage in writing and assume that they can make the same usage choices in speech situations that call for it. But we need to remind ourselves that "There really is no right or wrong usage. Usage choices are either appropriate for the situation or not appropriate" (Fisher, 1980, p. 63). Thus, while "book language" is preferred in most school writing, it is not appropriate in many social situations outside of school.

Teacher demonstration may be useful when particular aspects of usage are being attended to for the first time, when instructional time is short, or when the usage issue is too complex for the student to deal with any other way. While editing Delores's paper, for example, her teacher decided to call attention to usage in one of her sentences: "I like to go to school for I could be real smart." The teacher substituted *so* and *can* for *for* and *could* and said: "This is the way the sentence would be written in a book. Read it aloud so you can get a feel for how it sounds." In doing this, the teacher was developing Delores's intuitive knowledge of how words and tenses are used in standard English. Although Delores was a ninth grader, the teacher didn't talk with her about the differences between *for* and *so*, nor did she give Delores the rule about keeping tenses consistent within a sentence. (Again, it is doubtful that formal grammar instruction would be all that helpful here.) When Delores read her piece of writing to a small group of her classmates, she reproduced the standard usage and heard how the sentence sounded. Also notice how brief and focused this lesson was. Delores's teacher recognized that attending to more than one aspect of usage at a time only risked confusion.

Comparing usage is another useful technique, especially when the same difficulties with usage arise frequently in students' writings. Comparison usually requires collecting examples from students' work that illustrate problems with language usage before the lesson can be taught. For example, a teacher working with two girls, both of whom were dialect speakers, observed that they weren't using plural *-s* and past tense *-ed* endings consistently in their writing. Because they sometimes used these markers, the teacher assumed that the girls knew of their existence and function but not at a conscious enough level for them to make a choice about using the endings appropriately. The teacher looked through a number of the girls' recent compositions and located examples of missing plural and past tense markers. She wrote the sentences containing these examples on a piece of paper. Then she rewrote the sentences "as an author would in a book" (see Figure 12-3).

The teacher asked the girls to examine the pairs of sentences and explain differences in their own words. The girls had no difficulty locating the differences between their language and "book" language. They were also able to explain the differences as rules, i.e., that *-s* was used at the end of a word when talking about more than one and that *-ed* was used when talking about things that had already happened. If the girls hadn't been able to offer a hypothesis about the operation of plural and past tense markers, this teacher was prepared to ask them to look at the sentences and figure out how they would know in the future when to add *-s* or *-ed* to words in their writing.

First I had to wait in the waiting room until he call me.
First I had to wait in the waiting room until he called me.

I really don't like snow because when you are really dress up...
I really don't like snow because when you are really dressed up...

At home for the last three day...
At home for the last three days...

I'm going to take my camera and take pictures of my teachers and children and some friend too.
I'm going to take my camera and take pictures of my teachers and children and some friends too.

FIG 12-3   *Comparing usage*

Many points of usage may be taught in the same way, ranging from replacing "Me and Bobbie" with "Bobbie and I" and avoiding split infinitives ("She helped the children to fill the glasses correctly" rather than "She helped the children to correctly fill the glasses") to sophisticated discussions about appropriate usage when writing character descriptions or trying to capture the essence of a character in the character's dialogue. (In the latter case, of course, the students may need to study and replicate dialectical or nonstandard usage.) It is also interesting to compare usage in songs and poems that creates certain effects, such as a rhyme scheme. Students might, for example, compare the lines "We three Kings from Orient are. Bearing gifts we travel afar" with the sentence "We are three Kings from the Orient" and discuss what the lyric writer might have had in mind when deciding how to write the first line of the song.

The final technique, "lifting" text, is also useful, especially when you've already demonstrated or compared certain aspects of usage. Here teachers ask a group of students to edit for usage a text (one in need of editing) written by a student. As students change usage on their own, you might record their choices in writing. You might also issue specific challenges to them: "Let's take a look at the pronouns John used in his piece of writing. Which are used the way they would be in a book? Which are not? How would those be written in a book?"

We want to close this discussion of usage with a caveat. Teachers must be cautious when teaching standard English to nonstandard speakers. Language is very personal. It not only allows us to communicate, it also enables us to proclaim our membership in social and cultural groups. Questions about the use of standard or nonstandard dialects are questions of appropriateness, not correctness. Successful writers (and speakers) must learn that standard English is appropriate in certain contexts and that dialects may be appropriate in other contexts. When we encourage students to write for a range of purposes and audiences, we give them opportunities to use both standard and nonstandard language in their writing. In this way they learn grammatical usage appropriate to the social context, rather than "correct" usage.

Handwriting

"Handwriting is for writing" (Graves, 1978, p. 393). The only reason to learn handwriting is to communicate with others. If a student's handwriting doesn't require unusual effort from readers or from the student herself in producing it, there is little reason for the student to be receiving any special handwriting instruction. In general, students who write for audiences learn quickly that legible handwriting is important. Handwriting can, however, interfere with students' writing fluency. Handwriting difficulties can cause some students to write less or not at all. Other students focus so much attention on handwriting that they lose sight of what they wish to say. Poor handwriting may frustrate some students' efforts at communication and, in some cases, students may not be able to read their own handwriting, making revision and editing all but impossible. Although a thorough discussion of handwriting instruction is beyond the scope of this book, we wish to offer some advice on dealing with handwriting problems.

Some students need to be convinced to keep handwriting in perspective. Just as students should be encouraged to focus on ideas in initial drafts rather than on spelling, they should be encouraged to do the same with handwriting. Graves notes that "When handwriting flows, the writer has better access to his own thoughts and information" (1983, p. 181). Sometimes games can help. For example, if a student spends too much time neatly forming letters as he writes, conduct races for a week or so in the journal or during free writing: How many words can you write in how many minutes? Or, if the student's problem is that she spends a lot of time erasing and re-forming letters, have a "no eraser week" and have the students discuss and show what they did when erasers weren't allowed and how this "rule" affected their writing.

Some students need explicit handwriting instruction, but learning to print or to write in cursive does not require that students do handwriting exercises in isolation. Students can learn handwriting as they write meaningful text simply by being invited to write messages of their own and by being helped with those letter formations or letter sequences the teacher observes as being difficult. Students who need handwriting instruction ought to receive it while copying their own compositions for publication or, at the minimum, while copying something—a poem, for example—they have selected because they want their own copy of it.

Children who need help with their handwriting can be effectively and efficiently grouped for instruction, just as students with similar needs are grouped for instruction that addresses conventions. If you observe that several students are writing letters from the bottom up rather than from the top down, for example, work with them and have them copy or recopy whatever they've chosen. If students have difficulty writing a letter or connecting letters in cursive, demonstrate how to write the letter or letter series, let them try it out, and then have them focus on that letter or letter series in the next thing they copy. Before students make a final copy of their writing, have them underline in their rough copy the problem letter(s) they want to focus on; it will help them remember to make an extra effort when they encounter those letters.

Some students (like John, the boy whose spelling we have discussed at length in this chapter) may reverse letters in their writing, even in cursive writing. Reversals, which are common in young children's writing, are often the result of a lack of experience with print. The same is true of the reversals that older students make in both LD and remedial programs; these students are often no more experienced with print than a much younger, normally achieving child. (For more on this topic, see Nelson, 1980; F. Smith, 1982a; and Vernon, 1957.) Even good readers and writers may reverse letters, but this doesn't usually interfere with literacy development.

Problems with reversals may be exacerbated by the excessive attention they receive. Some students become so concerned about possible reversals they ask, "Is this the right way?" as soon as they've finished writing a letter they know causes them problems. In such cases, it's best to give students support they can use on their own so that some of the anxiety and pressure they have built up over the problem is relieved. For example, if a student regularly reverses *b* and *d*, consider putting some guide words featuring the letters, like *dog* and *cab*, nearby so that the student can refer to them. The best place to put the words might be on the upper corners of the student's desk, in this case, *dog* on the left and *cab* on the right so that the circular part of the words face outward from the desk. After a few months of increased success, ask the student if her image of the words on the desk is so good the cards can be removed. In any case, editing for reversals should come at the proofreading stage. Whatever your solution to the problem, it must reduce student anxiety.

Handwriting problems can also be the result of postural or motor difficulties that render handwriting very labored and difficult, consuming a great deal of students' energy. In such cases, your intervention may help a great deal. While positional guidelines for fluent handwriting may be consulted (see Graves, 1983, pp. 172–73 as an example), Graves recommends that a good way to figure out the source of difficulty is to sit next to students and imitate their handwriting. Thus, you should turn the paper at exactly the same angle and place it in the same relationship to your midline, distance yourself from the desk and paper in the same way, hold the pencil in the same way and apply similar pressure to the paper, and position both your elbow and back in the same way. Write for the same period of time that the child writes. You should be able to discover and change those positions that cause the student to labor so hard and to be fatigued. (If the student is left-handed, you might ask a left-handed adult to do this for you and to relate his observations. Consult Howell, 1978, or Enstrom, 1968, for left-handed guidelines.)

If the student appears to have motor problems, several things are worth mentioning. First, many motor problems will virtually disappear or at least improve through writing itself. In other words, sometimes the problem is also the cure. The only cure for a child who is having difficulty learning to ride a bike is to help her ride the bike. The same is often true of handwriting; a student's motor difficulties often resolve themselves through the constant, integrated practice that the writing muscles get as the student writes. As Graves says, "If children have enough writing time, and are in control of their topics, their handwriting improves" (1983, p. 178).

We have observed many students, including children with diagnosed physical difficulties such as cerebral palsy, improve their handwriting abilities through extended daily writing in journals and similar situations. When the children's regular teachers noticed improvement and inquired about the source of it, they were surprised to learn that the children did not go through an isolated handwriting program or visual motor training.

Occasionally, a student will have a handwriting problem that doesn't respond to instruction. In such cases, it may be wise to help the student learn another method for fluently recording ideas. Even young children can be taught to type (Kaake, 1983; J. L. Rowe, 1959a, b, c) and many fine typing tutorial software programs are available. Fluency, in particular, can be helped by learning to type. The average handwriting speed for the third and fourth graders in a study by Rowe was 1.6 words per minute in comparison to 42 words per minute at the typewriter. Students can also learn to compose at the typewriter or word processor.

WORKING TOGETHER

Students who struggle in school are the responsibility and concern of many individuals. Classroom teachers look for ways to accommodate the individual needs of struggling readers and writers without losing sight of the needs of the rest of the class. The presence of students who require more intensive, frequent, and individual support from their teachers often makes the difficult job of teaching that much more difficult (Allington, 1994b). Struggling readers and writers may also come to the attention of remedial and special education teachers who work with these students in resource room settings, segregated classes, or, increasingly, within the regular classroom. Speech-language pathologists or school psychologists may also be involved in consultative roles or, occasionally, providing direct service. When students struggle in school, parents strive to find additional means to support their children in school. In addition to their usual efforts to meet their children's basic emotional and physical needs, parents do what they can to support their child's reading and writing development. They may spend extra time reading and writing with their child or, if they can afford it (and, sometimes, even if they can't) parents may hire tutors or enroll their children in private schools. School trouble always has an impact on family dynamics, often creating tensions between parents, between parents and children, between parents and grandparents, and even among siblings (Dudley-Marling, 1990). And, of course, no one is more affected by school failure than students themselves. Students' life chances and self-esteem are closely related to school success. We can only imagine the pain felt by students who are forced to spend over a third of their waking hours in classrooms where people consider them less than adequate.

Learning problems affect the lives of teachers, parents, administrators, school support staff, and students. Yet there is often little sense that the various parties to school failure are in it together. There is often little communication—and less cooperation—between remedial and special education teachers, regular classroom teachers, and school support staff (Five, 1995; Jordan,

1994). Administrators often dictate policies (e.g., standardized tests, common curricula, local or regional district standards) that severely constrain teachers' abilities to accommodate the needs of individual learners (Dudley-Marling & Dippo, 1995). Teachers report to parents, but rarely offer parents a meaningful role in children's literacy education (Cairney & Munsie, 1995). It is rarer still for either teachers or parents to benefit from students' perspectives on their school struggles.

It's not hard to explain the lack of cooperation and collaboration among those with an interest in struggling readers and writers. Teacher education programs that seldom teach the skills or dispositions needed for collaboration, administrative structures that isolate teachers in their classrooms, working conditions that place impossible demands on school staff, and different views of the meaning of literacy and reading and writing instruction all mitigate against collaborative efforts on behalf of students' literacy learning. Still, it stands to reason that if parents, teachers, administrators, and students could find ways to work together, the prospects for students developing into readers and writers able to fulfill their intentions in a range of communicative settings would be greatly enhanced.

13

Developing Collaborative Relationships

In this chapter we talk about improving the quality of literacy instruction for struggling readers and writers by developing collaborative relationships among teachers, parents, administrators, and students. We'll give special attention to working in situations where people's beliefs about literacy and literacy learning present a barrier to effective collaboration. We begin by discussing the development of collaborative relationships with our teaching colleagues.

Collaboration Among Teaching Colleagues

Political, pedagogical, and economic factors are coming together to change the relationships between special education and remedial teachers and their colleagues who work in regular classrooms. Instead of relieving regular classroom teachers of the responsibility of teaching reading and writing to some students, special education and remedial education teachers are being asked to share responsibility for reading and writing instruction with regular classroom teachers. Special education and remedial teachers may be expected to work in consultative roles or, more likely, work with struggling readers and writers within the regular classroom (Jordan, 1994). The sharing of responsibility for struggling learners can lead to more consistent, intense, and frequent reading and writing instruction for students who need it. *Forced* collaboration, however, may lead to conflict among teachers who have disparate goals for literacy and different approaches to teaching and/or to reading and writing instruction. In this section we discuss some of the ways special and regular classroom teachers can work more closely together as well as some of the problems that can emerge when we attempt to collaborate with colleagues whose beliefs about literacy and literacy instruction may be very different from our own.

Effective collaboration between regular classroom teachers and resource teachers is most likely if there is a shared responsibility for initial assessment, goal setting, and other decision making. Sometimes special education and remedial teachers make no effort to involve children's classroom teachers in decision making. (See, for example, Five, 1995.) It's unrealistic, however, to expect regular classroom teachers to feel much responsibility for a student's reading and writing instruction if they don't have a voice in decisions affecting that instruction (Alvarez, 1981). Classroom teachers know a great deal about the reading and writing development of their students and often have a clearer view of what a struggling student needs to learn in order to be a more effective reader/writer. Yet, except for making the referral, many classroom teachers have few opportunities to participate in either placement or instructional decisions for remedial students or students with learning disabilities, even though these students will spend the majority of their time—if not all of their time—in the regular classroom (Five, 1995).

Collaboration among resource teachers and regular classroom teachers begins with the initial assessment of students' reading and writing development. Even if the classroom teachers or resource teachers with whom we are working do not share our beliefs about reading and writing instruction, they still have vital information to contribute. Resource teachers, for example, can ask classroom teachers to listen to see if students' oral reading miscues make sense or not. Or classroom teachers could ask resource teachers to focus their assessment on whether a student's miscues change the meaning of a text and what strategies that student seems to use when she gets stuck on a word. Classroom teachers are in a particularly good position to comment on the range of purposes for which students read and write. Classroom teachers' familiarity with the reading and writing development of normally achieving children can be especially valuable to resource teachers who work almost exclusively with *problems*. Together resource and regular classroom teachers can reflect on students' writings by asking questions like, "Does the student remark on important aspects of her world in writing?" and "What does the student's spelling tell us about his knowledge of sound/letter relationships?" These kinds of questions ensure that we'll get a rich description of students' reading and writing development and not just a catalogue of students' deficits. These sorts of assessment questions may also broaden the ways some teachers view reading and writing. In general, regular classroom teachers can collaborate in the range of assessment strategies discussed in Chapters 4 and 5.

If possible it is useful for resource teachers to observe students as they read, write, and respond to reading and writing instruction in their regular classroom, sharing what they observe (e.g., "Did you notice the comic book Mark was reading before class?") with the classroom teacher. Common sense indicates that resource teachers should focus their observations and commentaries on the student's reading and writing and not on the teacher or the instructional program, no matter what their opinion. It would be tempting to comment on the nature of reading and writing events in some classrooms (or in the resource room), but this would only damage the relationship between classroom and resource teachers and, more seriously, risk the student's relationship with his teachers.

When teachers who share responsibility for students' reading and writing development work together to identify students' strengths and needs, they are better able to develop a cooperative plan for a reading and writing program. They can decide together, for example, when—and if—students work in the resource room. They can also discuss how the classroom teacher could offer more intense, frequent, and individualized reading and writing instruction (Allington, 1994b). It could be decided, for example, that periods of sustained silent reading be implemented for all students as a means of increasing the amount of time students with reading difficulties have to engage in reading *and* the amount of time teachers have to provide individual support and direction (Dudley-Marling, 1996). The instructional strategies in this book can be used with individual students or small groups within a regular classroom setting, although some teachers might need some help to see how this is possible. The Writing and Reading Workshop routines we discussed in earlier chapters, for example, provide frequent opportunities for teachers to address students' individual learning needs.

Some teachers, overwhelmed by the increasing demands to teach more things to more students, find it nearly impossible to free up time to provide any additional support and direction for individual students in their classrooms. These teachers would be most grateful for an additional pair of hands, which resource teachers can provide by working with struggling readers and writers *within* the regular classroom. Resource teachers working in the regular classroom could, for example, provide individual support and direction (e.g., assisted reading or repeated reading) to any student who needs it during sustained silent reading times, meet with literature-sharing groups, conduct writing conferences, do reading and writing minilessons with small groups, and so on. They might also help establish reading buddies, peer tutoring (Bartnicki, 1995), literature-sharing groups (Short & Pierce, 1990), collaborative writing, or peer editing as ways to provide peer support to struggling learners within classroom settings. Resource teachers might also increase the possibility for individual support and direction in the regular classroom by helping organize volunteers (e.g., parents, grandparents, high school students) to work with struggling readers and writers in their classrooms.

Classroom teachers would also welcome the help of resource teachers in preparing instructional materials to help meet the needs of struggling readers and writers. Resource room teachers could, for example, prepare lists of frequently misspelled words for individual or whole class use or they could prepare occasional cloze tasks for in-class use as needed. They might also help identify appropriate literature for struggling readers or locate text sets for literature-sharing groups.

We also need to be sympathetic to classroom teachers who would like to increase the amount of reading and writing that goes on in their classroom—our primary goal—but find it difficult to balance this need with the demands of teaching math, social studies, physical education, sex education, problem solving, and so on. The amount of reading and writing during the day could be increased if teachers work together to find ways for students to read and write "across the curriculum" (Atwell, 1990; Pappas et al., 1990). Ideally, resource room and regular classroom teachers might collaborate on a thematic unit that is carried out in both the regular classroom and resource room. Teachers may resist new ideas for teaching reading and writing because they feel they barely have time to do what they are already doing. Often this is because teachers view reading and writing as skills that are taught in particular blocks of time. Working together, resource room and classroom teachers can discover ways to integrate reading and writing instruction throughout the day and across the curriculum.

Teachers who share responsibility for children's literacy education may also consider various models of co-teaching as a means of both supporting each other and taking better advantage of each person's expertise. (See Gelzheiser & Meyers, 1990, and Scala, 1993, for excellent examples of this.) Sands, Kozleski and French (in press) propose the following co-teaching formats (slightly adapted here) which address how two teachers might interact during instruction. Note that planning roles should also be negotiated.

One person teaches, one assesses or coaches. One professional holds instructional responsibility while the other assesses students in the class or peer-coaches the teacher. Either person may take either role and may switch roles at any time.

One person teaches the group, one teaches individuals. One person provides individual help and guidance to students while the other professional provides instruction to the group.

Simultaneous teaching. The content is divided and each professional provides instruction on one part to half the students at a time. Students switch places, and the instructor provides the same content to the other group.

Parallel teaching. Both professionals cover the same content to portions of the larger group of students.

Re-teaching. One person instructs students who have already learned previous content while the other works with students who did not learn the content, either re-teaching or adapting it so that the students learn it.

Tag team teaching. Presenters take turns, one on, one off. The person who is not presenting at the moment may fill a variety of roles (from data collection to individual student assistance).

Speak and add teaching. Both presenters are "on stage" at the same time. One leads, the other supports. The lead person is in charge of the content and makes process decisions. The support person adds examples, humor, or other perspectives.

Speak and chart teaching. This format extends "speak and add" in that the person in the support role acts as a neutral documenter who records ideas on an easel, overhead projector, or chalkboard.

Duet teaching. This format represents the epitome of co-teaching and is only possible with skilled professionals who have done extensive collaborative planning. Both presenters talk—they alternate or finish sentences for one another. They use physical proximity as a tool. They choreograph the physical space—they avoid blocking the speaker and subtly cue each other with looks, proximity, hand gestures, voice tempo, and intonation. They stay focused all the time, each attentive to the other and to the students.

To collaborate effectively resource and classroom teachers need to be able to show each other that they are supporting aspects of reading and writing that both consider important. Students are often referred for remedial or special education because of problems with spelling, for example. If spelling is *the* issue for the regular classroom teacher, resource teachers need to be able to show what they're doing to support students' spelling development. If doing phonics drills is important for getting along in the classroom reading program, resource room teachers also need to be able to demonstrate how their whole language program addresses phonics. Resource teachers in particular may have to be open to the possibility that sometimes they will have to teach students the *skills* needed to do the reading exercises in the regular classroom. Whole language teachers want students to learn to read a range of texts, but they also want students to experience success within their regular classroom reading program even if they disagree with the philosophy underpinning that program. Teachers must be certain that they never hold students hostage to their beliefs.

Teachers often report that it's difficult to find mutually convenient times to meet with each other, and there can be little argument that all teachers have busy schedules. It may be difficult to find large blocks of time for teachers to meet, but there are usually lots of shorter time periods during the day when teachers are available. Frequent two- or three-minute meetings are sometimes more effective anyway. A resource teacher, for example, can share a sample of a student's work or briefly review a student's reading or writing progress just before school, between classes, during preparation periods, during recess, and so on. If teachers are unable to find convenient meeting times, they should both write down several times during the day when they are available for five minutes. It's unlikely that they won't be able to find five minutes during the day to meet. Other teachers will be especially willing to meet regularly with us if they come to expect that something useful will emerge. But be brief! If we habitually take lots of our colleagues' time, we may encounter an increasing reluctance to meet in the future.

Collaborating with Parents

Research indicates that parents do much to actively support their children's language learning through listening, prompting, questioning, modeling, demonstrating, and jointly constructing meaning with their children. (See Pellegrini & Yawkey, 1984, and Feagans, Garvey, & Golinkoff, 1984, for reviews of this research.) However, educators have tended to ignore parents' contributions to children's reading and writing development despite evidence that significant literacy learning occurs in the home even before students enter school (Durkin, 1966; Taylor, 1983; Teale & Sulzby, 1986; Wells, 1986). "Many of the same parents who fulfilled [a] rich and complex role in spoken language development . . . begin to fulfill more limited roles in the literacy learning of their children once school age is reached" (Cairney & Munsie, 1995, p. 2). Recent talk about home-school partnerships has led many educators to consider more active parent involvement in children's literacy learning. Too often, however, parent involvement means *training* parents to be either teachers-in-the-home (e.g., Cairney & Munsie, 1995; McGilp & Michael, 1994) or teacher-helpers in the school (e.g., Lamme, 1981; Williams & Bellomo, 1995). Positioning parents as trainees or helpers is unlikely to create the mutual trust and respect necessary for the development of collaborative relationships. Worse, the "parents-as-literacy-teachers" model of parent participation risks schools intruding into the lives of families (Bloome, 1995; Dillon, 1989), perhaps even transforming relationships between parents and their children, while denying the value of home literacy practices different from the school's (Bloome, 1995; Dillon, 1989; Shockley et al., 1995; Taylor, 1994). What's needed, we think, are respectful alternatives to "parents-as-teachers" or "parents-as-teacher-helpers."

We begin with a brief description of a parent-teacher literacy initiative that suggests the possibility of real partnerships in which teachers offer support to parents, but actually listen to and use what parents have to say. We then discuss some general principles that we believe ought to underlie any efforts by schools to involve parents in school literacy programs.

Engaging Families

In *Engaging Families: Connecting Home and School Literacy Communities,* Shockley, Michalove, and Allen detail the efforts of two teachers (Shockley and Michalove) to work with parents to create literacy connections between the home and the school (1995). Several times a week Shockley and Michalove's first and second graders brought home books they had chosen. Families were encouraged to spend some time reading and talking about the books their children brought home and then record bits of their conversations in a journal to which teachers responded. Journals provided a place for students to grow as writers and provided a stimulus for students to think about and discuss books they had read. Journals were also used by parents to communicate directly to teachers about literacy issues or, in some cases, just to chat. Teachers used the journals to comment on student/parent responses to books they'd read and, sometimes, to offer parents supportive advice. For example, when a parent worried that the book her daughter had chosen had "too many difficult words for her right now," her teacher suggested "that this is probably . . . one of those times . . . that it would be best for you just to read to her" (Shockley et al., 1995, p. 42). Parents further contributed to the school literacy program by writing stories about family experiences in a class book of "Family Stories."

Shockley et al. indicate that this home-school literacy initiative was very successful. To the degree that children participated in parallel literacy practices at home and at school, "children spent more time engaged in reading, writing, and literate talk" (Shockley et al., 1995, p. 15). What makes this initiative noteworthy, however, isn't teachers sending books home for children to read with their parents or parents and their children collaborating on reading response journals. Many teachers do these things. What's remarkable about *Engaging Families* is the tone of the initiative. First of all, the teachers listened to what parents had to say. When a parent used the journal to indicate her intention to use "easy words" that her son knew to make up stories for him to read, the teacher didn't invoke whole language dogma about the integrity of texts to discourage the parent. Rather she responded, "I'd say give it a try. Let me know how it goes. . . ." (Shockley et al., 1995, p. 67). Similarly, when a parent's journal entries indicated that she focused the discussion of books her son read on the "moral" of the story, the teacher did not draw on theory about student ownership or reader response to deter the parent. Instead, she supported this mother's effort. We suspect that if a parent had rejected storybook reading in favor of alternative literacy practices—reading the Bible or morality tales, for example—the teachers would have been equally supportive. Teachers also invited parents to comment on children's reading and development as part of the *Engaging Families* project.

The *Engaging Families* initiative did not seek to train parents to do school with their children. Teachers offered advice to be sure, but they were cautious not to overwhelm parents with information. Notably, the tone of teachers' advice was respectful and supportive. Instead of *do's* or *musts* or *shoulds* teachers offered: "I wonder how it would work if . . . ," "You might try . . . ," "I noticed that _____ is having trouble with. . . . One way to help is . . ." This isn't a matter of form, however. Parents were able to take "You might try . . . " as the advice of an equal partner because the entire initiative signaled to parents that teachers took what they had to say seriously.

It seems to us that this kind of respect by educators for what parents have to say is all too rare. Underlying these teachers' stance that parents and teachers could enter into a partnership of equals is the assumption that parents care about their children's education and the belief that parents possess useful knowledge. It seems to us that these assumptions are crucial to the success of any home-school literacy project.

Some Guiding Principles for Working with Parents

Emerging from programs like the *Engaging Families* initiative are some principles which we think should be the basis of any home-school literacy projects. The principles we present here are adapted from Cairney and Munsie (1995).

THE STARTING POINT FOR HOME-SCHOOL COOPERATION IS A SENSE OF PARTNERSHIP AND MUTUAL RESPECT

Despite increased public criticism for schools as a whole, parents are generally supportive of their own children's teachers and the school they attend (e.g., Barlow & Robertson, 1994). It's not clear, however, that teachers always have the same respect for parents. Many educators are too quick to cite parental ignorance, apathy, or neglect for children's struggles in school and too slow to recognize the Sisyphean struggles of many parents to provide emotional and material support to their children in the face of extraordinary stresses. (See Taylor & Dorsey-Gaines, 1988.) We believe that the faith Shockley and Michalove had in the knowledge, caring, and abilities of parents is a necessary precondition for developing collaborative relationships with parents. If we cannot communicate our trust to parents it isn't likely they will give their trust to us.

HOME-SCHOOL COLLABORATIONS SHOULD FULFILL THE NEEDS OF PARENTS

There are a range of ways parents can be supportive of their children's schooling. Many parents, overwhelmed by the demands of jobs and family, support their children's literacy development by showing an interest in their child's schooling and providing emotional and material support to their children. Other parents may be able to find the time to participate in various school functions. They may, for example, support teachers' programs by helping to raise funds for classroom resources (e.g., books), staff book publishing programs (Williams & Bellomo, 1995), listen to students read in the classroom, or help teachers prepare teaching materials. Parents may be able to share their talents as authors, poets, musicians, storytellers, and craftsmen (McGilp & Michael, 1994). Many parents can be involved in joint decision making about literacy initiatives in and out of the classroom. Whatever their level of involvement parents mustn't be made to feel that they're just "the help." There must be something in it for them beyond a demonstration of altruism. They must be able to learn and contribute with the sense that what they have to say and do will make a difference. Home-school literacy programs limited to exploiting the labor of parents as classroom volunteers offer little to parents and, by communicating a lack of respect, may foreclose the possibility of real collaboration.

THE OVERRIDING PURPOSE OF HOME-SCHOOL LITERACY INITIATIVES IS TO BRING ABOUT POSITIVE LITERACY BENEFITS FOR CHILDREN

As we've said throughout this text, the goal of literacy instruction for struggling readers and writers is to increase students' ability to use reading and writing in a range of communicative settings. The goal of parent involvement is to provide the possibility of additional support and direction for developing readers and writers, not to relieve teachers. Actively involving parents in instructional and assessment decisions supports literacy learning by offering teachers and parents a broader perspective on students as learners and increases students' opportunities to engage in reading and writing (Jordan, 1994). We take for granted that parent involvement is an asset to teachers and students, but, like Shockley and Michalove, we do not blame parents if they do not fulfill *our* expectations.

HOME-SCHOOL LITERACY INITIATIVES SHOULD BE RESPONSIVE TO THE NEEDS OF PARENTS

Teachers can offer parents specific, helpful suggestions for supporting their children's development as readers and writers. The tone of such advice should be respectful (e.g., "You might try . . . ," "Something I do sometimes . . .") and should respond to parents' intentions. For example, we are certainly in a position to offer parents advice on responding to children's oral reading miscues, but, in general, we should offer our advice only if it matches parents' intentions. If parents ask, we can give some direction, but, if they don't ask, why should we presume to tell them how to interact with their children? Our eagerness to share 101 reading strategies with parents can also be read as a lack of faith in what parents know. We shouldn't forget that most of what we've learned about reading with children at home has come from studies of parents, so parents do know something about reading with their children. (David Dillon [1989] likens telling parents how to read with their children to selling real estate to Native Americans.) We should also be open to the very real possibility that parents can teach us something about family literacy to share with other parents and, perhaps, build on in the classroom. This suggests that parent–teacher discussions about family literacy might be preferable to a teacher lecture, for example.

Teacher advice should also be sensitive to parents' needs to create and sustain particular kinds of relationships with their children. Many parents, for example, resent the intrusion of homework that reduces opportunities for parents to interact with their children (Samway, 1986). Homework can also reduce the amount of time students have available to learn other skills not developed in school but considered important by parents. Parents of struggling students sometimes find that reading and writing with their children merely exacerbates existing tensions over schooling. School literacy can also push out—or at least devalue—other home-based literacy practices. In general, constructing parents as teachers can detrimentally affect parents' relationships with their children. Teachers should also be careful not to contribute to the construction of idealized "super parents" who meet all the demands of work and family while also having the skill, time, and energy to tutor their own children. Parents unable to meet these expectations—and most aren't—will only learn to feel inadequate, resentful, or both.

With these caveats in mind, there are ways teachers may be able to support parents' efforts to increase children's opportunities to engage in meaningful reading and writing. For example:

- Teachers might encourage parents to read aloud to their children, regardless of age. If parents aren't able to read to their children themselves (e.g., some parents work at nights, others may lack confidence in their own literacy, and so on) they might arrange for siblings, baby sitters, or grandparents to read to them. If we think it's necessary, we might also let parents know about the positive effect reading to children can have on their reading and language development (e.g., Teale, 1978; Wells, 1986). We might also suggest resources on reading aloud to children like Jim Trelease's (1995) *Read-Aloud Handbook*, perhaps including these resources in our classroom library for parents to borrow.

- If parents are uncertain about how to respond to their child's oral reading miscues, we might suggest, for example, that they could minimize miscues by reading the text to the child first, before their son or daughter reads it to them. If *parents are interested* we could demonstrate the technique of assisted reading to them to support their children's reading (Hoskisson, Sherman & Smith, 1974). We might urge parents not to limit the amount of discussion of a text or the accompanying pictures. We could recommend that they avoid criticism and allow their child plenty of "wait time" or "thinking time" before providing assistance with words. Again, if *parents express an interest* we might demonstrate strategies like "Read on a little" (Bartlett, Hall & Neale, 1984). If nothing else, we would like to help parents learn to respond to children's oral reading in a way that makes reading enjoyable for parents and children alike (Bartlett, Hall & Neale, 1984).

- Teachers could remind parents of the range of reading or writing opportunities they might take advantage of to encourage their children to read and/or write. A particularly successful activity we've seen used with groups of parents (this could be done on parents' nights at school) to broaden their notions of reading and writing begins by inviting parents to write down everything—no matter how insignificant it may seem—that they've read or written in the last day or so. After a discussion of everyone's lists parents are asked how they might have included their children in these various reading and writing events. Typically, parents suggest strategies like offering children a section of the newspaper to read, letting the child read/follow recipes, look for road signs, and so on. This sort of activity also demonstrates to parents that they can easily support their child's literacy development within the flow of daily activities.

- We might remind parents that books aren't the only worthwhile sources of reading material. Parents might be relieved to hear that magazines and comic books, for example, can be valuable for encouraging reading. We might also let parents know whenever we discover a new children's book we particularly like and encourage them to do the same. A class newsletter might be a good place to share the news that "Mrs. Sedgewick discovered a new book by Steven Kellogg. . . ." Parents' nights are also a good place for parents to share some of their favorite children's books. It is also worthwhile to make available to parents (maybe in the class library) anthologies about children's and adolescents' literature.

- When parents are interested in locating children's books to read with their sons and daughters, we might encourage them to visit local libraries. If some parents aren't comfortable using libraries, we could arrange for the librarian to give parents a tour of the facilities. We could use the class newsletter to keep parents informed about school book fairs and special reading programs at libraries. We might remind parents of younger children about story reading times at the local public library. We could recommend bookstores that have particularly good selections of children's and adolescents' literature. (Teachers need to be sensitive, however, to the reality that not all parents can afford to buy books at bookstores.) Some children's bookstores also feature story times and visits by authors of children's and adolescents' literature. You might even consider establishing a book-lending library for parents at school (Brieling, 1976) if parents don't have easy access to other sources of books.

- When parents worry about the effects of television and video games on children's reading habits, teachers could suggest family reading times. Some families we know set aside thirty minutes every night for everyone to read, but even fifteen minutes a night is worthwhile. If parents seem skeptical, we could tell them that seeing their parents regularly reading has been shown to have a positive effect on children's reading development (O'Rourke, 1979).

- If parents are interested in writing with their children, we might suggest writing letters to grandparents or letting children help prepare grocery lists. Some families keep regular journals that provide a record of family events as well as a model for writing. When the Dudley-Marling family took a trip to England their father bought each member of the family a journal and, at the end of each day, everyone spent about fifteen minutes writing a little bit about what they had done that day. Vacation journals could be used for any trip, even a trip to visit grandparents and, who knows, journal writing could become a habit.

- Another idea parents can use to encourage their children to read and write is to write to their children. Some parents stick notes in their child's lunch box. Many families have blackboards or bulletin boards in the kitchen where family members exchange written messages. When parents get in the habit of sending written messages to the children, their children often get in the habit of writing back.

- For parents who want to help children with their writing we might provide editing checklists (McGilp & Michael, 1994) as a guide for helping children edit their work.

One caution is in order here. Reading and writing are often a source of considerable stress between parents and their LD or remedial children. Therefore, it's important that parents be encouraged to focus on reading and writing experiences with their children that are especially likely to be natural and enjoyable. Parents should not be encouraged to teach reading or writing skills but rather to help their children find as many opportunities as possible for purposeful and enjoyable reading and writing. The sorts of ideas we have shared here involve parents in time-honored ways in their children's literacy development and minimize stress for both parents and children. In some cases, however, parents may find any involvement in their child's reading and writing program stressful. Other parents—those who work nights, for example—may have relatively little time to read and write with their children. Teachers should be alert to these possibilities and consciously avoid making parents feel guilty if they aren't able, or willing, to participate in their child's reading and writing program.

Collaborating with Administrators

Principals and other school administrators can be valuable partners. They can provide the physical resources and support that significantly affect school literacy programs (Barnard & Hetzel, 1976). In general, administrators only need to be convinced that a teacher's literacy program is thoughtful, coherent, and based on the real needs of children. Therefore, whole language teachers should make every effort to address the beliefs and expectations about literacy and literacy instruction of the administrators—principals, supervisors, curriculum consultants, and so forth—with whom they work. Let them know what's going on in your reading and writing program and your rationale for your approach to literacy instruction. Administrators are often grateful to receive the latest information on reading and writing instruction and may be interested in several books on whole language written for administrators (Head-Taylor, 1989; Weaver & Henke, 1992; Wortman & Matlin, 1995). Principals and superintendents feel the pressures for "accountability," so we must offer evidence (in the form of student work and, perhaps, research summaries) that our literacy program addresses students' instructional needs, including the needs imagined by those to whom the principal is accountable. If local and state agencies mandate standardized tests as measures of literacy development, we may need to provide principals with evidence (i.e., research) that supports the effectiveness of whole language programs in terms of standardized test scores (e.g., Dahl & Freppon, 1995; Freppon & Dahl, 1991; Freppon & Headings, in press; K. Goodman, 1986b; Singer, McNeil, & Furse, 1984; Teale, 1978; Wells, 1986). Our ability to provide support for our literacy programs—and, perhaps, our willingness to at least demonstrate some ability to compromise—will go a long way toward enlisting the support of the administrators with whom we work.

We may also find ways to solicit the active involvement of school administrators in our reading and writing programs. We know principals, for example, who regularly read to students in their schools. Others routinely stop by classes to listen to students share their writing or perform plays they've written. Asking principals to work with struggling students in the classroom helps teachers provide additional support for these students while demonstrating the nature and effect of their reading and writing programs. Teachers might also consider inviting district administrators and even school board members to observe in their classes as a way of demonstrating the thoughtfulness and the effectiveness of their literacy programs.

Principals and other school administrators can also be invaluable allies for helping to establish schoolwide literacy programs, such as sustained silent reading, paperback book programs, or writing fairs. Schoolwide literacy programs can broaden the literacy experiences of LD, remedial, and normally achieving students throughout the school. Efforts by the principal in support of schoolwide literacy programs may prevent, or at least minimize, future reading and writing failures.

Administrators can help establish volunteer programs, arrange for time to consult with teachers and other school staff, locate community resources, and establish schoolwide information-sharing networks. They can also help you develop parent programs, arrange in-service sessions, encourage collaboration by school staff, and seek donations of reading and writing materials, if necessary.

We imagine some readers chuckling to themselves, "They've never met my principal." No, we haven't, and we know from our own experience that not all principals are equally supportive of their teachers. We acknowledge the possibility of administrators hostile to whole language instruction and serious consequences for appearing to buck official or unofficial reading and writing policies (Edelsky, in press). If we are able to enlist the support of our principals and other administrators, however, it will help us better meet the needs of struggling readers and writers throughout the school, even minimizing future problems.

Collaborating with Students

Teaching is a quintessentially collaborative experience. Teachers can invite, facilitate, motivate, support, and direct, but unless students learn—and learning *always* requires the participation of learners—teachers can't really claim that any teaching has occurred. Learning is the student's prerogative. To claim that we taught but students didn't learn is, from our perspective, an odd notion that contradicts our understanding of what it means "to teach." Teaching requires that we enlist students' participation in reading and writing, not through the use of artificial incentives and rewards, but by demonstrating to students the power of literacy to affect their lives and the world in which they live.

Teachers should always begin by communicating their goals for literacy to students and invite students to share their goals. Teachers might profitably involve struggling learners in goal setting, materials selection, scheduling, evaluation, and program planning. The importance of student input is most apparent with older students, but even our youngest students can offer valuable input into the educational decisions that will affect their lives.

This does not mean that students get to decide *whether* they learn to read and write. We just need to find common ground with students that recognizes their role in learning to read and write. Teachers might, for example, ask students what books they would like to read and what they'd like to learn about (again, not *whether* they'd like to learn about American history but *what aspects* of U.S. history they would like to explore in greater depth). We also believe that students can and should participate in the decisions that are made at IEP conferences. Students can, for example, give us their views about whether we support their reading and writing development in the regular classroom or a resource room setting. (Not all students will have the same view.) Students can participate in parent-teacher conferences, perhaps even taking an active role in sharing what they have learned. Students can also participate in the assessment of their learning (see Ames & Gahagan, 1995; Atwell, 1982; Rhodes & Shanklin, 1993; Rhodes, 1995) and the evaluation of our reading and writing program. Which instructional strategies have they found to be most helpful? Are there strategies they find ineffective or even insulting? We imagine few students would have much good to say about "high-interest, low-vocabulary" books, for example. Or, if we're considering the introduction of word processors into our writing program, we might request student input. If we think students have too little information to provide input, we can at least let them evaluate the effectiveness of such innovations as the word processor after they've been introduced as part of the curriculum.

Involving students in educational decision making increases the prospect of students' active participation in their reading and writing programs and their development as readers and writers. In general, we should treat students as partners in developing and implementing reading and writing curricula. As we've noted throughout this book, students must actively participate in their reading and writing development. We can't succeed without their commitment and participation.

Students can also collaborate among themselves. The older students become, the more they come to rely on people their age for companionship and interpersonal support and the more they can be placed in positions of responsibility for helping students their own age and younger. However, that does not mean that trusted adults don't have an impact. In fact, we're convinced that interpersonal relationships between students at school thrive only in the context of positive interpersonal relationships between a teacher and students.

Teachers can encourage good interpersonal relationships between students in many ways; they will foster academic achievement and changes in attitudes in the process. Encouraging respect between students and a helpful attitude between students is an important first step. An urban teacher whom one of the authors studied sometimes seated children in the classroom in such a way that the seating arrangement provided support (Clarke, Davis & Rhodes, 1995). For example, the teacher seated a very bright and empathetic girl next to another girl who was socially withdrawn and had very low academic performance. With the teacher's and the first girl's quiet but steady attention and encouragement, the second girl slowly began to try to do her assignments, raise her hand in class, and interact with other children.

Relationships between students can also be cultivated within literacy events and can, in the process, directly affect reading and its development. We have, for example, marveled at how fifth-grade Title I children worked very hard to select and prepare a book for their first-grade Title I book buddies and how they beamed when their students enjoyed their sessions with them. As teachers, we have all experienced learning something better while teaching it; cross-age tutoring provides the same benefit to the older child. In fact, research shows that those who are tutored and those who tutor both gain in knowledge or skill and attitude (Cohen, Kulik & Kulik, 1982; Osguthorpe & Scruggs, 1986; Scruggs, Mastropieri & Richter, 1985), including in situations where the tutor is a special education student and the tutored student is either normally achieving or receiving special education services (Maheady, Harper & Mallette, 1991).

Leland and Fitzpatrick report on cross-age tutoring between average and below-average sixth-grade readers and kindergartners in which students read and wrote together weekly for forty-five-minute periods (1994). By the end of the year, the sixth graders reported that they enjoyed reading and writing more, their parents reported that they read at home much more frequently, their teachers reported that comprehension had improved and they read at school frequently, and the librarian reported a considerable increase in the number of books checked out by the students. Labbo and Teale reported positive results as well when struggling fourth-grade readers read trade books to kindergartners (1990). And middle schoolers who had missed the magic of good picture books when they were younger gained a great deal from reading them to young children in a nearby school (Robb, 1993). It is recommended that students receive training in tutoring techniques; there are some programs available that assist teachers in designing such training, including a videotape (Cameron & Limbrick, no date).

Paired reading or peer buddy reading is another literacy event that is built on and enhances interpersonal support among students. Robb writes of her experience working with seventh- and eighth-grade struggling readers for whom paired reading was a key to their reading development (1993). Before students read their trade books in pairs each day, Robb modeled reading strategies (e.g., mental imaging, rereading) and as students read, they supported each other's use of the strategies.

Discussing books is another literacy event that depends on and enhances interpersonal relationships among students. Peterson and Eeds argue that students must learn to "dialogue" about good books rather than simply to discuss them (1990). They state:

> . . . Dialogue requires personal investment and cannot be pursued in a passive state. . . . Meaning evolves in dialogue through heartfelt responding that seeks to cooperatively disclose meaning. People in dialogue need each other. They collaborate one-with-the-other, striving to comprehend ideas, problems, events, feelings. Working together, partners in dialogue call one another forth as they seek to comprehend the world. (p. 14)

But probably most important of all, especially for students who struggle with reading, is to create an environment in which students can enjoy reading with each other and begin to see reading itself as a possible vehicle for human connection and companionship. In an insightful exploration of reading with struggling readers, Eidman-Aadahl found that her "basics" class at the high school believed that reading "would entail lost friendships" because it was viewed as such a solitary activity (1988). As she helped her students "open" the definition of reading and as she found ways to help them recognize and implement reading as a social activity, she found that they began to change their notions about reading and their roles as readers.

Collaborating with Others

There are many people within the school and community who can contribute to students' reading and writing programs. School librarians, for example, can be very helpful in the selection and acquisition of reading materials. For those of us who haven't had courses in children's and/or adolescents' literature, librarians' assistance in locating books appropriate to students' background, experience, and reading ability is invaluable. Librarians can also support classroom reading programs by ordering text sets for literature-sharing groups. Many librarians are also well acquainted with microcomputer technology and can support teachers' efforts in this area. Some librarians are accomplished storytellers or oral readers who would be more than happy to perform for your class as a way of engaging students' interests in literature.

Speech and language therapists, because of their expertise in oral language development, can help resource room and regular classroom teachers create rich language learning environments that provide fertile ground for literacy development. Other school staff—consultants, school psychologists and guidance personnel, clerical and custodial staff—may be willing to share skills or interests that can contribute to your language program. When Dudley-Marling taught third grade he discovered a computer consultant who was a masterful storyteller. He arranged for her to visit his class on a biweekly basis, and she regularly captivated his students with her spellbinding stories. We have also encountered school custodians and secretaries who regularly shared their musical talents with students in their schools.

People from the community can contribute to school literacy programs in much the same way. You can probably discover children's authors, poets, storytellers, and musicians who are willing to share their skills with your class or, perhaps, the entire school. Williams and Bellomo were able to enlist senior citizens to record books on tape for students to listen to (1995). Community volunteers can provide some of the labor for book-publishing programs (Williams & Bellomo, 1995). We may also be able to recruit peer tutors from among the students in our school. Schools of education at local colleges or universities are a good source of potential classroom volunteers. If you use volunteers in your classroom, it's important that you require regular, long-term commitments and clear expectations of how they will work in your classroom.

Strategies for Dealing with Imposed Curricula

Whole language teachers, students, and administrators often have to work together to cope with curricula that have been imposed on them. Often teachers may be expected to use the same "skill building" reading series. Children may be tested according to their mastery of skills addressed in these programs and teacher evaluations linked to student success. Resource room and classroom teachers may labor under skills-oriented IEPs developed by someone else (Five, 1995). And all LD and remedial teachers who function as resource teachers must give consideration to the regular classroom curriculum, which may include a skills-oriented approach to reading and/or writing.

These curricular constraints cannot be ignored. The success of LD and remedial students in the regular classroom, teaching evaluations, and, in extreme cases, continued employment may depend on teachers' ability to deal with curricula over which they have little control. It is much more common, however, for regular classroom teachers to have to deal with mandated curricula. They often have to learn how to implement holistic reading and writing programs within the framework of an imposed curriculum. In this section we will discuss some strategies for dealing with imposed curricula.

Teachers who feel constrained by imposed curricula should first check their perceptions. Are they, in fact, required to adhere slavishly to a curriculum to the exclusion of any other approach to reading and writing? In most cases they are not. We've known many teachers who have satisfied their principals or other administrators with explanations of how and why they would like to either supplant or supplement the adopted reading program. These explanations addressed principals' legitimate concerns that classroom literacy programs make sense for students.

If a principal or supervisor is reluctant to permit a departure from the adopted curriculum, teachers should not give up. They should continue to lobby for the freedom to implement meaningful reading and writing activities in their classroom. Ohanion, for example, described her efforts to obtain her principal's permission to read books with her students during the lunch hour (1994). The principal agreed to this proposition on the condition that the assigned reading time continue to focus on the teaching of reading skills. Ohanion's students ate their brown bag lunches while Ohanion read to them and they looked at books on their own. We don't suggest that teachers give up their lunch period, but extraordinary efforts are occasionally required to introduce the reading and writing of actual texts into the classroom.

Most teachers do have freedom, perhaps more than they realize. Even where imposed curricula exist, these curricula only indicate that teachers should address certain content or standards, use certain materials, and so on. Teachers are rarely required to do nothing else, although Ohanion's experience reminds us that this can happen. In all but the rarest cases, teachers do have the opportunity to encourage meaningful reading and writing, even within the context of a skills-oriented curriculum.

If teachers are required to use skills-based reading and writing programs, they don't usually have to use these programs exclusively. They can devote a segment of the reading or language arts period to more meaningful activities, such as journal writing and sustained silent reading, which involve students in the reading and writing of actual texts. As we noted earlier, regular classroom teachers can also be encouraged to teach reading and writing "across the curriculum," incorporating meaningful reading and writing opportunities in content areas.

If teachers examine what they do with their skills-based programs, they find that they already make choices about what to use and not to use in the curriculum. No teacher we know uses materials exactly as they are written. Many teachers, for example, skip the *enrichment* or *language extension* portions of the basal reader teacher's guide and choose to spend their time on skills exercises and worksheets. Teachers could continue to use the basal reader and move toward more meaningful reading and writing if they made different choices. Teachers could choose to skip the skills exercises and worksheets and spend their time instead on the enrichment and extension activities. Those activities often feature meaningful reading and writing or at least offer the potential for incorporating the reading and writing of texts into the curriculum.

Even when teachers must use mandated skills exercises and worksheets, they can spend less time at it. In our experience, students spend lots of time doing worksheets that could be completed in relatively short periods of time. When children are given a reward for satisfactorily completing worksheets, they finish worksheets that formerly took up to thirty minutes to complete in as little as five minutes with no apparent effect on performance. Many students may find the opportunity to read their favorite stories sufficient reward for completing tedious worksheets (Deardorff, 1982). We're not advocating worksheets or behavioral rewards. It's just that if teachers find they must use skills worksheets in their classes, these can be done more quickly than they usually are so that extra time is available for real reading and writing.

Some teachers may be fearful of abandoning skills-oriented writing and reading instruction because of the effect this might have on their students' performances on the achievement tests that are often used to gauge the skill of students and teachers. This is a reasonable concern. Standardized reading and writing tests, which may focus on isolated skills, are widely administered throughout North America. Teachers concerned about the effects of introducing a more meaningful approach to written language instruction on children's test performance should reassure themselves by remembering that holistic approaches to reading and writing do attend to what are referred to as "skills" like punctuation, spelling, and word recognition (Hansen, 1987). Writing skills or conventions are addressed during editing, when it becomes necessary to standardize writing for the sake of readers. As we have noted, readers must consider graphophonic rules, but children learn and use them as they read, not before they read. Teachers who encourage meaningful reading and writing will positively affect students' performance on reading achievement tests (e.g., Dahl & Freppon, 1995; Freppon & Dahl, 1991; Weaver, 1994). On the other hand, there will always be some students who develop into effective readers although they never do well on skills tests (Altwerger & Resta, 1986; Jackson, 1981).

Students may also need help dealing with imposed curricula. Throughout this book we've stated our position that the mastery of isolated, fragmented skills is not a prerequisite to successful reading and writing. We believe that students will learn the skills necessary for reading and writing as they read and write. But in some cases, isolated skill instruction may be necessary, not as a strategy for teaching students to read and write but as a strategy for helping LD and remedial students survive in resource rooms or classrooms where "doing skills" is required.

Obviously we want to do everything we can to promote the reading and writing development of our students. However, it's also important that our students reach a point where they no longer need us. They must learn to function within the context of ordinary reading and writing curricula. Sadly, in some classrooms or resource rooms it isn't enough to be able to read and write real text for real reasons. In these settings, reading and writing competence requires that students demonstrate the mastery of various skills, e.g., sound-blending, syllabication, capitalization, and so on.

In some instances, the LD or remedial student may understand the skill but have problems with worksheets or tests. Sometimes, the format is problematic. At other times, students do not perceive that an exercise calls for the very knowledge they apply in their reading and writing. We once encountered a student who struggled endlessly over worksheets that required her to circle the words that rhymed from a list of words. We knew this student could produce rhymes. We had heard her make up rhymes in her LD classes. It turned out that the student was confused by the visual aspects of the task—some of the words that rhymed were spelled quite differently (e.g., *make-steak*).

Teachers of struggling readers and writers should attempt to identify the specific kinds of problems their students have with reading and writing through observing and talking with the students involved. If it appears that the task itself might be the problem, they can address this explicitly. It may be a case of teaching the student how to go about completing a particular worksheet rather than teaching the skill. In rare cases, it may be necessary to teach skills like sound-blending to struggling students directly. When this happens, teachers should remember that what they are doing is teaching "school survival skills" and not reading. Be honest with students when this happens. Don't deceive them into believing that what you are doing is teaching reading, but do tell them that they may have to learn some things that make little sense if they're going to succeed in a particular situation. If such skills instruction is attempted, it should not be done until the student has achieved a reasonable level of fluency and has discovered that reading and writing are meaningful and purposeful. At that point, it may be possible to help students make a connection between the skill as it is being taught and something they already know and do in reading and writing.

14 *Sharing Expectations About Reading and Writing Development*

Differing expectations about reading and writing instruction, what it means to be literate, and even the meaning of schooling can be a major barrier to collaboration among parents, teachers, administrators, and students. Students come to school with expectations of schooling shaped by the beliefs of their parents, portrayals of schooling in the media, and the experience of siblings. Students who expect drills and exercises to play a central role in schooling, for example, may be unsettled by teachers who expect students to play a significant role in shaping the reading and writing curriculum. Parents may be concerned about reading and writing programs different from "the way they were taught." Principals can be expected to be anxious about teachers who depart from the prescribed literacy curriculum. Whole language teachers may also have to overcome negative stereotypes about whole language instruction. Skeptical portrayals of whole language in the media and some professional journals may lead many parents, administrators, and even other teachers to expect that you, as a whole language teacher, will not attend to fundamental reading and writing skills.

Clearly communicating our beliefs about literacy and literacy instruction is a key to avoiding some of the misunderstandings that threaten effective collaboration among students, parents, administrators, and teachers. We need to be clear about our goals for reading and writing instruction and how we expect to achieve those goals. We also need to explicitly address some of the myths about whole language instruction that may imperil collaboration: that is, whole language teachers *do* teach phonics; whole language teachers *do* teach spelling; whole language teachers *do* teach punctuation; whole language teachers *do* teach word recognition (Dudley-Marling, 1995; Edelsky et al., 1991; Goodman, 1993; Newman & Church, 1990). Laissez-faire instruction in the name of whole language is, quite simply, bad teaching. Thus it is important that we articulate how we expect to teach our students to read and write and our rationale for teaching this way. Further, our explanations must be free of the jargon that distances whole language teachers from their colleagues, parents, and the general public.

The trick is, of course, to share our views without staking out hardened positions that signal that we're not really interested in collaboration. We must try to find ways to communicate our beliefs and invite others to share theirs. We need to convince parents and fellow teachers that we are interested in their views and that we are willing to work together to establish shared goals for reading and writing instruction and the means to achieve those goals. Whole language teachers' strong views about reading and writing cannot be allowed to translate into inflexible positions that make it impossible to work with people with different sets of beliefs about literacy and literacy instruction. Whole language teachers need to be flexible and open to the possibility of compromise. Communicating expectations about literacy learning is the first step in developing collaborative relationships. The goal is not, however, to convert people to our beliefs, although most people are more likely to listen to our views on literacy and literacy learning if we take their beliefs seriously. Collaboration depends on mutual respect.

The Expectations of Parents

Successful collaboration with parents depends on teachers' willingness and ability to articulate the nature of their literacy programs. In any case, parents have a *right* to know what teachers will be doing to support their child's literacy development and why. We believe that much of the public criticism of schools can be traced to poor communication. Parental demands for standardized testing, more homework, and back-to-basics curricula may have more to do with parents' desires to have a window on what goes on in the classroom than any fundamental disagreement over curriculum or philosophy. In our experience, when schools do an effective job sharing what they do with parents, accountability through testing, homework, and standardized curricula is rarely an issue.

Therefore, it is in the best interests of teachers and children to offer parents a clear description of our instructional program along with an appropriate rationale. If, for example, we tell our parents that, in certain situations, students' invented spellings will be accepted, we must also explain our position that it makes little sense to worry about correct spelling with students who produce very little writing *because* they are overly concerned with spelling conventions. We might remind parents of their own willingness to accept misarticulations and ungrammatical utterances when their children were learning to use oral language. It is useful to share writing samples from students in previous years with parents to show how accepting invented spellings can have a positive effect on children's writing fluency. These same samples of children's writing can also be used to demonstrate to parents how invented spellings typically evolve over time. Teachers must also be clear about the deliberate strategies they will be using in their classrooms to support students' spelling development. Similarly, we shouldn't tell parents "we don't teach phonics here." Instead, we should tell them exactly what we will be doing to develop students' knowledge and use of graphophonic information.

Periodic newsletters, parent conferences, IEP staffings, open houses, meetings with groups of parents, and telephone calls are some of the possibilities for communicating with parents that we will describe in more detail. Whatever means teachers use to communicate their expectations with parents, the tone of these communications must provide room for parents to share their views. Teachers must also be alert to the possibility that sharing information can make parents feel like second-class partners who know less, encouraging passivity when what we desire is a partnership (G. Goodman, 1989). Probably the best way to guard against this situation is to be sure that information sharing occurs in a broader context of collaboration in which parents and teachers share information with each other. One-way communication will never be congenial to developing collaborative relationships.

The Printed Word

Jane Murphy, a first-grade teacher from a Toronto-area school, has put together a three-ring binder full of children's work, classroom photographs, and articles on the teaching of writing. The binder also includes Jane's goals for her writing program and some information about the structure of writing instruction in her classroom. Jane circulates the binder among her parents throughout the early part of the school year. Jane's parents have a clear understanding of what she does and why; they are very supportive of her program. Parents are also invited to share written comments on the binder. This could easily become the basis of an ongoing written dialogue between parents and teachers regarding the classroom literacy program and the development of collaborative strategies (Shockley et al., 1995). Visitors to Jane Murphy's classroom also get a sense of her writing program by looking through the binder.

Many teachers send home letters to parents explaining various aspects of their reading and writing programs. Sandra Wilde, for example, provides several examples of letters to parents discussing both spelling development and teachers' spelling programs (1992). Figure 13-1 is a letter from Dudley-Marling to the parents of his third-grade students that attempts to give an overview of his instructional program and the central place of reading and writing in that program. Of course, such a brief description of an instructional program risks misunderstanding unless followed up by additional information.

Routine class newsletters can also function as a means of informing parents about what their children are doing in school and what they might do at home to support classroom instruction. A newsletter might be a good place for an ongoing discussion of invented spellings, for example. Newsletters are also a good place to celebrate the achievements of students. A student-prepared newsletter in Dudley-Marling's third grade acknowledged students' accomplishments in reading and writing. When students prepare the classroom newsletter they not only keep parents informed about the classroom literacy program, but also demonstrate its possibilities.

Students might also write individual letters to their parents as a way to document what they have done in school and their progress as readers and writers. Students in a remedial reading class in Denver, for example, take time each day to make a few notes on a calendar to record what they have done in class before they return to their regular classrooms. Every two weeks they use these notes to write letters to their parents explaining what they have done and what they have learned during the previous two weeks. In another class for emergent readers, students share what they are doing in school by dictating a group letter to their parents, which is copied and sent home. This serves as both a source of information for parents and reading material for students.

Teachers might also consider sharing with parents pamphlets, articles, and books about whole language that are accessible to parents. In Ontario, for example, the Federation of Women Teachers' Associations of Ontario publishes a pamphlet for parents describing whole language. Inexpensive pamphlets on whole language might be distributed to parents on back-to-school nights or during parent-teacher conferences to supplement teachers' presentations. Many of the books in Scholastic's "Bright Idea" series, all of which can be read by parents in an hour or so, provide excellent summaries of whole language theory and practice. We recommend especially *What's Whole in Whole Language?* (Goodman, 1986), *The Craft of Children's Writing* (Newman, 1984), *Reading Begins at Birth* (Doake, 1988), *Spel . . . Is a Four Letter Word* (Gentry, 1987) and *When School Is a Struggle* (Dudley-Marling, 1990). Some teachers or schools keep a library of books and articles about literacy for parents to borrow.

A note of caution on the use of print resources: Not all parents are equally fluent or interested readers, so the use of written material may not always be effective. Worse, an overreliance on printed materials may encourage feelings of inferiority in some parents, foreclosing any possibility of parent-teacher collaboration.

Phone Calls

Telephone calls can be a useful way to supplement and clarify information shared with parents by other means. A phone call which begins, "Mr. Thompson, I was wondering if you had a chance to read the note I sent home about our spelling program and if you had any questions," minimizes misunderstandings by giving parents an opportunity to raise any questions and concerns about how the literacy program we have outlined will help their children overcome their struggles with reading and writing. This provides an opportunity for teachers to explain how their approach to reading and writing instruction responds to the individual needs of children. Parents of struggling students are interested in a general description of the reading and writing program in their child's class, but they are even more interested in the kind of reading and writing instruction they can expect for their children. Parents need to be reassured that we have given thought to their child's individual needs. If Anne has always had a difficult time with spelling, her parents will want to know exactly how we expect to support Anne's spelling development.

Phone calls are also a personal way to reassure parents of struggling students for whom school has been a particularly painful experience. Since their child's schooling will have been a negative experience for many of these parents, we should make every effort to stress the positive in our phone conversations without pretending that there haven't been problems. We also need to accept the possibility

Dear Parents:

I'd like to take this opportunity to introduce myself and share a bit about our classroom program. This is my first year at Norwood and my first year as a Grade 3 teacher. I have, however, 7 years of previous teaching experience in primary and over 10 years experience teaching adults. Reading, writing, and oral language development are my special areas of interest. I expect to stress oral and written language in all areas of the curriculum including math, science, and social studies.

Let me tell you a bit about our program. Every day starts with reading, about 30 minutes of which is devoted to students reading silently. Students are also encouraged to write something about what they've read each day and to share their reading with other students. Additionally, there are opportunities to read throughout the day in science, math, and the computer and listening centers. I also work individually with students who need extra help in reading and I expect them to do some work with reading partners in which students support each other. Our goal in reading is for students to improve their reading fluency, to read as widely as possible, and to have opportunities to talk about what they are reading with each other. Specific goals, of course, vary according to the needs of individual students.

The writing program emphasizes frequent opportunities for students to write. Each day writing begins with a brief lesson on some aspect of writing (for example, selecting writing topics, spelling, or writing organization). Then students are given about 30 minutes for writing. During this time I work individually with students. Students are also encouraged to seek help from each other and share what they've written with their fellow students. Students also have regular opportunities to write throughout the day during reading, science, math, and so on. We also have a message corner in the classroom where students can post notes they have written to me or to each other. Our goal in writing is to encourage students to write for a variety of purposes and audiences.

The math program combines group instruction with centers where students work in small groups or individually either independently or with the teacher. Our math program stresses the use of manipulative materials and, according to school board and Ministry guidelines, focuses on geometry, measurement, and number (that is, addition, subtraction, multiplication, etc.). Currently, we are working on committing addition and subtraction facts to memory and place value (including addition with "carrying" and subtraction with "borrowing").

Ours is basically a center-based program in which students work at centers where they usually are expected to carry out an experiment or series of activities. For example, we are currently doing a science unit on plants. Students visiting the science center this week are doing a series of activities with bean seeds, sweet potatoes, and carrots.

Students visit three or four centers each day. Center times range from 30–45 minutes. Each week students are scheduled to visit the science center 3 times, the math center 4 times, listening center once, computer center once, art center twice, reading corner twice, and

FIG 14-1   *Introductory letter to parents about the classroom program (Part 1)*

writing center twice. Once a week students have a free choice period during which they can visit the center of their choice. I expect to increase the amount of student choice as the year goes on.

We also will be going to gym on Mondays, Wednesdays, and Fridays. During gym we will do a variety of activities which encourage the gross and fine motor development of our students. This week, for example, we are doing parachute activities. In North County Schools students begin French instruction in Grade 3. Our class will have French each day after morning recess from 10:30–10:50.

The students will also be going to a music teacher once a week on Friday afternoons. But since I play the guitar we will be doing some music every day. Typically, I write out the lyrics to new songs on chart paper to provide students with additional opportunities for reading. I also will be reading orally to students several times each day. Last week we enjoyed one of the "Bunnicula" books and this week we are reading the first in the "Boxcar Children" series.

Evaluation is a very important part of our program. I began the year by doing a careful evaluation of each student's reading, writing, and math skills. I insure continuing evaluation by picking four students to observe closely each day (two in the morning and two in the afternoon). I also will be having regular reading and writing conferences with students and trying to examine samples of students' writing each week. For the students' part, I expect them to keep a record of their reading and their center visits in their notebooks.

Finally, I am anxious to involve parents as much as possible in our program. Parents are free to visit our classroom ANY TIME they wish and I expect to invite parents to contribute to our program in a variety of ways. This letter, for example, will be followed by a survey asking parents to participate in the evaluation of their child's development.

Thank you very much.

Sincerely,

FIG 14-1 *Introductory letter to parents about the classroom program (Part 2)*

that some parents will use phone calls as an opportunity to vent their anger—not at us, but at a system that has caused them and their families so much pain. (See Dudley-Marling, 1990.) Should a phone call become an occasion for parental catharsis, teachers need to be prepared not to take it personally.

Phone calls are also an occasion to ask parents for their input. We can learn from parents about their children's interests and abilities. Parents can tell us about children's reading and writing at home. When Dudley-Marling taught third grade, for example, he learned during a phone conversation that Jennifer, who was a reluctant writer in class, spent much of her free time at home writing stories. Parents can also tell us what they think their children should be learning, giving teachers an opportunity to discuss how reading and writing instruction in their classrooms addresses parents' concerns (e.g., "Yes, Mr. French, I'm also concerned that my students learn to be good spellers, so each day we . . .").

Telephone calls are more likely to be effective if they are regular and if we notify parents that it will be our habit to call them from time to time to discuss their child's progress and/or our literacy program with them. Parents who equate phone calls from teachers with "more bad news" will almost certainly welcome a "good news" phone call. Sending parents a note that you will be calling as a matter of routine may lessen the possibility of parents assuming a defensive posture the moment they hear, "Mrs. Tanney, this is Sarah's teacher. . . ."

Large class sizes and excessive demands on teachers may make it seem that routine telephone calls to parents are unrealistic. However, if we make just one phone call a night it should be possible to talk to all of our parents every two or three months. If this is still too burdensome—after all, some parents may keep us on the phone for a half an hour or more—we might consider phoning only those parents whose children have struggled learning to read and write. Of course, all the students with whom remedial and special education teachers work struggle in school, but smaller class sizes may make it relatively easier to phone parents regularly.

Parent Conferences and Open Houses

Parent conferences and open houses can be useful occasions for sharing information about your reading and writing program. An open house at the beginning of the year may, for example, feature slide presentations of the previous year's program with specific examples of students' reading and writing. Some teachers use these times to engage parents in reading and writing as a means of demonstrating the potential power of their literacy program. Open houses are also a good time to talk with parents about any concerns they have with your program. Parent gatherings are another opportunity for teachers to communicate to parents what they do and why.

Individual parent conferences are also a good place for keeping parents informed about your literacy program and their child's progress. However, it's important that the information shared with parents be precise, accurate, and provide opportunities for parents to share their perceptions of their child's reading and writing development. Very general comments about a student's progress usually leave parents less than satisfied. Teachers who regularly observe their students as they read and write and carefully document their observations will have lots of detailed information to share with parents.

Open houses and parent-teacher conferences are problematic for many parents and teachers. Teachers are often disappointed by poor parent turnouts that they take as an indication of parents' lack of interest in their children's education.

Parents, for their part, often find little of value in parent-teacher gatherings beyond an opportunity to signal their interest to teachers. Parents come to show they care, not because they find these events particularly rewarding. The opportunity to demonstrate their credentials as "interested parents" isn't enough to attract many parents overburdened by the demands of work and family. Although parents are interested in their children's education, they're less likely to be interested in meetings, committees, or other formal functions (Thompson, 1992). The chance to signal their interest is also insufficient motivation for other parents to overcome a discomfort with schools that derives from their own negative experiences with school (Potter, 1989). This may be especially true of many parents of struggling readers and writers who struggled in schools themselves.

We have two pieces of advice about parent-teacher meetings. First of all, teachers should assume that all parents care about their children's education (Shockley et al., 1995). There are many possible explanations for parents staying away from open houses, parent conferences, and "meet the teacher" nights, the least likely of which is that the parents don't care. If teachers use a variety of means to communicate with parents, then school-based, parent-teacher meetings aren't so crucial. Additionally, teachers should make every effort to make coming to school worth the effort. Parents are much more likely to come to school events if they believe that this is an opportunity for them to share something with teachers. They may also be interested in hearing presentations on children's literature, for example, or talking among themselves about reading at home. Involving students in parent-teacher conferences, perhaps by asking students to lead the discussion of their reading and writing program, may also increase the interest of parents in teacher conferences. Finally, we need to help create school cultures that are welcoming. Teachers must work with principals and parents to create school climates in which parents and teachers do not see each other as adversaries.

The IEP Conference

Special education teachers—and, on occasion, regular classroom and remedial reading teachers—routinely participate in IEP meetings in which general instructional plans and strategies are developed for individual students. These conferences offer another opportunity for teachers to share about their programs and to develop collaborative relationships with parents. This would be a good place to involve parents in setting goals, program planning, and the sharing of responsibilities. Parents might, for example, take responsibility for doing assisted reading with their child each day or helping their son or daughter write weekly letters to grandparents. Regrettably, parents are usually relegated to the role of observers at IEP conferences, squandering a valuable opportunity for collaboration.

Classroom Visits

Classroom visits are an unbeatable way for parents to learn about what goes on in their child's classroom. Visiting parents have the opportunity to observe teachers and students working and learning together and to see samples of students' work. Additionally, parents may discover an idea or two they can use to encourage and support reading and writing at home. Ideally, we'd like parents to come back again and again. In our experience, parents are more likely to visit if teachers make a conscious effort to make them comfortable. Comfortable furniture (not everyone enjoys sitting in tiny chairs), warm greetings, and something to do (parents might be given a choice to either sit back and observe or work with students) encourage frequent visits. We would also bet that the practice of assigning clerical tasks to parents when they visit classrooms discourages many parents from coming at all and, in any case, denies them the opportunity to see what's going on. Classroom doors that are always open (literally) are also much more inviting. Teachers might also ask parents what can be done to make schools and classrooms more inviting. We could easily imagine a parent advisory group being charged with the purpose of creating parent-friendly classrooms. This would enable teachers to learn from parents what makes them feel welcome and unwelcome.

Home Visits

Although home visits are time consuming, they offer teachers an opportunity to meet with children and parents on their home ground where both are more likely to be at ease (Potter, 1989). During home visits teachers can share information about their classroom programs, discuss a student's progress, and exchange ideas with parents on students' current and future reading and writing development. Despite the potential value of home visits, we need to be sensitive to the possibility that some parents may feel that they are an intrusion (Potter, 1989). Some families have every reason to fear home visits as unwelcome surveillance by public employees, and at least one state is trying add the role of "immigration officer" to teachers' official duties. In general, it is probably best to give parents choices about where they meet with teachers. One school we know, for example, uses parent sign-up sheets to schedule home visits which are limited to around twenty minutes per visit. All indications are that these visits have had a positive effect on the relationships between parents and teachers.

Finally, it is unlikely that teachers can affect parents' expectations with a single newsletter, phone call, or face-to-face meeting. Frequent communication about our goals and teaching methods will be necessary. Open communication with parents will diminish the prospects of conflict while improving the prospects of collaboration. In turn, parents' participation in their child's literacy program will affect the way parents think about reading and writing (Williams & Bellomo, 1995). Parent-teacher contacts will be most effective if teachers are explicit about their goals and the direction of their literacy program and if they share concrete examples of students' work. Parents who understand what teachers are doing and why are far more likely to work with their child's teacher, and, of course, parents and teachers working together will lead to a better understanding of individual children and how best to support their literacy development.

The Expectations of Teachers and Administrators

Efforts should also be undertaken to share expectations about literacy and literacy instruction with administrators, regular classroom teachers, and others with whom teachers work. Misunderstandings between special education and remedial teachers, for example, and other professional educators may permanently damage working relationships, leading to ineffective instructional situations for students and, occasionally, negative teaching evaluations. It is also important, therefore, that teachers have some sense of the expectations and beliefs of other educators with whom they work. The objective here isn't to reach consensus, although some compromises may be necessary. Instead, the goal is to achieve a level of understanding and respect that makes collaboration possible and enables the different parties to anticipate areas of potential conflict and address them *before* problems arise.

Probably the best method for communicating expectations is frequent personal contact. Talk with teachers and administrators as often as you can and let them know, generally, what you will be doing and why. You can do this naturally. It's quite natural, for example, to discuss with other teachers the reading and writing of students for whom you share instructional responsibility. Most principals are pleased to have the opportunity to hear what's going on in classrooms in their schools.

It is especially useful to share samples of students' work with the teachers and administrators with whom we work. We might draw their attention to developmental changes, and briefly share what we expect to do to encourage continued reading and writing development. We have to be careful not to overwhelm our colleagues with too much detail and avoid our natural desire to sell our point of view. Overzealous whole language teachers can turn their colleagues off. Avoid using jargon in your discussions with teachers and administrators, even the phrase "whole language." Instead of saying, "I'm a whole language teacher . . ." describe the kinds of literacy experiences you provide for your students. Also avoid excessive enthusiasm. Many people are put off by jargon and by bandwagons. Just let teachers and administrators know that what you are doing is providing what you believe encourages literacy development in the students with whom you are working. It may also be necessary to make it clear to your principal and fellow teachers that you are not ignoring aspects of reading that they feel are important. You still teach spelling, phonics, word recognition, and punctuation. It's just that your approach to language arts instruction may be different from that of some of your colleagues.

If you feel you need to demonstrate the effectiveness of programs, let your students find ways to share their work. You might display students' work in the halls outside your classroom and encourage students to share their reading and writing in their other classes. Maybe invite teachers and administrators to visit your classroom before the school day begins. Some teachers encourage visits by providing coffee and donuts before school to encourage their colleagues to visit their classrooms every so often. Special education or remedial teachers might offer to teach lessons in the regular classroom, and regular classroom teachers can invite special education and remedial teachers to observe their lessons and even to co-teach. The teachers' lounge is a good place to share some of your successes. Teachers might be impressed to hear, for example, that, after years of resistance to writing, little Jason is churning out books. Other teachers may be especially interested to discover that writing done by remedial students or students with learning disabilities may be as good as or better than the writing done by normally achieving students in their classes. Teacher-research projects (e.g., Bissex & Bullock, 1987; Cochran-Smith & Lyle, 1993; Goswami & Stillman, 1987; Olson, 1990) documenting the efficacy of whole language practices, and/or summaries of whole language research may overcome the skepticism of other teachers or principals. Participating on key committees, especially curriculum development and textbook selection committees, is another way to define expectations and, of course, influence school policy (e.g., Rhodes & Shanklin, 1989; Stephens, 1991; Weaver, 1994). Using opportunities like these can communicate your approach to reading and writing instruction and, if done artfully, may influence colleagues and invite collaboration.

It can also be useful to share and discuss articles on reading and writing instruction with other teachers and with the principal. You might also leave copies of interesting articles about reading and writing in the teachers' lounge or in other areas likely to be used by teachers. Some schools have a system for circulating interesting books and articles. You might also make staff aware of interesting speakers or conferences in your area. If teachers express an interest in something you've shared (e.g., "spelling in a whole language program") you might offer to hold a miniworkshop or suggest a study group. This all works especially well if everyone on the staff gets into the act, in which case you may discover principals and teachers discussing articles from journals like *The Reading Teacher* or *Language Arts* in the faculty lounge or during staff meetings.

Patience is one of the keys to sharing expectations and setting the stage for the development of collaborative relationships. We often need to remind ourselves that our goal is to communicate our expectations and find ways to work with our colleagues, not convert everyone to our point of view. Even this relatively modest goal can take several years, maybe even longer for new teachers. If you do affect colleagues' beliefs about reading and writing, it will only happen after you've earned their respect and trust.

The Expectations of Students

Effective collaborative relationships with the parents, teachers, and administrators with whom we work does not depend on developing a common set of beliefs about the meaning of literacy. We do not need to change people's beliefs to work with them. In the case of students for whom learning to read and write has been a struggle, however, changing their beliefs about the processes by which people read and write is often an explicit goal of our reading and writing instruction. Students who equate the skills of drills and exercises with all reading practices, for example, need to revalue the role their background knowledge and experience play in making sense of texts. Often our instruction challenges students' sense of the value of literacy in their lives. Ken Goodman believes that changing students' expectations about the value of reading and writing in their lives is *the* primary goal of reading and writing instruction for struggling students. He says:

> Revaluing is essential. If those [struggling] pupils are to become literate, they must lose the loser mentality. They must find the strength and confidence to take the necessary risks, to make the literacy choices, and to enter into functional literacy events. Whole language teaching helps pupils value what they can do and not be defeated by what they can't do; it helps them trust themselves and their linguistic intuitions, to become self-reliant in their sense of what they are reading. Whole, relevant, meaningful language . . . can help them build productive meaning-seeking strategies. Eventually they will come to realize that making sense is all that reading and writing are about. (K. Goodman, 1986, p. 56)

Every instructional strategy in this book is intended to encourage students to revalue reading and writing as meaningful, purposeful processes. Still, some older students may need to be shown how your instructional program meets their needs to do well on standardized tests, learn "proper" punctuation and spelling, and get good grades in other classes.

REFERENCES

AARDEMA, V. (1975). *Why mosquitoes buzz in people's ears.* New York: Dial.

AARON, I. E., & HUTCHISON, S. M. (1993). Best books for children from four countries for 1992. *Reading Teacher, 47,* 212–221.

ADAMS, M. (1990). *Beginning to read: Thinking and learning about print.* Cambridge, MA: MIT Press.

ADAMS, P. (1973). *There was an old lady who swallowed a fly.* New York: Grosset and Dunlap.

AFFLERBACH, P. (1993). STAIR: A system for recording and using what we observe and know about our students. *Reading Teacher, 47,* 260–263.

ALEJANDRO, A. (1994). Like happy dreams—Integrating visual arts, writing, and reading. *Language Arts, 71,* 12–21.

ALLEN, J., & EISELE, B. (1990). Yelling for books without losing your voice. *The New Advocate, 6,* 117–130.

ALLEN, J., & HANSEN, J. (1986). Sarah joins a literate community. *Language Arts, 63,* 685–691.

ALLEY, G., & DESHLER, D. (1979). *Teaching the learning disabled adolescent: Strategies and methods.* Denver, CO: Love Publishing.

ALLINGTON, R. (1980). Poor readers don't get to read much in reading groups. *Language Arts, 57,* 872–876.

ALLINGTON, R. L. (1993). Literacy for all children: Michael doesn't go down the hall anymore. *Reading Teacher, 46,* 602–606.

ALLINGTON, R. L. (1994a). The schools we have. The schools we need. *Reading Teacher, 48,* 14–29.

ALLINGTON, R. L. (1994b). What's special about special programs for children who find learning to read difficult? *Journal of Reading Behavior, 26,* 95–115.

ALLINGTON, R. L., & BROIKOU, K. A. (1988). Development of shared knowledge: A new role for classroom and specialist teachers. *Reading Teacher, 41,* 806–811.

ALLINGTON, R. L., & McGILL-FRANZEN, A. (1989). Different programs, indifferent instruction. In D. K. Lipsky & A. Gartner (Eds.), *Beyond separate education: Quality education for all* (pp. 75–97). Baltimore, MD: Paul Brookes.

ALMASI, J. F. (1995). The nature of fourth graders' sociocognitive conflicts in peer-led and teacher-led discussions of literature. *Reading Research Quarterly, 30,* 314–351.

ALTWERGER, B., & RESTA, V. (1986). *Comparing standardized test scores and miscues.* Paper presented at the annual meeting of the International Reading Association, Philadelphia, PA.

ALTWERGER, B., & RESTA, V. (1994). *Miscue analysis profile software.* Katonah, NY: Richard C. Owen.

ALTWERGER, B., EDELSKY, C., & FLORES, B. M. (1987). Whole language: What's new? *The Reading Teacher, 40,* 144–154.

ALVAREZ, M. C. (1981). A cooperative reading plan starts from within, involves the entire school. *NAASP Bulletin, 65,* 67–74.

AMES, C. K., & GAHAGAN, H. S. (1995). Self-reflection: Support students in taking ownership of evaluation. In C. Dudley-Marling & D. Searle (Eds.), *Who owns learning? Questions of autonomy, choice, and control* (pp. 55–66). Portsmouth, NH: Heinemann.

ANGLETTI, S. R. (1991). Encouraging students to think about what they read. *Reading Teacher, 45,* 288–296.

APPLEBEE, A. N., LANGER, J. A., & MULLIS, V. S. (1988). *Who reads best? Factors related to reading achievement in grades 3, 5, and 11* (Report No. 17–R–01). National Assessment of Educational Progress. Princeton, NJ: Educational Testing Service.

APPLEBEE, A. N., LEHR, F., & AUTEN, A. (1981). Learning to write in the secondary school: How and where. *English Journal, 70,* 78–82.

ARMBRUSTER, B. (1992). On answering questions. *Reading Teacher, 45,* 724–725.

ARMBRUSTER, B., & WILKINSON, I. A. G. (1991). Silent reading, oral reading, and learning from text. *Reading Teacher, 45,* 154–155.

ARMBRUSTER, B., ANDERSON, T. H., & OSTERTAG, J. (1989). Teaching text structure to improve reading and writing. *Reading Teacher, 43,* 130–137.

ARONSON, E. (1978). *The jigsaw classroom.* Beverly Hills, CA: Sage Publications.

ASHER, S. (1987). *Where do you get your ideas?* New York: Walker & Co.

ASTMAN, J. A. (1984). Special education as a moral enterprise. *Learning Disability Quarterly, 7,* 299–308.

ATWELL, M. A. (1988). Predictable books for middle-school children. In L. K. Rhodes & C. Dudley-Marling, *Readers and Writers with a difference.* Portsmouth, NH: Heinemann.

ATWELL, M. A., & RHODES, L. K. (1984). Strategy lessons as alternatives to skills lessons in reading. *Journal of Reading, 27,* 700–705.

ATWELL, N. (1982). Making the grade: Evaluating writing in conference. In T. Newkirk and N. Atwell (Eds.), *Understanding writing* (pp. 137–144). Chelmsford, MA: Northeast Regional Exchange.

ATWELL, N. (1987). *In the middle: Writing, reading, and learning with adolescents.* Portsmouth, NH: Boynton/Cook.

ATWELL, N. (Ed.). (1989). *Workshop 1: Writing and literature.* Portsmouth, NH: Heinemann.

ATWELL, N. (1990). *Coming to know: Writing to learn in the intermediate grades.* Portsmouth, NH: Heinemann.

AU, K. H. (1979). Using the experience-text-relationship method with minority children. *Reading Teacher, 32,* 677–679.

AUEL, J. M. (1980). *Clan of the cave bear.* New York: Crown.

AUEL, J. M. (1982). *Valley of the horses.* New York: Crown.

BALAJTHY, E. (1984). Using student-constructed questions to encourage active reading. *Journal of Reading, 27,* 408–411.

BARCHERS, S. I. (1993). *Readers theatre for beginning readers.* Englewood, CO: Teacher Ideas Press.

BARLOW, M., & ROBERTSON, H. J. (1994). *Class warfare: The assault on Canada's schools.* Toronto, Canada: Key Porter Books.

BARNARD, D. P., & HERTZEL, R. W. (1976). The principals' role in reading instruction. *Reading Teacher, 29,* 386–388.

BARONE, D. (1990). The written response of young children: Beyond comprehension to story understanding. *The New Advocate, 3,* 49–56.

BARTLETT, R., HALL, J., & NEALE, S. (1984). A parental involvement project in the primary schools of South Oxfordshire. *Reading, 18,* 173–177.

BARTNICKI, O. (1995). Reading with friends: A peer-tutored reading program. In C. Dudley-Marling & D. Searle (Eds.), *Who owns learning? Questions of autonomy, choice, and control* (pp. 41–51). Portsmouth, NH: Heinemann.

BASS, R. J., JURENKA, N. A., & ZIRZOW, E. G. (1981). Showing children the communicative nature of reading. *Reading Teacher, 34,* 926–931.

BATH, S. R. (1992). Trade-book minigroups: A cooperative approach to literature. *Reading Teacher, 46,* 272–275.

BAUMANN, J. F., JONES, L. A., & SEIFERT-KESSELL, N. (1993). Using think-aloud to enhance children's comprehension monitoring abilities. *Reading Teacher, 47,* 184–193.

BAYER, A. S. (1990). *Collaborative-apprenticeship learning: Language and thinking across the curriculum, K–12.* Katonah, NY: Richard C. Owen.

BECK, I. L., & MCKEOWN, M. G. (1981). Developing questions that promote comprehension: The story map. *Language Arts, 58,* 913–917.

BECK, I. L., MCCASLIN, E. S., & MCKEOWN, M. G. (1981). Basal readers' purpose for story reading: Smoothly paving the road or setting up a detour? *Elementary School Journal, 81,* 156–161.

BEEBE, M. J. (1980). The effect of different types of substitution miscues on reading. *Reading Research Quarterly, 15,* 324–326.

BEED, P. L., HAWKINS, E. M., & ROLLER, C. M. (1991). Moving learners toward independence: The power of scaffolded instruction. *Reading Teacher, 44,* 648–655.

BEERS, C., & BEERS, J. (1977). Three assumptions about learning to spell. *Elementary School Journal, 19,* 238–242.

BEERS, J. W. (1980). Developmental strategies of spelling competence in primary school children. In E. H. Henderson & J. W. Beers (Eds.), *Developmental and cognitive aspects of learning to spell* (pp. 35–45). Newark, DE: International Reading Association.

BENNETT, J. (1993). Seeing is believing: Videotaping reading development. In L. K. Rhodes & N. L. Shanklin, *Windows into literacy: Assessing learners K–8* (pp. 344–348). Portsmouth, NH: Heinemann.

BERGLAND, R. L., & JOHNS, J. L. (1983). A primer on uninterrupted sustained silent reading. *Reading Teacher, 36,* 534–539.

BISSEX, G. (1980). *GNYS AT WRK: A child learns to read and write.* Cambridge, MA: Harvard University Press.

BISSEX, G. L., & BULLOCK, R. H. (Eds.). (1987). *Seeing for ourselves: Case-study research by teachers of writing.* Portsmouth, NH: Heinemann.

BIXBY, M., ET AL. (1983). *Strategies that make sense: Invitations to literacy for secondary students.* Columbia, MO: Teachers Applying Whole Language.

BLACHOWICZ, C. L. Z. (1991). Vocabulary instruction in content classes for special needs learners: Why and how? *Reading, Writing, and Learning Disabilities, 7,* 297–308.

BLACHOWICZ, C. L. Z., & LEE, J. J. (1991). Vocabulary development in the whole literacy classroom. *Reading Teacher, 45,* 188–195.

BLANTON, W. E., WOOD, K. D., & MOORMAN, G. (1990). The role of purpose in reading instruction. *Reading Teacher, 43,* 486–493.

BLOOME, D. (1995, August). *Cultural politics and language in and from the classroom.* Paper presented at the annual Whole Language Umbrella Conference, Windsor, Ontario.

BLOOME, D., & EGAN-ROBERTSON, A. (1993). The social construction of intertextuality in classroom reading and writing lessons. *Reading Research Quarterly, 28,* 305–332.

BLOOME, D., HARRIS, L. H., & LUDLUM, D. E. (1991). Reading and writing as sociocultural activities: Politics and pedagogy in the classroom. *Topics in Language Disorders, 11,* 14–27.

BLOOME, L., & LAHEY, M. (1978). *Language development and language disorders.* New York: Wiley.

BONNE, R., & MILLS, A. (1961). *I know an old lady.* New York: Rand McNally.

BOOKMAN, M. O. (1983). *Spelling as a cognitive-linguistic developmental process: A study of two subgroups of learning disabled adults.* Doctoral dissertation, University of Colorado at Boulder.

BOS, C. S. (1982). Getting past decoding: Assisted and repeated readings as remedial methods for learning disabled students. *Topics in Learning and Learning Disabilities, 1,* 51–75.

BRADDOCK, R., LLOYD-JONES, R., & SCHOER, L. (1963). *Research in written composition.* Urbana, IL: National Council of Teachers of English.

BRANSFORD, J. D., & JOHNSON, M. K. (1972). Contextual prerequisites for understanding: Some investigations of comprehension and recall. *Journal of Verbal Learning and Verbal Behavior, 11,* 717–726.

BRENNEMAN, R. (1985, September). A debatable idea. *Notes Plus, 3.*

BRIDGE, C. (1979). Predictable materials for beginning readers. *Language Arts, 56,* 503–507.

BRIELING, A. (1976). Using parents as teaching partners. *Reading Teacher, 30,* 187–192.

BRIGGS, R. (1970). *Jim and the beanstalk.* New York: Coward, McCann, & Geoghegan.

BROWN, A. (1978). Knowing when, where and how to remember: A problem of metacognition. In R. Glaser (Ed.), *Advances in instructional psychology.* Hillsdale, NJ: Erlbaum.

BROWN, H., & CAMBOURNE, B. (1987). *Read and retell.* Portsmouth, NH: Heinemann.

BRUCE, B. (1978). What makes a good story? *Language Arts, 55,* 460–466.

BRUINSMA, R. (1980). Should lip movements and subvocalization during silent reading be directly remediated? *Reading Teacher, 34,* 293–295.

BRYAN, R. (1971). *When children speak.* San Rafael, CA: Academic Therapy.

BURKE, C. L. (1982). Save the last word for me. In J. Newman (Ed.), *Whole language activities.* Halifax, NS: Dalhousie University.

BURKE, C. L. (1985). Editors' table. In J. C. Harste, K. M. Pierce, & T. Cairney (Eds.), *The authoring cycle: A viewing guide* (pp. 69–75). Portsmouth, NH: Heinemann.

BURNS, J., & SWAN, D. (1979). *Reading without books.* Belmont, CA: Fearon Pitman.

BUTTERY, T. J., & POWELL, J. V. (1978). Teacher verbal feedback during primary basal reading instruction. *Reading Improvement, 15,* 183–189.

CADIEUX, S. (1982). Letting children lead the way. In T. Newkirk and N. Atwell (Eds.), *Understanding writing* (pp. 63–67). Chelmsford, MA: Northeast Regional Exchange.

CAIRNEY, T. H., & MUNSIE, L. (1992). *Beyond tokenism: Parents as partners in literacy.* Portsmouth, NH: Heinemann.

CALHOUN, M. (1975). *Old man Whickutt's donkey.* New York: Parents' Magazine Press.

CALKINS, L. M. (1983). *Lessons from a child.* Portsmouth, NH: Heinemann.

CALKINS, L. M. (1986, 1994). *The art of teaching writing.* Portsmouth, NH: Heinemann.

CALKINS, L. M., & HARWAYNE, S. (1991). *Living between the lines.* Portsmouth, NH: Heinemann.

CAMBOURNE, B. L., & ROUSCH, P. D. (1982). How do learning disabled children read? *Topics in Learning and Learning Disabilities, 1,* 59–68.

CAMERON, M., & LIMBRICK, L. (1992). *Peer power: Using peer-tutoring to help low-progress readers in primary and secondary schools.* Katonah, NY: Richard C. Owen.

CARBO, M. (1978). Teaching reading with talking books. *Reading Teacher, 32,* 267–273.

CARBO, M. (1981). Making books talk to children. *Reading Teacher, 35,* 186–189.

CARLBERG, C., & KAVALE, K. (1980). The efficacy of special versus regular class placement for exceptional children: A meta-analysis. *Journal of Special Education, 14,* 295–309.

CARLE, E. (1969). *The very hungry caterpillar.* New York: Philomel.

CARR, E., & OGLE, D. (1987). K-W-L plus: A strategy for comprehension and summarization. *Journal of Reading, 30,* 626–631.

CASANAVE, C. P. (1988). Comprehension monitoring in ESL reading: A neglected essential. *TESOL Quarterly, 22,* 283–302.

CASSIDY, J. (1981). Grey power in the reading program—a direction for the eighties. *Reading Teacher, 35,* 287–291.

CASSIDY, J. (1984). The concept kit. *Reading Today, 35,* 287–291.

CASTEEL, C. P., & ISOM, B. A. (1994). Reciprocal processes in science and literacy learning. *Reading Teacher, 47,* 538–545.

CAULEY, L. B. (1983). *Jack and the beanstalk,* New York: G. P. Putnam.

CHANEY, J. H. (1993). Alphabet books: Resources for learning. *Reading Teacher, 47,* 96–104.

CHOMSKY, C. (1972). Stages in language development and reading exposure. *Harvard Educational Review, 42,* 1–33.

CHOMSKY, C. (1976). After decoding: What? *Language Arts, 53,* 288–296.

CHOMSKY, C. (1978). When you still can't read in third grade: After decoding, what? In S. J. Samuels (Ed.), *What research has to say about reading instruction.* Newark, DE: International Reading Assocation.

CHRISTIAN-SMITH, L. K. (1988). Girls' romance novel reading and what to do about it. *The New Advocate, 6,* 177–185.

CLARK, F. L., ET AL. (1984). Visual imagery and self-questioning: Strategies to improve comprehension of written material. *Journal of Learning Disabilities, 17,* 145–149.

CLARKE, M. A., DAVIS, W. A., RHODES, L. K., & BAKER, E. (1995). *Creating coherence: High achieving classrooms for minority students.* Preliminary report of research conducted under U.S. Department of Education, OERI Field Initiated Studies Program, Grant R117E30244. Denver, CO: University of Colorado, Denver.

CLAY, M. (1970). *Stones: Concepts about print test.* Portsmouth, NH: Heinemann.

CLAY, M. (1972). *Sand: Concepts about print test.* Portsmouth, NH: Heinemann.

CLAY, M. (1982). *Observing young readers.* Portsmouth, NH: Heinemann.

CLAY, M. (1991). Introducing a new storybook to young readers. *Reading Teacher, 45,* 264–273.

CLEARY, L., & LUND, N. (1993). Debunking some myths about traditional grammar. In L. M. Cleary & M. D. Linn (Eds.), *Linguistics for teachers* (pp. 38–72). New York: McGraw-Hill.

CLOSE, E. G. (1990). Seventh graders sharing literature: How did we get here? *Language Arts, 67,* 817–823.

CLYDE, J. A. (1981). *Open-ended sentence questionnaire on writing.* Unpublished paper. Elizabeth, CO: Elizabeth Elementary School.

CLYMER, T., & MARTIN, P. M. (1980). *The partridge and the fox.* Lexington, MA: Ginn.

COCHRAN-SMITH, M., & LYTLE, S. L. (1993). *Inside/outside: Teacher research and knowledge.* New York: Teachers College Press.

COHEN, P., KULIK, J., & KULIK, C. (1982). Educational outcomes of tutoring: A meta-analysis of findings. *American Educational Research Journal, 19,* 237–248.

COHEN, R. (1983). Self-generated questions as an aid to reading comprehension. *Reading Teacher, 36,* 770–775.

COLES, G. (1987). *The learning mystique: A critical look at "learning disabilities."* New York: Pantheon.

COLLIER, J. L., & COLLIER, C. (1977). *My brother Sam is dead.* New York: Scholastic.

COMMIRE, A. (Ed.). (since 1971). *Something about the author: Facts and pictures about contemporary authors and illustrators of books for young people.* Detroit, MI: Gale.

CONRAD, L. (1993). Improving the report card ritual. In L. K. Rhodes & N. L. Shanklin, *Windows into literacy: Assessing learners K–8* (pp. 398–407). Portsmouth, NH: Heinemann.

CORDEIRO, P., GIACOBBE, M. E., & CAZDEN, C. (1983). Apostrophes, quotation marks, and periods: Learning punctuation in the first grade. *Language Arts, 60,* 323–332.

COSTELLO, S. (1992). Retrospective miscue analysis: In the classroom. In K. S. Goodman, L. B. Bird, & Y. M. Goodman (Eds.), *The whole language catalogue: Supplement on authentic assessment* (pp. 152–153). Santa Rosa, CA: American School Publishers.

CRAFTON, L. K. (1982). Comprehension before, during and after reading. *Reading Teacher, 36,* 293–297.

CRAFTON, L. K. (1983). Learning from reading: What happens when students generate their own background information? *Journal of Reading, 26,* 585–592.

CRAFTON, L. K., ET AL. (1980). Language instruction: From theoretical abstractions to classroom implications. *Occasional Papers in Language and Reading.* Bloomington, IN: Language Education Department, Indiana University.

CRISCUOLO, N. P. (1978). Activities that help involve parents in reading. *Reading Teacher, 32,* 417–419.

CROCKER, M. (1983). On doing projects. In J. Newman (Ed.), *Whole language: Translating theory into practice* (pp. 150–161). Halifax, NS: Dalhousie University.

CROCKER, M. (1985). Creating a vertical file. In J. Newman (Ed.), *Whole language: Theory into use* (pp. 150–161). Portsmouth, NH: Heinemann.

CUDD, E. T., & ROBERTS, L. (1989). Using writing to enhance content area learning in the primary grades. *Reading Teacher, 42,* 392–404.

CULLINAN, B., JAGGAR, A., & STRICKLAND, D. (1974). Oral language expansion in the primary grades. In B. Cullinan (Ed.), *Black dialects and reading* (pp. 50–55). Urbana, IL: National Council of Teachers of English.

CULLINAN, B. (1989). *Literature and the child.* New York: Harcourt Brace Jovanovich.

CUMMINGS, P. (Ed.). (1992). *Talking with artists.* New York: Bradbury.

CUNNINGHAM, D., & SHABLAK, S. (1975). Selective reading guide-o-rama: The content area teacher's best friend. *Journal of Reading, 18,* 380–382.

CUNNINGHAM, P. (1978). "Mumble reading" for beginning readers. *Reading Teacher, 31,* 409–411.

DAHL, K. L., & FREPPON, P. A. (1995). A comparison of innercity children's interpretations of reading and writing instruction in the early grades in skills-based and whole language classrooms. *Reading Research Quarterly, 30,* 50–74.

DALTON, B., WINBURY, N. S., & MOROCCO, C. C. (1990). "If you could just push a button": Two fourth grade boys with learning disabilities learn to use a computer spelling checker. *Journal of Special Education Technology, 10,* 177–191.

D'ANGELO, K. (1982). Correction behavior: Implications for instruction. *Reading Teacher, 35,* 395–399.

DAVEY, B. (1983). Think aloud: Modeling the cognitive process of reading comprehension. *Journal of Reading, 27,* 44–47.

DAVEY, B., & PORTER, S. M. (1982). Comprehension-rating: A procedure to assist poor comprehenders. *Journal of Reading, 26,* 197–201.

DAVIDSON, J. L. (1982). The group mapping activity for instruction in reading and thinking. *Journal of Reading, 26,* 52–56.

DEARDORFF, B. (1982). Confessions of a skills teacher. *Learning, 11,* 42–43.

DEFREECE, B. (1993). "With our combined efforts, we may help her grow." In L. K. Rhodes & N. L. Shanklin, *Windows into literacy: Assessing learners K–8* (pp. 298–304). Portsmouth, NH: Heinemann.

DEKKER, M. M. (1991). Books, reading, and response: A teacher-researcher tells a story. *The New Advocate, 4,* 37–46.

DE LA MARE, W. (1959). *Jack and the beanstalk.* New York: Knopf.

DELPIT, L. D. (1988). The silenced dialogue: Power and pedagogy in educating other people's children. *Harvard Educational Review, 58,* 280–298.

DEREGNIERS, B. S. (1987). *Jack the giant-killer.* New York: Atheneum.

DESHLER, D. D., ET AL. (1980). *An epidemiological study of learning disabled adolescents in secondary schools: Social status, peer relationships, activities in and out of school, and time use* (Research report No. 18). Lawrence, KS: University of Kansas Institute for Research in Learning Disabilities.

DESHLER, D. D., ET AL. (1984). Academic and cognitive interventions for LD adolescents: Part II. *Journal of Learning Disabilities, 17,* 170–178.

DILLON, D. (1989). Dear readers. *Language Arts, 66,* 7–9.

DIMARTINI, S. (1987). *Teaching reading through Mother Goose.* Lakewood, CO: LINK.

DOAKE, D. D. (1988). *Reading begins at birth.* Richmond Hill, Ontario: Scholastic.

DOIRON, R. (1994). Using nonfiction in a read-aloud program: Letting the facts speak for themselves. *Reading Teacher, 47,* 616–624.

DONELSON, K. L., & NILSEN, A. P. (1989). *Literature for today's young adults.* Glenview, IL: Scott Foresman.

DREHER, M. J., & SINGER, H. (1980). Story grammar instruction unnecessary for intermediate grade students. *Reading Teacher, 34,* 261–268.

DUDLEY-MARLING, C. (1985). Perceptions of the usefulness of the IEP by teachers of learning disabled and emotionally disturbed children. *Psychology in the Schools, 22,* 65–67.

DUDLEY-MARLING, C. (1990). *When school is a struggle.* New York: Scholastic.

DUDLEY-MARLING, C. (1995). Whole language: It's a matter of principles. *Reading and Writing Quarterly, 11,* 109–117.

DUDLEY-MARLING, C. (1996). Explicit instruction within a whole language framework. In E. McIntyre & M. Pressley (Eds.), *Teaching skills in a whole language classroom: The role of explicit instruction.* Norwood, MA: Christopher Gordon.

DUDLEY-MARLING, C., & DIPPO, D. (1995). What learning disability does: Sustaining the ideology of schooling. *Journal of Learning Disabilities, 28*, 408–414.

DUDLEY-MARLING, C., & OPPENHEIMER, J. (1995). Writing and ownership: A critical tale. *The International Journal of Qualitative Studies in Education, 8*, 281–295.

DUDLEY-MARLING, C., & SEARLE, D. (1991). *When students have time to talk.* Portsmouth, NH: Heinemann.

DUDLEY-MARLING, C., KAUFMAN, N. J., & TARVER, S. G. (1981). WISC and WISC-R profiles of learning disabled children: A review. *Learning Disability Quarterly, 4,* 307–319.

DUNCAN, P. H. (1993). I liked the book better: Comparing film and text to guide critical comprehension. *Reading Teacher, 46*, 720–725.

DUNDAS, V., & STRONG, G. (1991). *Readers and writers and parents learning together.* Katonah, NY: Richard C. Owen.

DUPUIS, M. M., LEE, J. W., BADIALI, B. J., & ASKOV, E. N. (1989). *Teaching reading and writing in the content areas.* Glenview, IL: Scott Foresman.

DURKIN, D. (1966). *Children who read early.* New York: Teachers College Press.

DUVOISIN, R. (illus.). (1962). *The miller, his song, and the donkey.* New York: McGraw-Hill.

DYCK, N. J., & COX, L. (1981). Should LD students underline their texts? *Academic Therapy, 17,* 83–87.

DYSON, A. H. (1989). *Multiple worlds of child writers: Friends learning to write.* New York: Teachers College Press.

EDELSKY, C. (1984). The content of language arts software: A criticism. *Computers, Reading, and Language Arts, 1,* 8–11.

EDELSKY, C. (1991). *With literacy and justice for all: Rethinking the social in language and education.* Philadelphia, PA: The Falmer Press.

EDELSKY, C. (1994, November). *On justice, equity and petards.* Paper presented at the annual meeting of the National Council of Teachers of English, Orlando, FL.

EDELSKY, C. (in press). *With literacy and justice for all: Rethinking the social in language and education.* (2nd ed.). Philadelphia, PA: The Falmer Press.

EDELSKY, C., & SMITH, K. (1984). "Is that writing—or are those marks just a figment of your curriculum?" *Language Arts, 61,* 24–32.

EDELSKY, C., ALTWERGER, B., & FLORES, B. (1991). *Whole language: What's the difference?* Portsmouth, NH: Heinemann.

EDWARDS, B. (1991). "Wouldn't Pa be amazed!" Connecting with literature through conversation. *The New Advocate, 4,* 247–263.

EEDS, M., & PETERSON, R. (1991). Teacher as curator: Learning to talk about literature. *Reading Teacher, 45,* 118–126.

EIDMAN-AADAHL, E. (1988). The solitary reader: Exploring how lonely reading has to be. *The New Advocate, 1,* 165–176.

EINSEL, W. (1962). *Did you ever see?* New York: Scholastic.

ELKIN, B. *Why the sun was late.* New York: Parents Magazine Press.

ELTING, M., & FOLSOM, M. (1980). *Q is for duck.* New York: Houghton Mifflin.

ENGLISH PROFILES HANDBOOK. (1990). Victoria, Australia: Ministry of Education. (Available from TASA, Fields Lane, P.O. Box 382, Brewster, NY 10509; phone: 914–277–4900.)

ENSTROM, E. A. (1968). Left-handedness: A cause for disability in writing. *Journal of Learning Disabilities, 1,* 410–414.

EPPS, D., MCGUE, M., & YSSELDYKE, J. E. (1982). Inter-judge agreement in classifying students as learning disabled. *Psychology in the Schools, 19,* 209–220.

EPPS, D., YSSELDYKE, J. E., & MCGUE, M. (1984). "I know one when I see one"—differentiating LD and non-LD students. *Learning Disability Quarterly, 7,* 89–101.

EVANS, K. M. (1992). Reading aloud: A bridge to independence. *The New Advocate, 5,* 47–57.

FADER, D. (1976). *The new hooked on books.* New York: Berkley Books.

FARR, R. (1992). Putting it altogether: Solving the reading assessment puzzle. *Reading Teacher, 46,* 26–37.

FARRIS, P. J. (1989). Story time and story journals: Linking literature and writing. *The New Advocate, 2,* 179–185.

FEAGANS, L., GARVERY, C., & GOLINKOFF, R. (Eds.). (1984). *The origins and growth of communication.* Norwood, NJ: Ablex.

FIELDING, L., & ROLLER, C. (1992). Making difficult books accessible and easy books acceptable. *Reading Teacher, 45,* 678–685.

FIGUEROA, R. A., RUIZ, N. T., AND GARCIA, E. (1994). *The optimal learning environment (OLE) research project in the Los Angeles Unified School District: Report #1, Reading outcome data.* Santa Cruz, CA: California Research Institute on Special Education and Cultural Diversity.

FISH, S. (1980). *Is there a text in this class?* Cambridge, MA: Harvard University Press.

FISHER, C. (1980). Grammar in the language arts program. In G. S. Pinnell (Ed.), *Discovering language with children* (pp. 60–64). Urbana, IL: National Council of Teachers of English.

FITZGERALD, J. (1983). Helping readers gain self-control over reading comprehension. *Reading Teacher, 37,* 249–253.

FIVE, C. L. (1995). Ownership for the special needs child: Individual and educational dilemmas. In C. Dudley-Marling & D. Searle (Eds.), *Who owns learning? Questions of autonomy, choice, and control* (pp. 113–127). Portsmouth, NH: Heinemann.

FLYNN, R. M., & CARR, G. A. (1994). Exploring classroom literature through drama: A specialist and a teacher collaborate. *Language Arts, 71,* 38–43.

FORESTER, A. D. (1977). What teachers can learn from "natural readers." *Reading Teacher, 31,* 160–166.

FOWLER, G. L. (1982). Developing comprehension skills in primary students through the use of story frames. *Reading Teacher, 36,* 176–179.

FRACTOR, J. S., WOODRUFF, M. C., MARTINEZ, M. G., & TEALE, W. H. (1993). Let's not miss opportunities to promote voluntary reading: Classroom libraries in the elementary school. *Reading Teacher, 46,* 476–484.

FREDERICKS, A. D., & RASINSKI, T. V. (1989–90). Working with parents. (A series of columns.) *Reading Teacher, 43–44.*

FREDERICKS, A. D., & RASINSKI, T. V. (1990a). Factors that make a difference. *Reading Teacher, 44,* 76–77.

FREDERICKS, A. D., & RASINSKI, T. V. (1990b). Involving parents in the assessment process. *Reading Teacher, 44,* 346–349.

FREEDMAN, B., & REYNOLDS, E. G. (1980). Enriching basal reader lessons with semantic webbing. *Reading Teacher, 33,* 677–684.

FREEMAN, E. B., & PERSON, D. G. (1992). *Using nonfiction trade books in the elementary classroom.* Urbana, IL: National Council of Teachers of English.

FREPPON, P. A., & DAHL, K. L. (1991). Learning phonics in a whole language classroom. *Language Arts, 68,* 190–197.

FREPPON, P. A., & HEADINGS, L. (in press). Keeping it whole in whole language. In E. McIntyre & M. Pressley (Eds.), *Balanced instruction: Strategies and skills in whole language.* Norwood, MA: Christopher Gordon.

FRIEDMAN, M. I., & ROWLS, M. D. (1980). *Teaching reading and thinking skills.* New York: Longman.

FRITH, U. (1980). *Cognitive processes in spelling.* New York: Academic Press.

FRITZ, J. (1982). *Homesick: My own story.* New York: Putnam.

FROST, R. (1978). *Stopping by woods on a snowy evening.* (Ill. by Susan Jeffers.). New York: Dutton.

FURNAS, A. B. (1991). Yes, you can! In S. Stires (Ed.), *With promise: Redefining reading and writing for "special" students* (pp. 3–7). Portsmouth, NH: Heinemann.

GAGNE, E. D., & MEMORY, D. (1978). Instructional events and comprehensions: Generalization across passages. *Journal of Reading Behavior, 10,* 321–335.

GALE, J. (1975). *Neat and scruffy.* Toronto, ONT: Ashton Scholastic.

GAMBRELL, L. B. (1980). Think-time: Implications for reading instruction. *Reading Teacher, 34,* 143–146.

GAMBRELL, L. B. (1978). Getting started with sustained silent reading and keeping it going. *Reading Teacher, 32,* 328–331.

GANSCHOW, L. (1981). Discovering children's learning strategies for spelling through error pattern analysis. *Reading Teacher, 34,* 676–680.

GASKINS, R. W. (1992). When good instruction is not enough: A mentor program. *Reading Teacher, 45,* 568–572.

GEE, J. (1990). *Social linguistics and literacies: Ideology in discourses.* Bristol, PA: The Falmer Press.

GEE, J. (1994). First language acquisition as a guide for theories of learning and pedagogy. *Linguistics and Education, 6,* 331–354.

GELTZHEISER, L. M., & MEYERS, J. (1990). Special and remedial education in the classroom: Theme and variations. *Reading, Writing, and Learning Disabilities, 6,* 419–436.

GENTRY, J. R. (1987). *Spel…is a four-letter word.* Portsmouth, NH: Heinemann.

GENTRY, J. R., & HENDERSON, E. H. (1978). Three steps to teaching beginning readers to spell. *Reading Teacher, 31,* 632–637.

GERBER, M. (1984). Orthographic problem solving ability of learning disabled and normally achieving students. *Learning Disability Quarterly, 7,* 157–164.

GERBER, M., & HALL, R. (1981). *Development of orthographic problem-solving in LD children* (Technical Report No. 37). University of Virginia: Learning Disabilities Research Institute.

GIACOBBE, M. E. (1986). *Intensive writing workshop.* Denver: Public Education Coalition.

GIFF, P. R. (1987). *Laura Ingalls Wilder: Growing up in the little house.* New York: Puffin.

GILLES, C., DICKENSON, J., McBRIDE, C., & VanDOVER, M. (1994). Discussing our questions and questioning our discussions: Growing into literature study. *Language Arts, 71,* 499–508.

GLASS, G. V. (1983). Effectiveness of special education. *Policy Studies Review, 2,* 65–78.

GLAZER, J. I., & LAMME, L. L. (1990). Poem picture books and their uses in the classroom. *Reading Teacher, 44,* 102–109.

GOATLEY, V. J., BROCK, C. H., & RAPHAEL, T. E. (1995). Diverse learners participating in regular education "Book Clubs." *Reading Research Quarterly, 30,* 352–380.

GOLD, P. C. (1984). Cognitive mapping. *Academic Therapy, 19,* 277–284.

GOLDEN, J. M. (1984). Children's concept of story in reading and writing. *Reading Teacher, 37,* 578–584.

GOLDENBERG, C. (1993). Instructional conversations: Promoting comprehension through discussion. *Reading Teacher, 46,* 316–326.

GOODMAN, G. (1989). Worlds within worlds: Reflections on an encounter with parents. *Language Arts, 66,* 14–20.

GOODMAN, K. S. (1968). The psycholinguistic nature of the reading process. In K. S. Goodman (Ed.), *The psycholinguistic nature of the reading process* (pp. 13–26). Detroit, MI: Wayne State Press.

GOODMAN, K. S. (1973). Miscues: Windows on the reading process. In K. S. Goodman (Ed.), *Miscue analysis: Applications to reading instruction* (pp. 3–14). Urbana, IL: National Council of Teachers of English.

GOODMAN, K. S. (1982). Revaluing readers and reading. *Topics in Learning and Learning Disabilities, 1,* 87–93.

GOODMAN, K. S. (1986a). Basal readers: A call for action. *Language Arts, 63,* 358–363.

GOODMAN, K. S. (1986b). *What's whole in whole language?* Richmond Hill, Ontario: Scholastic-TAB.

GOODMAN, K. S. (1993). *Phonics phacts.* Portsmouth, NH: Heinemann.

GOODMAN, K. S., SHANNON, P., FREEMAN, Y. S., & MURPHY, S. (1988). *Report card on basal readers.* Katonah, NY: Richard C. Owen.

GOODMAN, Y. M. (1982). Retellings of literature and the comprehension process. *Theory into Practice, 21,* 301–307.

GOODMAN, Y. M. (1984). The development of initial literacy. In H. Goelman, A. Oberg, & F. Smith (Eds.), *Awakening to literacy* (pp. 123–152). Portsmouth, NH: Heinemann.

GOODMAN, Y. M., & ALTWERGER, B. (1985). Bookhandling knowledge task. In *Bookshelf Teacher's Resource Book* (pp. 131–133). Jefferson City, MO: Scholastic.

GOODMAN, Y. M., & BURKE, C. L. (1980). *Reading strategies: Focus on comprehension.* New York: Holt, Rinehart & Winston.

GOODMAN, Y. M., WATSON, D. J., & BURKE, C. L. (1987). *Reading miscue inventory.* Katonah, NY: Richard C. Owen.

GORDON, C. J. (1980). *The effects of instruction in metacomprehension and inferencing on children's comprehension abilities.* Doctoral dissertation, University of Minnesota, Minneapolis, MN.

GORDON, C. J., & BRAUN, C. (1980). Using story schema as an aid to reading and writing. *Reading Teacher, 37,* 116–121.

GOSWAMI, D., & STILLMAN, P. (Eds.). (1987). *Reclaiming the classroom: Teacher research as an agency for change.* Portsmouth, NH: Boynton/Cook.

GOSWAMI, U., & BRYANT, P. (1990). *Phonological skills and learning to read.* Hillsdale, NJ: Erlbaum.

GOURLEY, J. (1984). Discourse structure: Expectations of beginning readers and readability of text. *Journal of Reading Behavior, 16,* 169–188.

GRAFF, H. (1979). *The literacy myth.* New York: Academic Press.

GRAHAM, S., & VOTH, V. P. (1990). Spelling instruction: Making modifications for students with learning disabilities. *Academic Therapy, 25,* 447–457.

GRANGER, L., & GRANGER, B. (1986). *The magic feather.* New York: E.P. Dutton.

GRANOWSKY, A., MIDDLETON, F. R., & MUBMORD, J. H. (1979). Parents as partners in education. *Reading Teacher, 32,* 826–830.

GRANT, R., GUTHRIE, J., BENNETT, L., RICE, M. E., & McGOUGH, K. (1994). Developing engaged readers through concept-oriented instruction. *Reading Teacher, 47,* 338–340.

GRAVES, D. (1977). Spelling texts and structural analysis methods. *Language Arts, 54,* 86–90.

GRAVES, D. (1978). Handwriting is for writing. *Language Arts, 55,* 393–399.

GRAVES, D. (1983). *Writing: Teachers and children at work.* Portsmouth, NH: Heinemann.

GRAVES, D. (1994). *A fresh look at writing.* Portsmouth, NH: Heinemann.

GRAVES, D., & HANSEN, J. (1983). The author's chair. *Language Arts, 60,* 176–183.

GRAVES, M. F., COOKE, C. L., & LaBERGE, M. J. (1983). Effects of previewing difficult short stories on low ability junior high school students' comprehension, recall, and attitudes. *Reading Research Quarterly, 18,* 262–276.

GREENE, F. (1979). Radio reading. In C. Pennock (Ed.), *Reading comprehension at four linguistic levels* (pp. 104–107). Newark, DE: International Reading Association.

GREENE, M. (1978). *Landscapes of learning.* New York: Teachers College Press.

GRICE, H. P. (1978). Logic and conversation. In P. Cole & J. L. Morgan (Eds.), *Syntax and semantics, Vol. 3* (pp. 41–58). New York: Academic Press.

GRIFFIN, M., & JONGSMA, K. (1980). Analyzing retelling and oral reading: Adaptions of the Reading Miscue Inventory. In M. Griffin & K. Jongsma (Eds.), *Reading: Evaluative teaching* (pp. 96–181). Toronto: Ginn.

GRUBER, J. E., & VONECHE, J. J. (1977). *The essential Piaget.* New York: Basic Books.

HADAWAY, N. L., & YOUNG, T. A. (1994). Content literacy and language learning: Instructional decisions. *Reading Teacher, 47,* 522–527.

HAGERTY, P. (1992). *Readers' workshop: Real reading.* Richmond Hill, Ontario: Scholastic.

HAHN, A. L. (1985). Teaching remedial students to be strategic readers and better comprehenders. *Reading Teacher, 39*, 72–77.

HALIDAY, M. A. K. (1978). *Language as social semiotic.* Baltimore, MD: University Park Press.

HALLAHAN, D. P., & KAUFFMAN, J. M. (1976). *Introduction to learning disabilities: A psycho-behavioral approach.* Englewood Cliffs, NJ: Prentice-Hall.

HAMMOND, W. D. (1982). The quality of reading miscues. In J. J. Pikulski & T. Shanahan (Eds.), *Approaches to the informal evaluation of reading* (pp. 23–29). Newark, DE: International Reading Association.

HANCOCK, M. R. (1992). Literature response journals: Insights beyond the printed page. *Language Arts, 69*, 36–42.

HANCOCK, M. R. (1993). Exploring and extending personal response through literature journals. *Reading Teacher, 46*, 466–474.

HANDEL, R. D. (1992). The partnership for family reading: Benefits for families and schools. *Reading Teacher, 46*, 116–126.

HANSEN, J. (1987). *When writers read.* Portsmouth, NH: Heinemann.

HARBER, J. R. (1979). The effectiveness of selected perceptual and perceptual-motor tasks in differentiating between normal and learning disabled children. *Learning Disabled Quarterly, 2*, 70–75.

HARBER, J. R. (1982). Perceptual and perceptual-motor test scores are not a clue to reading achievement in second graders. *Reading Horizons, 22*, 207–210.

HARE, B. A. (1977). Perceptual deficits are not a clue to reading problems in second grade. *Reading Teacher, 31*, 624–627.

HARRIS, K. R., GRAHAM, S., & FREEMAN, S. (1988). The effects of strategy training and study conditions on metamemory among learning disabled students. *Exceptional Children, 54*, 332–338.

HARSTE, J. (1982). Say something. In J. Newman (Ed.), *Whole language activities.* Halifax, NS: Dalhousie University.

HARSTE, J., & BURKE, C. (1978). Toward a socio-psycholinguistic model of reading comprehension. *Viewpoints in Teaching and Learning, 54*, 9–34.

HARSTE, J., & BURKE, C. (1980). Understanding the hypothesis: It's the teacher that makes the difference. In B. P. Farr and D. J. Strickler (Eds.), *Reading comprehensions; Resource guide* (pp. 111–123). Bloomington, IN: Indiana University Reading Programs.

HARSTE, J., BURKE, C., & DEFORD, D. (1976). An instructional development activity for teachers: Making whole language reading games. In J. Harste & M. A. Atwell (Eds.), *Mainstreaming, the special child, and the reading process* (pp. 236–245). Bloomington, IN: Indiana University School of Education.

HARSTE, J., WOODWARD, V., & BURKE, C. (1984). *Language stories and literacy lessons.* Portsmouth, NH: Heinemann.

HARTMAN, D. K., & HARTMAN, J. A. (1993). Reading across texts: Expanding the role of the reader. *Reading Teacher, 47*, 202–211.

HARWAYNE, S. (1992). *Lasting impressions: Weaving literature into the writing workshop.* Portsmouth, NH: Heinemann.

HAWKING, S. (1988). *A brief history of time: From the big bang to black holes*. New York: Bantam.

HEAD-TAYLOR, G. (1989). *The administrator's guide to whole language*. Katonah, NY: Richard C. Owen.

HEATH, S. B. (1983). *Ways with words: Language, life, and work in communities and classrooms*. New York: Cambridge University Press.

HEINE, P. (1991). The power of related books. *Reading Teacher, 45,* 75–77.

HEINIG, R. B. (1992). *Improvisation with favorite tales: Integrating drama into the reading/writing classroom*. Portsmouth, NH: Heinemann.

HENDERSON, E. H., & BEERS, J. W. (1980). *Developmental and cognitive aspects of learning to spell*. Newark, DE: International Reading Association.

HENDERSON, L. C., & SHANKER, J. L. (1978). The use of dramatics versus basal reader workbooks for developing comprehension skills. *Reading World, 17,* 239–243.

HENNINGS, D. G. (1982). A writing approach to reading comprehension—Schema theory in action. *Language Arts, 59,* 8–17.

HENNINGS, D. G. (1992). *Beyond the read aloud: Learning to read through listening to and reflecting on literature*. Bloomington, IN: Phi Delta Kappa Educational Foundation.

HENRY, G. (1974). *Teaching reading as concept development: Emphasis on affective thinking*. Newark, DE: International Reading Association.

HEPLER, S. (1991). Talking our way to literacy in the classroom community. *The New Advocate, 4,* 179–191.

HERRMANN, B. A. (1992). Teaching and assessing strategic reasoning: Dealing with the dilemmas. *Reading Teacher, 45,* 428–433.

HESS, J. B. (1968). There's more than talk to choral reading. *Grade Teacher, 85,* 107–109.

HIEBERT, E. (1981). Developmental patterns and interrelationships of preschool children's print awareness. *Reading Research Quarterly, 16,* 236–260.

HILL, B. C., & RUPTIC, C. (1994). *Practical aspects of authentic assessment*. Norwood, MA: Christopher Gordon.

HINTON, S. E. (1980). *The outsiders*. New York: Dell.

HIRSH, M. (1972). *How the world got its color*. New York: Crown.

HITTLEMAN, D. R. (1983). *Developmental reading, K–8*. Boston, MA: Houghton Mifflin.

HOFFMAN, J. V. (1979). On providing feedback to reading miscues. *Reading World, 18,* 342–350.

HOFFMAN, J. V. (1981). Is there a legitimate place for oral reading instruction in a developmental reading program? *Elementary School Journal, 81,* 305–310.

HOFFMAN, J. V. (1992). Critical reading/thinking across the curriculum: Using I-charts to support learning. *Language Arts, 69,* 121–127.

HOFFMAN, J. V., & CLEMENTS, R. (1984). Reading miscues and teacher verbal feedback. *Elementary School Journal, 84,* 423–439.

HOFFMAN, J. V., ROSER, N. L., & BATTLE, J. (1993). Reading aloud in classrooms: From the modal toward a "model." *Reading Teacher, 46,* 496–503.

HOGE, S. (1983). A comprehension-centered reading program using reader selected miscues. *Journal of Reading, 27,* 52–55.

HOLDAWAY, D. (1979). *Foundations of literacy.* Portsmouth, NH: Heinemann.

HOLLINGSWORTH, P. M. (1970). An experiment with the impress method of teaching reading. *Reading Teacher, 24,* 112–114.

HOLLINGSWORTH, P. M. (1978). An experimental approach to the impress method of teaching. *Reading Teacher, 31,* 624–626.

HOLMES, D., & PEPER, R. 1977. An evaluation of spelling error analysis in the diagnosis of reading disability. *Child Development, 48,* 1709–1711.

HOLT, J. (1982). *How children fail* (2nd ed.). New York: Delacorte Press/Seymour Lawrence.

HONG, I. K. (1981). Modifying SSR for beginners. *Reading Teacher, 34,* 888–891.

HOSKISSON, K., SHERMAN, M., & SMITH, L. L. (1974). Assisted reading and parent involvement. *Reading Teacher, 27,* 710–714.

HOWELL, H. (1978). Write on, you sinistrals! *Language Arts, 55,* 852–56.

HRESKO, W. P. (1988). *Test of early written language.* Austin, TX: Pro-Ed.

HUCK, C. (1976). *Children's literature in the elementary school.* New York: Holt, Rinehart & Winston.

HUCK, C. (1979). Literature for all reasons. *Language Arts, 56,* 354–355.

HUGHES, M., & SEARLE, D. (1991). A longitudinal study of spelling abilities within the context of the development of writing. In J. Zutell and S. McCormick (Eds.), *Learning factors/teacher factors: Issues in literacy research and instruction* (pp. 159–168). Chicago, IL: National Reading Conference.

HUGHES, M., & SEARLE, D. (in press). *Spelling over time: Working with children's understanding of children's spelling from K–6.* York, ME: Stenhouse.

HUNT, L. (1970). The effect of self-selection, interest, and motivation upon independent, instructional and frustrational levels. *Reading Teacher, 24,* 146–151.

IDOL-MAESTRAS, L. (1983). *Getting ready to read: Guided probing for poor comprehension.* Unpublished paper.

INNOCENTI, R. (1991). *Rose Blanche.* New York: Stewart, Tabori, & Chang.

INVERNIZZI, M., & WORTHY, M. J. (1989). An orthographic-specific comparison of the spelling errors of learning disabled and normal children across four grade levels of spelling achievement. *Reading Psychology, 10,* 173–188.

JACKSON, L. A. (1981). Whose skills system? Mine or Penny's? *Reading Teacher, 35,* 260–262.

JACOBS, J. (1975). *Jack and the beanstalk.* New York: Henry Z. Walck.

JOHNS, J. L. (1975). Strategies for oral reading behavior. *Language Arts, 52,* 1104–1107.

JOHNS, J. L. (1982). Therapy for round robin oral reading. *Reading Horizons, 22,* 201–203.

JOHNSON, N. M., & EBERT, M. J. (1992). Time travel is possible: Historical fiction and biography—passport to the past. *Reading Teacher, 45,* 488–495.

JOHNSON, R. J., JOHNSON, K. L., & KERFOOT, J. F. (1972). A massive oral decoding technique. *Reading Teacher, 25,* 421–423.

JOHNSON, T. D., & LOUIS, D. R. (1987). *Literacy through literature*. Portsmouth, NH: Heinemann.

JOHNSTON, J. S., & WILDER, S. L. (1992). Changing reading and writing programs through staff development. *Reading Teacher, 45*, 626–631.

JONES, J. R. (1981). Advising parents on reading. *Reading, 15, 27*–30.

JONGSMA, E. A. (1980). *Cloze instruction research: A second look*. Newark, DE: International Reading Association.

JORDAN, A. (1994). *Skills in collaborative classroom consultation*. London: Routledge.

KAAKE, D. M. (1983). Teaching elementary age children touch typing as an aid to language arts instruction. *Reading Teacher, 36*, 640–644.

KAMEENUI, E. J. (1993). Diverse learners and the tyranny of time: Don't fix the blame; fix the leaky roof. *Reading Teacher, 46*, 376–383.

KAROLIDES, N. J. (Ed.). (1992). *Reader response in the classroom: Evoking and interpreting meaning in literature*. New York: Longman.

KEELER, M. A. (1993). Story map game board. *Reading Teacher, 46*, 626–628.

KELLOGG, S. (1991). *Jack and the beanstalk*. New York: Morrow Junior Books.

KELLY, P. R. (1990). Guiding young students' response to literature. *Reading Teacher, 43*, 464–470.

KETTEL, R. P. (1981). Reading road quiz: A literature game show that develops readers. *Reading Teacher, 34*, 815–817.

KIEFER, B. (1991). *Getting to know you: Profiles of children's authors featured in Language Arts 1985–1990*. Urbana, IL: National Council of Teachers of English.

KIMMELMAN, L. (1981). Literacy ways toward enjoyable thinking. *Language Arts, 58,* 441–447.

KIPLING, R. (1973a). *How the leopard got his spots*. New York: Walker.

KIPLING, R. (1973b). *How the rhinoceros got his skin*. New York: Walker.

KIPLING, R. (1976). *How the camel got his hump*. New York: Spoken Arts.

KIRBY, D., & LINER, T. (1981). *Inside out: Developmental strategies for teaching writing*. Portsmouth, NH: Boynton/Cook.

KITAGAWA, M. M. (1982). Improving discussions or how to get the students to ask the questions. *Reading Teacher, 36, 42*–45.

KOSKINEN, P. S., WILSON, R. M., GAMBRELL, L. B., & NEUMAN, S. B. (1993). Captioned video and vocabulary learning: An innovative practice in literacy instruction. *Reading Teacher, 47*, 36–43.

KREVISKY, J., & LINFIELD, J. L. (1974). *The bad speller's dictionary*. New York: Random House.

KUCER, S. B., & RHODES, L. K. (1986). Counterpart strategies: Fine tuning language with language. *Reading Teacher, 40, 186*–193.

KUTIPER, K., & WILSON, P. (1993). Updating poetry preferences: A look at the poetry children really like. *Reading Teacher, 47*, 28–35.

LABOO, L. D., & TEALE, W. H. (1990). Cross-age reading: A strategy for helping poor readers. *Reading Teacher, 43*, 362–369.

LAMME, L. L. (1979). Song picture books: A maturing genre of children's literature. *Language Arts, 56,* 400–407.

LAMME, L. L. (1981). Parents, volunteers, and aides: Human resources for a literature program. In L. Lamme (Ed.), *Learning to love literature* (pp. 73–82). Urbana, IL: National Council of Teachers of English.

LAMME, L. L. (1990). Exploring the world of music through picture books. *Reading Teacher, 44,* 294–300.

LANCASTER, W., NELSON, L., & MORRIS, D. (1982). Invented spellings in Room 112: A writing program for low-reading second graders. *Reading Teacher, 35,* 906–1911.

LANDES, S. (1989). The poetry of chapter titles. *The New Advocate, 2,* 159–168.

LANGER, J. A. (1981). From theory to practice: A prereading plan. *Journal of Reading, 25,* 152–156.

LANGER, J. A. (1982). Facilitating text processing: The elaboration of prior knowledge. In J.A. Langer and M.T. Smith-Burke (Eds.), *Readers meets author: Bridging the gap* (pp. 149–162). Newark, DE: International Reading Association.

LANGER, J. A. (1994). A response-based approach to reading literature. *Language Arts, 71,* 203–211.

LAPP, D., & FLOOD, J. (1993). Are there "real" writers living in your classroom? Implementing a writer-centered classroom. *Reading Teacher, 48,* 254–258.

LASASSO, C. (1983). Using the *National Enquirer* with unmotivated or language-handicapped readers. *Journal of Reading, 26,* 546–548.

LASS, B. (1984). Do teachers individualize their responses to miscues? A study of feedback during oral reading. *Reading World, 23,* 242–254.

LAURITZEN, C. (1982). A modification of repeated readings for group instruction. *Reading Teacher, 58,* 456–458.

LEAL, D. J. (1993). The power of literary peer-group discussions: How children collaboratively negotiate meaning. *Reading Teacher, 47,* 114–120.

LEHR, F. (1984). ERIC/RCS report: Student-teacher communication. *Language Arts, 61,* 200–203.

LELAND, C., & FITZPATRICK, R. (1994). Cross-age interaction builds enthusiasm for reading and writing. *Reading Teacher, 47,* 292–301.

LERNER, J. (1993). *Learning disabilities: Theories, diagnosis, and teaching strategies* (6th ed.). Boston, MA: Houghton Mifflin.

LEWIS, M. E. B. (1982). Use of the thematic approach to curriculum development for learning disabled students: Assumptions and applications. *Learning Disabilities: An Interdisciplinary Journal, 1,* 25–33.

LEWIS, M., WRAY, D., & ROSPIGLIOSI, P. (1994). "...And I want it in your own words." *Reading Teacher, 47,* 528–536.

LINDFORS, J. W. (1987). *Children's language and learning.* Englewood Cliffs, NJ: Prentice-Hall.

LINDQUIST, A. A. (1982). Applying Bloom's taxonomy in writing reading guides for literature. *Journal of Reading, 25,* 768–774.

LIPSON, M.Y., & WIXSON, K. K. (1991). *Assessment and instruction of reading disability: An interactive approach.* New York: HarperCollins.

LOUGHLIN, C. E., & MARTIN, M. D. (1987). *Supporting literacy: Developing effective learning environments.* New York: Teachers College Press.

MACKEY, M. (1990). Filling the gaps: The Baby Sitters Club, the series book, and the learning reader. *Language Arts, 67,* 484–489.

MAHEADY, L., HARPER, G. F., & MALLETTE, B. (1991). Peer-mediated instruction: A review of potential applications for special education. *Reading, Writing and Learning Disabilities, 7,* 75–103.

MAIER, A. (1980). The effect of focusing on the cognitive processes of learning disabled children. *Journal of Learning Disabilities, 13,* 143–147.

MANDLER, J. M., & JOHNSON, N. S. (1977). Remembrance of things parsed: Story structure and recall. *Cognitive Psychology, 9,* 111–157.

MANNING, M., MANNING, G., & LONG, R. (1994). *Theme immersion: Inquiry-based curriculum in elementary and middle schools.* Portsmouth, NH: Heinemann.

MANZO, A. (1969). The request procedure. *Journal of Reading, 12,* 123–126.

MAREK, A. (1989). Using evaluation as an instructional strategy. In K. Goodman, Y. Goodman, & W. Hood (Eds.), *The whole language evaluation book* (pp. 189–212). Portsmouth, NH: Heinemann.

MARING, G. H. (1978). Matching remediation to miscues. *Reading Teacher, 31,* 887–891.

MARINO, J. (1981). Spelling errors: From analysis to instruction. *Language Arts, 58,* 567–572.

MARSHALL, K. (1983). The reading problem: Some sensible solutions. *Learning, 12,* 50–60.

MARTIN, B. (1970a). *Brown bear, brown bear, what do you see?* New York: Holt, Rinehart & Winston.

MARTIN, B. (1970b). *"Fire, fire," said Mrs. McGuire.* New York: Holt, Rinehart & Winston.

MARTIN, B., & BROGAN, P. (1972). *Sounds of language readers.* New York: Holt, Rinehart & Winston.

MARTINEZ, M. (1993). Motivating dramatic story reenactments. *Reading Teacher, 46,* 682–688.

MASON, G. E. (1981). High interest-low vocabulary books: Their past and future. *Journal of Reading, 24,* 603–607.

MATEJA, J. (1982). Musical cloze: Background, purpose, and sample. *Reading Teacher, 35,* 444–448.

MATEJA, J., & WOOD, K. D. (1983). Adapting secondary level strategies for use in elementary classrooms. *Reading Teacher, 32,* 813–817.

MAYA, A. Y. (1979). Write to read: Improving reading through creative writing. *Reading Teacher, 32,* 813–817.

MAYER, M. (1975). *Just for you.* New York: Golden Press.

MAYHER, J. S. (1990). *Uncommon sense: Theoretical practice in language education.* Portsmouth, NH: Boynton/Cook.

MCCAULEY, J. K., & MCCAULEY, D. S. (1992). Using choral reading to promote language learning for ESL students. *Reading Teacher, 45,* 526–533.

McClure, A. A. (1985). Predictable books: Another way to teach reading to learning disabled children. *Teaching Exceptional Children, 17,* 267–273.

McConaughy, S. H. (1980). Using story structure in the classroom. *Language Arts, 57,* 157–165.

McCormick, S. (1977). Should you read aloud to your children? *Language Arts, 54,* 139–143.

McCormick, S. (1981). Assessment and the beginning reader: Using student-dictated stories. *Reading World, 21,* 29–39.

McCracken, R. A. (1971). Initiating sustained silent reading. *Journal of Reading, 14,* 521–524.

McCracken, R. A., & McCracken, M. J. (1978). Modeling is the key to sustained silent reading. *Reading Teacher, 31,* 406–408.

McElmeel, S. L. (1988). *An author a month (for pennies).* Englewood, CO: Libraries Unlimited.

McGee, L. M., & Tompkins, G. E. (1983). Wordless picture books are for older readers too. *Journal of Reading, 27,* 120–123.

McGee, M. M., & Richgels, D. J. (1985). Teaching expository text structure to elementary students. *Reading Teacher, 38,* 739–748.

McGill-Franzen, A. (1993). "I could read the words!": Selecting good books for inexperienced readers. *Reading Teacher, 46,* 424–426.

McGill-Franzen, A., & Allington, R. L. (1991). The gridlock of low reading achievement: Perspectives on practice and policy. *Remedial and Special Education, 12,* 20–30.

McGilp, J., & Michael, M. (1994). *The home-school connection: Guidelines for working with parents.* Portsmouth, NH: Heinemann.

McGovern, A. (1975). *The secret soldier: The story of Deborah Sampson.* New York: Scholastic.

McKee, D. (1976). *The day the tide went out.* New York: Abelard-Schuman.

McKenzie, G. R. (1979). Data charts: A crutch for helping pupils organize reports. *Language Arts, 56,* 784–788.

McKeown, M. G., Beck, I. L., & Worthy, M. J. (1993). Grappling with text ideas: Questioning the author. *Reading Teacher, 46,* 560–566.

McNaughton, D., Hughes, C. A., & Clark, K. (1994). Spelling instruction for students with learning disabilities: Implication for research and practice. *Learning Disability Quarterly, 17,* 169–185.

McNaughton, S. (1981). The influence of immediate teacher correction on self-corrections and proficient oral reading. *Journal of Reading Behavior, 13,* 365–371.

McNulty, F. (1979). *How to dig a hole to the other side of the world.* New York: Harper & Row.

Medway, P. (1981). *Finding a language: Autonomy and learning in school.* New York: Writers and Readers.

Mellon, J. C. (1975). *National assessment and the teaching of English.* Urbana, IL: National Council of Teachers of English.

MEYER, B. J., & FREEDLE, R. O. (1979). Effects of discourse type on recall. *Prose Learning Series Research Report no. 6.* Tempe, AZ: Arizona State University.

MEYER, B. J., BRANDT, D. H., & BLUTH, G. J. (1980). Use of author's textual schema: Key for ninth-graders' comprehension. *Reading Research Quarterly, 16,* 72–103.

MICCINATI, J. (1981). Use visual imagery to enhance recall of information. *Reading World, 21,* 139–143.

MICCINATI, J., & PHELPS, S. (1980). Classroom drama from children's reading: From the page to the stage. *Reading Teacher, 34,* 269–272.

MILLER, G. M., & MASON, G. E. (1983). Dramatic improvisation: Risk-free role playing for improving reading performance. *Reading Teacher, 37,* 128–131.

MILLER, L. D., & WOODLEY, J. W. (1983). Retrospective miscue analysis: Procedures for research and instruction. In *Research in reading in the secondary school* (pp. 10–11, 53–67). Tucson, AZ: University of Arizona.

MILLS, H., O'KEEFE, T., & STEPHENS, D. (1992). *Looking closely: Exploring the role of phonics in one whole language classroom.* Urbana, IL: National Council of Teachers of English.

MOE, A. J., & HOPKINS, C. J. (1978). Jingles, jokes, limericks, poems, proverbs, puns, puzzles, and riddles: Fast reading for reluctant readers. *Language Arts, 55,* 957–965.

MOFFETT, J. (1968). *Teaching the universe of discourse.* Boston, MA: Houghton Mifflin.

MOLDOFSKY, P. B. (1983). Teaching students to determine the central story problem: A practical application of schema theory. *Reading Teacher, 36,* 740–745.

MONSON, R. J., & MONSON, M. P. (1994). Literacy as inquiry: An interview with Jerome C. Harste. *Reading Teacher, 47,* 518–521.

MOORE, J. C., JONES, C. L., & MILLER, D. G. (1980). What we know after a decade of sustained silent reading. *Reading Teacher, 33,* 445–450.

MOORE, P. (1971). *The missing necklace.* Glenview, IL: Scott, Foresman.

MOREY, W. (1965). *Gentle Ben.* New York: Avon Books.

MORRIS, J. (1987). *Create your own whole language games.* Lakewood, CO: LINK.

MORROW, L. M. (1990). Assessing children's understanding of story through their construction and reconstruction of narrative. In L. M. Morrow & J. K. Smith (Eds.), *Assessment for instruction in early literacy* (pp. 110–134). Englewood, NJ: Prentice-Hall.

MORROW, L. M., & PARATORE, J. (1993). Family literacy: Perspective and practices. *Reading Teacher, 47,* 194–200.

MORROW, L. M., & SMITH, J. K. (1990). The effects of group setting on interactive storybook reading. *Reading Research Quarterly, 25,* 213–231.

MOSEL, A. (1968). *Tikki tikki tembo.* New York: Holt, Rinehart, & Winston.

MOSS, J. (1978). Using the "focus unit" to enhance children's response to literature. *Language Arts, 55,* 482–488.

MOSS, J. (1982). Reading and discussing fairy tales—old and new. *Reading Teacher, 35,* 656–660.

MOSS, J. (1984). *Focus units in literature: A handbook for elementary school teachers.* Urbana, IL: National Council of Teachers of English.

Moss, J. F., & Oden, S. (1983). Children's story comprehension and social learning. *Reading Teacher, 36,* 784–789.

Moustafa, M. (1993). Recoding in whole language reading instruction. *Language Arts, 70,* 483–487.

Moyer, S. B. (1982). Repeated reading. *Journal of Learning Disabilities, 15,* 619–623.

Murray, D. (1968). *A writer teaches writing.* Boston, MA: Houghton Mifflin.

Murray, D. (1990). *Shoptalk: Learning to write with writers.* Portsmouth, NH: Heinemann.

Myers, J. (1992). The social contexts of school and personal literacy. *Reading Research Quarterly, 27,* 297–333.

National Association for the Education of Young Children. (1988). NAEYC position statement on the standardized testing of young children, three through eight years of age. *Young Children, 43,* 42–47.

Neill, K. (1980). Turn kids on with repeated readings. *Teaching Exceptional Children, 13,* 63–64.

Nelson, H. (1980). Analysis of spelling errors in normal and dyslexic children. In U. Frith (Ed.), *Cognitive processes in spelling* (pp. 475–493). New York: Academic Press.

Newman, J. (1978). Oral reading miscue analysis is good but not complete. *Reading Teacher, 31,* 83–85.

Newman, J. (1984). *The craft of children's writing.* Portsmouth, NH: Heinemann.

Newman, J., & Church, S. M. (1990). Myths of whole language. *The Reading Teacher, 44,* 20–26.

Newsom, S. D. (1979). Rock 'n roll 'n reading. *Journal of Reading, 22,* 726–730.

Nichols, J. (1978). Foiling students who'd rather fake it than read it or how to get students to read and report on books. *Journal of Reading, 22,* 245–247.

Nicholson, T., Bailey, J., & McArthur, J. (1991). Context cues in reading: The gap between research and popular opinion. *Reading, Writing, and Learning Disabilities, 7,* 33–41.

Noble, T. H. (1980). *The day Jimmy's boa ate the wash.* New York: Dial Press.

Norton, C. (1991). *Through the eyes of a child.* New York: Merrill.

Norton, D. (1977). A web of interest. *Language Arts, 54,* 928–932.

Norton, D. (1990). Teaching multicultural literature in the reading curriculum. *Reading Teacher, 44,* 28–40.

Nutter, N., & Safran, I. J. (1983). *Sentence combining and the learning disabled student.* ERIC Document No. 252–94.

Nutter, N., & Safran, I. J. (1984). Improving writing with sentence combining exercises. *Academic Therapy, 19,* 449–455.

Ogle, D. (1986). K-W-L: A teaching model that develops active reading of expository text. *Reading Teacher, 39,* 564–570.

Ohanian, S. (1994). *Who's in charge? A teacher speaks her mind.* Portsmouth, NH: Heinemann.

Ohlhausen, M. M., & Jespen, M. (1992). Lessons from Goldilocks: "Somebody's been choosing my books but I can make my own choices now!" *The New Advocate, 5,* 31–46.

OLSON, M. W. (1990). The teacher as researcher: A historical perspective. In M. W. Olson (Ed.), *Opening the door to classroom research* (pp. 1–20). Newark, DE: International Reading Association.

O'ROURKE, W. J. (1979). Are parents an influence on adolescent reading habits? *Journal of Reading, 22,* 340–343.

OSGUTHORPE, R. T., & SCRUGGS, T. E. (1986). Special education students as tutors: A review and analysis. *Remedial and Special Education, 7,* 15–26.

PAGE, W. D., & PINNEL, G. S. (1979). Developing purposes for reading. *Today's Education, 68,* 52–55.

PALINSCAR, A., & BROWN, A. (1984). Reciprocal teaching of comprehension-fostering and comprehension-monitoring activities. *Cognition and Instruction, 1,* 117–175.

PAPPAS, C. C., KIEFER, B. Z., & LEVSTIK, L. S. (1990). *An integrated language perspective in the elementary school.* New York: Longman.

PARSONS, L. (1990). *Response journals.* Portsmouth, NH: Heinemann.

PATERSON, K. (1977). *Bridge to Terabithia.* New York: Avon.

PEARSON, P. D., & GALLAGHER, M. C. (1983). The instruction of reading comprehension. *Contemporary Educational Psychology, 8,* 317–344.

PEARSON, P. D., & JOHNSON, D. D. (1978). *Teaching reading comprehension.* New York: Holt, Rinehart, & Winston.

PEARSON, P. D., & SPIRO, R. (1980). Toward a theory of reading comprehension instruction. *Language Disorders and Learning Disabilities, 1,* 71–88.

PEARSON, P. D., HANSEN, J., & GORDON, C. (1979). The effect of background knowledge on young children's comprehension of explicit and implicit information. *Journal of Reading Behavior, 11,* 201–209.

PEET, B. (1989). *Bill Peet: An autobiography.* Boston, MA: Houghton Mifflin.

PELLEGRINI, A., & YAWKEY, T. (Eds.). (1984). *The development of oral and written language in social contexts.* Norwood, NJ: Ablex.

PETERSON, R., & EEDS, M. (1990). *Grand conversations: Literature groups in action.* Richmond Hill, Ontario: Scholastic-TAB.

PFLAUM, S. W., ET AL. (1980). The influence of pupil behaviors and pupil status factors on teacher behaviors during oral reading lessons. *Journal of Educational Research, 74,* 99–105.

PFLAUM, S. W., & BRYAN, T. H. (1982). Oral reading research and learning disabled children. *Topics in Learning and Learning Disabilities, 1,* 33–42.

PIAGET, J. (1971). *Biology and knowledge* (B. Walsh, Trans.). Chicago, IL: University of Chicago Press. (Original work published 1967.)

PIERCE, K. M., & SHORT, K. G. (1994). Environmental issues and actions. *Reading Teacher, 47,* 328–335.

PIGDON, K., & WOOLLEY, M. (1993). *The BIG picture: Integrating children's learning.* Portsmouth, NH: Heinemann.

PITTS, M. M. (1983). Comprehension monitoring: Definition and practice. *Journal of Reading, 26,* 516–522.

POOLEY, R. C. (1974). *The teaching of English usage.* Urbana, IL: National Council of Teachers of English.

POOSTAY, E. J. (1984). Show me your underlines: A strategy to teach comprehension. *Reading Teacher, 37,* 828–830.

POPLIN, M. S. (1983). *Learning disabilities at the crossroad.* Paper presented at the annual meeting of the Claremont Reading Conference, Claremont, CA. ERIC reproduction No. ED 229 958.

POPLIN, M. S. (1988). The reductionist fallacy in learning disabilities: Replicating the past by reducing the present. *Journal of Learning Disabilities, 21,* 389–400.

POTTER, G. (1989). Parent participation in the language arts program. *Language Arts, 66,* 21–28.

QUISENBERRY, N. L., BLAKEMORE, C., & WARREN, C. A. (1977). Involving parents in reading: An annotated bibliography. *Reading Teacher, 31,* 34–39.

RAND, M. K. (1984). Story schema: Theory, research and practice. *Reading Teacher, 37,* 377–382.

RANKIN, E. F. (1974). *The measurement of reading flexibility.* Newark, DE: International Reading Association.

RAPHAEL, T. E. (1982). Question-answering strategies for children. *Reading Teacher, 36,* 186–190.

RAPHAEL, T. E. (1986). Teaching question answer relationships, revisited. *Reading Teacher, 36,* 516–523.

RAPHAEL, T. E., & McKINNEY, J. (1983). An examination of 5th and 8th grade children's question-answering behavior: An instructional study in metacognition. *Journal of Reading Behavior, 15,* 67–86.

RAPHAEL, T. E., & McMAHON, S. I. (1994). Book club: An alternative framework for reading instruction. *Reading Teacher, 48,* 102–116.

RAPHAEL, T. E., & PEARSON, P. D. (1982). *The effect of metacognitive awareness training on children's question-answering behavior.* Technical Report No. 238. Urbana, IL: Center for the Study of Reading.

RAPHAEL, T. E., & WONNACOTT, C. A. (1981). *The effect of metacognitive training on question-answering behavior: Implementation in a fourth grade developmental reading program.* Paper presented at the National Reading Conference, Dallas, TX.

RASINSKI, T. (1989). Fluency for everyone: Incorporating fluency instruction in the classroom. *Reading Teacher, 42,* 690–693.

RASSMUSSEN, C. (1962). *Let's say poetry together and have fun.* Minneapolis, MN: Burgess.

RAWLS, W. (1974). *Where the red fern grows.* New York: Bantam.

RAWLS, W. (1976). *Summer of the monkeys.* New York: Doubleday.

READ, C. (1975). *Children's categorization of speech sounds in English.* Urbana, IL: National Council of Teachers of English.

READENCE, J. E., BEAN, T. W., & BALDWIN, R. S. (1981). *Content area reading: An integrated approach.* Dubuque, IA: Kendall/Hunt.

RECHT, D. R. (1976). *The self-correction process in reading. Reading Teacher, 29,* 632–636.

REID, D. K., & HRESKO, W. P. (1981). *A cognitive approach to learning disabilities.* New York: McGraw-Hill.

REID, D. K., HRESKO, W. P., & HAMMILL, D. D. (1981). *Test of early reading ability.* Austin, TX: Pro-Ed.

RHODES, L. K. (1979). Comprehension and predictability: An analysis of beginning reading materials. In R. F. Carey & J. C. Harste (Eds.), *New perspectives on comprehension*. Bloomington, IN: Monographs in Language and Reading Studies, *3*, 100–131.

RHODES, L. K. (1981). I can read! Predictable books as resources for reading and writing instruction. *Reading Teacher, 34*, 511–518.

RHODES, L. K. (1993). *Literacy assessment: A handbook of instruments*. Portsmouth, NH: Heinemann.

RHODES, L. K. (1995). Students and teachers: Sharing ownership and responsibility in reading. In C. Dudley-Marling & D. Searle (Eds.), *Who owns learning? Questions of autonomy, choice, and control* (pp. 29–39). Portsmouth, NH: Heinemann.

RHODES, L. K., & HILL, M. W. (1983). Home-school cooperation in integrated language arts programs. In B. A. Bushing & J. I. Schwarz (Eds.), *Integrating the language arts in the elementary school* (pp. 179–188). Urbana, IL: National Council of Teachers of English.

RHODES, L. K., & NATHENSON-MEJIA, S. (1992). Anecdotal records: A powerful tool for ongoing literacy assessment. *Reading Teacher, 45*, 502–509.

RHODES, L. K., & SHANKLIN, N. L. (1989). *A research base for whole language*. Lakewood, CO: LINK.

RHODES, L. K., & SHANKLIN, N. L. (1993). *Windows into literacy: Assessing learners K–8*. Portsmouth, NH: Heinemann.

RHODES, L. K., & SHANNON, J. (1982). Psycholinguistic principles in operation in a primary learning disabilities classroom. *Topics in Learning and Learning Disabilities, 1*, 33–42.

RICHARDSON, J. E. (1976). *A risky trip*. Beverly Hills, CA: Benzinger.

RICHGELS, D. J., & MATEJA, J. A. (1984). Gloss II: Integrated content and process for independence. *Journal of Reading, 27*, 424–431.

RICKELMAN, R. J., & HENK, W. A. (1990). Children's literature and audio-visual technologies. *Reading Teacher, 43*, 682–684.

RILEY, J. D. (1979). Teachers' responses are as important as the questions they ask. *Reading Teacher, 32*, 534–537.

ROBB, L. (1993). A cause for celebration: Reading and writing with at-risk students. *The New Advocate, 6*, 25–40.

ROBINSON, F. P. (1961). Study skills for superior students in secondary schools. *Reading Teacher, 15*, 29–33.

ROBINSON, H. A. (1983). *Teaching reading, writing, and study strategies: The content areas*. Boston, MA: Allyn & Bacon.

ROGINSKI, J. (1985). *Behind the covers*. Englewood, CO: Libraries Unlimited.

ROLLER, C. M. (1994). Teacher-student interaction during oral reading and rereading. *Journal of Reading Behavior, 26*, 191–209.

ROLLER, C. M., & BEED, P. L. (1994). Sometimes the conversations were grand, and sometimes... *Language Arts, 71*, 509–515.

ROSE, M. C., CUNDICK, B. P., & HIGBIE, K. L. (1983). Verbal rehearsal and visual imagery: Mnemonic aids for learning disabled children. *Journal of Learning Disabilities, 16*, 352–354.

ROSENBLATT, L. M. (1978). *The reader, the text, the poem.* Carbondale, IL: Southern Illinois University Press.

ROSS, P. A. (1978). Getting books into those empty hands. *Reading Teacher, 31,* 397–399.

ROWE, J. L. (1959a). Readin', TYPIN', and 'rithmetic. *Business Education World, 3,* 9–12.

ROWE, J. L. (1959b). Readin', TYPIN', and 'rithmetic. *Business Education World, 39,* 19–21.

ROWE, M. B. (1974). Relation of wait-time and rewards to the development of language logic, and fate control: Part one—wait time. *Journal of Research in Science Teaching, 11,* 81–94.

ROWE, M. B. (1986). Wait time: Slowing down may be a way of speeding up. *Journal of Teacher Education, 37,* 43–50.

RUDDELL, R. B. (1978). Developing comprehension abilities: Implications from research for an instructional framework. In S. J. Samuels (Ed.), *What research has to say about reading instruction.* Newark, DE: International Reading Association.

RUMELHART, D. E. (1975). Notes on a schema for stories. In D. G. Bobrow & A. Collins (Eds.), *Representations and understandings.* New York: Academic Press.

RYAN, E. G., & TORRANCE, E. P. (1967). Training in elaboration. *Journal of Reading, 11,* 27–32.

RYLANT, C. (1985). *The relatives came.* New York: Bradbury Press.

SACCARDI, M. (1993). Children speak: Our students' reactions to books can tell us what to teach. *Reading Teacher, 46,* 318–324.

SADOSKI, M. C. (1980). Ten years of uninterrupted sustained silent reading. *Reading Improvement, 17,* 153–156.

SADOW, M. (1980). The use of story grammar in the design of questions. *Reading Teacher, 35,* 518–523.

SAMUELS, S. J. (1979). The method of repeated readings. *Reading Teacher, 32,* 403–408.

SANDS, D., KOZLESKI, E. B., & FRENCH, N. (in press). *Special education for the 21st century: Making schools inclusive communities.* Pacific Heights, CA: Brooks Cole Publishing.

SARASON, S. (1982). *The culture of the school and the problem of change.* Boston, MA: Allyn & Bacon.

SAUL, W., & JAGUSCH, S. A. (1991). *Vital connections: Children, science and books.* Portsmouth, NH: Heinemann.

SAWYER, J. M. (1993). Motivating children's at-home reading with book swaps. *Reading Teacher, 47,* 269–270.

SCALA, M. A. (1993). What whole language in the mainstream means for children with learning disabilities. *Reading Teacher, 47,* 222–229.

SCHAUDT, B. A. (1983). ERIC/RCS: Another look at sustained silent reading. *Reading Teacher, 6,* 934–936.

SCHELL, L. (1988). Dilemmas in assessing reading comprehension. *Reading Teacher, 42,* 12–16.

Scheverman, B., Jacobs, W. R., McCall, C., & Knies, W. C. (1994). The personal spelling dictionary: An adaptive approach to reducing the spelling hurdles in written language. *Intervention in School and Clinic, 29*, 292–299.

Schieffelin, B. B., & Gilmore, P. 1986. *The acquisition of literacy: Ethnographic perspectives.* Norwood, NJ: Ablex.

Schiller, C. (1973). I'm OK, you're OK. Let's choral read. *English Journal, 62,* 791–794.

Schneeberg, H. (1977). Listening while reading: A four year study. *Reading Teacher, 30,* 629–635.

Schoof, R. N. (1978). Four color words: Comic books in the classroom. *Language Arts, 55,* 821–827.

Schuck, A., Ulsh, F., & Platt, J. (1983). Parents encourage pupils (PEP): An inner-city parent involvement reading program. *Reading Teacher, 36,* 524–527.

Schumaker, J., et al. (1982). Multipass: A learning strategy for improving reading comprehension. *Learning Disability Quarterly, 5,* 295–304.

Schwartz, S. S., & MacArthur, C. A. (1990). They all have something to say: Helping learning disabled students write. *Academic Therapy, 25,* 459–471.

Scieszka, J. (1989). *The true story of the three little pigs.* New York: Viking Kestrel.

Scollon, R., & Scollon, S. (1981). *Narrative, literacy, and face in interethnic communication.* Norwood, NJ: Ablex.

Scruggs, T. E., Mastropieri, M., & Richter, L. L. (1985). Tutoring interventions with behaviorally disordered students: Social and academic benefits. *Behavioral Disorders, 10,* 283–298.

Searle, D. (Personal communication, July 6, 1995).

Sears, S., Carpenter, C., & Burstein, N. (1994). Meaningful reading instruction for learners with special needs. *Reading Teacher, 47,* 632–638.

Sebesta, S. L., Calder, J. W., & Cleland, L. N. (1982). A story grammar for the classroom. *Reading Teacher, 36,* 180–184.

Segel, E. (1990). Side-by-side storybook reading for every child: An impossible dream? *The New Advocate, 3,* 131–137.

Shanklin, N. K. (1981). *Relating reading and writing: Developing a transactional theory of the writing process.* Bloomington, IN: Monographs in Teaching and Learning, School of Education, Indiana University.

Shannon, P. (1993). Developing democratic voices. *The Reading Teacher, 47,* 86–94.

Shannon, P., & Goodman, K. S. (1994). *Basal readers: A second look.* Katonah, NY: Richard C. Owen.

Shapiro, H. R. (1992). Debatable issues underlying whole-language philosophy: A speech-language pathologist's perspective. *Language, Speech, and Hearing Services in the Schools, 23,* 308–311.

Shapiro, H. R. (1993). Response to Fawcett and Norris. *Language, Speech, and Hearing Services in the Schools, 25,* 44–46.

Shaughnessy, M. D. (1977). *Errors and expectations: A guide for the teacher of basic writing.* New York: Oxford University Press.

SHOCKLEY, B. (1993). Extending the literate community: Reading and writing with families. *The New Advocate, 6,* 11–24.

SHOCKLEY, B., MICHALOVE, B., & ALLEN, J. (1995). *Engaging families: Connecting home and school literacy communities.* Portsmouth, NH: Heinemann.

SHORT, K. G. (1993). Visual literacy: Exploring art and illustration in children's books. *Reading Teacher, 46,* 506–516.

SHORT, K. G., & BURKE, C. L. (1991). *Creating curriculum.* Portsmouth, NH: Heinemann.

SHORT, K. G., & PIERCE, K. M. (1993). Beginnings: Connecting our past, present, and future. *Reading Teacher, 47,* 46–56.

SHORT, K. G., & PIERCE, K. M. (Eds.). (1990). *Talking about books.* Portsmouth, NH: Heinemann.

SHUMAN, R. B. (1982). Reading with a purpose: Strategies to interest reluctant readers. *Journal of Reading, 25,* 725–730.

SIEGEL, M. G. (1984). *Reading as signification.* Unpublished doctoral dissertation, Indiana University.

SILVERSTEIN, S. (1974). *Where the sidewalk ends.* New York: Harper & Row.

SILVERSTEIN, S. (1981). *A light in the attic.* New York: Harper & Row.

SIMMONDS, E. P. M. (1992). The effects of teacher training and implementation of two methods for improving the comprehension skills of students with learning disabilities. *Learning Disabilities Research and Practice, 7,* 194–198.

SINGER, H. (1978). Active comprehension: From answering to asking questions. *Reading Teacher, 31,* 901–908.

SINGER, H., MCNEIL, J. D., & FURSE, L. L. (1984). Relationship between curricular scope and reading achievement in elementary schools. *Reading Teacher, 37,* 608–612.

SIPE, L. R. (1993). Using transformations of traditional stories: Making the reading-writing connection. *Reading Teacher, 47,* 18–26.

SKOLNICK, D. F. (1992). Reading relationships. *The New Advocate, 5,* 117–127.

SKRTIC, T. M. (1991). The special education paradox: Equity as the way to excellence. *Harvard Educational Review, 61,* 148–186.

SLOYER, S. (1982). *Readers' theater: Story dramatization in the classroom.* Urbana, IL: National Council of Teachers of English.

SMITH, C. F. (1978). Read a book in an hour. *Journal of Reading, 23,* 25–29.

SMITH, F. (1973). *Psycholinguistics and reading.* New York: Holt, Rinehart & Winston.

SMITH, F. (1975). *Comprehension and learning: A conceptual framework for teachers.* New York: Holt, Rinehart & Winston.

SMITH, F. (1978). *Reading without nonsense.* New York: Teachers College Press.

SMITH, F. (1981). Demonstrations, engagement and sensitivity: A revised approach to language learning. *Language Arts, 58,* 103–112.

SMITH, F. (1982a). *Understanding reading.* New York: Holt, Rinehart & Winston.

SMITH, F. (1982b). *Writing and the writer.* New York: Holt, Rinehart & Winston.

SMITH, F. (1983a). The uses of language. In F. Smith (Ed.), *Essays into literacy* (pp. 51–58). Portsmouth, NH: Heinemann.

SMITH, F. (1983b). Reading like a writer. *Language Arts, 60,* 558–567.

SMITH, F. (1986). *Insult to intelligence: The bureaucratic invasion of our classrooms.* Portsmouth, NH: Heinemann.

SMITH, S. L. (1979). *No easy answer: The LD child at home and at school.* New York: Bantam.

SMITHERMAN, G. (1995). "Students' right to their own language": A retrospective. *English Journal, 84,* 21–27.

SPEARE, E. G. (1983). *The sign of the beaver.* New York: Dell.

SPIEGEL, D. L. (1992). Blending whole language and systematic direct instruction. *Reading Teacher, 46,* 38–44.

SPIEGEL, D. L., & ROGERS, C. (1980). Teacher responses to miscues during oral reading by second-grade students. *Journal of Educational Research, 74,* 8–12.

SQUIRE, J. R. (1983). Composing and comprehending: Two sides of the same basic process. *Language Arts, 60,* 581–589.

STAHL, S. A. (1992). Saying the "p" word: Nine guidelines for exemplary reading instruction. *Reading Teacher, 45,* 618–625.

STALLMAN, A. C., & PEARSON, P. D. (1990). Formal measures of literacy assessment. In L. M. Morrow & J. K. Smith (Eds.), *Assessment for instruction in early literacy* (pp. 7–44). Englewood Cliffs, NJ: Prentice-Hall.

STANSELL, J. C. (1987). Reader-selected vocabulary procedure (RSVP): An invitation to natural vocabulary development. In D. Watson (Ed.), *Ideas and insights: Language arts in the elementary school* (pp. 76–77). Urbana, IL: National Council of Teachers of English.

STANSELL, J. C., & DEFORD, D. E. (1981). When is a reading problem not a reading problem? *Journal of Reading, 25,* 14–20.

STEIN, N. L., & GLENN, C. G. (1979). An analysis of story comprehension in elementary school children. In R. O. Freedle (Ed.), *New directions in discourse processing.* Norwood, NJ: Ablex.

STEPHENS, D. (1985). Uncharted land: Reading comprehension research with the special education student. In A. Crismore (Ed.), *Landscapes: A state of the art assessment of reading comprehension research.* Final report HUSDE-C-300-83-0130. Bloomington, IN: Language Education Department, Indiana University.

STEPHENS, D. (1991). *Research on whole language: Support for a new curriculum.* Katonah, NY: Richard C. Owen.

STEVENS, K. (1982). Can we improve reading by teaching background information? *Journal of Reading, 25,* 326–329.

STIRES, S. (Personal communication, November 23, 1991).

STOTSKY, S. (1974). Sentence combining as a curricular activity: Its effect on written language development and reading comprehension. *Research in the Teaching of English, 8,* 30–71.

STOTSKY, S. (1983). Research on reading/writing relationships: A synthesis and suggested directions. *Language Arts, 60,* 627–642.

STRICKLAND, D. S. (1972). Black is beautiful vs. white is right. *Elementary English, 49,* 220–223.

STROM, L. (1980). Open to suggestion: Vocabulary game for the content areas. *Journal of Reading, 23,* 582–583.

STUBBS, M. (1982). Written language and society: Some particular cases and general observations. In M. Nystrand (Ed.), *What writers know: The language, process, and structure of written discourse* (pp. 31–55). New York: Academic Press.

SULZBY, E. (1991). Assessment of emergent literacy: Storybook reading. *Reading Teacher, 44,* 498–500.

SWABY, B. (1984). FAN out your facts on the board. *Reading Teacher, 37,* 914–916.

TAUBENHEIM, B., & CHRISTENSEN, J. (1978). Let's shoot "Cock Robin"! Alternatives to round robin reading. *Language Arts, 55,* 975–977.

TAYLOR, B. M. (1980). Children's memory for expository text after reading. *Reading Research Quarterly, 15,* 399–411.

TAYLOR, B. M., & SAMUELS, S. J. (1983). Children's use of text structure in the recall of expository material. *American Educational Research Journal, 20,* 517–528.

TAYLOR, D. (1991). *Learning denied.* Portsmouth, NH: Heinemann.

TAYLOR, D. (1993). *Family literacy: Young children learning to read and write.* Portsmouth, NH: Heinemann.

TAYLOR, D. (1994, May). *The ideologies and ethics of family literacy pedagogies: A postformal perspective.* Paper presented at the Annual Conference of the International Reading Association, Toronto.

TAYLOR, D., & DORSEY-GAINES, C. (1988). *Growing up literate: Learning from inner-city families.* Portsmouth, NH: Heinemann.

TAYLOR, K. K. (1984). Teaching summarization skills. *Journal of Reading, 27,* 389–393.

TAYLOR, N. D., & CONNOR, O. (1982). Silent vs. oral reading: The rational instructional use of both processes. *Reading Teacher, 35,* 440–443.

TCHUDI, S. (1991). *Travels across the curriculum: Models for interdisciplinary learning.* New York: Scholastic.

TCHUDI, S. (Ed.). (1993). *The astonishing curriculum: Integrating science and humanities through language.* Urbana, IL: National Council of Teachers of English.

TEALE, W. (1978). Positive environments for learning to read: What studies of early readers tell us. *Language Arts, 55,* 922–932.

TEALE, W., & SULZBY, E. (Eds.). (1986). *Emergent literacy: writing and reading.* Norwood, NJ: Ablex.

TEMPLE, C. A., & GILLET, J. W. (1984). *Language arts: Learning processes and teaching practices.* Boston, MA: Little, Brown.

TEMPLE, C. A., NATHAN, R. G., TEMPLE, F., & BURRIS, N. A. (1993). *The beginnings of writing.* Boston, MA: Allyn & Bacon.

THOMPSON, F. (1992, April). *Making homework: Models of homework and family involvement.* Paper presented at the Annual Conference of the American Educational Research Association, San Francisco, CA.

THORNDYKE, P. W. (1977). Cognitive structures in comprehension and memory of narrative discourse. *Cognitive Psychology, 9,* 77–110.

THORNE, B. (1993). *Gender play: Girls and boys in school.* New Brunswick, NJ: Rutgers University Press.

TIERNEY, R. J., & LaZANSKY, J. (1980). The rights and responsibilities of readers and writers: A contractual agreement. *Language Arts, 57,* 606–613.

TOLAR, S. B. (1991). Extra readings: Reading outside the classroom. *Reading Teacher, 44,* 526–527.

TOLSTOY, A. (1968). *The great big enormous turnip.* New York: Franklin Watts.

TOMPKINS, G. E., & McGEE, L. M. (1983). Launching nonstandard speakers into standard English. *Language Arts, 60,* 463–469.

TOVEY, D. R. (1979). Teachers' perceptions of children's reading miscues. *Reading Horizons, 19,* 302–307.

TOVEY, D. R. (1981). Children's perceptions of oral and silent reading. *Reading Horizons, 22,* 72–80.

TRELEASE, J. (1985). *The read-aloud handbook.* New York: Penguin.

TRELEASE, J. (1995). *The read-aloud handbook.* (Rev. ed.). New York: Penguin.

TRUE, J. (1979). Round robin reading is for the birds. *Language Arts, 56,* 918–921.

TSUCHIYA, Y. (1988). *Faithful elephants.* Boston, MA: Houghton Mifflin.

TURBILL, J. (1983). *Now we want to write!* Rozelle, NSW, Australia: Primary English Teaching Association. Distributed by Heinemann.

VACCA, J. (1981). Reading with a sense of writer: Writing with a sense of reader. *Language Arts, 58,* 937–941.

VACCA, R. T. (1981). *Content area reading.* Boston, MA: Little, Brown.

VACCA, R. T., & VACCA, J. A. (1993). *Content area reading.* New York: Harper-Collins.

VAWTER, J. M., & VANCIL, M. (1980). Helping children discover reading through self-directed dramatization. *Reading Teacher, 34,* 320–323.

VERGASON, E. L. (1974). Be your own Boswell. In P. A. Geuder, L. K. Harvey, D. Lohd, & J. D. Wages (Eds.) *They really taught us how to write* (pp. 35–36). Urbana, IL: National Council of Teachers of English.

VERNON, M. D. 1957. *Backwardness in reading.* Cambridge: Cambridge University Press.

VILLAUME, S. K., WORDEN, T., WILLIAMS, S., HOPKINDS, L., & ROSENBLATT, C. (1994). Five teachers in search of a discussion. *Reading Teacher, 47,* 480–487.

VOGT, M. (1991). An observation guide for supervisors and administrators: Moving toward integrated reading/language arts instruction. *Reading Teacher, 45,* 206–211.

VUKELICH, C. (1984). Parents' role in the reading process: A review of practical suggestions and ways to communicate with parents. *Reading Teacher, 37,* 472–477.

VYGOTSKY, L. (1986). *Thought and language,* ed. by A. Kozulin. Cambridge, MA: MIT Press.

WALLEY, C. (1993). An invitation to reading fluency. *Reading Teacher, 46,* 526–527.

WATSON, D. (1978a). Reader-selected miscues: Getting more from sustained silent reading. *English Education, 10,* 75–85.

WATSON, D. (1978b). *Recording, decoding, will the real reader stand up?* Speech given at National Conference on the Language Arts in the Elementary School, Indianapolis, Indiana.

WATSON, D. (1987). Skinny books. In D. Watson (Ed.), *Ideas and insights: Teaching the English language arts, K–6.* Urbana, IL: National Council of Teachers of English.

WATSON, D., BURKE, C., & HARSTE, J. (1989). *Whole language: Inquiring voices.* Portsmouth, NH: Heinemann.

WEAVER, C. (1982). Welcoming errors as signs of growth. *Language Arts, 59,* 438–444.

WEAVER, C. (1990). *Understanding whole language.* Portsmouth, NH: Heinemann.

WEAVER, C. (1994). *Reading process and practice: From socio-psycholinguistics to whole language.* (2nd ed.). Portsmouth, NH: Heinemann.

WEAVER, C., & HENKE, L. (Eds.). (1992). *Supporting whole language: Stories of teacher and institutional change.* Portsmouth, NH: Heinemann.

WEENER, P. (1983). On comparing learning disabled and regular classroom children. *Journal of Learning Disabilities, 14,* 227–232.

WELLS, G. (1986). *The meaning makers: Children learning language and using language to learn.* Portsmouth, NH: Heinemann.

WEPNER, S. B. (1990). Holistic computer applications in literature-based classrooms. *Reading Teacher, 44,* 12–19.

WEPNER, S. B. (1993). Technology and author studies. *Reading Teacher, 46,* 616–619.

WHALEY, J. F. (1981). Story grammars and reading instruction. *Reading Teacher, 34,* 760–771.

WHITIN, D. J., & WILDE, S. (1992). *Read any good math lately? Children's books for mathematical learning, K–6.* Portsmouth, NH: Heinemann.

WHITIN, P. (1994). Opening potential: Visual response to literature. *Language Arts, 71,* 101–107.

WIENCEK, J., & O'FLAHAVAN, J. F. (1994). From teacher-led to peer discussions about literature: Suggestions for making the shift. *Language Arts, 71,* 488–498.

WILDE, S. (1992). *You kan red this! Spelling and punctuation for whole language classrooms.* Portsmouth, NH: Heinemann.

WILKINSON, I. A. G. (1991). Silent reading, oral reading, and learning from text. *Reading Teacher, 45,* 154–155.

WILLIAMS, B., & BELLOMO, C. (1995). Parents and schools: Partners in literacy. *Primary Voices K–6, 3,* 26–34.

WINKELJOHANN, R., & GALLANT, R. (1979). Queries: Why oral reading? *Language Arts, 56,* 950–953.

WIXSON, K. K., BOSKY, A. B., YOCHUM, M. N., & ALVERMAN, D. E. (1984). An interview for assessing students' perceptions of classroom reading tasks. *Reading Teacher, 37,* 346–352.

WOLF, S. A. (1993). What's in a name? Labels and literacy in readers theatre. *Reading Teacher, 46,* 540–545.

WOLFRAM, W. (1995). Dialect awareness and the study of language. In A. Egan-Robertson & D. Bloome (Eds.), *Students as researchers of language and culture in their own communities.* Cresskill, NJ: Hampton Press.

WOLFRAM, W., & CHRISTIAN, D. (1989). *Dialects and education: Issues and answers.* Englewood Cliffs, NJ: Prentice-Hall.

WOLLMAN-BONILLA, J. E. (1994). Why don't they "just speak?" Attempting literature discussion with more and less able readers. *Research in the Teaching of English, 28,* 321–358.

WONG, B. (1985). Questions about a text: What you ask about is what children learn. *Reading Teacher, 37,* 287–293.

WONG, B., & JONES, W. (1982). Increasing metacomprehension in learning disabled and normally achieving students through self-questioning training. *Learning Disability Quarterly, 5,* 228–240.

WOOD, M. L. (1983). Shared reading. In J. Newman (Ed.), *Whole language activities.* Halifax, NS: Dalhousie University.

WOODLEY, J. (1990). *Reading miscue inventory disk.* Katonah, NY: Richard C. Owen.

WORTHAM, S. (1993, February). *The reification of classroom discourse: The experience-near examples as commodities.* Paper presented at the annual Ethnography in Education Forum, Graduate School of Education, University of Pennsylvania, Philadelphia, PA.

WORTMAN, B., & MATLIN, M. (1995). *Leadership in whole language: The principals' role.* York, ME: Stenhouse.

YOAKLEY, C. B. (1974). One approach to the process. In P. A. Geuder, L. K. Harvey, D. Lohd, & J. D. Wages (Eds.), *They really taught us how to write* (pp. 46–49). Urbana, IL: National Council of Teachers of English.

YOUNG, E. (1990). *Lon Po Po.* New York: Scholastic.

YOUNG, T. A., & VARDELL, S. (1993). Weaving readers theatre and nonfiction into the curriculum. *Reading Teacher, 46,* 396–406.

YSSELDYKE, J. E., ET AL. (1982). Similarities and differences between low achievers and students labeled learning disabled. *Journal of Special Education, 16,* 73–85.

YSSELDYKE, J. E., & ALGOZZINE, B. (1983). LD or not LD: That's not the question! *Journal of Learning Disabilities, 16,* 29–31.

YSSELDYKE, J. E., & CHRISTENSON, S. L. (1987). *The instructional environment scale.* Austin, TX: Pro-Ed.

ZARAGOZA, N., & VAUGHN, S. (1992). The effects of process writing instruction on three 2nd-grade students with different achievement profiles. *Learning Disabilities Research and Practice, 7,* 184–193.

ZARAGOZA, N., & VAUGHN, S. (1995). Children teach us to teach writing. *The Reading Teacher, 49,* 42–47.

ZINSSER, W. (Ed.). (1990). *Worlds of childhood: The art and craft of writing for children.* Boston, MA: Houghton Mifflin.

ZUCKER, C. (1993). Using whole language with students who have language and learning disabilities. *Reading Teacher, 46,* 660–670.

ZUTELL, J. (1978). Some psycholinguistic perspectives on children's spelling. *Language Arts, 55,* 844–850.

ZVIRIN, S. (1994). Disabled kids: Challenges and choices. *Book Links, 3,* 44–49.

AUTHOR INDEX

Aardema, 222
Aaron, 107
Adams, P. 208
Afflerbach, 44
Alejandro, 220
Aliki, 208
Allen, 309
Allen, J., 90, 120
Alley, 25, 77
Allington, 20, 24, 26, 27, 115, 151, 165, 301, 305
Allsburg, 224
Almasi, 212
Altwerger, 3, 27, 29, 72, 320
Alvarez, 304
Ames, 315
Anderson, 183
Angletti, 217
Applebee, 102, 132
Armbruster, 154, 183, 227, 228
Aronson, 225
Asher, 224
Atwell, M., 93, 108, 140, 145
Atwell, N., 20, 215, 217, 238, 245, 247, 266, 305
Au, 137
Aual, 223
Auten, 132

Badiali, 148
Bailey, 199
Baker, 76, 112
Baldwin, 148, 173, 232
Barlow, 309
Barnard, 313
Barone, 216, 217
Bartlett, 311
Bass, 112
Bath, 76

Battle, 113
Baumann, 172
Bayer, 23
Baylor, 224
Bean, 148, 173, 232
Beck, 180, 231
Beebe, 185
Beed, 212
Beers, 66, 273
Bellomo, 308, 310, 318, 330
Bergland, 164
Bissex, 214, 279, 280
Bixby, 214
Blachowicz, 139, 143, 190, 198
Blanton, 132, 133, 134
Bloome, D., 5, 6, 11, 14, 19, 308
Bloome, L., 271
Blume, 108
Bluth, 179
Bogt, 79
Bonne, 108, 164, 208
Bookman, 272
Bos, 158, 160
Braddock, 294
Brandt, 179
Bransford, 128
Braun, 179
Brenneman, 213
Bridge, 109
Brieling, 312
Briggs, 223
Brock, 213
Brogan, 162
Brown, 77, 169, 177, 214
Bruce, 180
Bruinsma, 166
Bryan, P., 198

Bryan, R., 162
Bryan, T., 54, 155
Bullock, 332
Burke, 11, 13, 23, 45, 55, 70, 74, 124, 126, 154,
    155, 185, 196, 197, 213, 221, 266
Burns, 125
Burris, 18, 62, 65, 272
Burstein, 158, 185
Buttery, 209

Cadieux, 168
Cairney, 307, 302, 309
Calder, 179
Calhoun, 223
Calkins, 20, 236, 238, 240, 242, 243, 245, 246,
    253, 260, 261, 266, 270, 290
Cambourne, 54, 155, 155, 213
Cameron, 316
Carbo, 159, 160
Carlberg, 26
Carle, 108, 204
Carpenter, 158, 185
Carr, 135, 214
Casanave, 78
Cassidy, 224
Casteel, 126
Cavley, 223
Cazden, 290, 291
Chaney, 106
Chomsky, 159, 160, 161, 295
Christenson, 79, 151
Christian, 294
Christian-Smith, 103, 108
Church, 21, 322
Clark, F., 25, 169, 172
Clark, K., 283
Clarke, M., 76, 79, 112, 316
Clay, 72, 138, 208
Cleary, 294
Cleland, 179
Close, 213, 217
Clyde, 254
Clymer, 140
Cochran-Smith, 332
Cohen, 316
Coles, 25
Collier, C., 149
Collier, J., 149
Commire, 224
Connor, 151
Cook, 148, 149
Cordeiro, 290, 291
Costello, 196
Cox, 174
Crafton, 149, 209, 222
Crocker, 124, 225, 256

Cudd, 184
Cullinan, 107, 294
Cummings, 224
Cundick, 172
Cunningham, 166, 173

Dahl, 21, 198, 199, 314, 320
Dalton, 286
D'Angelo, 185
Davey, 170, 172
Davidson, 220
Davis, 316
Davis, 76, 79, 112
Deardorf, 319
DeFord, 121, 146, 221
Dekker, 216, 217
Delamore, 223
Delpit, 16, 294
Deregniers, 223
Deshler, 25, 77, 134
Deshler, 25
Dicinson, 212
Dillon, 308, 311
Dimartini, 205, 206
Dippo, 302
Doake, 325
Doiron, 113
Donelson, 107
Dorsey-Gaines, 309
Dreyer, 226
Dudley-Marling, 9, 21, 25, 29, 81, 127, 163, 239,
    242, 243, 258, 270, 322, 325, 327
Duncon, 223, 301, 302, 305
DuPuis, 148
Durkin, 307
Duvoisin, 223
Dyck, 174
Dyson, 23, 114

Ebert, 121
Edelsky, 2, 3, 6, 11, 23, 29, 322
Edward, 214
Eeds, 23, 114, 119, 211, 307
Egan-Robertson, 6, 11
Eidman-Aadahl, 317
Einsel, 202
Eisele, 120
Elkin, 222
Elting, 108, 206
Enstrom, 299
Epps, 25
Evans, 112

Fader, 107
Farr, 31
Farris, 217

Faulkner, 295
Feagans, 307
Felknor, 74
Fielding 105, 106
Figeuroa, 28
Fish, 5
Fisher, 296
Fitzgerald, 172
Fitzpatrick, 316
Five, 24, 301, 303, 318
Flood, 235, 239
Flores, 3
Flosom, 108
Flynn, 214
Folsom, 206, 207
Folstoy, 203
Forester, 112
Fowler, 180, 181
Fractor, 102
Fredericks, 38
Freedle, 180, 181
Freedman, 220
Freeman, 107, 274
French, 306
Freppon, 32, 198, 199, 314, 320
Friedman, 232
Frith, 224, 272
Furnas, 97
Furse, 105, 122, 314

Gagne, 137
Gahagan, 315
Gale, 191, 192
Gallagher, 91
Gallant, 151, 152
Gambrell, 159, 164, 168
Ganschow, 281
Garcia, 28
Garvey, 307
Gee, 2, 6, 11, 13, 15, 29, 77
Gelzheiser, 306
Gentry, 273, 325
Gerber, 62, 272, 275
Giacobbe, 278, 290, 291
Giff, 224
Gilles, 212
Gilmore, 15
Glass, 26
Goatley, 213
Gold, 220
Golden, 180
Goldenberg, 212
Golinkoff, 307
Goodman, G., 322
Goodman, K., 6, 7, 19, 21, 55, 62, 72, 74, 110,
    172, 198, 314, 322, 325, 333

Goodman, Y., 13, 45, 55, 70, 155, 185, 196, 213
Gordon, 128, 179
Goswami, 198, 332
Graff, 2
Graham, 272, 273, 282, 283
Granger, B., 26
Granger, L., 26
Grant, 122
Graves, 20, 59, 60, 61, 148, 149, 236, 238, 239,
    243, 242, 249, 269, 270, 273, 283, 298, 299
Greene, F., 161, 177
Greene, M., 240
Grice, 10
Griffin, 53
Gruber, 21
Guthrie, 122

Haber, 25,
Hagerty, 118
Hall, 272, 274, 311
Hallahan, 25
Halliday, 10
Hammill, 70, 71
Hammon, 54, 55
Hampton, 135
Hancock, 216, 217
Hanh, 228
Hansen, 90, 128, 135, 269, 320
Hare, 25
Harris, K., 273
Harris, L., 5, 6
Harste, 70, 154, 155, 177, 213, 221
Hartman, D., 221
Hartman, J., 221
Harwayne, 109, 236, 238, 240, 246, 253, 259,
    261, 262, 253, 266
Hawking, 8, 9
Hawkins, 94
Head-Taylor, 313
Headings, 314
Heath, 5, 10, 213
Heine, 222
Heinig, 214, 215
Hendersen, 214, 272, 273
Heney, 221
Henke, 313
Hennings, 112, 114
Hermann, 171, 172
Hess, 162
Hetzel, 313
Hiebert, 70
Higbie, 172
Hill, 38, 79, 90
Hinton, 223
Hirsh, 222
Hittleman, 122

Hoffman, 113, 151, 152, 174, 175, 176, 225
Hoge, 197
Holdaway, 173
Hollingsworth, 158, 159, 160
Holmes, 272
Holt, 19
Hong, 165
Hopkins, 111
Hoskisson, 311
Howell, 299
Hresko, 70, 71, 72, 134
Huck, 102, 104, 107, 112
Hughes, C., 283
Hughes, M., 65, 273, 279
Hunt, 73, 132
Hutchinson, 107

Idol-Maestras, 145
Innocenti, 106
Invernizzi, 62, 272
Isom, 126

Jackson, 320
Jacobs, 223
Jagger, 295
Jagusch, 107, 120
Jespen, 131
Johns, 152, 164, 185
Johnson, D., 228
Johnson, K., 161
Johnson, N., 121, 128, 178, 179
Johnson, R., 161
Johnson, T., 220, 221
Johnston, 79
Jones, 145
Jones, 164, 165, 269, 172
Jongsma, 53
Jordan, 301, 303, 310
Jurenka, 112

Kaake, 300
Kameenui, 28
Karolides, 211
Kaufman, 25
Keeler, 221
Kellogg, 208, 223, 224
Kelly, 217
Kerfoot, 161
Kettel, 221
Kiefer, 123, 224
Kimmelman, 222
Kipling, 222
Kirby, 217, 268
Kitagawa, 169, 209, 213
Koskinen, 159

Kozleski, 306
Krevisky, 286
Kucer, 184
Kulik, C., 316
Kulik, J., 316

Labbo, 316
LaBerge, 148, 149
Lahey, 271
Lamme, 109, 308
Lancaster, 273
Landes, 178
Langstaff, 208
Langer, 102, 136, 211, 212
Lapp, 235, 239
LaSasso, 111
Lauritzen, 161
Lazansky, 271
Lee, 148, 190, 198
Lehr, 132
Leland, 316
Lerner, 25
Levskik, 123
Lewis, 125, 180
Lima, 226
Limbrick, 316
Lindfors, 20
Liner, 217, 268
Linfield, 286
Linquist, 169
Lloyd-Jones, 294
Long, 127
Lopson, 79
Loughlin, 78
Lovis, 220, 221
Ludlum, 5, 6
Lund, 294
Lytle, 332

MacArthur, 239, 282
Mackey, 108
Maier, 173
Mandler, 178, 179
Manning, G., 127
Manning, M., 127
Manzo, 169, 175
Maring, 185
Marino, 281, 283
Marshall, 53, 180, 181
Martin, B., 108, 162, 163, 203, 207
Martin, M., 78
Martin, P., 140
Martinez, 102, 214
Mastripeiri, 316
Mateja, 173, 205

Matlin, 313
Maya, 110
Mayer, 108
Mayher, 198
McArthur, 199
McBride, 212
McCaslin, 135
McCauley, 162
McClure, 108, 109, 222
McConaughy, 180
McCormick, 72
McCraken, M., 164
McCraken, R. 164
McElmeel, 224
McGee, 109, 179, 180, 18, 295
McGill-Franzen, 20, 24, 26, 27, 108
McGilp, 307, 310, 313
McGough, 122
McGovern, 149
McGue, 25
McKee, 222
McKenzie, 225, 264
McKeown, 135, 180, 231
McKinney, 228
McMahon, 119
McNaughton, 283
McNeil, 105, 122, 314
McNulty, 212
Medway, 169
Mellon, 67
Memory, 137
Meyer, 179, 180, 181
Meyers, 306
Miccinati, 172
Michael, 307, 310, 313
Michalove, 308, 309, 310
Micinatte, 214
Miller, 164, 165, 196, 214
Mills, 108, 164, 199, 205, 208
Modlofsky, 180
Moe, 111
Moffett, 259, 294
Monson, M., 126
Monson, P., 126
Moore, J., 164, 165
Moore, P., 217
Moorman, 132, 133, 134
Morey, 190
Morris, 221, 273
Morrison, 295
Mosel, 214
Moss, 125, 180, 222
Moustafa, 198
Mullis, 102
Munsie, 302, 307, 309

Murray, 23, 238, 240, 241, 244, 255
Myers, 6, 16, 26
Myers, W., 224

NAEYC, 70
Nathan, 18, 62, 65, 272
Nathenson-Mehia, 44
Neale, 311
Neill, 161
Neuman, 159, 322, 325
Newman, 21, 58
Newsom, 109
Nichols, 221
Nicholson, 199
Nilsen, 107
Noble, 290
Norland, 165
Norton, C., 107
Norton, D., 107, 125
Nutter, 259

Oden, 180
O'Flahaven, 212
Ogle, 135
Ohanion, 318, 319
Ohlhausen, 131
O'Keefe, 199, 205
Olsos, 332
Oppenheimer, 239, 242, 243
O'Rourke, 312
Osguthorpe, 316
Ostertag, 183

Page, 133
Paliscar, 169, 177
Pappas, 123, 305
Parsons, 216
Paterson, 178, 224
Pearson, 70, 128, 228
Peet, 224
Peetoom, 122
Pellegrini, 307
Peper, 272
Person, 107, 173
Peterson, 23, 119, 211, 317
Pflaum, 54, 155
Phelps, 214
Piaget, 18
Pierce, 23, 107, 119, 226, 305
Pigdon, 124
Pinkney, 224
Pinnel, 133
Pitts, 170
Pooley, 296
Poostay, 174

Poplin, 18, 19, 83
Porter, 172
Potter, 330
Powell, 209

Quackenbush, 208

Rand, 180
Rankin, 77
Raphael, 119, 213, 228, 229
Rasinski, 38, 158, 160
Rasmussen, 162
Rawls, 220, 223, 232, 287
Read, 18, 62, 272
Readence, 148, 173, 232
Reed, 94,
Reid, 70, 71, 134
Resta, 27, 320
Reynolds, E., 220
Reynolds, Q., 224
Rhodes, 17, 29, 35, 42, 44, 47, 53, 54, 55, 61, 70,
    71, 72, 73, 74, 76, 78, 79, 93, 104, 108,. 109,
    110, 112, 140, 145, 184, 207, 315, 316, 332
Richardson, 191, 194
Richgels, 173, 179, 180, 181
Richter, 316
Rickelman, 147, 159
Riley, 230
Robb, 106, 112, 316
Roberts, 184
Robertson, 309
Robinson, 232
Roginski, 224
Roller, 94, 105, 106, 190, 212
Rose, 172
Rosenblatt, 10, 132, 133, 211
Roser, 113
Rospigliosi, 180
Ross, 130,131
Rousch, 54, 155
Rowe, J., 300
Rowe, M., 169
Ruddell, 230
Ruiz, 28
Rumelhart, 178
Ruptic, 38, 79, 90
Ryan, 209
Rylant, 106, 224

Saccardi, 73
Sadoski, 164
Sadow, 180
Safran, 259
Samuels, 160, 161, 179
Samway, 311

Sands, 306
Saul, 107, 120
Scala, 306
Schaudt, 164
Schell, 54
Schevermann, 272, 286
Schieffelin, 15
Schiller, 162
Schneeburg, 158
Schoof, 111
Schwartz, 239, 282
Scollon, R., 15
Scollon, S., 15
Scruggs, 316
Searle, 65, 258, 272, 273, 284
Sears, 158
Sebesta, 179
Seifert-Kessel, 172
Shablak, 173
Shanker, 214
Shanklin, 10, 12, 17, 29, 35, 47, 53, 54, 70, 72, 78,
    315, 332
Shannon, J., 109
Shannon, P., 2, 110
Shapiro, 24
Shaugnessy, 132
Sherman, 311
Shinn, 25
Shockley, 308, 309, 310, 324, 329
Short, 23, 106, 107, 119, 124, 125, 126, 226, 305
Shumaker, 25, 145
Shuman, 102, 111, 133
Silverstein, 162
Simon, 240
Simonds, 228
Singer, 105, 122, 169, 179, 213, 314
Sipe, 225
Skrtic, 26
Sloyer, 161, 162
Smith, C., 225
Smith, F., 12, 18, 20, 22, 70, 112, 132, 133, 135,
    157, 217, 235, 292, 299
Smith, K., 6
Smith, L., 311
Smith, S., 156
Smitherman, 294, 295
Speare, 219
Spiegel, 21, 24, 219
Spiro, 173
Stahl, 198
Stallmen, 70
Stansell, 121, 146, 198
Stein, 178
Steiner, 256
Stephens, 17, 29, 134, 199, 205, 332

Stephens, 332
Stevens, 148
Stillman, 332
Stires, 267
Stotsky, 259
Strickland, 295
Strom, 221
Stubbs, 132
Sulzby, 72, 307
Swan, 125

Taubenheim, 151
Taylor, B., 179
Taylor, D., 26, 307, 308, 309
Taylor, K., 215
Taylor, N., 151
Tchudi, 120, 122, 123, 126
Teale, 314
Teale, 102, 111, 307, 311, 316
Temple, 18, 62, 65, 272
Thorndyke, 178
Thorne, 239
Tierney, 271
Tolar, 111
Tompkins, 109, 295
Tompson, 329
Torrance, 209
Tovey, 191
Traver, 25
Trelease, 311
True, 151
Turbill, 170

Vacca, J., 47, 148
Vacca, R., 47, 148, 161, 179, 232, 233
Vancil, 214
Vandover, 212
Vardell, 162
Vaughn, 239, 254, 274, 291
Vawter, 214
Verason, 256
Vernon, 299
Villaume, 213
Voigt, 224
Voth, 272, 282, 283
Vygotsky, 91

Walley, 162
Warner, 25
Watson, 23, 45, 55, 58, 74, 110, 126, 128, 155, 196, 197
Weaver, 6, 10, 17, 20, 21, 23, 27, 29, 67, 198, 313, 332
Wells, 307, 314, 311
Wener, 25
Wepner, 148, 218
Westcott, 208
Whaley, 180
Whitin, 107, 120
Wieneek, 212
Wilde, 6, 18, 65, 67, 107, 120, 171, 236, 272, 273, 274, 284, 286, 289, 290, 292, 324
Wilder, 79
Wilkinson, 154
Williams, 308, 310, 318, 330
Wilson, 159
Winkejohann, 151, 152
Wixson, 79
Wolf, 214
Wolfram, 294
Wollman-Bonilla 213
Wong, 134, 145, 169
Wonnacott, 228
Wood, K., 132, 133, 134, 173
Wood, M., 174
Woodruff, 102
Woodward, 70
Wooley, 124, 196
Worthy, 62, 231, 272
Wortman, 14, 15, 313
Wray, 180

Yawkey, 307
Yoakley, 255
Young, 162, 173, 214
Ysseldyke, 25, 26, 79

Zaragoza, 239, 254, 274, 291
Zinsser, 224
Zirzow, 112
Zucker, 118
Zutell, 272, 273
Zvirin, 107

SUBJECT INDEX

activating background knowledge. *See* prereading strategies
administrators. *See* collaboration; communicating expectations
already-known statements, 135–136, 143, 174, 213–214
alternative presentation modes, 147–148
anecdotal records. *See* assessment
art (as a means of sharing). *See* graphic sharing
assessment. *See also* collaboration, with teachers
    anecdotal records, 43–44, 54, 116
    graphic sharing. *See* graphic sharing
    literature logs. *See* literature logs
    of attitudes and interests, 72–73
    of early reading and writing, 70–72, 89
    of instructional environment, 78–80
    of literary aspects, 76–77
    of oral reading. *See* Reading Miscue Inventory
    of perceptions, 73–74
    of products of reading and writing, 3, 41
    of reading comprehension, 8, 39, 52–54
    of reading flexibility, 40
    of silent reading, 58, 73
    of social aspects, 75–76
    of spelling development, 39, 60, 62–66, 69, 272
    of students' perceptions of reading and writing, 40
    of writing, 13, 59–70
    of writing conventions, 60, 61–62, 67–68, 69
    principles of, 33, 35–40
    processing words, 54–58
    reading and writing interview, 45–49, 52, 61, 73–74
    retellings, 53
    sample evaluations of writing, 68–70
    self-assessment, 45, 76
    status of class, 44–45
    think-alouds, 52

assisted reading, 157, 158–60, 193, 311
Attention Deficit Disorder, 17–18
attitudes, 39. *See also* attitudes and interests, assessment of role of audience in
authoring cycle profile, 61
Author's Chair, 61
Authors' Circle, 266–267

background knowledge, role in reading, 19, 121. *See also* pre-reading strategies, increasing background knowledge
Bad Speller's Dictionary, 286
basal readers, 110
behaviorism, 26
book introductions, 138–139

capitalization, 67–68. *See also* punctuation, assessment of writing conventions
CD-ROM, 102, 104, 147, 148
choral reading, 117, 162–163
cloze, as an assessment strategy, 58. *See also* instructional cloze
collaboration, *See also* assessment, self-assessment
    with administrators, 313–314
    with parents, 72, 159, 307–313
    with students, 79, 314–316
    with teachers, 303–307
communicating expectations
    to administrators, 331–332
    to parents, 323–331
    to students, 332–333
    to teachers, 331–332
community of readers/writers, 22–23, 209, 210
comprehension. *See also* assessment of reading comprehension, reading comprehension rating, 172
Concepts About Print Tests, 72
conceptually grounded vocabulary, 143

conferencing. *See also* roving conferences
    for reading, 114, 167–170
    for writing, 260–267, 275–276
    questions for, 168–169
confirming, role of in reading, 12–13
confronting student beliefs, 154–157, 254–255
constructivist view of learning, 18–19
Content Reading Interview, 47
context, 10. *See* pragmatics
co-teaching, 306–307
criteria for selecting reading materials. *See* selecting
    reading materials, teacher support
cross-age tutoring, 316

data charts, 264–266
dealing with imposed curricula, 318–321. *See also*
    writing topics, coping with assigned
DEAR. *See* sustained silent reading
debate, 37
demonstration
    as an instructional strategy, 92–94, 112–114,
        130, 134, 156, 247. *See also* writing
        processes
Denver Reading Attitude Survey, 73
development. *See also* spelling development, punc-
    tuation development
    language learning principles, 20–23, 29
    of oral language, 18, 21
    of punctuation, 67–68
    of reading and writing, 20–21
dialect, 191, 294, 295–96
discovery
    as an instructional strategy, 92–94
drafting, 240–241
dramatization, 214–215

eclecticism, 28–29
editing
    of writing, 242–243, 286–287, 293, 313
Emergent Reading and Writing Evaluation, 71–72
environment. *See* literacy learning environment
environmental print, 103–104
expectations. *See* communicating expectations
expository texts
    teaching about, 148, 179, 180–184
extensions
    of texts, 114, 117, 215

feedback. *See* responding to reading and writing,
    reading miscues
five finger method for book selection, 131
flexibility, 40, 93

games as an instructional strategy, 204, 281
    as a means of sharing, 221
glossing, 173

goals and objectives. *See* instructional planning,
    purpose of reading/writing instruction
Goldilocks strategy for selecting books, 131
gradual release of responsibility model of instruc-
    tion, 91–97
grammar instruction. *See* grammatical usage
grammatical usage, 39, 258, 294–297. *See also*
    editing
graphic
    organizer, 148, 173, 220
    sharing, 54, 219–221
graphophonic prediction check, 202
Guide-O-Rama, 173
guided use, 94–96
guidelines for selecting reading materials. *See*
    selecting reading materials

handwriting, 298–300
hangman, 281
high-interest, low-vocabulary books, 105, 110
holistic education, ix–x
holistic teaching. *See* holistic education
home visits, 330
homework, 311
hooked on books program, 107
Hooked on Phonics, 198

I-Charts, 174, 175, 176, 225, 226
immersing students in print. *See* literacy learning
    environment
independent
    reading, 115
    use, 96–97. *See also* ownership
Individual Education Plan, 81, 89–91, 101, 121,
    315, 318
    IEP conferences, 315, 329
innovating on the author's structure, 205–206, 217
inquiry curriculum, 125–127, 226
instructional
    cloze, 187–189, 204–205. *See also* substitution
        lessons
    environment scale, 79
instructional planning
    a holistic approach, 82, 83–89
    behavioral objectives critiqued, 82, 83, 84, 90
    developing learner objectives, 86, 87
    developing summary statements, 83–85
    developing teaching goals, 86–87
    on-going evaluation, 81–82, 87–89
    role of assessment in, 33, 49–51, 87–88, 91–97,
        116, 119
    written goals and objectives, 81–83
interdisciplinary curricula, 122–125
    resources for, 124, 125, 137
interests, 39
interviews. *See* assessment

invented spelling, 272. *See also* assessment of spelling development

jigsaw
    as an instructional strategy, 224

knowledge rating sheet, 143

language
    cues. *See also* reading miscues
        graphophonics, 6–7, 11, 186, 189, 198–201, 202
        pragmatics, 9–10, 11
        semantics, 8–9, 11, 189
        syntax, 7–8, 11
    experience stories, 275
    learning, principles of. *See* development, language learning principles
    phycological process, 11–14, 82–83, 211
    social process, 14–16, 27, 28, 35, 39, 82–83
    system, 5–10
learning disabilities
    approaches to teaching, 25–29
    compared to remedial learners, 25
    nature of, 25–26, 145
librarians, 317
libraries, classroom, 102–104, 111
lifting examples of student work, 95–96, 258, 293
literacy learning environments, nature of, 20–21, 40, 78, 111, 115, 115–116, 243–246, 290–291, 311. *See also* assessment of instructional environment, collaboration with parents
literary aspects of reading and writing, 40, 93, 101. *See also* assessment of literary aspects
literature
    circles. *See* oral sharing of texts
    logs, 54, 119, 215–217
    role in writing, 245–246
    sharing. *See* oral sharing

mapping. *See* semantic webbing
matching
    as an instructional strategy, 203–204
metacognition, 40, 77
minilessons
    reading, 118
    writing. *See* writing workshop minilessons
miscue analysis. *See* reading miscue analysis
mumble reading, 166

narratives. *See* story grammar
neurological impress method. *See* assisted reading
newsletters
    as a means of communicating with parents, 125, 312, 324

note taking, 94, 95, 174
nudging, 266

observation. *See* assessment
OLE project, 28
oral reading, 112–114, 117, 118, 151–154, 275, 311
oral sharing
    of reading texts, 113, 114, 118, 119, 211–215, 317
    of text sets, 221–227
    of writing, 117, 267–268
ownership, 19–20, 59, 60, 61, 105, 113, 109, 132–133, 145, 235, 239, 241, 249, 270, 314–317. *See also* assessment, self-assessment, writing topics

paired reading, 159, 316–317
paragraphs, writing, 257
parent conferences, 58, 328
parents. *See* collaboration, communicating expectations
perceptions, 39
phone calls
    as a means of communicating with parents, 325
phonics, 5, 6, 10, 21, 29, 99, 186, 200, 320. *See also* language cues, graphophonics
pointing, 158, 201–202
politics of literacy. *See* language as a social process
portfolios, 49
post organizer, 232
predictable books, 107–109, 117, 157, 205
predicting, role in reading, 11–12, 128
prep, 136–137
prereading strategies
    activating background knowledge, 134–144
    establishing purposes, 132–134
    increasing background knowledge, 145–146, 149
    previewing text, 113, 144–145
    previewing topics, 134–138
    previewing vocabulary, 139–144
prescribed curricula. *See* dealing with imposed curricula
procedural aspects of reading and writing, 39
proofreading. *See* editing
publishing, 266, 267–270
punctuation, 39, 67–68, 289–294
    development, 290–291
    rules, 292. *See also* assessment of writing conventions
purpose
    of reading and writing instruction, 1–2, 16, 86, 150–151, 157, 185
puzzle strategy, 184, 257

QARs (question-answer relationships), 228–230
questioning. *See also* conferencing
    as a prereading strategy, 113, 136, 144–145
    in reading, 117, 153, 155, 188, 231
    interpreting, 227
    learning to answer questions, 213, 227, 228–230
    self-questioning, 145
    taxonomies of, 228

radio reading, 161
Read Aloud Handbook, 311
readability, 103, 104, 110, 131
reader selected miscues, 197–198
Readers' Theater, 161–162, 214, 217
reading
    across the curriculum, 120–122. *See also* inter-
        disciplinary curricula
    aloud. *See* oral reading
    centers. *See* libraries
    comprehension, 23, 39, 134, 185. *See also*
        assessment of reading comprehension
    conference. *See* conferencing in reading
    conference questions. *See* conferencing
    development. *See* development
    fluency, 154–155
    materials. *See* guidelines for selecting reading
        materials
    miscues
        examples of miscue analysis, 55–57
        in summary statements, 84–85
        meaning of, 36, 55, 84
        of poor readers, 54, 155, 185, 189
        reader-selected miscues, 58
        teacher feedback to, 190–196
    readiness. *See* assessment of early reading and
        writing
    related texts, 113
    social practice. *See* language as a social process
    strategies, 187–188
    transactional process. *See* language as a psycho-
        logical process
    workshop, 118–120
Reading Activity Logs, 114
Reading Miscue Inventory, 55–58
    limitations of, 58
    variations, 55. *See also* reading miscues, retro-
        spective miscue analysis
Reading and writing
    interview. *See* assessment reading and writing
        interview
    relationship, 99
reciprocal teaching, 177–178
record keeping, 41–51. *See also* assessment anec-
    dotal records, portfolios
regenerating texts, 205

rehearsal, for writing, 240
repeated reading, 114, 118, 157, 160–164
ReQuest, 178
responding to reading and writing, 217. *See also*
    reading miscues
retellings as an instructional strategy, 214. *See also*
    assessment of reading comprehension
retrospective miscue analysis, 196–198
revising writing, 241–242, 251–252
round robin reading, 151–152
roving conferences, 170

say something, 213
scaffolding. *See* book introductions
school wide literacy programs, 314
selecting reading materials. *See also* basal readers
    big books, 109, 117
    expository texts, 104
    guidelines for, 104–105
    non-book materials, 110–111
    paperback books, 104–105
    readability formulas, 103, 104
    song books, 104, 109
    student-written materials, 110–111
    teacher support for, 129–132, 167
    textbooks, 110
    trade books, 102–104, 106–107
    wordless picture books, 109
semantic webbing, 123, 148, 232
sentence
    combining, 254
    composing, 257–258
    expansion, 258–260
sequencing text parts, 202–203
sharing of writing, 243–244
silent reading, compared to oral reading, 151–154,
    156. *See also* sustained silent reading, as-
    sessment of silent reading
size-up, 145
sketch to stretch, 219–220
skills. *See* phonics
skinny books, 110, 220
spellers, commercial, 273, 282
spelling. *See also* invented spelling, assessment of
    spelling development
    correct, 65
    development, 62–66, 272–274
    instruction for letter-name spellers, 279–280
    instruction for phonemic spellers, 276–279
    instruction for prephonemic spellers, 274–277
    instruction for transitional spellers, 280–284
    placeholder spelling, 284–285
    poor spellers, 273
    role of memorization in, 273
    spelling lists, 282–284

SQ3R, 233
standards, role in assessment, 37
story grammar, 148, 178–179, 180–184
story starters, 239
students. *See* collaboration, communicating
    expectations
study reading, 232–233
substitution lessons, 189–190
survey, 145
sustained silent reading, 115, 157, 164–166

talking books, 159
teacher-guided probing technique, 145
teachers
    as learners, 24. *See also* collaboration, communi-
        cating expectations, dealing with imposed
        curricula
    as readers and writers, 23, 112–114
Test of Early Reading Ability, 71
text
    features. *See* story grammar, expository texts
    sets. *See* oral sharing of text sets
thematic units. *See* integrated curricula
think-alouds, 94, 170–172, 174, 227
topic introduction. *See* pre-reading strategies,
    previewing topics
topics. *See* writing topics

underlining, 174
usage. *See* grammatical usage

vertical files, 124
vocabulary
    development. *See* pre-reading strategies, preview-
        ing vocabulary
    prediction, 140–142

voice. *See* ownership
voice-print match, 158
volunteers, 314

whole language, as a set of beliefs, 2–3
word
    recognition, 39, 54–58, 71, 198–204. *See also*
        repeated reading
    substitution, 258–259
wordless picture books, 109–110
worksheets, 93, 209, 313
writing
    conferences. *See* conferences for writing
    folders, 249
    interview. *See* assessment reading and writing
        interview
    leads, 252–253
    miscues, 36
    process, 239
        demonstrating, 250–253
    topics
        brainstorming, 248–249
        coping with assigned topics, 239, 249
        demonstrating, 23
        effect on assessment, 59
        selecting, 247–250, 261–262
writing workshop, 80, 113, 237–274
    minilessons, 237, 246–260, 278, 280, 281,
        292
    procedures for, 246–247
written
    conversation, 262–263, 276
    sharing of texts, 215–218